Contemporary Mexican Painting in a Time of Change

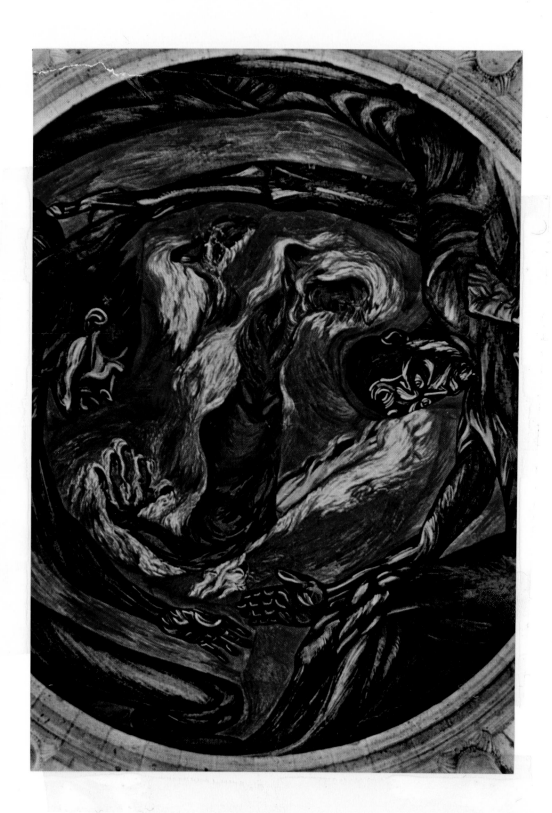

Contemporary Mexican Painting in a Time of Change

by Shifra M. Goldman

University of Texas Press   Austin and London

The Texas Pan American Series

Requests for permission to reproduce material from
this work should be sent to Permissions, University of
Texas Press, Box 7819, Austin, Texas 78712.

The Texas Pan American Series is published with the
assistance of a revolving publication fund established
by the Pan American Sulphur Company.

Frontispiece: José Clemente Orozco, *Man of Fire*,
1938–1939, fresco. Hospicio Cabañas, Guadalajara.
Courtesy of the Orozco family. Photo courtesy Instituto
Nacional de Bellas Artes.

Library of Congress Cataloging in Publication Data

Goldman, Shifra M   1926–
    Contemporary Mexican painting in a time of change.

    (The Texas Pan American series)
    Based on the author's thesis, University of Califor-
nia, Los Angeles, 1977 published under the title:
Nueva presencia, the human image in contemporary
Mexican art.
    Bibliography: p.
    Includes index.
    1. Painting, Mexican.   2. Painting, Modern—20th
century—Mexican.   3. Mural painting, Mexican.
4. Mural painting—20th century—Mexico.
5. Nationalism and art—Mexico.   I. Title.
ND255.G64   759.972   80-17107
ISBN 0-292-71061-5

To my parents, Sylvia and Abraham Meyerowitz, and my son, Eric Garcia

Contents

Illustrations

Foreword

by Raquel Tibol

Shifra M. Goldman's critical investigation of Nueva Presencia provides a panorama of antecedents and immediate consequences, as she considers the particular acts and works of that group in the light of its contradictions, its successes, its confusions and contributions. In consequence this study acquires a singular force in the current juncture of Mexican culture and, since the literature on Mexican art of the recent decades is very limited, it fills a great vacuum.

Shifra M. Goldman begins by recognizing that despite economic dependence Mexico knew how to offer resistance to the importation of artistic styles and maintained strong national character in the visual arts. In fact, the Mexican School, which was profoundly humanistic, had succeeded in establishing a new kind of realism, in spite of the powerful influence of the School of Paris and other rich cultural currents from Europe and the United States. The product of an unusual graft—the nationalistic Mexican Revolution on the flesh of European internationalism—Mexican humanism made itself unique by its extroversion. Orozco the social critic, Rivera the chronicler, Siqueiros the seeker of justice—the ethical predispositions are various, but the artistic product of the founders who originally channeled the Mexican movement is identified by its objectivity; the imagination acts in an extrapersonal field.

In Mexican pictorial humanism the individual is inseparable from the social and historical type. Siqueiros remarked on this in his celebrated article of 1945, "No hay más ruta que la nuestra" ("Ours is the only way"), in which he referred to the "national and international importance of modern Mexican painting," considering it "the first bud of a great reform in the art of the contemporary world." The phrase "Ours is the only way," long considered a slogan of suffocating narrowness, was really the pronouncement of a theory, controversial if you like, but one of the most substantial theories set forth in Mexico. After a brief analysis of the market, of the social patterns of artistic production, of the subjects, the professional principles, the organization of production and instruction, of multiplication and publication, and then of the artistic product during Antiquity, the Middle Ages, and the Renaissance, Siqueiros argued that "the end of the Renaissance opened a long period of decadence in the representational arts." Siqueiros expressed the opinion that this decadence was far from being eliminated in Latin America, where "the representational arts express the most extreme intellectual colonialism." But for Siqueiros there was an exception to this decadence: the modern Mexican pictorial movement, "a movement which has not remained abstractly theoretical," but since the early 1920s has "raised itself up by good practices," since it interpreted the drama caused by the exploitation, misery, hunger, and sickness of the Mexican people. In fact, Mexican social painting did not conform to a more or less metaphorical humanism, but had discarded in advance all ideological and partisan compromises. Pictorial compositions on current events made by the Mexicans were of interest not only to Mexicans but affected people of democratic consciousness all over the world.

The Mexican art movement emerged in a period of sharp and dynamic class realignment. Humanistic painting had set itself in the main zone of contact between the classes. The themes were new and were treated in a new style. Besides, because of the contradictory interests of the Mexican governments and their necessity of national reaffirmation, as well as the known anti-imperialist and independence-oriented elements characteristic of a bourgeoisie which aspired to strengthen and modernize itself, the mural movement had a period of popularity and vigorous expansion.

If Mexican muralism forms an essential chapter in the development of world art, it is because great subjects, which concerned very large groups of people, were interpreted with unusual sensitivity and with an attitude expressive of social values, and since the artists who produced it were highly trained, its expression had real formal strength and great aesthetic value.

In later years the mural movement lacked social and historical opportunities to continue its growth and development. The dominant sectors of the bourgeoisie shut off certain aspects of public debate which stilled its ideological heartbeat. The mural painters found themselves unable to continue to develop their movement. The social and economic circumstances of Mexico after World War II pushed art toward the small studio, to a cloistered and solitary existence which was often undesired. Shifra M. Goldman correctly states that during the period 1955–1965 Mexican artists were pressured and conditioned, emotionally as well as philosophically, to change the sense of rebellion which had characterized the movement in its open confrontations with the oligarchy and with imperialistic interests.

It might appear that the neohumanist painters of Nueva Presencia (also known as Los Interioristas) allied themselves with postrevolutionary Mexican realism, of the gigantic murals and popular graphic art. Even a superficial analysis shows that the connections are few: the Mexican School made pronouncements which it confirmed in painting; Nueva Presencia made pronouncements which liberated painting from any fixed positions. Mexican realism always exerted itself to be explicit, didactic, and for the people; Nueva Presencia was exclusive and cut itself off from the people. Realism adapted its ethical content to social and political tendencies which dominated its times; Nueva Presencia clung anarchically to ideological improvisation. The realists never forgot the academy—they stylized it; the artists of Nueva Presencia detested the academic—they broke with it. For these reasons we can affirm that Nueva Presencia is not an orthodox descendant of Mexican realism but rather an unorthodox continuation of the Mexican contemporary art movement.

The relationship between this new humanism and abstract expressionism Goldman considers crucial, since, like abstract expressionism, this type of figurative imagery could also, and perhaps only, externalize psychic residues but not penetrate to the spirit of the human social drama. If the forms aspire to enter the social realm, to make a genuine protest, to be effective in raising social consciousness, they must possess solidity, precision, and firmness and reveal a deep attraction for the subjects they aim to attack. The naturalism of Nueva Presencia was characterized by ambiguity and by the break between its pictorial imagery and its social intentions. The group never managed to formulate the response to which it aspired, but it did know how to cultivate its own type of antiformalist figuration, and express the spiritual and even the philosophical, intentionally giving up illustration and anecdote.

Interiorismo had its predetermined directions and its limitations, but it succeeded in setting itself up as the Mexican branch of neoexpressionism, since it somehow knew how to take to itself the crisis through which the continent was living. It presented itself simultaneously as a stylistic option and as a way out for those who wanted to refer to current events and situations, in a particular artistic style, without giving up the commercial gallery, the museum, and the rest of the cultural apparatus of the dominant class.

Los Interioristas took their position between the problems and interests affecting emerging social forces and the dominant stylistic tendencies of formalism. They worked toward new necessities without daring an extreme break which would have carried them to ideological compromises which surely they had no wish to make. They limited themselves to being militant nonconformists. They did not aspire to enlighten, but merely to liberate feelings, though they renounced the idea of art as a means of producing happiness. Those who adopt a controversial attitude do not celebrate but rather discuss, protest, or insult.

A poetic manuscript by Leonel Góngora summarizes the sentiments of that individualistic rebellion without a program: "Things that fill us with enthusiasm because they are part of our time; things that fill us with despair because they are part of our time; things that fill us with anguish because they form part of the epoch; things that fill us with happiness because we live them; things that fill us with pain because we suffer them; things that fill us with lassitude because they attack that which we love; things that fill us with love because we feel them; things that fill us with veneration because they form part of our history."

Feelings emerged from the interior of an individual and conditioned his vision of the outer world. It was not a question of perceiving visible reality literally but rather of achieving an interpretation of very general matters by means of a strong artistic style in which painting and drawing were used to give a dramatic emphasis, which did not disdain the powers of caricature but actually assumed them. The deformation of caricature reinforces the aggressiveness of images which make vehement criticisms of the society of their time, calling in fact for greater spiritual dignity.

In this respect Los Interioristas differed from the Italian artists' group The Pro and the Con which in 1961 had produced a series of drawings and prints on the common theme "La violenza ancora" ("violence again"). It happened that in Italy, as in Mexico and the United States, at that time there was much talk of a "new image of man," of a new objectivity, of a new figurative art. Renato Guttuso, the outstanding figure of that Italian group, believed that a truthful representation of man should grasp his totality, from his intestines to his heart, from his ideas to his face, from his acts to his anxiety, and did not renounce the hope of a future in which it might be possible to propose that the splendors of beauty were the

splendors of human dignity. The Italians rejected the caricaturing aspect of expressionism because they felt it was fundamentally superficial in its characterization. Since they wished to jolt the conscious and unconscious mind, they turned to pictorial and graphic violence. The wars in Algeria and Vietnam and the struggles for liberation in black Africa caused them to inscribe on their pages angry, painful, conscience-stricken drawings. The Italians assimilated reality freely because they wanted to totally confront the internal and external beings. Their attempt clashed with avant-garde ideologies and with a set of established values which were not all obsolete.

The artists of Nueva Presencia, like those of The Pro and the Con, had the courage to recognize and remember some of these values. Both believed that with the lines of a drawing one could discover unexplored aspects of the human condition. Painting and drawing are not just things of beauty but are sometimes terrible cultural acts which try to remold life in order to change and perfect it. No wonder, then, that Goldman seeks the motives for a rather general inclination among Los Interioristas toward the grotesque, the macabre, mutilations. She analyzes the reasons for the dominance of draftsmanship over the purely pictorial, for the compositional need to revive forms consecrated by Orozco or by Siqueiros without admitting the themes that motivated them; for the break, during the 1950s, with consecrated styles. She examines the relationship of Los Interioristas with existentialism, the connections between neofiguration and Pop Art, and how surrealist elements appeared with their provocative overtones.

Thus one sees clearly that Nueva Presencia was the fruit of the necessity to oppose an art of new meaning to the formalist currents which had gained great power in previous years. However, the dichotomy between meaning and form was not carried to its ultimate consequences, but was resolved by a kind of fusion of opposites. Los Interioristas understood humanism as the representation of the human being, and they agreed also with Mauricio Lasansky that many painters took shelter behind the term *humanism* in order to continue to cultivate a reactionary academicism, a melodrama of inflated substance and little meaning. That was not, and could not be, the opposite of pure aesthetic speculation. Melodrama can sometimes achieve real grandeur in painting, but *horror vacui* deserves the same disdain as "good taste." Los Interioristas violated the principles of refinement to achieve a more direct and engaged communication.

To express new ideas they needed new forms, forms with the power to give direction not only to a new style but also to a new function. They sought to release energies with new forms which were already familiar to the spectator's eye due to the prestige of their origins, but yet not recognizable as a particular influence from the past. The new attitude carried an additional obligation to cultivate a personal style, even though it meant turning to earlier European art to achieve it. Individuality had become a sensitive point with these artists, for prestige and sales depended on it, and it was the artists' Achilles' heel for those who wished to manipulate them.

It was Ben Shahn who said (and it was repeated by Jack Levine) that nonobjective art was the art of the cold war. Goldman has returned to the question (as has Eva Cockcroft) of the styles which have had ideological acceptance in the United States, where the most extreme individualism has been especially glorified, as have purely formal and technical experimentation.

The cultural distortions produced by the period of McCarthyism oblige us now to rewrite the history of art in the United States, the history not only of the art of the United States itself but also of that of Latin America, which was artificially devalued. Falsifications must be removed from our depictions, falsifications which have been supported by those interested in eradicating from art the bitter realities of Latin America, punished by reactionary violence, and restricting the liberating force of art with its chastizing and transfiguring power over human conduct.

The ideological struggle and artistic competition were so strong that they required the erection of barricades. They made of art a force affecting events. Thus seen, *interiorismo* was an expressionist style, since it was conceived and had its short development in a state of protest. One must not forget that expressionism is reborn (with variations imposed by time and circumstances) each time artists decide to oppose the established system with their art, using it as an instrument of their rage, even though in the ferocity of their accusations they descend to the irrational.

In the period of the Cold War, Goldman observes the enthusiastic support Mexican intellectuals, including the artists, offered the triumphant Cuban Revolution. But she sees that at the same time Mexican cultural officials gave in to the pressures of the Organization of American States and the multinational corporations, all this in the framework of capitalistic development patronized by the United States.

Interiorismo did not receive the benefits of government support or foundation fellowships or the allegiance of the populace. In an unfortunate time of ascendant individualism, it was a shared adventure in the Mexican cultural environment, which at the beginning of the 1960s offered a restricted art market and a timid cultural outlook. If it pleases us now to retrace analytically with Shifra Goldman the chapters of this adventure, it is because we cannot but recognize that it was a sincere attempt, full of youthful eagerness, to move toward a better world.

Mexico City, April 1980
(Translated by Terence Grieder)

Preface

The research for this study was compiled from four major sources of information: (1) interviews with artists, art critics, and gallery owners; (2) archives of artists, critics and historians, and galleries; (3) libraries of government institutions and universities; (4) newspaper and periodical libraries.

Among newspaper and periodical libraries, the most important was the Hemeroteca Nacional, Mexico City. In addition, I used materials from the Art Library and University Research Library at the University of California, Los Angeles; the Brand Library, Glendale, California; the Library of the Instituto de Investigaciones Estéticas, Universidad Nacional Autónoma de México, Mexico City; and the Los Angeles Central Library.

Archives consulted include those of Arnold Belkin (the most extensive), Mexico City; Shelly Wexler Bickford (Cober Gallery), formerly of San José, California; Departamento de Artes Plásticas of the Instituto Nacional de Bellas Artes, Mexico City; Leonel Góngora, Amherst, Massachusetts; Francisco Icaza, Mexico City; Galería Mer-Kup, Mexico City; José Muñoz Medina, Mexico City; Selden Rodman, Oakland, New Jersey; Wenger Collection, La Jolla, California; Joseph Young's Zora Gallery archive, Los Angeles; and Héctor Xavier, Mexico City.

A list of taped and untaped interviews conducted between 1972 and 1976 can be found in the bibliography. All statements attributed to artists and not otherwise identified derive from these interviews. In addition, the bibliography contains a list of letters and the archives in which they are located.

I owe a special debt of gratitude to three people: Julius Kaplan, without whose patience and encouragement this work might not have been completed; Arnold Belkin, who gave generously of his time and permitted access to his archives; and Raquel Tibol, who shared her knowledge and insight with me on many occasions. My thanks to Jean Franco, Arnold Rubin, Terence Grieder, and Stanton L. Catlin, who read and criticized the manuscript. Thanks are also due to Leonel Góngora, Vita Giorgi, Jaime Mejía and Lety Arroyo de Mejía, Selden Rodman, Joseph Young, Shelly Wexler Bickford, Sig and Muriel Wenger, Silvan Simone Gallery, Galería Mer-Kup, and Gloria Taracena, who have helped in different ways. Finally I wish to express my gratitude and appreciation to Carolyn Cates Wylie and Suzanne Comer for skilled editorial assistance and thoughtful suggestions.

Introduction

There is a painful irony in the new image of man that is emerging, however fragmentarily, from the art of our time. An observer from another planet might well be struck by the disparity between the enormous power which our age has concentrated in its external life and the inner poverty which our arts seeks to expose to view . . . the shape of man as revealed in our novels, plays, painting and sculpture . . . a creature full of holes and gaps, faceless, riddled with doubts and negations, starkly finite.[1]

Man has been incapable of love, wanting in charity, and despairing of hope. He has not molded a life of abundance and peace; and he has charred the earth and befouled the heavens more wantonly than ever before. He has made of Arden a landscape of Death. In this landscape we dwell; and with these images we must live.[2]

TO PROMOTE THE ONLY ART WHICH HOLDS MEANING FOR OUR CONTEMPORARIES; the art which does not separate man as an individual from man as an integral part of society. No one, especially the artist, has the right to be indifferent to the social order.[3]

Los Interioristas (The Insiders), or Nueva Presencia (New Image), as they later became known, were a group of Mexican artists subscribing to a basic philosophy who created a publication and exhibited together in various configurations for about two years. Canadian-born artist Arnold Belkin and Mexican artist Francisco Icaza jointly published the five issues of the *revista-cartel* (magazine-poster) *Nueva Presencia*, which publicly articulated the principles around which the artists grouped themselves. This publication, though intended as a monthly, actually appeared at irregular intervals from August 1961 to August–September 1963. Its demise was practically contemporaneous with the demise of the group. Issue No. 1 of the broadside, illustrated with the works of Belkin and Icaza, functioned as a manifesto, setting forth its principles in the form of a call to "artists, art students, thinkers and educators, professionals, and all social classes" to re-

ject art of "good taste" produced for the market or for political speculators, academic art, and intellectualized criticism, and to subscribe to an art that clearly and directly affirmed its involvement with the individual as an integral part of society. The precursors who embodied these universal principles in their art were, according to the manifesto, Grünewald, Michelangelo, El Greco, and Orozco.

Though the group of artists who firmly considered themselves members of Los Interioristas numbered only seven (see Fig. 1), the total number of artists who exhibited under their banner and identified with their concepts in more than a casual way was sixteen: Arnold Belkin, Rafael Coronel, Francisco Corzas, José Luis Cuevas, Leonel Góngora, Gastón González César, José Hernández Delgadillo, Francisco Icaza, Ignacio (Nacho) López, Benito Messeguer, Francisco Moreno Capdevila, José Muñoz Medina, Emilio Ortiz, Antonio Rodríguez Luna, Artemio Sepúlveda, and Héctor Xavier.

The artists of Los Interioristas/Nueva Presencia, most of whom were born between 1930 and 1936, were of a generation shaped by the tensions and traumas of the post–World War II period— the Cold War, atomic and hydrogen bombs that threatened instant world annihilation, and a general mood of moral and social disequilibrium. The decade of the 1960s, at the beginning of which Nueva Presencia was formed, became an era of world-scale rebellion for change on the part of students and young people, from the United States civil rights sit-ins in the early part of the decade to the demonstrations that took place in the late sixties in Paris, Berlin, Rome, Tokyo, San Francisco, Chicago, and other major cities, including the infamous massacre of students in Tlatelolco, Mexico City, in 1968. The degree to which the art forms and public pronouncements of Nueva Presencia were shaped and conditioned by contemporary historical and social forces is one of the themes explored in the following pages. A number of questions present

themselves. In the land of social realism and revolutionary muralism, why did it appear necessary in the 1960s to reaffirm a socially oriented
art? It would appear a redundancy. What shifts
had taken place in the focus of Mexican art from
the inception of the mural movement to the formation of Nueva Presencia? What role did Rufino
Tamayo and other easel painters play in this re-
direction? What external artistic influences entered Mexico, and to what degree were they
integrated or rejected? How important was the
role of Mexico's nearest and most powerful
neighbor, the United States, in these shifts?
These questions, as well as the thematic and stylistic concerns of Nueva Presencia and their importance and influence in Mexico, are discussed
below.

Of all the nations of Latin America, Mexico
was the first to experience, at the beginning of
the twentieth century, a major revolution, which
not only changed the political and social conditions of life for a large number of people, but also
produced a tremendous flowering of intellectual
and creative energy that decisively changed the
course of Mexican culture. It took the direction
of an intensive nationalism in reaction to the im-
itative, European-oriented culture of the Porfirio
Díaz regime. Under government patronage, muralism became part of a vast educational program
directed toward the neglected rural areas of Mexico as well as the cities in an effort to educate the
great masses of people set in motion by the revolution. Like all aspects of culture in this period,
the plastic arts engaged the participation and enthusiasm of the most advanced and talented personalities of the nation. The earliest phase of
Mexican cultural nationalism, of which muralism was the strongest manifestation, can be described as extroverted and humanistic. Plastic
expression was influenced by José Vasconcelos'
Bergsonian and Diego Rivera's Marxist humanism. Rivera's most poetic and epic works and
José Clemente Orozco's most positive depictions
of the revolution (as well as his biting denuncia-

1. Los Interioristas. *From left to right:* Francisco Icaza,
Leonel Góngora, Arnold Belkin, Francisco Corzas, José
Muñoz Medina, Artemio Sepúlveda (Emilio Ortiz not
included). Mexico City, 1961. Courtesy Belkin Archives; photo by Vázquez Castellanos.

tions of church and wealth) were produced in
this period. A second phase occurred when the
first flush of revolutionary fervor and idealism
was tempered by disillusionment at government
betrayals of the revolution. The *callista* betrayal
is reflected in some of Orozco's post-1926 Preparatoria murals; in sections of Rivera's murals
in the central staircase of the Palacio Nacional;
and explicitly in David Alfaro Siqueiros' 1932
Los Angeles mural *Portrait of Mexico Today*
(original title: *Delivery of the Mexican Bourgeoisie That Emerged from the Revolution into
the Hands of Imperialism*).

Another direction in Mexican art, which remained a subcurrent until after World War II,
was expressed in the work of artists like Manuel
Rodríguez Lozano, Frida Kahlo, and Rufino Tamayo. Its character was lyrical and internal
rather than epic and dramatic. The artists felt
directed toward a world of images fed by the
subconscious. Painters (and poets) dealt with
themes of solitude, emptiness, night, the cosmos,
and what has been widely called "the tragic
sense of life." In addition to the external liberation from oppression that had keynoted earlier
nationalism (and continued to be expressed in

the Mexican School), Mexican thought now expressed self-liberation. From objective activism it shifted to subjective introspection—what has been named *ensimismamiento* (self-absorption).[4] In the complex kaleidoscope of modern Mexican art, dominated by revolutionary muralism, the subjective tendency—though drawing its imagery from Mexican sources—proclaimed itself as universal and international and opposed to what it considered the narrow nationalism and indigenism of the mural movement. The most respected artistic personality for this point of view was, and has continued to be, Tamayo. It is significant in understanding the contradictions inherent in Nueva Presencia that the two living Mexican artists its members most respected were the polar opposites Siqueiros and Tamayo. The overriding esteem in which they held Orozco can perhaps be explained by the balance he struck between extroverted social statement and individualistic humanism.

What was the character of Mexican muralism? As an art form it was dedicated to certain didactic propositions: teaching the ideals and the history of the 1910 revolution and previous struggles for freedom and independence; elevating and glorifying the great indigenous heritage of Mexico, which had been suppressed and denigrated since the sixteenth century; and projecting the *mestizo* concept of the Mexican "race"—the view that modern Mexican civilization was not simply Spanish but the result of the encounter and eventual fusion of two cultures and the physical fusion of two peoples. In addition to this purely nationalistic concern, the majority of muralists espoused left-wing socialist or communist ideals and were antifascist, anti-imperialist, and antimilitaristic.

Above all, mural art was wedded by its very nature to the proposition that art should be public: available to the masses of people rather than the private property of wealthy collectors. It should be understood that essentially Mexico lacked a middle class when it emerged from its

semifeudal state in the first portion of the twentieth century and therefore a priori had a very small clientele for easel paintings. Historically the upper classes, landowners, and the church had patronized European artists on the assumption that Mexico was a barbarian nation without culture. It was natural that the newly evolved mural movement, translating a historical situation into a point of principle, should eschew this limited audience and address itself with murals to the main body of the population, whose interests the muralists had made their own.

From the 1920s to the 1960s, muralism was the great artistic manifestation of Mexican nationality. For thirty of those years it completely dominated the spectrum of the plastic arts, overshadowing easel painting, sculpture, and architecture as the most typical expression of the Mexican spirit. Along with its offspring, neorealistic easel painting and graphic arts, it crystallized into the "Mexican School" with common denominators in theme and style. During the 1950s, muralism engaged in violent confrontation with nonnationalistic, nondidactic, and formally oriented painting. During the entire period from 1920 to 1960, Mexico itself was changing from a largely agricultural to a modern industrial-commercial nation with a growing working class and bourgeoisie concentrated in the cities. Though it is one of the most highly developed of Latin American countries, it is still an underdeveloped nation compared to the great industrial powers of Europe and the United States, with whom it has manifold and complex connections. Its demographic distribution, in addition, presents a lopsided picture. Major urbanization is concentrated in Mexico City, now a sprawling metropolis of twenty million people, and a series of provincial cities that only recently have begun to come to the fore economically and culturally. As a result, there is a growing gap between urban concentrations of wealth and the increasing impoverishment and isolation of the rural areas.

The monolithic structure of galleries and plastic arts organizations, essentially governmental and centralized in Mexico City, has begun to give way in recent years to a more pluralistic spectrum of exhibition possibilities with the rise of private galleries. One of my contentions is that the increasing availability of galleries and the increasing importance of middle-class patronage in the post–World War II period has encouraged the development and popularity of abstract and non-objective easel painting.[5] In contrast to the prewar period, we find two major currents in contemporary art: abstraction, and neofiguration in a non–social realist vein. Totally nonobjective painting is practiced by a small minority, though it is on the increase.

By the 1950s many painters of the Mexican movement had fallen into decorative patterns, repeating motifs that had been created by the progenitors of the movement. "A decade or more ago," said eminent Mexican critic Luis Cardoza y Aragón in 1961, "I foresaw the academicism that was hardening into a mold."[6] Partial responsibility for what has been called *nationalismo pintoresco* (picturesque nationalism) lies with the taste of former revolutionaries transformed into bourgeois *nouveaux riches* or government bureaucrats, with nostalgic attachment to the idealized "old days" and a sentimental desire for paintings of revolutionary heroes and picturesque folklore. Neither Orozco nor Siqueiros catered to this taste; Rivera, at times, did. However, according to critic Antonio Rodríguez, it is to the mediocre talents of the later generations of muralists that we owe a body of uninspired murals and easel paintings.[7]

For forty years the ideas of the muralists had been part of the intellectual climate of the Mexican art world, and they could not fail, even after the objective circumstances had changed, to leave their residue in the consciousness of the younger artists. Even those overtly opposed to the basic propositions of the mural movement and the Mexican School were affected. This helps to explain the continued existence of mu-

ral activity by dedicated easel painters and abstractionists. Also it must be noted that despite the fulminations against easel painting in the 1923 "Social, Political, and Aesthetic Declaration of the Syndicate of Technical Workers, Painters, and Sculptors" (the manifesto of the mural movement), easel painting was, and continued to be, an important part of the artistic creation of the most active muralists.

Despite the hegemony of the Mexican School in the prewar period, international culture and artistic influences of a nonrealistic nature filtered into Mexico even in its most insular periods. Among these were the contact with Dada in the twenties and the even more eventful arrival of surrealism in the forties. Concerning the latter, Mexico had always been a land of the fantastic and supernatural (owing to its still living and vibrant pre-Columbian heritage), and the fusion of its "natural surrealism" with the programmatic European movement is apparent in the rich variety of surrealistic modes in contemporary art. Cubism, futurism, and their variations were part of the artistic equipment of Rivera and Siqueiros when they returned from Europe in the early 1920s. The pervasive impact of Picasso, as assimilated by Tamayo and others, has also shaped the development of modern Mexican art. In the fifties, abstract expressionism and its European counterpart, informalism (known throughout Latin America as *informalismo*), began to show their influence in the work of younger artists. Though European informalism had great influence in Mexico, it is important to delineate the influx in the fifties of an entire cultural pattern from the United States: an existentially oriented artistic philosophy that found its original locus in the Beat poets of San Francisco and the abstract expressionists of New York.

Mexico's particular variety of existential thought, which came into vogue during the 1950s, is most succinctly expressed in *The Labyrinth of Solitude* (*El laberinto de la soledad*, 1950), Octavio Paz's important essay on loneli-

2. Nacho López at the Galería Novedades with the exhibit "Fifty Jazz Images," 1962. Courtesy Nacho López.

ness and the Mexican personality.[8] Responsive to the new currents of Sartrian existentialism influential in the postwar period, but also evidencing a continuing *ensimismamiento*, Paz examines the nature of Mexican loneliness in a series of brilliant explorations of Mexican hermeticism, *machismo* (masculinity), indifference to death and violence, and sense of inferiority. His major theme is that of solitude, the profoundest fact of the human condition. Man, he says, is the only being who knows he is alone, and the only one who seeks out another. Man is nostalgia and a search for communion. Therefore when he is aware of himself he is aware of his lack of the Other, that is, of his solitude. Concern for collective humanity suffering from, or responding to, the injustices of oppression and exploitation (such as we find in the murals of Rivera and Siqueiros) yields to consideration of the agonies of the solitary individual facing the indifferent universe and constantly seeking the Other to complete and affirm his existence. The irremediability of the human condition is emphasized by the ultimate isolation of the individual within himself. *The Labyrinth of Solitude* was very popular in Mexico and well known to Nueva Presencia.

That these ideas were attractive to the generation of Mexicans nurtured in the fifties is evidenced by the acceptance of Beat influence, which penetrated Mexico by way of North American students who appeared, bearded and sandaled, in Mexican classrooms—particularly those of the English-language Mexico City College.[9] Arnold Belkin, co-founder of Nueva Presencia and Los Interioristas and a faculty member of the college, had his first contact with Beat culture in the late fifties. He writes: "There was a symposium at Mexico City College around '57 or '58 which opened with a reading of *Howl*, done by a student of mine (my students were older than I was, mostly being Korean War Vets). I became very aware of beat poetry . . . and tried to introduce [the poems] into Spanish. We were very aware of all the beat-oriented movements in poetry from Latin America."[10] Several years later Belkin translated Allen Ginsberg's *America* into Spanish for the Mexican-published bilingual magazine *El Corno Emplumado* and wrote to a friend in Los Angeles for a selection of Ginsberg and Lawrence Ferlinghetti poetry, then published by City Lights Books of San Francisco. Nor was Belkin the only one. In 1962, photographer Nacho López presented a joint exhibit with sculptor Pedro Cervantes titled "Fifty Jazz Images" (see Fig. 2). Though no reference was made to the Beat poets and jazz musicians who combined their arts in San Francisco poetry readings, the visceral and liberating qualities that jazz embodied for a generation of White bohemians in the United States is echoed by Cervantes: ". . . music of liberty, totally devoid of fear and inhibition, direct expression of the interior rhythm of intermittent man, anguished, explosive, adulating."[11] Francisco Icaza's 1963 series of drawings based on Albert Camus' *The Plague* also attests to the increasing importance in Mexico of Sartre and Camus' atheistic existentialism.

The Beat influence brought the spirit of antiestablishment rebellion to Mexico but, in contrast to the revolutionary politics of the mural movement, the rebellion often took a bohemian rather than a political form, as was consistent with the romantic-anarchic thrust of "beatitude." This was true for many Latin American avant-garde groups directly or indirectly linked with the Beat generation, albeit at a later date. The typical Beat antipathy toward existing political programs and ideologies was succinctly expressed by the inter-American movement Nueva Solidaridad (New Solidarity): "We do not believe in the Bolshevik Social Paradise, nor in the Eden of Private Capital, nor in the Myth of Superior Races."[12]

The point at which bohemian "antiestablishment" movements like the United States Beats and the British Angry Young Men fused and overlapped with the emerging movement known as the New Left is hard to determine, but that they shared certain characteristics is not in doubt. Deriving from Marx's early idealist writings, from William Morris, and from a number of contemporary Marxist intellectuals, the New Left movement included strains of anarchism, utopian socialism, nihilism, existentialism, and humanism. The very heterogeneity of the movement allowed artists with social interests to turn to art movements with a vaguely Marxian flavor whose nature could be determined by the artists themselves rather than a political party. Though no specific ties between Nueva Presencia and the New Left can be documented, there is little doubt that various members of Nueva Presencia shared many of the political and philosophical sympathies of the New Left. They were opposed to nuclear armament and United States intervention in Cuba and the Dominican Republic; they deplored poverty, social injustice, racism, violence, hypocrisy, and physical and spiritual degradation, and these themes frequently form the direct and indirect content of their artistic works.

Abstract expressionism (*informalismo*) became a distinct current in Mexico in the mid-fifties. Artists such as Lilia Carrillo, Manuel Felguérez, Fernando García Ponce, Vicente Rojo, and Luis García Guerrero (among others) showed the di-

verse influences of Maria Helena Vieira da Silva, Willem de Kooning, Jasper Johns, Antonio Tápies, Lucio Fontana, Afro (Basaldella), and Pierre Soulages as well as the expressive brushwork derived from Tamayo, Juan Soriano, Roberto Matta Echauren, and Siqueiros. The freer approach to paint application, surface texture, and brushwork derived from *informalismo* also affected many figural artists, as did stylistic influences from older masters like Velázquez, Rembrandt, Goya, Toulouse-Lautrec, Ensor, Nolde, and the German expressionists. Mexican artists affected by these trends included Alberto Gironella, Pedro Coronel, Enrique Echeverría, and Interioristas Rafael Coronel, Corzas, Icaza, and Belkin.

If *informalismo* can be understood as a subjective withdrawal into the self, a retreat into the subconscious from the fearful problems of reality in the postwar period, a mystical, individualized, existential response to the problems of "being," we can perhaps find points of contact beyond the stylistic between *informalismo* and the kind of neohumanistic figuration that appeared earliest in the work of Cuevas and found expression among a number of artists of his generation. The figurative imagery created by these artists (including those of Nueva Presencia) shared with *informalismo* the sense of personal isolation: the figure (like the "gesture" of abstract expressionism) making its solitary, painful stand against cosmic indifference; the violent distortion of the human body matching the evocation of personal emotion through violent paint application; the immediacy of expressive content overriding the importance of creating a "precious object"; and the reversion to exotic mysticism, whether derived from Zen, Freud, pre-Columbian religion, or folk magic. In both *informalismo* and neohumanism (one abstract, the other figurative), the art forms served as a polarity to realist objectivity. Both were negations of social realism in their particular ways. They were a retreat into the self as the source and solution of the problems of human existence.

Neohumanist art has been characterized as "post-ideological," i.e., without dogma or an encompassing ideology, and responsive to "today's crisis [which] is the crisis of life itself . . . inexplicable and incomprehensible."[13] Though I do not agree that any human crisis is inexplicable, or that any human society or activity can exist without an ideological framework, this formulation may very well correspond to the attitudes of the artists themselves. It is a description rather than an analysis of their state of mind. Withdrawal into subjectivity is often associated with a sense of apocalyptic crisis, one in which accepted verities of the social structure have crumbled and the individual is filled with helpless despair. This state of mind was consistent with the increasing alienation that accompanied the development of capitalism in postwar Mexico. If the muralists saw socialism as a promising alternative for their country's problems, the neohumanists, in the post-Stalin era, disengaged themselves from both capitalism and socialism and were thereby placed in the position of seeking causes and solutions within their individual psyches. This is clearly evident when one compares the suffering, isolated figural images of neohumanism with the optimistic and collectivist content of Rivera and Siqueiros. It is evidence that the retreat into self can apply as easily to figurative as to nonobjective art.

The irony of the situation is that Nueva Presencia's formation is directly related to a reaction against increasingly academic *informalismo*. This reaction on a world scale took the double form of neo-Dadaism (Pop art) and neohumanism, both of which sought new images of contemporary reality. The latter made itself manifest in the United States as early as 1959 with the exhibit "New Images of Man" at the New York Museum of Modern Art, followed by the appearance the following year of Selden Rodman's book *The Insiders: Rejection and Rediscovery of Man in the Arts of Our Time*, from which Los Interioristas derived their first name and much of their philosophy. In point of fact, Rodman's book can be seen as the link between the "New Images" show and Los Interioristas. Not only was Rodman very much aware of the show (from which he purchased a painting), but also Rico Lebrun and Leonard Baskin, both represented in "New Images," later formed artistic and personal ties with Los Interioristas through his intercession. These events signaled the resurgence of an "involved art" that avoided reverting to the style or content of the social realism of the 1930s. In Europe this resurgence was attested to by the 1960 appearance of the Munich-published art magazine *Tendenzen*, which linked prewar with postwar protest art; the organization in the early sixties of Imago—a loose confederation of international artists dedicated to bringing socially meaningful subjects back into art without any fixed manifesto—by André Verlon and Argentinian Antonio Berni (later associated with the Argentinian neofigurative group that paralleled Nueva Presencia); and the 1966 Vienna exhibit "Engaged Art—Socially Critical Graphics since Goya."[14]

In outlining the gradual and complex evolution of widespread subjectivity and individualism in Mexican philosophy and art during the half-century since the end of the Mexican Revolution, one further factor that should be considered is the possibility that abstract expressionism was publicized and popularized in Mexico and Latin America by various United States public and private agencies as part of the cultural and ideological penetration that characterized the period of the Cold War. Its purpose, according to this theory, was the replacement of social realism (whose strongest and most enduring expression was in Mexico) as a viable artistic possibility. It is pertinent to explore Mexican claims that the United States was engaged in "cultural imperialism" and that its activities distorted and deflected the natural development of modern Mexican art.[15] Whether the increased interest in abstract and nonrepresentational painting during the fifties and the active institutional support given abstract painters in 1960 were the result of individual predilections on the part of artists and art administrators, or were caused by the subtle pressures of the international art market and cultural imperialism, is discussed in detail below. The evidence indicates that both factors were operational, but there is little doubt that the international pressures were strong determinants of artistic direction.

To summarize, I am suggesting that Mexican painting in the sixties offered three distinct possibilities of development: (1) social realism, the universal socialist aesthetic that considers art a political instrument proceeding from dialectical and historical materialism; (2) figurative and abstract art without social or political considerations; and (3) neohumanist figurative art, which expressed the anguish of human existence but was politically and ideologically nonpartisan. This book explores the ways in which these trends are linked to particular historical periods in Mexican history, and the degree to which they have interacted to produce the contemporary human image in Mexican art.

Contemporary Mexican Painting in a Time of Change

The Mexican Mural Movement, Cultural Nationalism, and Social Realism

Mexican Muralism

Intellectuals had a complex relationship to the Mexican Revolution. Most came from the middle class, some from the *criollo* bourgeoisie (Mexicans of purely Spanish descent). Although their education and philosophy separated them from the most oppressed classes of farmers and workers who joined the revolution, the intellectuals espoused the people's cause, in which they saw their own reality reflected. In general, the intelligentsia observed this reality from the outside. In certain cases, however, intellectuals and artists participated in the revolution directly. With the exception of Diego Rivera, who spent the years between 1907 and 1921 in Europe (except for a brief return in 1910–1911), the progenitors of the mural movement, Dr. Atl (Gerardo Murillo), David Alfaro Siqueiros, Ramón Alva de la Canal, José Clemente Orozco, and others, were at the battlefronts or close to them. Thus the first-hand experiences of the revolution that permeated the artistic output of Orozco and Siqueiros were quite different from those of Rivera. The question might be asked whether the source of Rivera's optimism and idealism, as contrasted with Orozco's critical pessimism and Siqueiros' confrontive violence, might not be sought in these early experiences—in addition, of course, to temperamental differences. On the other hand, the Mexican intellectual, says Octavio Paz (a noted poet and essayist who has served his country for many years as a diplomat), occupies a very different position as far as the state is concerned than the intellectuals of Europe and the United States, who wield their influence from *outside* the government, with criticism. The Mexican intellectual's position is political action,[1] as in the case of José Vasconcelos and others up to the present day. The conjunction of intellectual and artistic pursuits and direct political participation on the highest policy levels has created an integration between art and politics inconceivable in the highly industrialized capitalist nations and has direct bearings on the social urgencies of the mural movement.[2] It is also expressed in the tug-of-war between social and personal expression that characterized Nueva Presencia.

The tenets of the Mexican mural movement are clearly stated in the manifesto issued in 1923 by the Syndicate of Revolutionary Painters, Sculptors, and Engravers of Mexico. The very fact that the artists agreed to organize themselves into a trade union and work collectively is significant of a new socialized attitude—one that conceived of the artist as a "cultural worker" rather than an elitist individual.[3] The most important question, when one is dealing with manifestos, is their effect on the form and content of the works produced under their guidance. The Syndicate manifesto is an ambitious document. Whether it was reflected in the early works of its adherents can be determined only by comparing its proposals with the works themselves. When it first appeared, it was pasted on street corners and telephone poles of Mexico City (a procedure also followed with the *Nueva Presencia* broadsides in the early sixties). As translated by Anita Brenner, portions of it read:

DECLARATION
Social, Political, and Aesthetic of

    The Syndicate of Technical Workers, Painters and Sculptors to the native races humiliated through centuries; to the soldiers made executioners by their chiefs; to the workmen and peasants flogged by the rich; to the intellectuals not fawners of the bourgeoisie . . .

    . . . THE ART OF THE MEXICAN PEOPLE IS THE GREATEST AND MOST HEALTHY SPIRITUAL EXPRESSION IN THE WORLD [and its] tradition our greatest possession. It is great because, being of the people, it is collective, and that is why our fundamental aesthetic goal is to socialize artistic expression, and tend to obliterate totally, individualism, which is bourgeois.

    We REPUDIATE the so-called easel painting and all the art of ultra-intellectual circles because it is aristocratic, and we glorify the expression of Monumental Art because it is a public possession.

We PROCLAIM that since this social moment is one of transition between a decrepit order and a new one, the creators of beauty must put forth their utmost efforts to make their production of ideological value to the people, and the ideal goal of art, which now is an expression of individualistic masturbation, should be one of beauty for all, of education and of battle.[4]

How these principles informed the works produced in the Escuela Nacional Preparatoria, and subsequent murals, is best answered by turning to the paintings themselves. Diego Rivera's first mural, *Creation*, for example, an encaustic executed in the Bolívar Auditorium of the Escuela Nacional Preparatoria in 1922, was a richly colored blend of Italo-Byzantine and cubist characteristics, far removed in its half-religious, half-philosophical content from the tenets of the Syndicate manifesto. Not until Rivera painted his murals in the Secretaría de Educación Pública (1923–1928) and the Escuela Nacional de Agricultura in Chapingo (1925–1927) did the tenets of the manifesto make themselves apparent. The content had been revolutionalized and mural technique and style changed decisively. There were clear references to prerevolutionary worker abuse and idealized images of revolutionary changes such as land distribution, rural teaching, and the union between workers and peasants.

José Clemente Orozco's first murals in the Escuela Nacional Preparatoria were painted under the conviction that "a painter who works within the Italian tradition of the fifteenth and sixteenth century can be more 'nationalist' than some other artist tickled silly at the sight of our Mexican pots and pans"[5] (a snide jibe at Rivera). This antifolkloric attitude persisted in Orozco's outlook; however, it should not be confused with antinationalism. In spite of the Italianate character of his first mural, *Maternity*, Orozco was profoundly nationalistic, albeit his conceptions of both the revolution and the conquest, in such works as *The Trinity*, *The Strike*, *Destruction of the Old Order*, and *Cortés and Malinche* were

individual and contrary to the nationalism and idealism of his contemporaries; they demonstrate his particular blend of iconoclasm and skepticism. His staircase murals on the theme of the origin of the Hispanic-American world accept neither of the prevailing views of the conquest: that of the *hispanistas*, who glorified Spain's civilizing contributions to a barbaric, blood-drenched world without mentioning the bloody conquest itself, nor that of the *indigenistas* (like Rivera), who conceived of an idyllic nativism before the conquest.

Despite the fact that he was the major theoretician of the mural movement from the beginning, Siqueiros' earliest mural (in the National Preparatory School) was rather less auspicious than those of his colleagues. His winged female hovering over sea shells and other abstract forms shows no evidence of the Mexicanist and revolutionary content so stingingly enunciated in the manifesto. *Burial of a Worker* (1924), however, begins to show an early maturity of style as well as a new content in the three workers carrying a bright blue coffin with an unobtrusive hammer and sickle on the cover.

Did the *tres grandes* ("big three"—Siqueiros, Rivera, and Orozco) express the tenets of the Syndicate's 1923 manifesto in their murals of the first decade? If we consider the *spirit* of the document rather than the express words, we can answer affirmatively. An artistic manifesto represents a literary core around which artists radiate for greater or lesser periods of time, embroidering on those of its concepts most translatable in terms of their individual genius—as can be demonstrated in the degrees of adherence to or variation from the manifestos of the futurists or surrealists. The Mexicans expressed the essence of their manifesto each within his individual temperament and style: Siqueiros dealt with working-class content, Orozco with the ideas and abuses of the revolution and the formation of the Mexican nation, Rivera with indigenous and popular culture, the history of the revolution, and the role of Yankee imperialism. Their styles were responsive to the search for new expression and the educational needs of postrevolutionary Mexico.

Mexican Muralists in the United States

Between 1930 and 1934, muralism entered an international phase as murals were painted in the United States by Rivera, Orozco, and Siqueiros and artists from all parts of the American continent visited Mexico. Though both Rivera and Orozco painted portable murals in the United States as late as 1939–1940 and Siqueiros held an experimental workshop in New York in 1936, they did no stationary murals after 1934. In spite of—or perhaps because of—the very unfavorable publicity attending the murals painted in these years and the destruction of Rivera's Rockefeller Center mural and two of Siqueiros' Los Angeles murals, the muralists were tremendously influential among younger, socially minded artists, who welcomed them as the avant-garde of the day. In effect, social realism became an international style in the thirties, finding disciples and followers in Latin America, the United States, and Europe. Though largely abandoned during World War II and the subsequent period of the Cold War and McCarthyism, the humanistic ethic remained valid for many figurative painters.[6] It underwent a number of permutations, disengaging itself from class alignments and substituting "universal" for class-derived human malaise, thus laying the basis for neohumanism.

The major precepts of the Mexican mural movement were translated into United States terms through the intervention of painter George Biddle, who wrote to his former Groton schoolmate, President Franklin D. Roosevelt, in May 1933 at the height of the Great Depression and urged him to initiate direct government patronage of the arts after the Mexican model: "The

Mexican artists have produced the greatest national school of mural painting since the Italian Renaissance. Diego Rivera tells me that it was only possible because Obregón allowed artists to work at plumber's wages in order to express on walls of government buildings the social ideals of the Mexican revolution."[7] Among the factors that propelled an entire generation of North American artists toward the Left and social protest painting was, first and foremost, the Depression. Beyond that were the imminence of World War II and the polarization of political and social forces throughout the world into communist and fascist camps, the return of former expatriates who had encountered socialist or Marxist theories in Europe, and the establishment of the WPA Federal Art Project, which represented an unprecedented and radical movement in the United States—the first time the training and economic support of artists had been federally subsidized.

The entire period of the Depression in the United States and the accompanying governmental support of the arts, under various WPA agencies and the Treasury Department, has only recently begun to be studied.[8] As a result of stylistic fluctuations and an adverse political climate, a curious myopia afflicted United States art historians and critics after the 1930s, causing the entire American Scene and social realist schools (including the WPA period) to be relegated to obscurity, thereby depriving us of both reasoned and objective critical analysis and historical information. The role of the Mexicans in this period, in fact the entire history of contact between United States artists and the Mexicans from the 1920s on, is fragmentary.

It is outside the scope of this work to examine Mexican influence in the United States in more than a cursory way; however, two important international contacts should be noted here. The first was Rico Lebrun, who was one of the United States artists participating in the Treasury Department mural program. There is no evidence to indicate that he worked directly with either Ri-

vera or Orozco. However, though he was studying fresco painting in Italy during the crucial
years 1930–1933 when the Mexicans were in the
United States, he did return to New York in 1933
and could hardly have avoided knowledge of the
"battle of Rockefeller Center," which terminated
in the destruction of Rivera's fresco in 1933.
Orozco's fresco series at the New School for Social Research in New York (1930–1931) would
also have interested an artist who had just spent
three years studying the technique and had made
a special trip to Orvieto Cathedral to see the Si-
gnorelli frescoes. Lebrun's decisive encounter
with Mexico occurred in 1952–1953, when he
taught at the Escuela Universitaria de Bellas Artes in San Miguel de Allende, where Siqueiros
had conducted classes for art students three
years earlier.[9] The Mexican artist with whom Lebrun felt true spiritual affinity, however, was
Orozco. Lebrun's 1959 mural *Genesis* in Pomona
College, Claremont, California (Fig. 11), has many
humanistic and symbolic resemblances to Orozco's 1930 mural *Prometheus* in the same location
and, in fact, is a pendant to it: in 1956 Lebrun
had expressed the desire to paint a mural in
close proximity to Orozco's.[10] There is little
doubt that the close friendship and mutual support between Lebrun and the Nueva Presencia
artists in the sixties derive from this common
source (Orozco), which led to a stylistic as well
as philosophical affinity.

The second important international contact
and another United States artist who directly
linked 1930s social realism with neohumanism
was former social realist Ben Shahn. Like Lebrun, Lithuanian-born Shahn was an immigrant
to the United States. Shahn first came to the attention of Diego Rivera through fifteen gouache
drawings and a tempera panel, on the case of
imprisoned labor leader Tom Mooney, that Rivera
admired in the Downtown Gallery in New York.
Rivera wrote the foreword to Shahn's catalog and
persuaded him to become an assistant for the
Rockefeller Center mural. Shahn's own 1937–

1938 fresco mural in Roosevelt, New Jersey, follows the undulant principle he learned from
Rivera—deep recessions of space alternating
with human and architectural projecting details.
Though Shahn's style is essentially linear, with
flat areas of color that often verge on abstraction,
he remained a realist. After the thirties his art,
according to his own testimony, turned from social realism to personal realism; however, he
continued to deal with social themes to the end
of his life, often in an allegorical manner. Both
Shahn and Lebrun were included in the three-
nation exhibition organized by Nueva Presencia
in Mexico City in September 1963 under the title "Neohumanism in the Drawing of Italy, the
United States, and Mexico."

Lebrun and Shahn were not the only artists involved in the changes occurring in the art world
of the 1930s, changes partially caused by the visit
of the Mexican muralists. Social conditions had
changed radically in the United States during
these years and so, according to a contemporary
evaluation, had attitudes toward the arts: "We are
living in a time of conscious and critical re-evaluation," said Cahill and Barr in 1934. "In the
depression art seems more of a luxury than ever
. . . one clear note in contemporary American
painting is a new emphasis upon social and collective expression" in which subject and human
interest have definitely been reinstated.[11] "It is to
the credit of a little group of Mexicans," said another observer, "that they have, without weaken-
ing of the abstract structure, restored painting
that is socially meaningful. . . . They have wid-
ened the boundaries of modern painting, showing how the grasp on formal organization can be
made to serve with mural-art limitations."[12] That
the Mexicans were considered under the aegis of
"modernist" painting in the 1930s is suggested in
the above appraisal. The "conservatives" of the
day worked in a neoclassical spirit with all the
traditional notions about form, space, and color;
they saw art as noble and scholarly and, if it was
good, slightly mystical. Not only were the Mex-

icans formally modernist, but their subject matter was contemporary.

Information is sparse about the North Americans immediately influenced by the Mexicans. Rivera's assistants in San Francisco, Detroit, and New York included Lucienne Bloch, English painter Viscount John Hastings, English sculptor Clifford Wight, Matthew Barnes, Stephan Dimitroff, Hideo Noda, Arthur Niendorf, and Ben Shahn. Artists whose murals exhibited a debt to Rivera included Edgar Britton and Mitchell Siporin (Chicago); Karle Kelpe (Illinois); William C. Palmer, Charles Alston, and Marion Greenwood (New York); and Edward Millman (Chicago). James Michael Newell (New York) was indebted to Rivera and Orozco; Charles White (Virginia) to Orozco. Siqueiros' assistants in Los Angeles included Millard Sheets and other members of the California Watercolor Society, Dean Cornwell, Reuben Kadish, Myer Shaffer, Philip (Goldstein) Guston, Sanford McCoy, and possibly his brother Jackson Pollock. Kadish, Shaffer, and Guston were employed by the Los Angeles WPA, but few of their murals produced during that period are still in existence. A photograph of a Shaffer mural painted in the City of Hope Hospital, Duarte, California, shows Siqueiros' influence in the utilization of strongly foreshortened columns and stagelike spatial organization similar to that of Siqueiros' 1932 mural *Portrait of Mexico Today*.[13]

After World War II an influx of United States student artists financed by the G.I. Bill of Rights studied in Mexico, particularly in the mural course presented by Siqueiros in San Miguel de Allende, Guanajuato (1948–1949), during which they worked on the mural *Monument to General Ignacio Allende* (never completed), which utilized Siqueiros' theories of polyangular perspective. Among them were instructors David Barajas (now living in Los Angeles), James Pinto (who worked with Lebrun on the Pomona College mural), and Raymond Brossard, and students Phil Stein (who stayed with the Siqueiros *taller* [workshop]), Robert Hansen (living in Los Angeles),

and Joe Lasker. Other United States artists participated in the Siqueiros mural *The March of Humanity on Earth and toward the Cosmos* (Mexico City, 1965–1971). A United States assistant was Mark Rogovin of Chicago, who is active, as Arnold Belkin has been, in the contemporary United States mural revival.

Nationalism and Indigenism

The terms *indigenism* and *nationalism* are frequently used in this study, and consequently a brief explication of their significance is in order here. Indigenism in most Latin American countries, especially Mexico, which had no large, visible Afro-American population like that of Brazil or the Caribbean countries, was synonymous with Indianism. Both Orozco and Siqueiros opposed archeological reconstruction and tourist-oriented picturesqueness; at the same time both invented a new mythology of the pre-Columbian heroes Quetzalcoatl and Cuauhtemoc, who served as vehicles for the expression of modern concepts. At the same time, Indianism affected Mexican literature, music, and dance. Indianism, like the European cult of the primitive, is essentially a form of antirationalism and anti-intellectualism. The "primitive" or "backward" peoples were supposed to be instinctual, less repressed than more "civilized" groups, closer to their animal natures, more exotic. This is the essence of D. H. Lawrence's novel *The Plumed Serpent*, written in 1926. Artists like Diego Rivera, who had lived in Paris, substituted the pre-Columbian for the African then popular in Europe as a result of the influence of Cubism. However, there is a basic difference between European artists who turned to the "primitivism" of peoples outside their psychological and physical space and Latin Americans who returned to a culture infused with Indian essence.

Likewise, there is a difference between the nationalism of the highly developed imperial nations of Western Europe and that of underdeveloped or colonial nations of the twentieth century. To achieve an insight into the special characteristics attending an explosion of cultural nationalism in a country attempting to achieve political independence and a national identity after years or centuries of foreign domination, we must turn to the writings of intellectuals deriving from these cultures. One of the most lucid and profound expositions of cultural nationalism, written in the early 1960s in reference to African nationalism, by a Black psychiatrist from Martinique who lived many years in North Africa, is pertinent here:

While the politicians situate their action in actual present-day events, men of culture take their stand in the field of history. . . . It is in fact a commonplace to state that for several decades large numbers of research workers have, in the main, rehabilitated the African, Mexican, and Peruvian civilizations. The passion with which native intellectuals defend the existence of their national culture may be a source of amazement, but those who condemn this exaggerated passion are strangely apt to forget that their own psyche and their own selves are conveniently sheltered behind a French or German culture which has given full proof of its existence and which is uncontested.[14]

It must be kept in mind that Mexico was a colonized nation from the sixteenth to the nineteenth centuries and, despite the 1810 war of independence that freed Mexico politically from Spain, the colonized mentality of the ruling classes maintained a position of imitation vis-à-vis European culture and a contempt for indigenous culture. In Mexico, as in Latin America generally, nationalism has been one of the greatest forces impelling change. It has been deeply entwined with a necessary sense of dignity, pride, and affirmation. To counter engendered feelings of inferiority, intellectuals have reconstructed the past and in so doing have created a mythology of ancient utopias. The Mexican painter who epitomized this tendency was Diego Rivera who, within a framework of Marxism, dialectically

compared the positive and negative forces operating in a historical period, with an emphasis on the positive. In his vast epic of Mexican history on the staircase of the Palacio Nacional, Mexico City, he created a Golden Age, where Quetzalcoatl is the prophet. Cultural reaffirmation alone, however, is not the full substance of Rivera's mural. Mexico's Indian population also composed the largest and most exploited class of the country—the rural base on which the entire economic structure rested. To revitalize this class, to set before it, in a mural, not only its ancient tradition idealized, but its power to reconstruct the present and control the future, was to continue the work that the military phase of the revolution had started. This is the true significance of Rivera's mural, which rests on a twin construct of nationalism and indigenism.

Nationalism and indigenism were also elements in the work of both Siqueiros and Orozco, but serving different purposes. Siqueiros' 1944 mural *Cuauhtemoc against the Myth* used the Aztec emperor as a symbol of the possibility of a struggle against seemingly overwhelming forces. On the surface, Orozco disdained the use of nationalism, partly because of his scorn for romanticized visions of Indian life "fit to flatter the tourist" and partly because of a middle-class snobbery directed at "hateful and degenerate types of the lower classes" that caused him to eschew the painting of "Indian sandals and dirty clothes."[15] Nevertheless his treatment of the positive aspects of the human condition often presented Quetzalcoatl and the revolutionary heroes Hidalgo and Zapata in heroic and grandiose terms.

Nevertheless, cultural nationalism can outlive its usefulness and become a hindrance to development, or—as occurred in Mexico—become an exotic anachronism as a result of changed social circumstances. If prolonged beyond its social and psychological necessities, nationalism becomes nostalgia. There are three major stages in the development of nationalism. First, the colonized artists are subject to unqualified assimilation into the culture of the imperialist power and produce works whose inspiration is European. This stage in Mexico corresponded to the Porfirian era before the Mexican Revolution, when, though not actually an occupied country, Mexico was given over to foreign economic exploitation with the collusion of its own upper classes and looked to Europe for its cultural norms. The second stage is one in which artists immerse themselves in native culture and history as described above. This phase corresponds to the two decades 1920 to 1940, which saw a flowering of nativist, nationalist culture as an affirmation of self-pride. This stage also has its dangers: the return to nativist traditions within a modern context is discovered to be alien and "exotic" to the people themselves, who no longer function within a traditional culture. Though they may be Indian peoples, their context is contemporary and their culture shows the effects of a series of adaptations to present circumstances. Thus traditional customs are only an outer garment, the fragmentary appearance of a deteriorated and decayed past culture—deceiving only the tourist seeking "local color" or the blinded nativist. Artists run the risk of being out of date by shutting themselves up with a stereotyped reproduction of details, by turning paradoxically toward the past and away from actual events. This was the danger into which Rivera, and the determined *riveristas* who duplicated his formulas, fell during his later years, and against which Orozco and Siqueiros warned. The final stage is one in which artists who wish to create authentic works of art realize that the truths about their nation are invested in its present realities.[16]

On the other hand, it is pertinent to consider the significance of a rejection of nationalism and indigenism in a country whose component of Indians constitutes the most exploited stratum of the nation, or a nation that is part of the "third world" of underdeveloped countries vis-à-vis the wealthy, industrialized Western nations. Such re-

jection, in my opinion, reflects the internationalist economic and cultural affiliations of the bourgeoisie and not the reality of the rural and urban working people. One could conclude, therefore, that the virtue or evil of a nationalist position is relative. Nationalism and ethnocentricity within a highly developed imperialist nation represent retrogressive, reactionary tendencies, particularly when imposed on subject peoples. For the subject peoples, nationalism may be a form of survival.

This does not gainsay or invalidate the role of the artist as a social critic in either society— a role that Orozco, Rivera, and Siqueiros frequently assumed. It does raise a question about the position of Tamayo and, ultimately, Cuevas, in rejecting nationalism (at least verbally) for an abstract universalism, and this will be treated within the proper context.

Social Realism

Without engaging the whole question of "realism," it is necessary to arrive at some understanding of social realism, a major countercurrent to abstraction and nonengaged art in the 1930s and 1940s. The possible relationship of social realism and neohumanism will be traced later.

I cannot do much more than establish a working definition of social realism, since the issue is still hotly debated on an international scale.[17] As a term, it is specifically tied to the twentieth century and the appearance in 1917 of the first socialist nation. The original term, *socialist realism*, is said to have been coined by Stalin in 1932 and formalized in a speech to the 1934 Soviet Writers Congress by Maxim Gorky.[18] Gorky suggested that myths were imaginative abstractions of fundamental ideas underlying a given reality. Realism, according to him, was the embodiment of this reality in an image; if amplified through the addition of the desired and the possible, it promoted a revolutionary attitude.[19] Gorky's attitude had nothing in common with Stalinist Zhdanovism, which lasted in the Soviet Union from the mid-1930s until 1956, ending with the Khrushchev "thaw" (though reverberations still exist). Zhdanovism demanded of the artist a "truthful, historically concrete representation of reality in its revolutionary development" and a contribution to the "ideological transformation and the education of workers in the spirit of socialism."[20] It was enforced by rigid rules governing art and literature and has been considered a temporary aberration and distortion peculiar to a stage of Soviet development. In point of fact, it is a vulgarization of Marxist theory to equate realistic content with formal naturalism. Realism has been a periodically recurring current in art in the sense that certain artists have endeavored to depict the actual conditions of life and not its idealization; however, these recurrences have employed distinct forms of expression. In addition, realist artists have often sought to express the hidden meanings of things—thus exaggerations of reality or fantastic symbols may be utilized by realistic artists. Historically considered, realism should refer to the *content* of art and not to its *form*. Gorky's concept of the myth-making function had already been demonstrated, for example, in the French Revolution's heroic portraiture and in Rivera's recreation of the pre-Columbian Golden Age, among others.

Though the terms *social* and *socialist* realism are loosely interchanged in common usage, the major difference would seem to be the social context in which each is practiced.[21] Following the traditional assumption that a socialist nation is one in which the working class has taken over the control of the state and the means of production, the socialist realist artist is one who works to express the ideology of the new ruling class (the working people) to aid the transformation to a socialist society, as the Russian constructivists did for a short period of time. The vulgarization of this idea in the Soviet Union consisted of in-

sisting that the artist portray only positive and heroic aspects of life, without allowing objectivity. In other words, it was a form of idealism rather than realism. To present achievement without struggle, accomplishment without error, theory without self-criticism, becomes the antithesis of the dialectical method. Symbolic of the distortion that occurred was the distance that separated the writings of Gorky himself, where the variations of Russian character and activity are masterfully presented, and the products of Zhdanov prescription.

Social realists, on the other hand, function within class-structured capitalist societies, where their role is one of opposition to the owning classes, who represent a minority of the population. Social, or "critical" realism, as it has been called, implies, in most cases, an individual rather than a collective protest against bourgeois society and, as such, can be said to date back to nineteenth-century romanticism. Social realist art in the United States during the 1930s dealt with the negative aspects of life during the Depression: strikes, poverty, malnutrition, injustice, state brutality, and racism. It portrayed struggle against these conditions but seldom presented socialist alternatives (and the works that did were often censored or even destroyed).[22]

Mexican social realism, the hallmark of the mural movement, falls somewhere between "social" and "socialist." The reasons for this are to be found in the specificities of the Mexican Revolution which, in certain of its phases, introduced a modicum of socialist theory into a bourgeois revolution. The relative freedom of expression Mexico offered its social realists during certain more enlightened periods can be judged by the fact that Rivera was able to recreate his 1933 Rockefeller Center mural entire, including the portrait of Lenin that caused its original destruction, in the Palacio de Bellas Artes a year later. However, not all periods were so propitious. Rivera's four movable fresco panels satirizing foreign tourism (now in the Palacio de Bellas

Artes) were never exhibited by the Hotel Reforma, which commissioned them in 1936. His 1947–1948 mural in the Hotel del Prado was vandalized and finally covered until he removed the phrase "God does not exist." Siqueiros' 1958 mural in the vestibule of the Teatro Jorge Negrete was halted before completion by a judicial order obtained under government pressure by the Asociación Nacional de Actores, which had commissioned it, because of its excessive militancy. The historically engendered Mexican ambivalence toward overt socialist content and criticism has nevertheless permitted a range of social realist works that could not have existed, for example, in the United States. It should be noted, however, that, despite the quantity of murals painted in the 1960s, the content has become increasingly innocuous and uncritical. This is not unrelated, in my opinion, to the increase in private and public galleries and the corresponding shift in interest from public to private art, i.e., easel painting instead of murals.

We can get a better notion of the particularities of Mexican social realism by examining the theoretical statements and artistic practice of Mexico's major social realist theoretician, Siqueiros, as well as the variants created by Rivera and Orozco. This is of particular interest since the Nueva Presencia artists affirmed their admiration for the progenitors of the mural movement (especially Orozco) and were moved by the same urgings of social conscience that gave rise to social realism. How important residual social realism was in the artistic expression of Los Interioristas remains to be explored.

Mexican social realism can be divided into two phases: that of the twenties and thirties and that of the late forties and fifties. The 1923 Syndicate manifesto, which was largely the work of Siqueiros, established the social and nationalist parameters of Mexican realism in its early phases, but its terminology deals primarily with political and social rather than aesthetic aims. In the work of Siqueiros a conjunction of theoretical content

and form is indicated in a lecture delivered to the John Reed Club of Hollywood in 1932. The two Los Angeles murals, *Street Meeting* and *Tropical America*, mentioned in this lecture only partially utilized the formal theories. Siqueiros did not discover Duco (pyroxilin) paint as a medium until 1933, nor did he use colored cement, documentary photographs, or electrical projectors until a later date. However, he related this methodology to his concepts of class struggle. Technical innovations were of use, he said, only if applied with revolutionary proletarian conviction, at which time they would produce "transcendental aesthetic effects (social and intrinsic as in absolute works of art) that correspond to the present state of social struggle of the enraged classes, to the epoch of imperialism, last stage of capitalist rule, and to the affirmative stages of the new society which is very near."[23] The innovations were to be achieved by a scientific and materialist approach to the art of painting, as contemporary as the modern industrial world in which we live. He proposed use of the airgun and air hammer to apply and roughen the mural ground; white waterproof cement instead of plaster to permit outdoor, unsheltered murals; the airbrush for paint application; the electrical projector to transfer designs to the wall; precolored cement mortar applied to the wall with a compressor instead of painted surfaces; and the photograph and movie camera to integrate documentary material into a previously developed design.

By 1939 Siqueiros had developed additional techniques, including the use of vinylite paints[24] which permitted a variety of different surface textures; active wall surfaces—concave and convex; the distortion of electrically projected tracings on the wall surface; the camera to analyze volumes, space, and the movement of volumes; and the optical illusions created by compounded polyangular and superimposed form in simulating motion as the viewer changes position. In this connection Siqueiros later stated: "For the first time in the history of the world we are taken over by the camera and the film [to deal with] the most subtle expanse of space, of volume in space, of movement in all its complexity and what is even more important, the subtlest objectives and subjectives of human drama. Without learning from photography and its various techniques there is no access to new realism in painting."[25] The references to documentary photography and the illusion of movement are not completely original. They might be considered a synthesis of cubist-futurist explorations of time-space with the photomontage techniques developed by the Berlin Dadaists—techniques which, unlike cubist-futurist collage, were used to emphasize socially critical subject matter. A further impetus was received from Siqueiros' 1932 friendship with Russian film director Sergei Eisenstein.

In the statement quoted above, Siqueiros used the term *nuevo realismo* ("new realism"), later changed to *neorealismo* (1951), which marked a new phase of his social realism. The timing corresponds to the international ascendancy of United States abstract expressionism and European informalism, and a parallel neorealism among writers, film-makers, and painters attracted to a documentary style. In Italy, for example, Roberto Rossellini produced neorealist films like the 1945 *Open City*, and younger realist painters (as well as abstractionists) formed the Fronte Nuovo delle Arte several years later. Among their ranks was Renato Guttuso, Italy's most outstanding realist, whose work was later included in the Nueva Presencia–organized exhibit "Neohumanism in the Drawing of Italy, the United States, and Mexico." Another factor influencing the reaffirmation of social realism might have been the Soviet response to Cold War politics; in the post-1946 era, the Zhdanov hard line was applied to the arts internationally. There is little reason to doubt that Siqueiros, as one of Mexico's leading Communist Party members, was sympathetic to the reaffirmation. However, like the European Communist artists Picasso and

Léger, he also felt free to voice his criticism of Soviet socialist realism and affirm his independent role. In a 1948 article, he put forth his theory of four currents in modern world art: naturalism or academic realism; nonrealism or Paris formalism; socialist prorealism, focused in the Soviet Union; and functionalism, or the embryo of a new realism, in Mexico. Academic realism, he felt, had no professional theoretical adherents in Mexico, while in the Soviet Union, the pictorial practices of the socialist prorealists did not correspond to their theories. In Mexico, he said, the major theoretical and pictorial battles were between abstraction and the new realism.[26] There is nothing really new in these opinions, since the major opposition between realism and abstraction had been formulated as early as Siqueiros' 1921 *Vida Americana* "Calls," written and published in Barcelona when he went to study in Europe after the revolution, and reiterated in the 1923 Syndicate manifesto. What is of interest is the clear separation between dogmatic Soviet socialist realism and Mexican social realism. And when one considers the body of truly outstanding work produced under the banner of social realism in Mexico, it becomes clear that social realism does not, a priori, have to be cliché, either in content or execution, despite the unmemorable track record of many United States social realists. In this respect I disagree with many United States critics who have equated controversial content with poor aesthetics. Even Siqueiros' most bitter public opponent, José Luis Cuevas, when speaking candidly, admits Siqueiros' formal mastery in the period he called his "golden age" (prior to 1947).[27] If this were not true it would be hard to understand the extraordinary reverence with which the *tres grandes* (especially Orozco and Siqueiros) are regarded by younger socially conscious artists in Mexico, not all of whom necessarily agree with their politics or philosophy in art.

Diego Rivera's turn to social realism occurred when he reassessed his contact with contemporary art upon his return from Europe in 1921. He chose to break with "modernist" art and synthesize influences from cubism, Italian pre-Renaissance and Renaissance murals, and Mexican folk, popular, and pre-Columbian art into a new form: his own brand of social realism. Summing up his philosophy in a 1927 visit to Russia, Rivera said: "The Russian masses were right to reject the Paris and Berlin form of art called "ultramodern"; . . . artists should have given them an art of high esthetic quality, containing all the technical acquisitions of contemporary art, but an art simple, clear, and transparent as crystal, hard as steel, cohesive as concrete, the trinity of the great architecture of the new historical stage of the world."[28] "Technical acquisitions" did not refer to media but to formal innovation, since Rivera used (with rare exceptions) traditional fresco, encaustic, tempera, or mosaic, to the end of his life. He was opposed to dispensing with subject matter, deeming that a painter's work would suffer impoverishment as a result. In effect, he dismissed the efforts of the Russian avant-garde, Kandinsky, Lissitsky, Malevich, and others, though he, like Siqueiros, criticized the Russian academic painters who shielded themselves behind mottoes of Marxist dialectical materialism.

Though Rivera's large forms and bold colors are attractive and accessible in ways that Siqueiros' and Orozco's dramatic or expressionistic allegories are not, his murals are not as easily decipherable by the untutored as his statement would lead one to suppose. The density and complexity of the murals at the Palacio Nacional, the Palacio de Bellas Artes, and the Detroit Institute of Arts require careful and patient examination on the pictorial level, while the allegorical levels demand a high degree of sophistication. Human beings are participants in vast, detailed, encyclopedic epics rolled out like an embroidered carpet for our inspection. The viewer is caught up in the plethora of pictorial information, the decorative rhythms, the stylizations, and the brilliant color. As in Balzac's human comedy, thousands of characters appear, each with a distinct personality playing a role in a social drama. Because of the formal discipline of cubism, the morphology is clear; the metaphysics is another matter. The masses have built great civilizations in the past despite their sufferings engendered by the class struggle and the power of the oppressors; they will build glorious civilizations in the future. Leaders and prophets have arisen—Quetzalcoatl, Hidalgo, Juárez, Lenin, Marx, Zapata—who show the path to the willing workers. The anonymous peasants and workers are the ultimate heroes of Rivera's dramas, and their image is sublimated and projected into the future by the central figure of the Palacio de Bellas Artes mural, who holds the micro- and macrocosms, the wheels of science, industry, and society, in his powerful gloved hand.

To fit Orozco into a mold of social realism would be, perhaps, too procrustean. By definition, social realism—though not a given style—assumes class consciousness and a sympathetic relationship with the working class. Many of Orozco's artistic conceptions were essentially personal and mystical—a kind of anticlerical Christian existentialism. That his was a personal vision, spontaneously and emotionally expressed, rather than one determined by a consistent ideology, is attested to in numerous instances, and perhaps explains his known idiosyncratic political changes. In a letter to Justino Fernández in 1940, he said: "What matters is to think in a high voice, to say things that are felt in the moment they are said"[29]—a statement that does not indicate adherence to a preconsidered political doctrine. He conceived of a painting, he said, as something apart from morality and immorality, good or bad, vice or virtue. He felt it should not relate to theories, anecdotes, or stories or contain opinions about religious, political, or social affairs; its emotion should be generated wholly through its concrete plastic existence.[30] In spite of these sentiments, Orozco responded to the world in which he lived with definite notions of morality, religion, and social affairs. Born in 1883, he lived through the destruction and disillusionment of a revolution (whose brutality he observed first-hand) and two world wars. One can well understand his consequent distrust of machinery and technology, his dislike of demagoguery, his apocalyptic vision of the world. He saw good and evil in terms of universals, condemning ancient and modern brutality, war, betrayal, injustice, hypocrisy, greed; exalting human rebellion, strength, beauty, and genius. The two poles of his morality are contained in the metaphors of the prostitute as decay and destruction, and Prometheus/Quetzalcoatl as enlightenment and transcendence. One will no more encounter the social causes of prostitution in Orozco than one does in Rouault!

In Orozco's works it is apparent, despite his statement, that form ("concrete plastic existence") is always secondary to moralizing content and that his style evolved at the service of his passionate expression of moral concerns. In his work we find the heroic figures of Prometheus (Pomona College, Claremont, California), the Man of Fire (frontispiece to this book), Father Hidalgo (Palacio de Gobierno, Guadalajara), Quetzalcoatl (Dartmouth College, Hanover, New Hampshire) and even a Quixote-like Cortés (Hospicio Cabañas, Guadalajara). His most poignant expression of despair with modern civilization is *Christ Destroying His Cross* (Dartmouth College). Toward the end of his life, Orozco turned more frequently to the darker aspects of Biblical imagery: Lazarus raised from the dead, the devil, the apocalypse. The clothing of contemporary concerns in allegorical, mythological, or religious dress is not a new phenomenon in art; it always assumes that the artist has a given point of view (a political attitude, using "political" in the broadest sense of the word), and Orozco is not exempt from the expression of such views. He obviously had theories, opinions, and a moral position.

At the same time, Orozco had the typical fear of the bourgeoisie confronted by the "masses." To him, they were a blind destructive force that might be utterly barbaric if not checked. This is suggested in the Preparatoria works; but his most devastating image appears in the Biblioteca Gabino Ortiz, Jiquilpan, Michoacán: in stark black and white the masses have become huge screaming mouths carrying flags and flinging stones: abstracted monsters. Unlike Maxim Gorky, whom he resembled in his open-eyed critical appraisal of the common people, Orozco found no redeemers or creative spirits in the "lower depths" of humanity. There is no dialectical interaction in his works, as there is in Rivera's, between the people and the "great men of history." In this sense Orozco is Nietzschean. The people are led toward the light unwillingly; they quarrel among themselves in the process. The victims shake their fists toward the heavens in existential despair. Orozco could not, like Rivera and Siqueiros, put aside the middle-class attitudes into which all three had been born and identify himself with their kind of heroic working-class ethic.

There were moments when Orozco approached social realism. His cartoons for the newspaper *La Vanguardia* (published by Dr. Atl during the revolution) and the Syndicate newspaper *El Machete* were frankly partisan. He caricatured the wealthy and the church in the Preparatoria murals, but also showed the workers attacking each other. His depiction of revolutionaries in the early period was often sympathetic, but just as often not. The murals at the New School for Social Research in New York included the portraits of Lenin and Stalin, assassinated Yucatecan governor Felipe Carrillo Puerto, Gandhi, and references to British imperialism in India. The Dartmouth College mural shows a Villa/Zapata figure explicitly attacked by United States imperialists and their Mexican allies. Often, however, the "class enemy" is not identified and the assumption is that evil (and good) are inherent in human nature. It is this aspect, perhaps, that made Orozco so attractive to the anti-ideological young artists of the fifties and sixties.

A Contemporary Overview:
The Seeds of Confrontation

As long as the Marxist or quasi-socialist theories of the mural movement coincided with the political aspirations of the burgeoning bourgeoisie, common cause was made with the muralists—or rather the more militant aspects of muralism were tolerated by the bourgeoisie as long as this class was small and relatively powerless and as long as it recognized that the needs of the people who made the revolution required response and satisfaction. As it grew in power, the ruling class gradually discountenanced the militant and revolutionary aspects of muralism and retained only the superficial, sentimental, and nostalgic. Out of the Mexican School grew the academic movement which catered to this taste in devitalized, decorative, "patriotic" murals and easel painting. The Mexican bourgeoisie was seconded in its taste by the rapidly growing torrent of tourists who sought "local color" in works of art.

The decade between 1940, when Lázaro Cárdenas concluded his presidential term, and 1950 can be considered a period of transition in both art and politics. It signaled the beginning of the decline in quality of muralism and public art and the start of the era of private easel painting. By the fifties, Orozco was dead and Rivera had frequently turned to insipid and decorative painting. Only Siqueiros was left to make a powerful statement in the lobby of the Hospital de la Raza in 1952–1956, after which his official commissions dwindled.

Although muralism was declining in quality, it continued to increase in quantity in the forties and fifties. In the period after 1940, in addition to government commissions for large housing tracts and medical, educational, and other public buildings, mural production received a strong impetus from the construction of private banks and industrial and commercial buildings. A sharp increase in the number of private commissions occurred in 1940, and the quantity continued to rise unevenly until its highest point in 1958, when 36 of the 63 murals painted during the year were for the private sector. Thereafter there was a decline until 1964, when 98 murals (22 for the private sector) were painted in one year.[1] This was a year of expanded government construction and restoration of numerous museums in Mexico City under the presidency of Adolfo López Mateos, and the great increase in murals is accounted for by the commissions for these buildings. Between 1964 and 1969, mural production continued to decline, dropping to 14 in the final year. In addition, when one considers the fact that only 289 artists were involved in the creation of 1,286 murals between the years 1905 and 1969, it becomes apparent that commissions have not been diffused among the growing artistic community, which was estimated at 12,000 painters in Mexico City alone by 1973. The complaints of the younger artists at their inability to receive mural commissions seem justified by these statistics and verify that a type of "monopoly" existed within the ranks of the mural movement.

Hastening the demise of the mural movement were not only the factors of social and political change within Mexico but also a barrage of hostile criticism from without. Since the forties, a campaign of vilification of the mural movement as illustrative, narrative, archaic, narrowly nationalistic, propagandistic, literal, and unimaginative has been conducted in Europe and the United States, resulting in the disparagement or outright elimination of the Mexican School in histories of modern art.

By 1962, many of the younger Mexican artists themselves were in full revolt against the academic tendencies and mediocrity that had become endemic in Mexico. However, the process of re-evaluation was not permitted to proceed in a wholly organic fashion. The role played by United States cultural imperialism will be considered separately; however, in Latin America itself there were three persons in the forefront of the attack against the mural movement: Mexican painters Rufino Tamayo and José Luis Cuevas (both of whom found their earliest and most important recognition in the United States and Europe) and South American critic Marta Traba. During the forties and fifties, Tamayo was the "prophet" of antimuralism (or antimessage art); in the sixties, Cuevas succeeded to his mantle, in the process denouncing Tamayo himself.

When Siqueiros died in 1974, Henry J. Seldis, art critic of the *Los Angeles Times*, wrote: "In large measure the contemporary Mexican artist's liberation from the strictures of Mexican muralism is based on Rufino Tamayo's long standing rebellion against its ideological emphasis . . . No school has formed around Tamayo, but two generations of Mexican artists have now followed his example of ridding themselves of the need of being political propagandists." He also quoted Mexican writer Ramón Xirau as saying: "Tamayo's work was there to tell us that a painting's value depends on and resides in its plastic qualities primarily. The painter is, above all, a painter and if his work should ever come to have social, moral and ethical facets these will be in the forms of overtones."[2]

Rufino Tamayo

Because of his key role in the confrontation of the fifties, when he espoused the cause of the abstractionists, it is pertinent to examine Tamayo's work and influence here. The major issue that he presented to the Mexican art world, in the name of rebellion, was the question of socially oriented realism versus "pure painting." In this respect he was the foremost representative of what we might call the "subjective-formalist" aspect of modern Mexican art, with roots in the "modernism" and "internationalism" of the late twenties—an aspect that had a renewed florescence in the fifties.

The body of Tamayo's work in easel paintings, murals, and graphics makes his essential qualities evident: harmonious groupings of forms, an ability to create compositions of great equilib-

rium, and a keen sensitivity to color all speak of an artist of great talent who has constantly refined his art. Thematically he has dealt with allegorical treatments of Mexican history, still life, technology, cosmic and metaphysical reflections on destiny, love and sensuality, and the female form. Formally he has not been so much an innovator as a superb synthesizer of influences from Gauguin, Cézanne, and Picasso, as well as modern Mexican painters, the folk arts, and pre-Columbian sculpture. His art differs from that of the *tres grandes* in that it has been apolitical and formalistically oriented. His philosophy has been politically antinationalistic; however, his art is probably more ethnologically nationalistic than that of Orozco and Siqueiros. It has certain points of resemblance to that of Rivera in the open use of indigenous elements, though Rivera used these historically rather than purely pictorially. Like Rivera, Tamayo often juxtaposed crystalline forms with organic rhythms, created rich patterns of color on a flat surface, and used shallow space and overlapped figures.

Though Tamayo came from a Zapotec Indian family, it took the advent of conscious indigenism after the revolution and his appointment by José Vasconcelos in 1921 as head of the Departamento de Dibujo Etnográfico of the Museo Nacional de Arqueología, where he was surrounded by Mexican folk arts and pre-Columbian sculpture, to awaken his interest in nativist form. This interest provided him with precisely those elements of his artistic vocabulary that make his art uniquely Mexican, despite his predilection for modernist European art.

Tamayo briefly attempted some rapprochement with the objective conditions of the Mexican art world in the thirties. He painted two fresco murals in 1933 and 1938. The first was called *Song and Music*; the second, *Revolution*, strongly influenced by Orozco, demonstrates Tamayo's strained effort to integrate himself into the mainstream of Mexican painting. Between the years 1930 and 1938 he had only two gallery shows in

Mexico,[3] but exhibited regularly in the United States. In 1938 he moved to New York, remaining there a number of years with regular visits to Mexico. In 1948 he received major recognition in Mexico when the Instituto Nacional de Bellas Artes presented a retrospective of his work, a move that reflected not only his increasing prominence abroad but also the changing climate in Mexico. The 1950 Venice Biennial showed his work in a special Tamayo Salon, and two years later he received a commission to paint two murals for the Palacio de Bellas Artes—the ultimate symbol of official canonization.

During his visits and residence in New York Tamayo was in personal contact with the international art movement for the first time. He met Marcel Duchamp, Stuart Davis, Reginald Marsh, Yasuo Kuniyoshi, Raphael and Moses Soyer, Ben Shahn, and Joan Miró. Most important, however, was the major Picasso exhibition at the Museum of Modern Art in 1940. It ushered in the period of profound synthesis between pre-Columbian folk motifs and Picasso, and laid the groundwork for Tamayo's mature style and most significant production. The so-called "howling dog" or "animal" series combines the agonized expressiveness of Picasso's *Guernica* with that of the famous West Mexico clay sculptures of dogs. These "humanized animals in a world without myth,"[4] singly or in pairs, screaming or howling in desolate landscapes, seem the epitome of loneliness, pain, and despair (Fig. 3).

Tamayo changed his style in the period during which he left his native land to live abroad. Responsive in a purely plastic way to the upheavals of the Spanish Civil War and the prevailing terror of the prewar European mood as seen through the filtered aesthetic echoes of these events in Picasso's masterpiece, he expressed his social awareness in an intensely personal style. He was convinced that explicit "message" painting was not his *métier* and was persuaded that he was interested only in "pure" painting. Commenting on the mural movement in relation to himself, he

said: "Although the painting of that initial period revealed some distinguished qualities, the preoccupation of its authors to produce, above all, art that was Mexican, even though in appearance only, led them to fall into the picturesque, and be careless of the really plastic problems. When I saw what was happening, . . . I reacted strongly against the established norms, and . . . initiated a movement tending to restore to our painting its pure qualities."[5]

The years 1946–1956 might be said to mark another thematic and stylistic period. Some of Tamayo's most significant and most profoundly philosophical themes appeared simultaneously with the liberation of his style. He evolved from the ponderous, two-dimensional images of the previous period to more fluid compositions with violently foreshortened figures moving backward and forward in deep space. With *Women Reaching for the Moon* (1946) the full psychological and plastic impact of this period was attained. In the paintings of this period there is a sense of yearning, of reaching for impossible attainments, of vacant landscapes and isolated humans, of alienation and possible fear, that Tamayo attributes, in retrospect, to a presentiment of the space age: "Back in the forties when I painted the pictures of howling, agonized dogs now owned by the Museum of Modern Art, although I took my forms from popular art, I was thinking of mounting world pressures that would soon erupt . . . Immediately after World War II and the bombings of Hiroshima and Nagasaki, I started thinking about the implications of a new space age and did the first paintings of constellations shooting through space."[6] Though statements made thirty years after the fact can claim prophetic insight, there is a strong possibility that Tamayo's surreal quality was as much influenced by artistic encounters, such as his admiration for Giorgio de Chirico and his friendship with Miró in New York (works like Miró's 1940s *Constellation* paintings come to mind), as by profound musings on the international situation.

3. Rufino Tamayo, *Animals*, 1941, oil on canvas, 30⅛ × 40 in. (76.5 × 101.5 cm.). Collection, The Museum of Modern Art, New York, Inter-American Fund.

4. Rufino Tamayo, *Cosmic Terror*, 1954, oil on canvas, 39⅜ × 29½ in. (100 × 75 cm.). Collection of the Museo de Arte Moderno, Mexico City. Courtesy Instituto Nacional de Bellas Artes.

By 1951, Tamayo's human forms had become less anatomical and more schematic, grotesque, and fanciful. The disjunctive shapes suggest movement or double imagery. A sense of terror enters, a greater degree of horror, and trembling, nightmarish, and hysterical qualities. *Inexperienced Smoker* (1953), *Cosmic Terror* (Fig. 4), and *Man Burning* (1955), which share this mood, may have their sources in the grotesque masks of Mexican popular art or in the ubiquitous *calavera* (skeleton, skull) (*Children*, 1956); their spiritual quality, however, derives from postwar sensibility and fears. After 1956 Tamayo's images are refined and reduced to almost monochromatic color in which he explores the color ranges possible within a schema of limited tonal changes.[7] He presents increasingly violent, fragmented figures alone in an alien cosmos—mechanized, dehumanized, brutalized images that have lost almost all semblance of humanity.

It should be apparent that Tamayo, while not overtly political, is far from being a "pure" painter existing in some kind of historical vacuum—his own statements to the contrary notwithstanding. His human imagery has been responsive to the events of his time. However, there are certain contradictions in Tamayo's art. Rejecting nationalism and indigenism, it is still steeped in precisely those indigenous elements of form and mythology that he rejected. He himself recognizes these contradictions and resolves them by claiming that the muralists produced only the *appearance* of Mexican life, and not its essence. This was not at all the case.

What is not expressed in Tamayo's formulation is a recognition of the *audience* for whom the muralists created. Tamayo's aesthetic choices were out of tune with the objective circumstances of the postrevolutionary period. It was not a period to encourage delicate sensibility or refined contemplation, but one of violence and action. The reaffirmation of Indian peasant culture was tied to the need for land reform and the abolition of residual feudalism. The nationalization of industry was tied to the creation of an urban working class that required literacy and universal education. The rising middle class, often composed of former revolutionaries, operated on principles of laissez-faire capitalism. The spectre of the perennial Latin American "strong man" always lurked in the shadows of political strife; the twelve-year hegemony of Plutarco Elías Calles (1924–1936) was a case in point. Artists who wished to address themselves to this panorama needed to make political statements. Instead, Tamayo's art was oriented toward the poetic and subjective experience, expressed not in the painted rendition of the objective world but as a particular way of feeling about the world. This mode might be lyrical or tragic, but it was always personal. It was an expression of the *ensimismamiento* that appeared in the work of the

generation that followed the *tres grandes*, poets as well as painters, who formed the nucleus of the literary/artistic group Los Contemporáneos (The Contemporaries), which published a cultural magazine of the same name from 1928 to 1931. In Tamayo's work we find the same themes expressed so eloquently by the poets: private anguish, solitude, interior emptiness, night, and death. Such works as Xavier Villarrutia's *Nostalgia de la muerte* (Nostalgia for Death, 1938), José Gorostiza's *Muerte sin fin* (Death without End, 1939), and Bernardo Ortiz de Montellano's *Muerte del cielo azul* (Death of the Blue Sky, 1937) are cases in point. Their preoccupation with self seemed almost counterrevolutionary in the fervor of postrevolutionary Mexico.[8]

Understandably, Tamayo's recognition and triumph in his own land coincided with the final ascension to power of the bourgeoisie in the 1940's post-Cárdenas period. Tamayo's art was accorded a central role as the expression of the shift from muralism to easel painting, despite the fact that he continued to paint murals. His art is very "Mexican" without being controversial like social realism; its "revolution" is wholly formal. Ironically, it is perhaps due to the taste for the "naïve," the "primitive," and the "exotic" that his work has achieved popularity with the Mexican middle and upper classes. It is symptomatic of the new international sophistication of the urban bourgeoisie that they are prepared to patronize an art that is "nationalistic" and "modernistic" at the same time, one that can decorate their homes without introducing disturbing social themes. If the old revolutionaries-turned-entrepreneurs were attached to the devitalized images of revolutionary heroes and nostalgic rural scenes, their children—university-trained professionals and bureaucrats—have turned to more contemporary modes.

For all his personal reserve, Tamayo has not held aloof from the artistic confrontations, often violent, that are so characteristic of the Mexican art world. Through public statements and interviews in the press in Mexico and abroad, he maintained his status as the much-admired symbolic rebel against the status quo for the younger generation of the fifties, an early "martyr to the cause," so to speak, though his actual relations with the younger artists, as with the older, have not always been cordial. His relationship with the Nueva Presencia artists was cool, and he was surprised to find Belkin and Icaza receptive to his work when they visited him in 1963.

Tamayo's painterly style, his rich and subtle use of color, his evocative mysticism (sublimated from the indigenous), and his utilization of pre-Columbian and folk art, as well as musical and tropical fruit forms, have left their impress on a number of younger artists, the most important of whom are Juan Soriano, Ricardo Martínez de Hoyos, Guillermo Meza, Pedro Coronel, and Cordelia Urueta. In addition, the diffusion of the surreal mode and the impact of European surrealism have been important in the work of these artists, as in Tamayo's. It would be difficult to be a colorist in Mexico and escape Tamayo's influence wholly, since Tamayo's color is so integrally of his land that any coloristic reference to Mexican subject matter is bound to evoke him in either his darker earthy or his more brilliant chromatic periods.[9]

How much influence did Tamayo have on the artists of Nueva Presencia? Directly, very little. There is no doubt that they were the heirs of Orozco and not Tamayo, and their art tended in the direction of the linear, the dramatic, and the expressive. But if one considers the elements of surreal fantasy (Ortiz), of the evocative (Corzas), of the metaphysical or existential (Góngora, Belkin, Icaza), of the nightmarish and terrifying and grotesque (Sepúlveda), of the monumental (Muñoz, Sepúlveda, González), or of the painterly (Messeguer, Corzas) in the works of the members of Nueva Presencia, some relationship to Tamayo and the atmosphere of Los Contemporáneos can be established. Teachers in the Escuela Nacional de Pintura y Escultura ("La Esmeralda"), the art

school through which most of the Nueva Presencia artists passed, included artists of both the Mexican School and Los Contemporáneos, as well as younger teachers who fused these several directions in their work.

José Luis Cuevas, Marta Traba, and the Great Mural Debate

In the sixties the campaign against the Mexican School found its most articulate expression in the lectures and writings of José Luis Cuevas and Marta Traba. Both are treated at greater length in succeeding chapters, but in order to outline the opposition to the mural movement, one characteristic example in which they undertook a frontal attack in tandem against the *tres grandes* will be discussed here.

It is significant that, unlike the younger generation of Mexican figurative painters, who exempted the *tres grandes* when they criticized the Mexican School, Traba and Cuevas chose to assail Rivera, Siqueiros, and even the sacrosanct Orozco. It is a rare Latin American critic who seriously undertakes to criticize and denigrate the entire *oeuvre* of the Mexican mural movement, as Traba has done. Most, like the distinguished Guatemalan-born critic Luis Cardoza y Aragón, believe the stage of the mural renaissance was a great and necessary one that continues to demonstrate its vitality and timelessness; however, they say, changed social conditions indicate the need to move on to new expression.[10] The question arises as to why Traba, a prominent and knowledgeable critic, the founder and first president of Bogotá's Museo de Arte Moderno, should have so consistently and vehemently attacked all aspects of muralism. It was precisely her vehemence and the fact that she had never personally seen the murals that called her objectivity into question. It is common knowledge that Argentinian-born Traba had been a disciple of Jorge Romero Brest, who, as virtual art dictator (he held the positions of director of the Museo Nacional de Bellas Artes in Buenos Aires and head of the privately endowed Instituto Torcuato Di Tella founded by collector Di Tella, from 1960 to 1970), imposed an implacable avant-gardism on Argentinian artists. Later, as protégé of the Pan American Union's Division of Visual Arts director José Gómez-Sicre (of whom more will be said later), Traba became a powerful taste-maker in Latin America as critic and lecturer. A number of artists and writers in Mexico considered the Romero Brest/Gómez-Sicre/Traba triumvirate as a conspiracy to change the direction of Mexican art.

Traba's point of view was well illustrated in the course of a three-cornered debate that included herself and José Luis Cuevas versus Mexican art critic Antonio Rodríguez. Traba maintained that Mexican muralism was "an enormous abscess that has infected all our countries" and predicated her argument on the grounds that political revolutionaries in Mexico were artistic reactionaries. Rivera's Chapingo murals (generally considered among his finest) used reactionary plastic elements like allegory, realism, and anecdotalism, she said. Even formal innovations like Siqueiros' polyangular compositions, Orozco's moments of high drama, and Rivera's happy relationships of volumes did not change the political and antiaesthetic attitudes of the muralists, in her opinion. They cast aside, she claimed, the revolution of contemporary art and placed their art at the service of the Mexican Revolution.[11] In later writing, Traba argued that future (political) revolutions in Latin America would occur not for economic reasons but as a result of a new sensibility that would seek new objectives and priorities for humanity. Artists would play an important role in such revolutions. The decisive role of the Latin American artist as a revolutionary, she maintained, would be in the confrontation of (aesthetic) values, not only in political episodes.[12] The equation of revolutionary plastic form with revolutionary politics (or the substitu-

tion of the former for the latter) is certainly not new; as a matter of fact, it is a rather tired argument. And it hardly seems applicable to the work of Rivera, whose complex mural compositions are firmly based on structural lessons derived from his long involvement with cubism.

Cuevas was in agreement with Traba; in his opinion the muralists had rejected painting and opted for a "cheap journalism and harangue." Formally and artistically, he said, the muralists were null and void.[13] That Cuevas' public diatribes against the muralists were part of his "plan of attack" against an older art form, and that his more candid opinions of the muralists, especially Orozco and Siqueiros, were far more favorable than this statement indicates, will be shown in Chapter 6. And that Cuevas' allies were generally chosen as part of self-serving publicity will also be shown. For the moment it is important to note that Cuevas was also a protégé of Gómez-Sicre, who first brought him to international prominence in 1954, and thus his alliance with Traba was natural.

Rodríguez, in his response to Traba/Cuevas, made precisely the accusation indicated above: he pointed out that Traba was close to Gómez-Sicre and that both had undertaken to be periodic and gratuitous critics of Mexican muralism. The Mexican mural movement, he continued, had produced dozens of murals since Rivera's death in 1957, some excellent, some good, some mediocre. That Mexican muralism no longer fulfilled the same function or followed the same course that it had originally was natural for a living art that was the product of historical circumstances. Muralism, Rodríguez claimed, continued to enjoy great prestige in Mexico, and every great painter aspired to it—including Cuevas himself.[14]

It is certainly true that younger artists have been interested in mural commissions. Some of them have responded to outmoded form by experimenting with new types of murals, among them Manuel Felguérez, whose 1961 mural in the

Cine Diana of Mexico City is a large abstract relief composed of diverse mechanical pieces and found objects. Benito Messeguer projected the idea of creating a mural in which laminations, tubes, metal rods, and plastics are combined with more traditional forms. Messeguer, in fact, is interested in a synthesis between contemporary Op and traditional mural forms, since he feels that muralism continues to be important in Mexico. Nor is Messeguer the only one interested in muralism. Among Nueva Presencia members, half have created independent murals or acted as mural assistants. In spite of this, the persistent pressure in the contemporary art world has been away from muralism and toward easel painting. Though other Nueva Presencia members did murals—Capdevila, Delgadillo, Muñoz, and Icaza— only Belkin is essentially a muralist in spirit, with a large body of mural work to his credit and a monumental urge even in easel painting that often expresses itself in huge canvases or even triptychs supporting one enormous figure. For the others, perhaps, muralism was an artistic challenge and an economic supplement, as well as a matter of prestige. Muralism is the "grand manner" of Mexican art, and there is a strong temptation for younger artists to "prove themselves" in this style. Cuevas has even mocked the seriousness of contemporary muralism, thus negatively validating its continuing vitality, by painting a satirical billboard-mural that he conceived as a "Hollywood happening."

Easel Painting: The *Tres Grandes*

In closing this overview of contemporary influences that set the stage for developments in the period 1955–1965, some mention must be made of the nonmural works of the *tres grandes* and the degree of importance they had for younger artists.

The predominant position of muralism has not precluded the creation of a large body of out-

standing easel paintings, drawings, and prints, not only by those artists whose personal predilection was easel painting, but by the muralists as well. Of these, the works of Orozco have been of special importance to contemporary artists, especially those of Nueva Presencia. However, none of the younger artists have drawn their whole inspiration from Orozco's nonmural production; in fact, they do not conceive of separating the murals from the paintings and graphics. Siqueiros' influence has also been of importance, but to a lesser degree. Primarily, Orozco and Siqueiros influenced the younger postwar artists whose works were concerned with "social engagement" or interest in the human condition. This group includes Los Interioristas and other artists such as Luis Nishizawa, Gilbert Aceves Navarro, Javier Arévalo, and Arnaldo Coen.

Orozco's earliest surviving body of paintings and drawings dates back to 1910. Among them is a series of thinly brushed watercolors of prostitutes in brothels or on the street made while he was still a student at San Carlos Academy. Resting, fighting, scheming, seductive, ugly, these images have little of the redeeming Christian symbolism of Nolde or the compassion of Rouault. The innocent schoolgirl mantrap (Fig. 5), the seductive dancers, the waiflike outcast learning her trade prefigure the corrupt ugliness of the practiced prostitute. Orozco's drawings of the seamier side of the Mexican Revolution reveal his antipathy to the camp follower and also speak metaphorically to the corruption of the male participants (see Fig. 41). Eventually the prostitute becomes a symbol for all human corruption: a shameless Jezebel infecting mankind with her evil. Orozco's 1934 mural *Catharsis* (Fig. 6) displays an almost pathological contempt for women that continued throughout his life and formed a polarity to his transcendental male images Prometheus and Quetzalcoatl (and their incarnations) who represent the finest and highest of the human spirit. The other types of women who appear in Orozco's work are subservient to

men: devoted mothers and wives resignedly see
their men off to war; patient *soldaderas* with
babies on their backs follow the men to the revolution; the Indian princess Malinche, who betrayed her people to aid her lover, appears at the
side of, but restrained by, Cortés. Two aspects of
femininity, the saintly suppliant woman and the
femme fatale, have thus been adapted from their
nineteenth-century prototypes to an indigenous
existence.[15]

When the newly organized Interioristas held
their first show at the Galerías CDI, Orozco was
the only nonliving artist included in the exhibit.
A pen and ink drawing from his 1945 series *The
Truth* appeared on the catalog cover, attesting to

5. José Clemente Orozco, *A Woman*, ca. 1910–1913,
charcoal drawing. Photo courtesy Instituto Nacional de
Bellas Artes.

6. José Clemente Orozco,
Catharsis, detail, 1934, fresco.
Palacio de Bellas Artes, Mexico
City. Courtesy Instituto Nacional
de Bellas Artes.

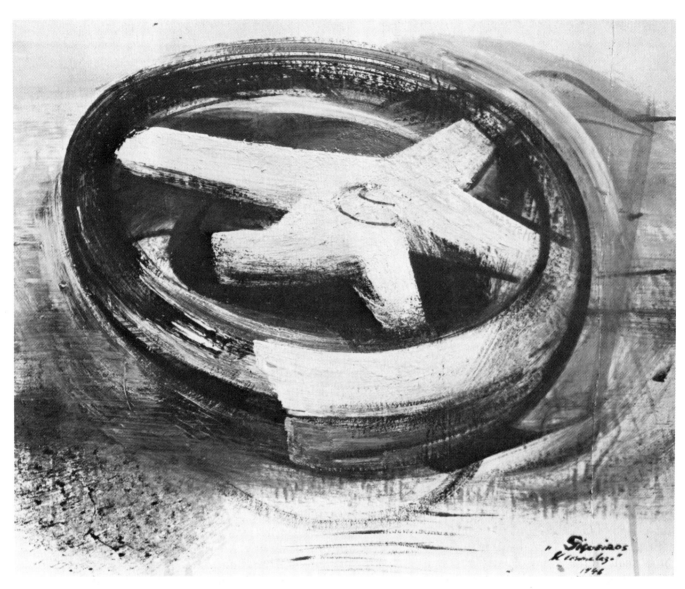

7. David Alfaro Siqueiros, *Rotation*, 1948, pyroxylin
on paper. 24¾ × 29⅞ in. (63 × 76 cm.). Private collection. Estate: MacKinley Helm.

8. David Alfaro Siqueiros, *Portrait of María Asúnsolo as a Child*, 1938, duco on plywood, 39⅜ × 29½ in. (100 × 75 cm.). Collection of María Asúnsolo; photo by Guillermo Zamora.

9. David Alfaro Siqueiros, *Landscape*, 1956, pyroxylin on masonite, 41 × 38⅝ in. (104 × 98 cm.). Collection of José Bertrand Cusiné; photo by Guillermo Zamora.

his importance and influence for a new generation of figurative artists. Caustic and sardonic, with an active wiry line, the drawings in this series dealt with beggars, clowns, devils, dancers, prostitutes, cabaret personalities, and fantastic animals. They deal as surely with human failings and gullibility as Goya's *Caprichos*. The spiritual kinship between Orozco and the younger Rico Lebrun, a draftsman of human dignity and agony, is apparent.

Like those of Orozco, many of Siqueiros' easel paintings, prints, and drawings are mural studies. Though the majority are figural, there exist a number of abstract works of great power that work out problems of spatial movement (Fig. 7). There is also a body of painting demonstrating a sensibility for portraiture and landscape (Figs. 8

and 9). For Siqueiros, painting style was as influential as the subject—perhaps more so. He used the highly manipulative possibilities of synthetic paints to create surface textures (sometimes several inches thick), volume, and striking value contrasts. Siqueiros' slashing baroque movement in space, dramatic chiaroscuro, and textural brushwork can be found in the works of a number of younger artists, among them Belkin, Nishizawa, and Federico Silva. Most important, perhaps, have been his technical innovations that revolutionized the art of painting. The introduction of new media must, of necessity, change the formal qualities of art by means of the wholly different properties of the paint. The synthetic resins have a wider range of effects than oil paint; they dry quickly, are soluble in water, can be thinned to the consistency of watercolor or thickened with additives such as marble dust and sand to form an almost sculptural surface, can be given a glossy or matte finish, can be applied in the traditional manner with brushes or painting knife, or sprayed, dripped, or allowed to run across a tilted surface for accidental effects. Though originally developed as a flexible, durable medium for outdoor murals, their use opened up a wide range of possibilities for easel paintings.

Siqueiros' artistic and political philosophy was much less popular with the younger artists than that of Orozco or Tamayo. However, he commanded tremendous power and prestige within the artistic establishment. His *taller* was a training ground for aspiring muralists. His former students and assistants taught in the major art schools of Mexico or were independent muralists. It was inevitable that, with the ascendancy of Cuevas in the late fifties as Mexico's most gifted younger artist, he and Siqueiros should symbolically represent the polarities of contemporary Mexican art. Cuevas represented a new sensibility and, even more than Tamayo (who has created a body of mural paintings), the transition from muralism to easel painting as a locus.

Rivera's influence was the most eroded of the *tres grandes*. His archeologicism brought him under attack in the antinationalistic fifties; his idealism was not consistent with the growing skepticism of the postwar world. Much of his easel painting after the forties was insipid, repetitive, and redolent with clichés. Nevertheless, his early interest in and extensive use of pre-Columbian and folk art forms brought them to the attention of the Mexican plastic consciousness. It is hard to say how widely this influence has been diffused, even among contemporary artists with the most "internationalist" of intentions. It was Rivera (long before Tamayo) who donated to the nation a vast collection of pre-Columbian art whose forms continue to appear in contemporary painting.

Tamayo's 1952 commission from the Mexican government to paint two murals in the Palacio de Bellas Artes (hitherto reserved for the *tres grandes*) marked a watershed of change in Mexican artistic life that reflected the changing character of Mexican society. The end of the Cárdenas regime (1934–1940) was also the end of Mexico's revolutionary phase and the beginning of the development of a national industrial and bureaucratic bourgeoisie controlling the government. This stage was marked by a moral and ideological crisis of society, the end of radical reforms, and the final separation of the bourgeoisie from the working classes.

It is generally accepted that the major growth of the bourgeoisie took place in the bonanza years 1940–1950, during and after World War II when shortages of imported goods caused the Mexican government to support diversified industrialization. At the same time, the rampant nationalization and anti–United States feeling of the pre-1940s period gave way to a new policy of encouraging foreign investment in Mexican industry—with the condition that such investment conform to Mexican law and usages, with no special concessions of the exploitative type usually granted by underdeveloped countries.

Between the small group of entrepreneurs, bankers, and financiers that made up the Mexican bourgeoisie and the mass of workers, semi-employed people, and destitute farmers was the nebulously defined middle class composed of technical workers, doctors, lawyers, engineers, sociologists, economists, government bureaucrats, and the growing segment of writers, professors, intellectuals, artists, and students. It was not the traditional middle class of developed countries, but a mobile stratum, socially and economically insecure, with little organization or political influence.[1] Correspondent with an increasingly international tendency of the Mexican entrepreneurial class, there was an augmented internal de-emphasis on nationalism and its corollary, indigenism. After 1940, official policy in

Mexico was no longer guided by the belief that there were continuing values in the Indian heritage. According to official thinking, Mexico was ready to take its place in the modern world, and its people needed to make the transition to modern attitudes and ways of living. The most obvious model was the United States, and though Mexican intellectuals pointed with alarm to the spiritual and cultural deficiencies of United States civilization, the material achievements of the United States exercised magnetic pull. By the mid-fifties, cultural nationalism of both varieties, objective and subjective, was under attack in favor of internationalism. While sections of the bourgeoisie aligned themselves with world capitalism and the last vestiges of socialist thought that colored the postrevolutionary period disappeared in actuality (if not in rhetoric) in official circles, important segments of the middle and working classes saw themselves (and the Mexican Revolution) as part of the prorevolutionary movements of Latin America and the national liberation movements of dependent countries throughout the world.

It is within this context that we must understand the enthusiasm and support for the Cuban Revolution of 1959. Just as artists and intellectuals of the 1920s identified their revolutionary aspirations with the 1917 Russian Revolution, so did their younger counterparts in the late 1950s see the resemblance of the Cuban to their own truncated revolution. After the disillusionments of the 1956 Stalin "revelations," the charismatic appeal of Fidel Castro and Ernesto "Che" Guevara won many admirers among the students and intellectuals who were to compose the Latin American counterpart of the New Left during the sixties. Pro-Cuban (though not necessarily pro-Marxist or procommunist) sentiments were one of the hallmarks of the New Left internationally, and, though many Latin Americans would have supported the Cuban Revolution from a purely nationalist "anti–Yankee imperialism" spirit, the conjunction of European, United States, and Latin American New Left sympathies highlights the increasingly international focus of Mexican intellectuals in the second half of the century.

At the termination of the Cárdenas period, the temporary identification of major artists with the political and economic goals of the Mexican state had begun to disintegrate, though muralists continued to paint "patriotic" and nationalist murals for the next two decades. It gradually became clearer that the role of the intellectual and the artist in Mexico was increasingly to be one of *criticism* rather than support of the state, and the criticism, unlike that of Mexico's social realists, was to be of an individual rather than a collective nature. Characteristically, it was not direct; it contained no explicit message and was not inspired by an established doctrine. The acts of "rebellion" in the Mexican art world during the 1950s are noteworthy for their unfocused quality and their lack of positive precepts. During this period social criticism disengaged itself from primary identification with the "working class" and the "exploited" and displayed the preoccupations characteristic of the international New Left, which was composed of the alienated and discontented "young intelligentsia" (as they were called by C. Wright Mills), who no longer saw the working class as the historic agency of change.[2] When Mexican art, which found its *raison d'être* in the values brought forth by the revolution, lost its vitality, it encountered the problem of the alienated artist—a situation that had occurred several decades earlier in Europe and the United States.

Galleries and Museums

Proliferation of the middle class after World War II also affected the Mexican art market. Between the years 1950 and 1960, the Mexican public began to interest itself in the acquisition of works of art. Rivera, Orozco, and Siqueiros already had a market for their works; only later did collectors begin to take an interest in Tamayo and the younger artists.

The complete lack of galleries in earlier years had worked great hardship on easel painters such as Tamayo, Carlos Mérida, and others who were contemporary with the early muralists. In 1926, Tamayo was forced to exhibit in a storefront location on Madero Street because no art galleries existed in Mexico City. In 1934, Inés Amor's private art gallery was founded. Under her firm direction, the Galería de Arte Mexicano consistently represented the major artists of the old and new generations, eventually giving Amor an unprecedented "political" and economic power in the Mexican art world from which she has been able virtually to dictate styles and trends and even to "freeze" certain of her artists into a lucrative phase of stylistic development.

By 1960, twenty-two private galleries had opened exhibitions in Mexico City, including the galleries Prisse, Proteo, Antonio Souza, and Juan Martín, which specialized in contemporary Mexican and international avant-garde trends. By 1964 more than forty different galleries offered the public an average of six openings a week, and by the early seventies Mexico City had eighty galleries. Easel painting had become a good investment and, in addition, gave the purchaser social prestige.[3] Despite this phenomenal growth, many of the younger artists, like Tamayo before them, made their artistic reputations abroad because both the private market and governmental commissions were dominated by known artists from the academic movement. "Cuevas," said gallery owner Antonio Souza in 1957, "is better known in Paris than here."[4] Not the least of Nueva Presencia's attractions for young artists in 1961 were its promotional and merchandising aspects, ably promoted by Arnold Belkin and Francisco Icaza both in Mexico and the United States. The record is replete with instances of their special efforts to establish and maintain gallery connections in New York and Los Angeles.

Parallel with the increase of private galleries,

various government dependencies established space adequate for exhibitions of easel paintings, graphics, and sculpture. By 1960, under the general supervision of the Instituto Nacional de Bellas Artes (INBA), an arm of the Secretaría de Educación Pública, exhibitions could be mounted not only at the Palacio de Bellas Artes (a pompous marble structure built at the turn of the century that also housed the Museo Nacional de Arte Moderno) but also at the Salón de la Plástica Mexicana, the Galería de la Ciudad de México, the Galería Chapultepec, the Galería José María Velasco, and the Galería José Clemente Orozco. Under the auspices of the Universidad Nacional Autónoma de México (UNAM) were the galleries of the Escuela Nacional de Artes Plásticas (San Carlos), the Museo Universitario de Ciencias y Artes, the Caso del Lago, and the Galería Aristos. In addition, the Organismo de Promoción Internacional de Cultura (OPIC), a cultural relations agency of the Secretaría de Relaciones Exteriores, not only circulated shows of Mexican art, but also acquired an extensive collection of works by younger artists. In 1964, the inauguration of the new Museo de Arte Moderno in Chapultepec Park affirmed governmental acceptance and institutionalization of easel painting. It is interesting to note that the Museo de Arte Moderno, unlike the new Museo de Antropología inaugurated the same year (also in Chapultepec Park), has no murals; its architecture seems symbolically to represent the shift from muralism to easel painting as the major trend in contemporary art.

The years 1955–1965 (marked by Cuevas' first international recognition at one end and the opening of an independent modern art museum at the other) seem to have encompassed a significant change in cultural emphasis: from government-sponsored, socially oriented public muralism to private ownership of art and the growth of an internal art market catering to the native middle class and the tourist trade. Not only was there increased private and public exhibition space for young as well as established easel painters, but the government-owned Salón de la Plástica Mexicana (founded in 1949) functioned as both exhibit space and marketplace, allowing artists to show their works without (or with low) gallery charges or sales commissions. A certain degree of interaction occurred between the private and public sectors of the art establishment; the resultant "taste-making" had its effects on the style and direction of young artists trying to gain recognition.

In line with the increasing internationalization of Mexican economic and social life, art exhibits presented in government institutions that had formerly been dedicated almost exclusively to national art began to take on a more international character. For example, in 1961, under the direction of Miguel Salas Anzures, head of the Departamento de Artes Plásticas of the INBA, the Museo Nacional de Arte Moderno had seven exhibitions of works from foreign countries (Czechoslovakia, Japan, Switzerland, India, Italy, Bulgaria, and Indonesia), while only three shows were Mexican-derived. The availability of and access to original works of art from all parts of the world contrasted markedly with the pre–World War II period, when artists relied upon travel, books, magazines, and occasional exhibits for their knowledge of international art trends.

Cultural Imperialism:
Latin America and Mexico

It would be naïve, in the light of revelations about the role of the United States Information Service (USIA), the Central Intelligence Agency (CIA), and United States multinational corporations in Latin America, to assume that the changes in direction taken by contemporary Mexican art occurred on a purely internal level or for purely aesthetic reasons. Since the 1967 exposures of CIA involvement in the covert funding of cultural organizations in both the

United States and abroad as a key part of United States foreign policy during the Cold War, we must consider the implications of cultural penetration on Latin American art. While there is no intent here to attempt an extensive itemization of this vast topic, some indication can be given of the possible effects this penetration had in the years 1955–1965, culminating in the 1965 Esso Salon in the Museo de Arte Moderno, and of the degree of involvement of some of the personae of Nueva Presencia.

This period was marked by increasing friction between the Mexican School and a wave of younger artists disinterested in socially responsive art. It was inevitable that social realism would become, as it had earlier in the United States, the target of those United States forces engaged in the Cold War. In the battle for cultural hegemony in Mexico, there was need for a major young talent who could be put forth as a symbol and spokesman against social realism, and this symbol was found in the person of José Luis Cuevas, who achieved his first international prominence with a 1954 show mounted by the Pan American Union in Washington, D.C., and through the personal support of José Gómez-Sicre, head of the Division of Visual Arts of the Pan American Union. Cuevas thereafter engaged in polemics against the Mexican School and social realism throughout Mexico, Latin America, and the United States.[5] It would be extreme to suggest that Cuevas was consciously involved in a political (rather than artistic) conspiracy to attack social realism; cultural formulations function much more subtly and are not always conceived of in political terms by artists themselves—though, as will be shown, they *may* be by cultural institutions. Rather, it might be said that Cuevas' precocious talent and personal egotism played a role in making him the figurehead for latent discontent and rebellion against the Mexican School. In addition, he was witty and articulate, and given to making pronouncements and writing extensively for the press. His personal vacillations and

his brief adherence to numerous groups rebelling against the "status quo" during these years emphasize the fact that his role can be seen as one of simple negation and his "rebellion" as of a wholly personal character. It can safely be said that Cuevas, concerned with the eternal "I," sought self-publication or gratification through his activities rather than an ideological stance.[6] In any case, with the support of Gómez-Sicre (and later Marta Traba), Cuevas' reputation as Mexico's most talented young artist and contemporary answer to social realism was established. It can be persuasively argued that Gómez-Sicre, as a very astute artistic critic, was simply following his aesthetic judgment in supporting Cuevas. Nevertheless, the 1964 Traba-Cuevas attack on Mexican muralism (discussed in Chapter 2) and their later conjunction in attacking Nueva Presencia when it became too consciously and outspokenly political, clarify the fact that the target was political art.

United States Cold War cultural politics has been incisively dealt with in two seminal articles written in the United States: Max Kozloff's "American Painting during the Cold War" and Eva Cockcroft's "Abstract Expressionism, Weapon of the Cold War."[7] Kozloff pointed out that the most concerted accomplishments of American (i.e., United States) art occurred during precisely the same period as the burgeoning claims of American world hegemony after World War II. Though American art never became a conscious mouthpiece for any agency, there was a parallel between the belief that America was the "sole trustee of the avant-garde 'spirit' and the U.S. government's notion of itself as the sole guarantor of capitalist liberty."[8] A new sophistication in bureaucratic circles brought the realization that the work of the American intelligentsia (and artists) could be used as a commodity in the struggle for American world dominance. It was revealed during the sixties that the CIA had covertly supported such domestic organizations as the Congress for Cultural Freedom (and its organ,

Encounter magazine); while abroad, exhibitions of United States avant-garde painting were made accessible under the sponsorship of the International Council of the Museum of Modern Art in New York, a Rockefeller-dominated institution. (If we can agree with the suggestion that cultural "warfare" aims indirectly to disrupt the symbol systems of living cultures and to infect them with the "conqueror's" values, that is, to attack the other's collective unconscious,[9] then we can see that cultural imperialism as a weapon of cold war could be a tool of neocolonialism in Latin America as easily as economic penetration.)

Kozloff felt that the similarity between the aims of American Cold War rhetoric and the heroicizing posture of the abstract expressionists (and their credo of personal liberty) was a coincidence. Cockcroft disagreed with this point of view and documented the "links between cultural Cold War politics and the success of abstract expressionism" which, she said, were carried out through the Museum of Modern Art, New York.[10] Specifically, she pointed out the relationship between the activities during World War II of Nelson Rockefeller's Office of the Coordinator of Inter-American Affairs and the Museum of Modern Art in providing exhibitions of contemporary American paintings to be shipped around Latin America, an area in which subsidiaries of Standard Oil of New Jersey had particularly lucrative investments. After the war (1952) the Museum of Modern Art launched its International Council, which promoted exhibits of avant-garde United States paintings—especially those of the abstract expressionists—for international exhibitions in such places as London, Paris, Tokyo, Venice, and (for Latin America) the prestigious São Paulo Biennials. Since the climate of the United States during the Cold War was virulently anticommunist and government agencies were prevented by red-baiting from carrying out such activities (especially since many of the artists involved had formerly been left-wing), the Museum of Modern Art served in a supranational

capacity to influence foreign intellectuals and artists and to present a strong propaganda image of the United States as a "free" society opposed to the "regimented" communist bloc. In the 1960s the Rockefeller interests launched the Council of the Americas and its cultural component, the Center for Inter-American Relations, specifically aimed at recovering respect for the United States in Latin America in the aftermath of the Cuban Revolution, the Bay of Pigs debacle, and the 1962 missile crisis.

In short, it can be said that since World War II, the artistic evolution of Latin America as a whole has been marked by internationalist trends, nearly all of European or North American origins. Abstract expressionism and informalism began to attain their position of prominence toward the end of the fifties and were more widely embraced by Latin American artists than any other style since the beginning of the nineteenth century. The spread of internationalism caused a reaction "against the schools of social revolutionary, social scene, and social commentary painting which, emanating from Mexico, prevailed during the 1930s and 1940s . . . abstract art [had] to a great extent replaced the social reformist or revolutionary interpretation of themes from Indian life as well as proletarian social motifs in general."[11] My purpose here is to indicate briefly some of the machinery of the change.

Over the years a number of subsidiaries of major North American corporations have assumed the role of cultural patronage in Latin America, primarily because international events sponsored directly by the United States government tended to be regarded as official propaganda, but secondarily for the purpose of creating favorable publicity for the companies concerned.[12] Under this category, for example, in 1959 the International Petroleum Company of Colombia (Intercol), an affiliate of Standard Oil of New Jersey, exhibited Colombian art objects in a Bogotá gallery as a "goodwill gesture." Public relations and press coverage snowballed, and the exhibit was brought to the Pan American Union, Washington, D.C., in 1960. Intercol, which had $100 million invested in Colombia, insisted that the art show was not tied in any way to its investment,[13] a statement that appears less than candid. In 1963, Intercol was a major supporter, along with other business interests like Colomotores, Panauto, Flota Mercante Grancolombiana, Braniff Airlines, and Shell and Phillips oil companies, in the foundation of the Museo de Arte Moderno in Bogotá under the direction of Marta Traba, and in 1965 it was involved with the Esso Salon, which sponsored competitive shows for Colombian artists under thirty-five years of age. In Mexico, we have the examples of the major collection of drawings and prints of General Motors of Mexico[14] and exhibits sponsored in its factories by the Ford Motor Company in Mexico. In Argentina, the Córdoba Biennial is sponsored by Kaiser Industries;[15] in Montevideo, General Electric also has entered the field of art patronage. In some cases art patronage by these transnational corporations has rivaled or even surpassed that of the national and provincial governments.

Concerning the effects of cultural penetration on Latin American artists, United States critic and historian Sam Hunter had this to say about the 1967 Córdoba Biennial: "Rarely, I think, has an exhibition so dramatically illustrated the erosion of local and provincial traditions and their supersession by international styles," a fact he considered to be the result of the "somewhat uncritical embrace of the ideology of 'advanced' art as a cultural 'cause' and form of individual liberation."[16] Hunter, however, viewed this erosion as essentially a passive process; he did not mention the active promotional role of United States cultural or business agencies. The homogenization and subversion of local artistic directions was also noted by the astute Mexican art dealer Inés Amor, who stated in 1964 that the "image of Mexico," always to be found in the work of painters doing "truly creative and lasting work" was not to be found in the work of beginning painters,

the majority of whom were following foreign influences.[17]

Some of the mechanics of the shift in artistic interests indicated above might be found in the role of international art competitions, which became important after World War II. The earliest and most important in Latin America was the São Paulo Biennial (first held in 1951), an American replica of the Venice Biennial. Winning a top prize at an international competition was important not only for the artist whose work it helped to launch or upgrade on the international art market, but for the country represented as well. In most cases the selection of artists for international competitions and the costs of shipping and handling were under the supervision of government agencies; however, in the case of the United States, these exhibits were managed and financed by the Museum of Modern Art.[18]

Inter-American competitions and exhibitions flourished with special vigor between 1956 and 1966. The Gulf-Caribbean Art Exhibition took place in 1956 at Houston's Museum of Fine Arts and the same year the Corcoran Gallery of Washington, D.C., presented Latin American Art; 1958 saw the First Interamerican Biennial of Painting and Prints of Mexico and the triennial Pittsburgh International (Carnegie Prize). In 1959 the Dallas Museum of Fine Arts presented "South American Art Today" and the Art Institute of Chicago showed "The United States Collects Pan American Art." In 1962 the First International Prize Competition was held by the Instituto Torcuato Di Tella of Buenos Aires, and the First American Biennial of Art was held in Córdoba, Argentina, sponsored by the Kaiser Industries of Argentina. In 1963 the First American Graphics Biennial took place in Chile. In 1964 Cornell University and the Solomon R. Guggenheim Museum sponsored a Latin American exhibit which was first shown in Caracas and then traveled to the United States, and in 1966 Yale University mounted the exhibit "Art of Latin America since Independence."[19] Other biennials and exhibits were held in the sixties in Guatemala, Costa Rica, Puerto Rico, Colombia, and Ecuador.

During two "vulnerable decades," 1950–1970, Latin American artists were offered inducements to change their styles and content in response to the large prizes and prestige of international competitions. The erosion of local development during these years is attested to by the 1961 São Paulo Biennial, where at least 80 percent of the art "belonged to some species of abstraction, and more than half to its latest modes," causing the viewer to wonder if this was the kind of painting and sculpture that now appealed to governments, and if the concept of "locality" and "roots" no longer played a role.[20] In 1960, for example, a traveling exhibition cosponsored by the Boston Institute of Contemporary Art (then directed by Thomas M. Messer) and Time, Inc. (the Luce interests), and assisted by Gómez-Sicre of the Pan American Union, featured eleven artists all of whom, with the exception of Ricardo Martínez (the only Mexican shown), were abstractionists.[21] Almost half the participants were from Argentina, where Jorge Romero Brest had made Buenos Aires a bastion of avant-garde art.

The culmination of United States corporate influence on Latin American art was the 1965 Esso Salons for Young Artists held in eighteen Latin American countries (with the obvious exception of Cuba). Organized at the suggestion of Humble Oil and Refining Company, a Rockefeller-dominated affiliate of Standard Oil, it was underwritten by the respective nationally based Esso companies (Latin American affiliates of Humble Oil) and organized by José Gómez-Sicre of the Pan American Union in conjunction with public and private fine arts institutions in the constituent countries. Each Salon was conceived as a national competition for artists under forty, with first and second prizes in both painting and sculpture. Winners participated in the Esso Salon of Young Latin American Artists held at the gallery of the Pan American Union (April 1965) at which they competed for an additional inter-

American prize. The jury for this competition was composed of United States experts, two of whom, Alfred H. Barr, Jr., of New York's Museum of Modern Art, and Thomas M. Messer of the Guggenheim, were connected with museums whose major sponsors (Rockefeller and Guggenheim) had made considerable fortunes in Latin American investments.

Historically Mexico has been one of the most outspoken of all Latin American nations against imperialism and neocolonialism, and it therefore comes as no surprise that Mexico's Esso Salon was surrounded by political as well as artistic controversy. Amid charges of irregularities in the selection of jurors (painters Tamayo and Orozco Romero, writers Rafael Anzures and Juan García Ponce, and art historian Justino Fernández), the two top painting prizes were awarded to abstractionists Fernando García Ponce and Lilia Carrillo, and the sculpture prizes to Guillermo Castaño, Jr., and abstractionist Olivier Seguin. As a result, a letter of protest signed by fifteen artists (including former Nueva Presencia members Icaza, Muñoz, Belkin, and González) was sent to the director of the Instituto Nacional de Bellas Artes sharply questioning the personnel of the selections committee and the jury, and the criteria used in awarding the prizes. It was felt that the selections committee and jury were proformalists; it was alleged that Tamayo had opposed awarding the painting prize to Benito Messeguer (also formerly of Nueva Presencia) because he (Tamayo) was opposed to the Nueva Presencia tendency; and finally that it was highly unethical for Juan García Ponce to sit on a jury that awarded his brother first prize.[22] (There is no doubt that some of these criticisms were in order; however, such eruptions were symptomatic of the heated debate and confrontation between realist and abstract art that raged for more than a decade and were given official recognition a year after the Esso Salon in a large exhibition at the Palacio de Bellas Artes called "¡Confrontación '66!")

On the political side, the abuses of the Esso Salon underlined the larger sense of indignation that a foreign company like Standard Oil (Esso) should undertake the invasion of national Mexican culture by establishing the competition and promoting distinct types of art. The role of the Pan American Union (Organization of American States) came under particular attack:

For a number of years the Organization of American States has maintained a silent struggle against the Mexican School of painting through the activities of the special organization which is directed by the critic Gómez Sicre . . . [though] Mr. Gómez Sicre has all the right in the world to the freedom of his aesthetic judgments. What is bad is that Mr. Gómez Sicre is a functionary of a supposedly impartial organization which has no right to protect a particular type of art . . . It is not an accident that a person with Gómez Sicre's ideas should be chosen by the OAS to "protect" painting on the Continent. Whether or not he is conscious of it, it is certain that his ideas about art result in favoring the political line of North American imperialism in Latin America. Since the Mexican School of painting is a nationalist and progressive manifestation it is in the interest of imperialism to combat it with all methods possible, because the abolition of nationalism is favorable to the penetration of Latin America . . . And this is the reason why "Standard Oil" is so interested in protecting the fine arts of Mexico.[23]

It can be inferred that the Instituto Nacional de Bellas Artes' sponsorship of an artistic competition underwritten by Esso Mexicana indicated the tacit approval of the Mexican government. Thus not only were Standard Oil and the Organization of American States apparently in collusion to influence the direction of Mexican art, as the magazine *Política* claimed, but the Mexican government itself was also involved, reflecting its increasingly capitalist orientation and partnership with United States finance. At the same time, the growth of a support system of art galleries, critics, and museums to accommodate an increasingly speculative collectors' art market is evidenced in the in-fighting surrounding the Esso Salon. Galleries such as Antonio Souza,

Proteo, and Juan Martín (whose artists were supported for the 1960 Mexican Interamerican Biennial and the 1961 São Paulo Biennial) were benefited in 1965 by the alliance between, for example, Tamayo and Juan García Ponce, the jurors whose choices determined the winners of the 1965 Esso Salon. It is reasonable to suppose that the aura surrounding the artists who became top prize winners in a national competition and whose works were thereby guaranteed the most extensive and prestigious exposure in the United States and Europe would have profitable consequences for the galleries that represented them. Thus the galleries and Esso can be considered to have had a "joint investment" in a Mexican "commodity": marketable art objects. The "profit" for the United States, of course, was not in dollars, but in the more subtle coin of consciousness-changing, of cultural infiltration, of deflection from a socially oriented, nationalistic, objective art (represented by social realism) to subjective or formalistically oriented art or to abstract art, which was liked only by a limited number of intellectuals. Since painting in Mexico was by far the most powerful of the revolutionary art forms, it was of major concern. The benefits of opposing the Mexican School, of cultivating "freedom of expression" without the restrictions of social responsibility, of furthering individualistic competition in the best traditions of "free enterprise" were demonstrated to younger artists seeking direction for their artistic development. To the impetus to abandon Mexico's traditional humanistic realism in favor of formalistic experimentation were added the rich inducements of international fame and financial compensation. In the insecure world of the contemporary artist, trying to achieve mastery of a discipline and make an aesthetic statement of some moment while simultaneously juggling these strivings with an eye to the market and the latest trends so as to be able, finally, to enter the cherished preserves of the middle class by achieving economic stability, the rewards of the Esso

Salon were a signpost. Temperamentally and philosophically the artist had been prepared for this striving by the flow of words over the previous ten years about the artist as rebel, romantic, and loner; about the need, above all, for absolute freedom of expression (a theme constantly reiterated by Tamayo); about the aesthetic achievements of, particularly, the abstract expressionists; and about the exhaustion, thematic and aesthetic, of the Mexican School. Tamayo's ascendancy, Cuevas' rapid rise to fame, the clear preference for abstraction evidenced by the prize awards of the Esso Salon—a series of overt and covert pressures and enticements—all had their effect on that level of consciousness that produces artistic choices.

Rebellion and Confrontation

Confrontation between the "old" and the "new" in Mexico became increasingly acute in the 1950s as the validity and the vitality of the Mexican School were challenged by younger artists. We have looked briefly at the economic and social aspects surrounding this change; the artistic tumult of the period deserves some chronological definition.

One of the earliest acts of rebellion against the realist school was that of a group of painters who in 1952–1953 loosely organized themselves against "official political art" at the small Galería Prisse. Included were Cuevas, Héctor Xavier, Enrique Echeverría, Alberto Gironella, Vlady, and José Bartolí. With no fixed program and no common plastic language, they were united only by the desire for change. The group had the backing of one of the most active promoters of internationalist contemporary art, Miguel Salas Anzures, who later, as director of the Departamento de Artes Plásticas of the Instituto Nacional de Bellas Artes, figured in the controversies surrounding the 1960 Mexican and the 1961 São Paulo biennials.

In 1955, German-born constructivist painter-sculptor-architect Mathias Goeritz, whose avant-garde and experimental art had caused him to become a focus of rebellion for young Mexican artists, held an International Confrontation of Experimental Art in the Galería Proteo that caused a general uproar and introduced a new note into the artistic ambience of Mexico. European painters Lucio Fontana, Francisco Nieva, Ogvind Fahlström, and Bernhard Schultze—the latter three of the fundamentally surrealist "Phases movement"—participated, as did United States abstract expressionist Paul Jenkins and Mexican artists Germán Cueto (leading spirit of the 1924 neo-Dada Estridentistas), Jesús Reyes Ferreira, and Juan Soriano. This artistic event was followed, five years later, by an influential article, "Estado de urgencia," by Parisian poet Edouard Jaguer, founder of the "Phases movement," in the pages of the Mexican magazine *Arquitectura*.[24] The two events were instrumental in developing a current of *informalismo* in Mexico.

Also in 1955, the Galería Proteo, considered a forum for independent artists, presented its Salon of Free Art, which included artists protesting the selections for the official winter Salon Nacional de Artes Plásticas. It included many of the Galería Prisse artists mentioned above as well as Mathias Goeritz, Carlos Orozco Romero, Tamayo, and Pedro Coronel.

In 1961, old and new vanguardists came together at the Galería Antonio Souza[25] under the auspices of the umbrella neo-Dada group called Los Hartos (The Fed-Ups), which had been organized the preceding year by Goeritz in protest against the emptiness of contemporary art. The protest lasted only a single day, but received international publicity. During its course, Goeritz, Reyes Ferreira, Pedro Friedeberg, Cuevas, and photographer Kati Horna joined with a number of personalities in various demonstrations. Cuevas displayed an all-white wall panel ironically titled *Panoramic Visions of Art*, Goeritz his abstract "metachromatic messages," and Friedeberg his well-known surreal furniture. Mutilated canvases and crushed automobiles were also on display, and a "70¢ egg" was destroyed, after which streams of water were poured on the floors and walls of the gallery.[26]

Mexico's two (and only) Interamerican Biennials, held in 1958 and 1960 in the Palacio de Bellas Artes, presented a microcosm of the controversy rocking the Mexican art world as the fifties came to a close. Within the two-year period between 1958 and 1960, the confrontation between social realism and its major counterstyle, abstract expressionism (tachism, informalism), became so acute that it splintered the art world, threatened to prevent the opening of the second Biennial, and eventually fractured the entire Biennial program; a third Biennial was planned, but never took place.

The 1958 First Interamerican Biennial of Painting and Prints of Mexico demonstrated the supremacy of the Mexican School and of realism. The four exhibits of homage mounted within the context of the Biennial were dedicated to Orozco, Rivera, Siqueiros, and Brazilian social realist Cándido Portinari. Tamayo was refused an homage exhibit and was therefore "represented" only by the three murals he had painted in the Palacio where the exhibit took place—which occasioned bitter letters. Other Mexican painters exhibited included Dr. Atl, muralists Juan O'Gorman and Jorge González Camarena, modernists Carlos Orozco Romero and Jesús Guerrero Galván, and younger artists Guillermo Meza, Juan Soriano, Cordelia Urueta, Ricardo Martínez, Ezequiel Negrete, and Olga Costa. Only Soriano could be considered a quasi-abstractionist.

Though the exhibit included such diverse figures as Jack Levine, Stuart Davis, Joseph Albers, Mark Tobey, and Morris Graves, the greater group of the United States artists represented were abstract expressionists—among them Sam Francis, Philip Guston, Willem de Kooning, Franz Kline, Adolf Gottlieb, Theodore Stamos, and Kenzo Okada. The exhibit constituted probably the largest exhibition of original works by these artists seen in Mexico up to that time. The Mexican School saw the growing popularity of abstract expressionism as an ideological challenge, but also as a spur forcing the social realists to re-examine their formal means. Expressing both these concerns, Siqueiros stated, at a meeting of the Frente Nacional de Artes Plásticas held directly before the opening of the Biennial, that it was necessary to develop the formal elements of realism, to enrich its conception, if realist artists hoped to do battle against abstractionism. Man needs the forms of his own time, he said, and in order to enrich realism, painters had to strip away the negative elements in his work and that of Rivera and Orozco; to reject superficial nationalism and folklorism. They had to paint figures that were less ideographic, more alive, more expressive, more psychologically oriented, truer.[27] Such a reorientation of realism might have been possible for an artist of the stature of Siqueiros in light of his life-long experimentation with the formal means of social realism, but it was not within the compass of most followers of the *tres grandes*, whose artistic vocabulary had already been exhausted.

If the 1958 Biennial was still largely dedicated to realism, with the exception of the United States entries, the 1960 Biennial represented a major change of direction, symbolized by the singular attention accorded Tamayo. His work was honored in a special salon and he was granted the International Award of Painting, not only for the merits of his art, as one observer noted, but as a token of apology to make him forget the insulting silence and disdain with which his work had been received in his own country for many years.[28] Among the works from eighteen countries exhibited in the halls of the Palacio de Bellas Artes and seventeen private galleries, there was a predominance of abstraction. It seemed as if the period of ferment that had preceded the 1960 Biennial reached combustion at that point, and when the smoke cleared, it became apparent that the monolithism of the Mexican School no longer existed. Social realism had proved itself too limited and unresponsive to changing conditions; or perhaps, more accurately, it was no longer in tune with changed conditions. It had failed to renew its plastic language and thus found itself impoverished and outmoded. However, there were also dangers in the ubiquitous informalism that seemed to dominate painting at the end of the decade. Critics spoke of the academization of abstract expressionism; of the host of mediocrities following this trend; of the great number of canvases inspired by the "decorativism" of Pierre Soulages or Alfred Manessier, Jackson Pollock or Willem de Kooning, Afro or Alberto Burri, with only a few exceptions of sensitive work; of the quantity of "dreary paintings," empty copies of United States painters who were copying Europeans.[29]

Given the quantity of academized informalism, and probably also responding to a deep and integral Mexican predilection for expressionism and the figurative (for with hindsight it can be seen that Mexican painters were not, with the exception of a small group that produced very fine geometrical or lyrical abstract canvases, really at ease with nonobjective painting), it was almost inevitable that a vanguard of new figurative expressionists should arise at the end of the fifties as a reaction to abstraction. As early as 1959, critic Margarita Nelken noted the reappearance (in the work of Cuevas and Icaza) of expressionism with unmistakably Mexican accents. She saw it as a reaction to the excessive dehumanization of plastic expression.[30] Five years later she documented thirty-eight artists who had developed in the vein of figurative expressionism traceable back to the nineteenth-century printmaker José Guadalupe Posada, the *tres grandes*, and other Mexican sources, as well as European expressionism from Goya to the German expressionists. Among this avant-garde she included Antonio Rodríguez Luna (a Spanish-born artist of an older generation), Cuevas, Icaza, Rafael Coro-

nel, Corzas, and Hernández Delgadillo, all of whom exhibited with Los Interioristas or Nueva Presencia.[31] Thus, at precisely the moment when nonobjective abstraction appeared to dominate painting, the groundwork was being laid for a new figurative art that differed from social realism in its existential subjectivity and surrealist overtones and employed a plastic vocabulary drawn from Orozco, European expressionism, and abstract expressionism itself. That Nueva Presencia included within its ranks some of the most talented adherents of the new figurative expressionism speaks to its cogency within the spectrum of Mexican painting of the sixties.

Two further occurrences set the stage for the emergence of Los Interioristas in 1961: (1) the imprisonment of Siqueiros in August 1960, just a month before the opening of the second Mexican Biennial, and (2) the choice of eight artists, all but one abstractionists, to appear at the 1961 São Paulo Biennial.

It is perhaps symbolic that the crucial years of artistic confrontation marking the immolation of social realism in Mexico were accompanied by the physical incarceration of its major practitioner and theorist. Between 1960 and 1964 Siqueiros served four years of the eight-year jail term to which he had been sentenced for "social dissolution." Since he was internationally known as Mexico's major artistic figure, his imprisonment caused reverberations among artists and intellectuals throughout the world and they rallied to his defense. Of direct consequence to the Mexican Biennial was the refusal of almost a hundred Mexican artists to participate in its activities as long as Siqueiros remained in prison. Seven of the foreign artists invited to the Biennial requested permission to visit Siqueiros in jail, a request that received no reply.[32] Among the younger Mexican artists, José Luis Cuevas not only protested Siqueiros' imprisonment in a telegram to the president of Mexico, but, along with Rafael Coronel, Arnold Belkin, and Francisco Icaza, abstained from participation in the Biennial. Significantly, it was during a visit by Belkin and Icaza to the imprisoned Siqueiros the following year that the concept of the first issue of *Nueva Presencia* was born. Siqueiros' imprisonment not only paralleled the existence of Nueva Presencia, but influenced its direction.

The storm that finally broke had been gathering since the first Mexican Biennial in 1958. The catalyst of change was the prestigious director of the Departamento de Artes Plásticas of the Instituto Nacional de Bellas Artes, Miguel Salas Anzures. During his tenure (1957–1961), Salas Anzures, who as early as 1952 had actively promoted contemporary art in Mexico, mounted a greater number of exhibits of foreign artists than any of his predecessors. He actively allied himself with the most avant-garde galleries of Mexico (especially Prisse, Antonio Souza, Proteo, and Juan Martín, which had been organized by the painters themselves), whose artists he supported and promoted. Among these artists were Pedro and Rafael Coronel, Cuevas, Alberto Gironella, Vlady, Enrique Echeverría, Manuel Felguérez, Lilia Carrillo, Waldemar Sjölander, Vicente Rojo, Luis Nishizawa, Myra Landau, Héctor Xavier, Nacho López, and Juan Soriano. In 1953 Salas Anzures had founded, along with abstract painter Vicente Rojo, the expensive and plush magazine *Artes de México*, an outgrowth of his brief directorship of *Artes Plásticas*, organ of the Frente Nacional de Artes Plásticas (of which he was secretary).[33] The 1958 and 1960 Biennials had taken place as a result of his persistent energy (the Biennial program terminated with his resignation), as had the creation of the Museo Nacional de Arte Moderno in the Palacio de Bellas Artes in 1958. (It was not until 1964, however, that a separate building was constructed in Chapultepec Park to house the new Museo de Arte Moderno.)

Doubtless the fury of controversy and the subsequent antagonism that surrounded the second Mexican Biennial had not been foreseen. The fact that Salas Anzures supported avant-garde artists, two of whom had won top prizes at the 1960 Biennial, exacerbated the antagonism. It is probable that Salas Anzures had decided by early 1961 who his choices for the sixth São Paulo Biennial would be, although these plans do not appear in the record since they never came to official fruition. The artists who eventually participated *hors concours* under his leadership came from the same group he had supported at the 1960 Mexican Biennial and, with the exception of one, were all abstractionists at the time: Gironella (the only figurative painter), Nishizawa, Rojo, Echeverría, Carrillo, Sjölander, Felguérez, and Vlady. Though the list includes some of the major nonobjective painters of Mexico, the fact that the great majority of Mexican painters were working in one or another mode of figuration would have caused tremendous criticism if this group had *officially* represented Mexico in Brazil.

In March 1961, Salas Anzures resigned from his position as director of the Departamento de Artes Plásticas for reasons that are not entirely clear.[34] What is certain is that on March 1, 1961, he received a letter from a high official of the Secretaría de Educación notifying him that the head of the Instituto Nacional de Bellas Artes had canceled his forthcoming exhibit titled "Reality and Abstraction," a show intended to place the diverse tendencies of Mexican art in confrontation. Seen negatively, such a show would have tended to confirm the biases of which Salas Anzures was accused; seen positively, it was a courageous attempt to keep the doors open to avant-garde art. In either case it would have accelerated controversy, and this, coming on the heels of the 1960 Biennial, the government apparently wished to prevent. Salas Anzures immediately tendered his resignation, which (contrary to what had happened on a previous occasion) was immediately accepted, perhaps with an eye to the fact that the São Paulo Biennial opened in September and the issue would arise once more. Functioning as an individual, Salas Anzures thereupon organized a "museum without walls," the Museo de Arte Contemporáneo de México, which, as its first action, prepared to send the eight artists mentioned above to São Paulo. Invited by Francisco Matarazzo Sobrinho, director of the Museu de Arte Moderna of São Paulo and founder of the São Paulo Biennials, forty works were exhibited at a "Salon Independiente" in a special hall. The *official* Mexican exhibit was a separate matter. The Instituto Nacional de Bellas Artes sent a special exhibit of Orozco works, paintings by Pedro Coronel, and exhibits of contemporary architecture, graphics, and painting. Cordelia Urueta won special mention for painting, while Francisco Moreno Capdevila and Héctor Xavier (later members of Nueva Presencia) were among the printmakers.

A matter that remains puzzling is Salas Anzures' relationship to governmental art policy. This concerns the invitation sent by an official of a foreign country to a group of artists whose organizer has ostensibly been discredited in his own country. Mexico is very sensitive about its image abroad and discourages the international airing of internal dissension. Why did Mexico permit a separate exhibit of "dissident" artists at the international São Paulo Biennial; why was it not considered an affront to the government? Though invited nations have been known to set up special exhibits outside the competition, in this case a group of individuals was permitted to do so. Did this have the tacit approval of the Mexican government?

The seemingly contradictory proceedings of the government with Salas Anzures underline the ambivalence of official policy toward the arts. Or perhaps it is more accurate to say that the government was attempting to mediate between opposing forces and was simply being pragmatic. The government continued to support the realist movement with which it had long been aligned and with which it was not politic to break in consideration of governmental revolutionary rhetoric. At the same time it promoted abstrac-

tion and other tendencies in its effort to present a modernized cultural demeanor on the world stage suitable to its new international cultural position.[35] Further considerations are that abstract painting, by its very nature, is nonpolitical, while the realists were very often political; and that the equation of abstractionism with liberation as the sign of an enlightened culture was still being promoted.

A posteriori, it can be seen that Salas Anzures functioned as the arts administrator who moved Mexican art into the modernist and internationalist arena in the crucial years starting in 1957. President Adolfo López Mateos (1958–1964) wanted to be known for his support of the arts. It is significant that it was during his time in office that the new Museo de Arte Moderno in Chapultepec Park supplanted the Museo Nacional de Arte Moderno established in 1958 in the Palacio de Bellas Artes by Salas Anzures. López Mateos also had the new Museo Nacional de Antropología constructed and other art structures updated and expanded. He was the president who put Siqueiros in jail in 1960, but he also pardoned him in 1964 so as not to leave a blot on his administration.

The sequel to the story of Salas Anzures' relationship to official government policy came three years after the "museum without walls" episode. In 1964, under President Gustavo Díaz Ordaz, a "floating" post was created for Salas Anzures in the higher echelons of the Secretaría de Educación; he was appointed to head a new program of activities for the Instituto Nacional de Bellas Artes that would totally revise the system of aesthetic education. Such a post placed him on a level with, or possibly even above, the head of the Instituto Nacional de Bellas Artes, and indeed there were indications that he would be its next director. Though he never received the latter post, one would assume that the government was not essentially opposed to his philosophy regarding the plastic arts or it would not have entrusted him with aesthetic education on a national level, or considered him to head an institution in which he had been forced to resign from a subordinate post.[36]

For artists working in an expressionistic-figurative vein in 1961—artists like Cuevas, who had won the First International Drawing Prize at the 1959 São Paulo Biennial and was considered Mexico's major young talent, and Rafael Coronel, who had his first one-person show at the Palacio de Bellas Artes in 1959 before he was thirty—a climate that favored nonobjective painting would represent a threat. They had before them the example of the United States and the fate of its realist painters since the rise and supremacy of abstract expressionism. Though they were associated with Salas Anzures in the "Museo," this factor might have prompted them to align them-

selves briefly with Los Interioristas. It was only natural that the response of a group of non–social realist figurative painters should have taken the form, if for nothing more than self-interest, of a collective that would bring their work to public attention. This is the bare bones of Los Interioristas. However, theirs was not simply a fly-by-night effort, a publicity stunt, a ploy to secure recognition and success; it was bolstered by a declaration of principles (albeit borrowed) and a manifesto that reflected the idealistic stance of its participants. Further, by limiting participation to artists who seemed to share their "ideology" and to certain stylistic characteristics, Los Interioristas produced the impression of a movement.

Insiders and New Imagists

4

Nueva Presencia as a concept, an ideology, a declaration of principles, and the germ of a collective, was the brainchild of two energetic, ambitious, idealistic, and highly articulate artists: Arnold Belkin and Francisco Icaza. It seems clear, from their recollections and those of other participants and observers of the events surrounding the publication of the first *revista-cartel* (magazine-poster), *Nueva Presencia* No. 1, in August 1961 and the first group exhibition of Los Interioristas in July 1961, that Belkin and Icaza worked in a complementary manner, assuming responsibilities as they arose. So integrated were their activities during the early period of enthusiasm that the specific roles devolving on each are hard to determine. What eventually emerges is Belkin's ideological role and Icaza's cohesive function for a group of artists (notoriously a noncohesive clan) who exhibited and worked together for over two years. Belkin and Icaza, who met during the boycott of the 1960 Mexican Biennial, also became close personal friends. Most remarkable of all the achievements that occurred between July 1961 and the last group show in November 1963 was the degree of unity sustained despite centrifugal tendencies resulting from outside pressures and internal petty jealousies and disagreements.

The roles of the two originators resulted from both external and personal circumstances. Canadian-born Belkin, temperamentally reserved, intellectual, conceiving of issues abstractly and in generic configurations, was still considered a "foreigner" (though he had lived in Mexico since 1948) and, within the subtleties of Mexican psychology, could not be at the "real center of things." Icaza, volatile and emotional, highly intelligent, well-educated and completely cosmopolitan, had lived abroad for most of his youth. Since he came of an ambassadorial family, he was automatically accepted as a member of the Mexican "aristocracy" when he returned permanently to Mexico in 1953. According to a contemporary observer, Icaza played a leading role

in the beginning, had a "Machiavellian type of mind," and was good at developing theories and convincing people of them. He was, however, a self-destructive person and eventually quarrelled with everyone.

Los Interioristas' first group exhibit and the publication of *Nueva Presencia* No. 1 were, according to Belkin, not connected events, though they shared a common parentage:

The term "Insiders," created by Rodman, unleashed a reaction in Mexico that had been developing during recent years. In my review of the above-mentioned book [*The Insiders*] for "Mexico en la Cultura" (*Novedades*, January 30, 1961), I proposed a re-evaluation of contemporary Mexican painting, affirming that the spirit of Orozco was not dead and that artists of the present generation, who were still unknown, were contributing a new humanism to painting.[1]

When the exhibition of paintings, drawings, and photography opened at the Galerías CDI on July 20, 1961, it was under the title "Los Interioristas." Concerning the magazine-poster, Belkin continues:

Icaza and I edited a magazine-poster dedicated "to man in the art of our time." The first issue on August 1, 1961, contained a manifesto in which we denounced an art of "good taste" and strove for an "art that had significance for our contemporaries." Since its publication coincided with the exhibition of "Los Interioristas," the manifesto was attributed to all the artists who had exhibited their works in the show.[2]

The artists exhibiting at the Galerías CDI who constituted the original Interioristas were Arnold Belkin, Rafael Coronel (who was discouraged by Inés Amor, his gallery representative, from continued participation with the group), Francisco Corzas, José Luis Cuevas, Francisco Icaza, Ignacio "Nacho" López, and Antonio Rodríguez Luna; the exhibit also included works by the late Orozco, as spiritual predecessor and inspiration. Belkin, Corzas, and Icaza formed the nucleus of the group in 1961; José Muñoz Medina, Emilio Ortiz, and Artemio Sepúlveda became "mem-

bers" in late 1961, Leonel Góngora, José Hernández Delgadillo, Francisco Moreno Capdevila,
and Benito Messeguer in 1962, and Gaston
González in 1963. On various occasions other artists exhibited with the group, but did not become
part of it. Antonio Rodríguez Luna, fifty-one
years old when Los Interioristas formed, Héctor
Xavier at forty, and Nacho López at thirty-seven,
were "elder statesmen" for the group: established
artists with mature styles who sympathized with
their aims, whose work was stylistically related,
and who exhibited with them on occasion, but
who came from an older tradition than the other
artists, who ranged from their mid-twenties to
early thirties.

"Insiders" and "New Images of Man"

The original source of inspiration for the formation of Los Interioristas (and the source of the
name) was the appearance in Mexico, in the aftermath of the turmoil surrounding the 1960
Biennial, of Selden Rodman's book (in English
only) *The Insiders: Rejection and Rediscovery of
Man in the Arts of Our Times.* Of the four artists
associated with the group who had boycotted the
Biennial—Cuevas, Coronel, Icaza, and Belkin—
Cuevas was the one most directly concerned
with publicizing the book, since an entire chapter was devoted to him as "Orozco's heir." He
brought it to the attention of Belkin, who wrote
an extensive and favorable review,[3] later reprinted in the *revista-cartel Nueva Presencia*
No. 2 in September 1961. Since Rodman's formulations gave initial impetus and definition to
Los Interioristas, it is worthwhile to outline his
philosophical and aesthetic concepts as they
were synthesized by Belkin and Icaza and the
group of artists attracted to them.

Selden Rodman, North American poet and
free-lance writer, had been interested in the
theme of *The Insiders* since the appearance of
his 1955 book, *The Eye of Man: Form and Con-*

tent in Western Painting, in which some of the
personae of *The Insiders* appear: Jack Levine,
Ben Shahn, and Rico Lebrun. In his 1959 trav-
elogue, *Mexican Journal: The Conquerors Conquered,* he recounted his search to discover
whether the spirit of Orozco was still alive in
Mexico and said that he considered the discovery in Antonio Souza's gallery of Cuevas' lithograph of a "grinning monster wearing a stovepipe
hat" as the first exciting work by a contemporary
Mexican he had seen to date.[4] This initial contact
led to a correspondence and friendship with
Cuevas that continued until the mid-sixties.
What also emerged clearly in *Mexican Journal*
was Rodman's antipathy to Siqueiros and Rivera
(given only passing reference in *The Insiders*),
and a qualified admiration of Tamayo, who was
classified as a non-Insider.

The Insiders posits the opposition of two types
of artists throughout history: non-Insiders, who
are concerned with ideation, symbolism, abstraction, and formal problems, and those "excep-
tional non-conformists" who defy the climate of
their time and initiate change: the Insiders. In
the modern period, the view that prevails is that
of Bernard Berenson's formalist credo: "Real artists do not bother about feeling and vision, but
only about learning how to draw and paint in a
more satisfactory way."[5] With Clive Bell, Roger
Fry, Clement Greenberg, and Thomas Hess, Rodman says, art has finally been brought to total
rejection of both human image and content. The
rediscovery of man in modern art begins with the
"forgotten master" Orozco, the first and greatest
Insider. By definition, an Insider is

an artist who feels drawn to values outside himself
strongly enough to examine them in his work.

Since "values outside himself" is taken to mean concern with the human condition, the Insider expresses
that concern in some form of representational imagery,
or (in the case of arts with abstract means), in an aesthetic vocabulary evocative of that condition.[6]

Since no examples of abstract Insiders are given
in the text, the means by which the human con-

dition would be expressed evocatively remain
unclear. On a formal level, the Insider is defined
as apt to be

more naturally a sculptor or draftsman than a painter
because he wishes to convey as directly and clearly as
possible his involvement with man. If he uses color at
all, it is primarily in an effort to intensify the emotion
behind the idea he is projecting, always as a comple-
ment to the drawing, never for its own sake. A deliberate defiance of the sensuous, atmospheric colorism of
the School of Paris may also be implied.

By the same token the Insider employs distortion
. . . to emphasize an imposed affliction or an inner
crisis.[7]

At this point a purely ideological note enters
Rodman's analysis: "He [the Insider] never depicts misery in the mass, as does the Communist
artist, because he conceives of evil and redemption in personal terms, soluble only through
the volition of the free spirit."[8] The Insider
may choose bums, workers, or peddlers as subject matter, but, unlike the social realist, he
chooses them precisely because they are unorga-
nizable and not subject to uplift and reform; they
are not victims of slum housing or juvenile de-
linquency, but of spiritual isolation and universal
indifference.[9]

This latter thinking is not reflected in Belkin's
review of The Insiders, nor did it find its way
into the theories of Los Interioristas—possibly
because Belkin himself felt uneasy with the formulation. During the years he had lived in Mexico and throughout his participation with Los Interioristas and Nueva Presencia, Belkin never
lost his identification with his left-wing Canadian background, his sympathy with working-
class issues and anti-imperialism. There is also
evidence in Belkin's murals (if not in his easel
paintings and drawings) that he did not view
misery and evil as soluble in purely personal
terms (as conceived by Protestant morality) or by
the volition of the free spirit (as suggested by
existentialism). His 1961 mural We Are All Guilty
(see Figs. 23, 24) presumes a communal sense of

responsibility for criminal behavior; it is more
sociological than individual.

Belkin's deletion of this aspect of Rodman's
thinking is significant. The deletion poses the
very dilemma faced by the young generation of
socially responsive artists in Mexico and elsewhere: how to pictorialize, or depict in plastic
terms, their enduring involvement with the misery, poverty, uncertainty, isolation, alienation,
and oppression they saw about them without
using the ideology or plastic vocabulary of social
realism. The problem was more acute in Mexico
than in other parts of the world, since social realism had remained a viable expression in the
work of Siqueiros, last of the tres grandes. As has
been shown in Chapter 3, the deflection of interest from social realism (which openly states the
nature of social problems like hunger, unemployment, discrimination, and war and identifies the
source as the capitalist system) to some more innocuous expression of social disorientation, or to
completely apolitical formalism, was the aim of
United States cultural imperialism. It was to encourage this deflection that abstract expressionism, with its introspective immersion in the self,
was encouraged in the United States and ex-
ported abroad. However, many of the younger
artists of Mexico had explicitly rejected abstract
expressionism. They felt the need of a new plastic language, new thematic material, and new solutions, but they were not prepared to ignore the
social realities about them. Their attitude posited
a serious breach between their ideas and those of
Rodman; however, in the first flush of excitement
about his book, the breach was probably not apparent. At the time, in an attempt to define an
alternate route to the two existing directions in
Mexican art (social realism and abstraction), the
future Interioristas turned uncritically to Rodman's formulations, prompted by their own predilections for draftsmanship, their sympathy with
the roster of artists he included, and his neo-
Renaissance "humanist-individualist" rhetoric.
Like all "enduring truths," his propositions had a

fine resonance until tested within a contemporary historical setting, especially that of an underdeveloped Latin American country.

Belkin's review particularly eulogized Rico Lebrun as the most admired of contemporary draftsmen and creator of an important mural (the 1960 *Genesis* in Pomona College, Claremont, California; see Fig. 11). He also defended José Luis Cuevas against the criticism that he was a draftsman and not a painter, and for his elimination of color. He compared him to Nacho López, one of Mexico's great photographers, who disdained the use of color in his photography.

The timing and implications of Rodman's book exceeded its intrinsic value as an art historical document. Most criticisms of Rodman found fault with his "original view of art history,"[10] which was full of shotgun judgments of paintings from many periods,[11] and his lack of plastic analysis. Such restrictions as stipulating that an Insider was more naturally a sculptor or draftsman than a painter, that color was secondary to drawing and distortion a necessary component, that multidimensional painting was superior to two-dimensional, were arbitrary to the last degree, and unworkable in that they committed a formalist "sin" in reverse: separation of content from formal means.

Rodman's predilections were clearly classical, with an overlay of expressionism for suitably individualized agony. Having passed through a phase as a collector of abstract expressionism, he was acute enough to realize that contemporary figurative artists could not return to a plastic vocabulary of the past; however, his stringent aesthetic requirements can be seen to have been as arbitrary as those of Clement Greenberg in respect to abstract expressionism.

Though eagerly embraced by Los Interioristas, Rodman's book served more as an organizational catalyst than a directional one. It served to coalesce an incipient trend that had been in formation since the mid-fifties, and for which Cuevas, to a certain degree, had been the model. It was

this trend that art critic Margarita Nelken had recognized as early as 1959 and formalized as a distinct Mexican expression in her 1964 book on the subject, *El expresionismo en la plástica mexicana de hoy*.

Abstract expressionism, almost at the point of demise in its own history, was the real target of Rodman's book, and in this he was not as solitary a voice in the United States as he was in Mexico. There had existed for some time, concurrent with the internationalization of abstract expressionism, what might be considered a countercurrent expression that achieved critical recognition with the important "New Images of Man" exhibit organized in 1959 by Peter Selz in New York's Museum of Modern Art. It is of no moment to argue whether Selz or Rodman had the original insight; what is important is the almost simultaneous recognition they gave a body of artists who had rejected formalism as a primary concern and were attempting to make some statement about the human condition. These artists used the human figure, but did not necessarily reject an avant-garde plastic vocabulary, including that of abstract expressionism. While Rodman, with some exception, had limited himself to the United States, Selz assembled an international roster of artists. "New Images of Man" appeared before the final draft of Rodman's book was complete and influenced its content; Balcomb Greene's painting *Seated Woman*, which Rodman purchased from the "New Images" show, and a quotation from a Greene manuscript which was printed earlier in the exhibit catalog appeared in *The Insiders* as well. Rodman was not totally uncritical of Selz, and wrote to Rico Lebrun in this vein after seeing "the whole meaning of your art warped by Selz's choices to conform to his world of faceless monsters."[12]

The tone of the Selz show was set by existential theologian Paul Tillich, who asked: "What has become of the reality of our lives?" and concluded that modern man is in danger of losing his humanity and becoming a thing among the things he produces. "The image of man," he said, "became transformed, distorted, disrupted and it finally disappeared in recent art." The artists wanted to regain that image and depict, as honestly as possible, the human predicament.[13] Perhaps the most truly existential images of the show, in a visual sense, were those of Alberto Giacometti, whose tall standing figures seemed to be pruned of all external vestiges save the most elementary. Many of the paintings and sculptures dealt with splintered, fragmented, scarred, corroded human forms whose textured surfaces seemed to derive from within, like blisters of anxiety boiling forth from some center of anguish and despair. Many of the works had obviously "primitivistic" references: Jean Dubuffet's *art brut* paintings based on children's scribblings, graffiti, and insane art; Cosmo Campoli's iconic forms taken from Aztec sculpture; or H. C. Westermann's mocking cubic constructions suggesting ancient idols. Others dealt with various types of metamorphosis, human-animal or human-insect (Kenneth Armitage, Theodore Roszak, and Germaine Richier); or human-machine aggregations (Eduardo Paolozzi). Some presented splintered, fractured bodies, or torsos with missing limbs (César Baldacchini, Leon Golub) or lonely figures lost in empty space, unrelating and uncommunicating (Nathan Oliveira, Richard Diebenkorn, Balcomb Greene), with impasto brushstrokes that owed a debt to abstract expressionism. The Pollocks that were included came from the black and white period suggestive of living forms, and the de Koonings were monstrous menacing images of women.

Leonard Baskin was represented in the show by sculptures dealing with death, *Man with a Dead Bird* and *The Great Dead Man*, and by pomposity-puncturing works of macabre humor, *Poet Laureate* and *Seated Man*. Rico Lebrun's death images concerned the theme of the Dachau and Buchenwald concentration camps (see Fig. 12). Though this theme has appeared repeatedly in postwar literature, it is surprising to find that few plastic artists have attempted to deal with it. Among the few are Lebrun and Argentinian-born United States graphic artist Mauricio Lasansky (who, however, was not included in the Selz show). Lebrun's rigid fragments of bodies and bones in almost abstract compositions manage to convey the horrors of the Nazi death pits.

For a variety of reasons, critics and reviewers in the United States were no more enthusiastic about "New Images of Man" than they were about Rodman's book. Both were too deviant from prevailing interests and fashions in the art world, which was still firmly dominated by abstract expressionism. Pop art, with all its attendant crudity and vigor, and its far more explicit scenes of violence, was still on the horizon.

Despite the adverse criticism, which, in some cases, may have derived from critical adherence to mainstream avant-garde art, "New Images of Man" was an important event. In the years since it took place, the increasing importance of artists such as Francis Bacon, Nathan Oliveira, Leon Golub, and others who were included in 1959 has confirmed that estimate. Figuration—indeed, realism itself, though of a new variety—again occupies center-stage, and is forcing a re-evaluation of critical judgments prevalent in the fifties. "New Images of Man" and *The Insiders*, despite discrepancies between them and internal weaknesses, have to be seen as interlocking events that were the first harbingers of an important international artistic movement that could not be seen in its full outlines until the 1970s, after passing through the crucible of the rebellious sixties. Selz's show brought together a diverse group of artists of varying ages, backgrounds, and concerns, working in a related vein; Rodman's book remedied Selz's Latin American myopia by including the Mexican humanists Orozco and Cuevas. In the final analysis, Rodman was a crucial link between the "New Image" of New York and that of Mexico, since none of the future Interioristas was aware of the New York show at the time it took place.

Nueva Presencia: Magazine/Poster

Five issues of the *revista/cartel Nueva Presencia* appeared between August 1961 and September 1963. Throughout its existence *Nueva Presencia* was planned, edited, and published under the major responsibility of Belkin and Icaza, and carried their signatures. The idea for its publication had arisen during a visit to Siqueiros in the Lecumberri prison early in 1961, after which Icaza suggested to Belkin that they publish a regular newsletter for Siqueiros. They then decided to make it a public expression, and finally the newsletter concept was abandoned. As it evolved, *Nueva Presencia* (whose title was taken from that of Belkin's January 1961 newspaper review of *The Insiders*, a title originally suggested by a journalist friend) was conceived both as a poster, in the style of the Syndicate broadsides that were pasted up around Mexico City, and as a monthly art magazine—an important function, considering the general lack of art magazines in Latin America. Thirty-five hundred copies were luxuriously printed (by the same printing establishment that produced the plush magazine *Artes de México*) in exchange for original art works by Belkin and Icaza, and were distributed at bookstores, libraries, campuses, galleries, and museums, without charge—a gesture conceived as an antiestablishment action. Dissemination, an important factor in determining impact, was aided by extensive coverage in newspapers and magazines, which, on occasion, reproduced an issue entire. This was facilitated by the fact that the 37-by-26-inch white poster, printed in black and one color, appeared on only one side of the paper. It folded three times upon itself to make a neat packet that opened like a book. In addition to being mailed abroad, it was often displayed at the group's exhibits. There is no doubt that *Nueva Presencia*, never a true art magazine in the broad sense of the term, became inextricably bound to Los Interioristas' image as a textual reference to their pictorial presentations. Not only did it give them a program and a sense of unity, but it effectively publicized their work and ideas far beyond the borders of Mexico City. It provided an organ for Los Interioristas just as *El Machete* had for the Syndicate; both were illustrated by the works of the artists. However, the political directions of the two publications were totally divergent. There is also little doubt that Belkin and Icaza thoroughly understood the promotional, public-relations, and merchandising advantages of *Nueva Presencia* for a group of young artists who were relatively unknown and who would benefit from the "group" format.

Nueva Presencia No. 1

The first issue of *Nueva Presencia* (Fig. 10), which appeared in August 1961, a month after the first Interioristas show, was the manifesto. Illustrated by Icaza's *Los Juanes No. 3* and Belkin's *The Accused*, its eleven-point program was in the form of a "Call":

1. WE CALL ALL ARTISTS:

   Painters, sculptors, architects, engravers, artists of the theatre and screen, photographers, writers, musicians, because their means of expression is communication.

   WE CALL STUDENTS OF ART:

   of architecture, philosophy, law, political science, economics, engineering, medicine, the sciences—and all those who study—because they have the future of the world in their hands.

   WE CALL THINKERS AND EDUCATORS,

   because they form the minds of our generation.

   WE CALL PROFESSIONALS.

   WE CALL ALL CLASSES OF SOCIETY,

   laborers, those who work the land, bureaucrats, merchants, politicians, financiers, because the manifestations of art are not made for any one class or any one group. WE ADDRESS THE MEN OF ALL NATIONS, the men of all races and

P R O P O S I T O S :

DESTACAR EL UNICO ARTE QUE ES SIGNIFICATIVO PARA NUESTROS
CONTEMPORANEOS; El Arte que no separa al hombre-individuo del hombre
como integrante social. Nadie tiene derecho a la indiferencia frente a la
organización social. MUCHO MENOS EL ARTISTA.

LOGRAR para el arte un cometido activo, como UNICA POSTURA
RESPONSABLE DEL ARTISTA FRENTE A SU TIEMPO.

ARNOLD BELKIN   FRANCISCO ICAZA

"LOS JUANES"   FRANCISCO ICAZA

NUEVA PRESENCIA

el hombre
en el arte
de nuestro
tiempo

1 AGOSTO DE 1961

TITULO EN TRAMITE   DERECHOS RESERVADOS   MENSUAL

1. LLAMAMOS A TODOS LOS ARTISTAS:
   A los pintores, escultores, arquitectos, grabadores, artistas escénicos y
   cinematográficos, fotógrafos, escritores y músicos, porque
   su medio de expresión es **la comunicación**.

   LLAMAMOS A LOS ESTUDIANTES DE ARTE,
   de arquitectura, filosofía, leyes, ciencias políticas, economía, ingeniería,
   medicina, ciencias —a todos los que estudian— porque
   tendrán el futuro del mundo en sus manos.

   LLAMAMOS A LOS PENSADORES Y A LOS EDUCADORES,
   porque forman las mentes de nuestra generación.

   LLAMAMOS A LOS PROFESIONISTAS.
   LLAMAMOS A TODAS LAS CLASES SOCIALES,
   a los obreros, a los que trabajan la tierra, a los burócratas, a los
   comerciantes, a los políticos y a los empresarios, porque las
   manifestaciones del arte no se hacen para una sola clase, ni para un
   solo grupo. **NOS DIRIGIMOS A LOS HOMBRES DE TODAS LAS NACIONES,**
   a los hombres de todas las razas y creencias.
   Porque el arte es el único medio de comunicación que posee un lenguaje
   universal.

10. *Nueva Presencia* No. 1, cover, August 1961.

creeds. Because art is the only means of communication which possesses a universal language.

Art has always been and will always be an instrument in the struggle for the peaceful evolution and
spiritual aggrandizement of the human species.

2. WE REJECT THE ART OF "GOOD TASTE."

Now is the time to denounce this nauseating art
which is nothing but a useless appendix to our
culture.

3. WE REJECT ART WHICH HAS SOLD ITSELF TO
MARKET SPECULATORS, THE POLITICAL CUR-
RENTS, OR TO WHAT IS FASHIONABLE.

4. WE REJECT ACADEMICISM.

We reject equally that which puts man in a false
position and that which denies his very existence.

5. WE REJECT THE INTELLECTUALIZED CRITIC.

The critic who uses art as a pretext to write literature. The critic who does not take a position, but
conforms to the established mode.

6. WE REJECT THE USELESS AND INCONSEQUEN-
TIAL THINGS THAT HAVE BEEN SAID AND
DONE IN THE NAME OF ART.

7. WE REJECT MYTHS.

A new presence demands new ideas. New ideas
have as their roots that which is most profound
and true in history.

8. THE ARTIST IS NOT A BUFFOON OF SOCIETY.

He is the denouncer of all the complacencies
which reign in the world. He who thinks he can
find in art a distraction to escape reality is mis-
taken.

9. WE STRIVE FOR PAINTING WHICH IS ANTI-
DECORATIVE, WHICH VIOLATES THE CON-
CEPTS OF "REFINEMENT" AND "GOOD TASTE."

"Good taste" is insipid. The greatest masterpieces
of the past never have been in "good taste." Grünewald, Michelangelo, El Greco, and Orozco had terrible "taste." The great painting of this century
should be antidecorative, antiaesthetic, anti-in-
tellectual. It should be raw, human, with social
responsibility, eloquent, real, complete, and universal.

10. WE STRIVE FOR ART WHICH COMMUNICATES
MOST DIRECTLY AND CLEARLY OUR BOND
WITH MAN.

11. WE SEEK TO PROMOTE THE ONLY ART
WHICH HOLDS MEANING FOR OUR
CONTEMPORARIES;

the art which does not separate man as an individual from man as an integral part of society. No one,
especially the artist, has the right to be indifferent
to the social order. WE SEEK TO SUCCEED IN OB-
TAINING FOR THIS ART AN ACTIVE COMMIT-
MENT AS THE ONLY POSITION TO BE TAKEN
BY THE RESPONSIBLE ARTIST IN OUR TIME.

The manifesto is a clear expository statement of
precepts that underline the fact that whatever
"packaging" motivations entered into the publication of *Nueva Presencia*, it was not prompted
by cynicism or a lack of idealism. *Nueva Presen-*

cia was separated from the Syndicate manifesto
both temporally and ideologically (though not
necessarily spiritually). Where the Syndicate
manifesto had been clear in its class alliances
(the native races, soldiers, workers, peasants, and
nonbourgeois intellectuals) and its goal of producing an art of ideological value to the people,
Nueva Presencia addressed itself to all classes
and groups without distinction and claimed that
art should be used for the peaceful evolution
of the human species. In contrast, *El Machete*,
tradepaper and political organ of the Syndicate,
featured a raised scythe and a militant verse on
its masthead:

The machete serves to harvest cane,
To open paths through timbered wilds,
Behead vipers, mow out tares,
And bow the merciless rich man.[14]

By 1961, the targets were "good taste," fashion,
art market speculators (collectors?), political
speculators (possibly a veiled reference to the
power of the social realists in established art circles), academicism (almost certainly referring to
both social realism and abstract expressionism),
and intellectualized critics: true indicators of the
middle-class milieu that surrounded the arts. Art
had become a commodity in the capitalist stage
of the Mexican state, and, like artists in highly
developed industrialized nations, the Mexicans
were becoming uneasy at the rise of a marketing
apparatus (galleries, museums, art critics, cura-
tors, and collectors/investors) that threatened to
affect the humanistic content of Mexican art. It is
one of the ironies of the time that the purpose
and the net result of Nueva Presencia was to
promote the success of another group of artists
within that same apparatus.

We have seen that the mural movement—certainly in the early works of the *tres grandes*—
found plastic means to express the ideology of
the Syndicate manifesto to a considerable degree.
It tried to be an art of "beauty for all, of education and of battle." It did create "monumental

art" that was a "public possession" and it even attempted to convert its participants to socialized, collective artistic expression and to obliterate bourgeois individualism, as its manifesto claimed. Was Nueva Presencia equally true to its manifesto? In my opinion it was, and the most striking example occurs in the opening paragraph. In addition to making no class distinctions among the people it addresses, it directs its particular message to two categories of society that were to be in the forefront of antiestablishment activities: students and professionals. Apparently, like the theoreticians of the New Left, Belkin and Icaza felt these two groups were the natural leaders of change; the most intelligent, the best prepared, and the most willing. (Perhaps this was so because they themselves were part of these groups, but that does not change the fact.) Those who study, they said, have the future of the world in their hands. In the structure of the manifesto, Belkin and Icaza abandoned not only "class division" but also "class struggle." In one sentence, they linked laborers with financiers and merchants (who might be supposed to have opposing interests), and they hoped to accomplish change through "peaceful evolution." This was in sharp contrast to the Syndicate, which threatened the "merciless rich man" with the machete. The mural movement expressed the force of armed struggle out of which it grew, while Nueva Presencia's iconography (of which much more will be said later) was more likely to suggest the anonymous, helpless victim at the mercy of unknown forces. "Peaceful evolution" suggests the philosophy of Gandhi and the tactic of non-violent civil disobedience that became important in the sixties; it is the ideology that gave birth to the methods so widely used by the United States civil rights and anti–Vietnam war movements.

In another sense, by affirming the artist's obligation to be responsive to the social order, the young humanists of the sixties aligned themselves with those of the twenties, while rejecting their political orientation. The choice of Orozco

as their guiding inspiration reaffirmed their connection with the mural movement, while at the same time identifying them with its most anarchic and iconoclastic spirit.

Nueva Presencia No. 2

The second issue of the broadside, which appeared in September 1961, introduced the major personalities of Los Interioristas and reprinted, as the source of its credo, Belkin's review of *The Insiders* and an article by Cuevas, "El arte actual se oriente hacia un nuevo humanismo" (Art Today Is Turning toward a New Humanism), accompanied by his drawing *Trodden Woman*. In his introduction to the issue, Belkin noted the return of figurative art with expressive content as a clear departure from both disengaged nonfigurative art and nationalistic social realism. In addition to Orozco's ink drawing *Wise Men* from the 1945 series *The Truth*, the issue also included works by the seven artists who had participated in the July Interioristas show.

The generally imprecise and romantic character of the first issue of *Nueva Presencia*, when contrasted to the second issue, did not escape the eyes of contemporary observers. The second number, said Julio González Tejada of *Mañana* magazine, was from all points of view much more interesting than the first. As was natural, it was much more serious, ideologically solid, intelligible, and useful than the first somewhat ingenuous message, which, because of its passion and romanticism and lack of rigor, was less successful.[15] González's criticism must be seen as a friendly admonition; he was a friend of Belkin and Icaza and worked for a magazine owned by the family of Icaza's wife. *Mañana* continued to give Nueva Presencia complete and excellent coverage. Not the least of the causes of Los Interioristas' success, in addition to the literary abilities of Belkin and Icaza themselves, was the support of critics like González, Raquel Tibol, Antonio Rodríguez, and Malkah Rabell. The appearance of three issues of *Nueva Presencia* between August and December 1961, and the lively polemical crossfire of artists and critics during the same period kept the group in the public eye. Their artistic exposure consisted only of the July exhibit at the Galerías CDI and a group show in October 1961 at the Escuela Nacional de Artes Plásticas (San Carlos), which, though it included Belkin, Icaza, Cuevas, Corzas, López, Rodríguez Luna, and Héctor Xavier, as well as others not part of the group, did not identify them as Interioristas. They did not exhibit again as a group until April 1962. As they became better known and invitations for individual and group shows began to proliferate, Belkin and Icaza found less time (or perhaps need) to publish *Nueva Presencia*: one issue appeared in 1962 and another in 1963. Their promotional energies were redirected into securing exhibits locally and internationally and preparing for them, as well as bolstering the faltering members of the group and strengthening it by the addition of new members.

Nueva Presencia No. 3

Activities on behalf of Siqueiros had started during the 1960 Mexican Biennial and had been germinal to Icaza and Belkin's friendship with each other and with Cuevas and Rafael Coronel, who also participated in the boycott. The *revista-cartel Nueva Presencia* had originally been conceived as a gesture of support to the imprisoned Siqueiros, although this was known only to a small group surrounding Belkin and Icaza. In November 1961, three months after the appearance of the manifesto, Belkin, Icaza, Cuevas, and Coronel participated in a delegation to Indian Prime Minister Jawaharlal Nehru, then on a state visit to Mexico, who they hoped would make a protest on behalf of Siqueiros, whom he knew personally. Prohibited from mentioning Siqueiros by governmental requirements, the artists involved presented to Nehru a portfolio of their works into the cover of which had been taped an original painting by Siqueiros.[16] At the end of the year, issue No. 3 of *Nueva Presencia* was openly

dedicated to Siqueiros on the occasion of his sixty-fifth birthday; it appeared on December 29, 1961. It included messages addressed to Siqueiros from fifty-five artists, writers, and intellectuals, covering a wide spectrum of political opinions. Under pressure from the government of President Adolfo López Mateos, a tight censorship had been clamped on the public media. Not even paid advertisements or announcements on behalf of Siqueiros were accepted by newspapers or radio stations. To publish privately and distribute an homage to a political opponent of the president of Mexico was an affront and challenge to authority that took considerable courage, but that must also have appealed to the antiauthoritarianism of Belkin and Icaza.[17]

Icaza and Belkin continued their activities on behalf of Siqueiros. On September 11, 1962, an "Open Letter to the Art Critics" in the name of "El Grupo Nueva Presencia" was distributed in three languages on the floor of a convention of the International Association of Art Critics in Mexico City, directing the critics' attention not only to Siqueiros' imprisonment but also to the fact that the content of his painting had been offered as criminal evidence by the court that convicted him.[18]

Excusing himself for his late response because of the constant demands and difficulties of prison life, Siqueiros wrote to Belkin and Icaza on December 24, 1962, thanking them for their efforts on his behalf and on behalf of the other persons jailed with him. He promised them a public declaration of what he considered the significance of the appearance of their antiabstractionist movement and "your great periodical *Nueva Presencia*," and hoped that ". . . my analysis will hit the mark about what I conceive as a very useful and eloquent theoretical-practical action in the development of the plastic arts of Mexico following our mural and printmaking effort."[19] Apparently the "declaration" never appeared; despite the warm tone of the letter there was a gap between Siqueiros and Nueva Presencia that Belkin later acknowledged, saying, "I don't think Siqueiros would have been too sympathetic anyhow."[20] There was too great a distance between the positions of Marxism and existentialism (to place the issues in large terms) to allow much sympathy between Siqueiros and Nueva Presencia. In addition, Siqueiros was committed to social realism and represented precisely those obstacles to artistic liberation that the younger generation opposed. The ambivalent relationship between Siqueiros and many of the younger artists, compounded of resistance to his powerful influence and admiration for him as artist and man, is illustrated by Icaza's summary of Siqueiros as a personality: "Siqueiros is a romantic. He thinks of himself as a hero, regenerating humanity. He is more innocent, and more honest than Diego was, less inclined to use dirty tactics to achieve his ends, less of a compromiser, opportunist—that's why he's in prison."[21]

There is good reason to believe that the continued activity of Los Interioristas on behalf of Siqueiros' release from jail was the real cause of the break with Cuevas, following which Cuevas was hostile to the group and publicly attacked it on a number of occasions. Initially, according to Belkin, Cuevas' disaffection took the form of opposition to the inclusion in the group of younger, unknown artists like Ortiz, Muñoz, and Sepúlveda; later he accused the younger artists of imitating him, and this became a reiterated part of his attack. The rupture became public in May 1962, when Cuevas, in a letter to the editor of *Excélsior*, not only disaffiliated himself from "the group of artists called 'Nueva Presencia'" but claimed that Orozco was an influence on his work only as an adolescent (which, considering Cuevas' precocity, was no doubt true) and much less important in the formation of his personality than the work of Sartre, Kafka, Beckett, Ionesco, and the movie comedies of Mack Sennett.[22] The surgery that skillfully separated Cuevas from Los Interioristas was left to other hands. In July 1962 a reprint of an article by Marta Traba, which had

originally appeared in Bogotá, was published in *Excélsior*—submitted by Cuevas. Traba undertook to criticize the imagery of Los Interioristas, which converted humans into monsters, and (paradoxically, considering that she was eulogizing Cuevas) claimed that they had plagiarized Cuevas' style. "José Luis Cuevas," she wrote, "is a great personality; the strangest, most powerful, and clearest of Latin American art," but the error of Los Interioristas was that "they all changed into Cuevas. From outright plagiarism to the most subtle borrowing, they all enlarge, deform, shade over penciled outlines, tint, like José Luis Cuevas." The real villain of the piece, however, was the specter of social realism: "To believe that the artist *must be* a deforming mirror to enlarge the horrors which weigh upon the human condition, would bring him to socialist realism . . . even if he achieved aesthetic results, which realism does not."[23]

While the strong influence of Cuevas' style and subject matter on some of the Nueva Presencia artists is apparent to even a casual inspection, this alone might not have caused such a strong rupture. Most artists probably consider it flattering to be copied rather than the reverse, and in a consumer market, it enhances the saleability of their names (though it must be admitted that Cuevas had a rabid fear of being copied by his contemporaries). Closer to the truth, perhaps, in view of the erratic swings of the Cuevas personality, is Icaza's version of the affair: he told Selden Rodman that Cuevas persuaded Marta Traba to attack Los Interioristas when José Gómez-Sicre frightened him into leaving the group after the Siqueiros issue of *Nueva Presencia* by writing him that he was being "used" by the Communists.[24]

The implication that *Nueva Presencia* was a "front" for any political ideology was sufficiently upsetting for Icaza to engage in his only public encounter in print with Cuevas. In it he claimed that Nueva Presencia was characterized by its independence of parties, politics, and government, and even, he added ironically, such entities sui generis as the Pan American Union.[25] This disengagement from existing political entities of all persuasions is very illuminating and clearly separates the historical context of young expressionists like Los Interioristas from that of the muralists and the Mexican School.

Nueva Presencia No. 4

During a two-year history, the artists who started their group career at the Galería CDI in July 1961 were to undergo a two-stage metamorphosis signalized by a change of names: from Interioristas (1961) to Nueva Presencia (1962). Though both terms, as well as *neohumanistas*, were present at the inception of the group and continued to be used interchangeably by critics and galleries, the emphasis on the use of a particular name symptomized a changing internal mentality, as well as personality clashes within the group.

One factor of significance is the degree to which political questions form a part of artistic experience in Mexico. Into this enter the traditional involvement of Latin American intellectuals, to an extent unknown in the United States, in the political life of their countries; the legacy of the mural movement, which had been the strongest cultural expression of Mexico and the most persistently political; and the colonized status of Latin American nations, which has made them particularly sensitive to transgressions against their sovereignty. Thus, not only did the members of Los Interioristas involve themselves publicly in activities on behalf of the imprisoned Siqueiros, but they also expressed their concern about United States attempts against the Cuban Revolution and interference in the Dominican Republic, and their final issue of *Nueva Presencia* in August–September 1963 engaged the issue of world peace, highly controversial at the time because of the hysterical atmosphere engendered in the fifties by the Cold War.

To the degree that Selden Rodman influenced—or was reflected in—the ideology of Nueva Pre-

sencia, we can say that the group continued to be Interioristas. However, by the time of the appearance of *Nueva Presencia* No. 2 (September 1961), there was already a cloud of doubt about the name. In February 1962 Icaza said: "I am not in agreement with this name 'Interioristas.' No such movement exists. All that exists is that it occurred to Selden Rodman to bring together diverse painters under the collective title: 'Insiders.' All that *does* exist is an affinity between all painters who are tired of the new academicism called abstract painting . . ."[26]

Questions about the name were also raised by two influential art critics who were, at the same time, sympathetic to the group: Antonio Rodríguez and Raquel Tibol. The former considered the appellation Interiorista very arbitrary, and suggested that an *interiorista* was a painter, writer, or poet principally concerned with an interior life, such as French writer Marcel Proust or Mexican painter Frida Kahlo, neither of whom looked for values outside themselves, as Rodman's definition suggested an Insider would do. There was no need, Rodríguez pointed out, for the young painters of Nueva Presencia to pigeonhole themselves within the definition invented by the creator of *interiorismo*.[27] The decision to change the group's name probably occurred shortly after the publication of Rodríguez's article; at any rate, the very next show, which took place April 11, 1962, at the Galería Mer-Kup in Mexico City, identified the group as "Nueva Presencia" and emphasized the metamorphosis by adding that this was its first collective exhibit.

Tibol also criticized Los Interioristas for their lack of self-definition and vacillating political emphasis. She challenged the designation of Orozco as an "Insider" and expressed her suspicion that Los Interioristas were creating an Orozco adapted to their needs, an Orozco from whom many fundamental factors of creative genius had been wrested in order to exalt his capacity to subjectivize the objective—which she considered the essential and definitive condition of the

Insider.[28] Though in essence Tibol was indirectly challenging Rodman, from whom Los Interioristas had uncritically accepted their principles, the point was well taken. Orozco cannot, in all accuracy, be considered introspective. Though often critical, he worked within the definitions and objectives of a *movement* that derived from the Mexican Revolution, and he did not, as Rodman suggests in *The Insiders*, stand aside from the events of 1910–1920 in order to express an impartial "rage or pity in the face of man's inhumanity."[29] Orozco did not conceive of inhumanity (i.e., "evil") as inherent in all persons; he clearly identified its sources in wealth or the abuse of power. The rich, the clergy, the generals, the labor leaders who betrayed their trust, and the brutalities of historical social systems were his targets. Orozco saw history as a clash of forces in which many were crushed and many confused, but during the course of which visionary leaders and thinkers arose who pointed out the path for those who were ready to follow. Comparing Cuevas (whom Rodman called Orozco's heir) with Orozco, for example, one is struck by the former's unrelieved pessimism and contempt for the human species. Even the constant inclusion of self-portraits indicates the subjective, autobiographical character of his inventions. Though there is no doubt about Cuevas' great gifts as an artist, he cannot be compared to Orozco in profundity—a profundity that depended precisely upon transforming the Mexican historical experience into a universal expression. Los Interioristas on the whole tried to combine extreme subjectivity (the work of art as a unique experience deriving from the psyche of a single individual—an attitude they shared with the abstract expressionists) and social objectivity (the artist "drawn to values outside himself" with the responsibility to communicate these to the audience); but these two goals were not always compatible, and they partially account for the internal wrangling and eventual disintegration of the group.

During the very period when Los Interioristas were re-evaluating their original premises and changing their self-designation, their influence and prestige as a "third movement" in art (neither social realist nor abstract) were spreading in the Latin American sphere, and even in the United States, primarily through the dissemination of issues of *Nueva Presencia*. By April 1962, the broadside was known in Colombia, Guatemala, Cuba, and other areas and the two enthusiastic editors were sure it would eventually reach even the dissatisfied nonconformists of the Soviet Union.[30] It was also in April 1962 that the Pan American Union opened an exhibition in Washington, D.C., called "Neo-Figurative Painting in Latin America," which was an acknowledgment of the international scope of the expressionistic neofiguration. Artists of five countries were included: from Argentina, three artists of a strongly defined neofigurative group with affinities to Nueva Presencia, Rómulo Macció, Luis Felipe Noé, and Jorge de la Vega (Ernesto Deira and Antonio Segui were omitted), as well as Carolina Muchnik; from Colombia, Fernando Botero and Carlos Granada; from Nicaragua, Armando Morales; from Panama, Alberto Dutary and Guillermo Trujillo; and from Mexico, José Luis Cuevas. In view of the coming public rupture between Cuevas and Nueva Presencia, it is perhaps significant that Cuevas was the only Mexican artist invited. But, in any case, the Pan American Union exhibit made it clear that a large number of artists in Latin America, as well as the Europeans and North Americans who comprised the "New Images of Man," were working in a direction that seemed to emphasize the grotesque aspects of modern humanity based on an artistic projection of existentialism and even anarchy. This exhibit of the early sixties can be seen as the last throb of the Beat spirit and the prelude to the decade of rebellion that, in its later phases, was led by the international adherents of the New Left. The spreading influence of Nueva Presencia and its international links can be attributed to these subcurrents that manifested themselves artistically in the years 1962–1963.

Published in April 1962, the fourth issue of *Nueva Presencia* was an affirmation and demonstration of the international character of neohumanism. The introduction breathes a new air of authority and sense of purpose: "Convinced that the great art of this century is being born simultaneously in all parts of the world, as also is being simultaneously born the restlessness, the seeking, of our generation—without the limits of frontiers, or of political affiliations—we have initiated a series of unifying activities with artists of other countries." This issue of *Nueva Presencia*, beginning with texts and the reproduced works of Leonard Baskin and Rico Lebrun, was envisioned as the first of a series of bilingual neohumanist documents.

Baskin's article, "La necesidad del prejuicio," was a partisan and frontal attack on the noncommunicative, undisciplined formalism of abstract expressionism. "There is no question," he said, "that the drive towards noncommunication in art is but one expression of man's growing inability to communicate in general." No doubt abstract expressionism offered its practitioners unparalleled freedom, but freedom, Baskin said, is the "recognition of necessity." Freedom means the control of reality, and control means mastery of all the tools with which we model the physical and intellectual environment that surrounds us. If freedom is not controlled, it may result simply in the expression of anarchic exuberance. Baskin was concerned with the broad issue of the artist's responsibility toward society. Is Trotsky's dictum true, he asked, that a decadent society must produce a decadent art, or can we overcome our own constraining *Zeitgeist*? He cited the indications of a new spirit in the figurative painting emerging in Chicago, San Francisco, and the "New Images of Man" show.[31]

Lebrun's "Apuntes sobre arte" (Notes on Art) were general statements about his artistic philosophy; the "Carta de Rico Lebrun" (Letter from Rico Lebrun) concerned his personal reactions to his first encounter with Nueva Presencia artists in Mexico City in February of that year. These texts, as well as the reproductions of Lebrun's *Woman of the Crucifixion* and three ink drawings from his *Inferno* series, make it easy to understand the tremendous influence Lebrun had on Los Interioristas, philosophically and artistically—especially on Belkin. He articulated their beliefs in original and powerful language and produced magnificent, tormented drawings of a monumental quality that were wholly centered on the human form: "I prefer the theme of the human figure and its predicament to whatever other structural or abstract proposition the former [themeless art] has; in all senses it has more life and richness of content. As mutilated and altered by life as the said image may be, or reduced in form and content by my own limitations as an artisan, I discover in it, nevertheless, here and there, accents of authenticity."[32]

Belkin's admiration of and contact with Lebrun predated the formation of Los Interioristas and was founded on the two characteristics of Lebrun's art that most closely resembled that of Orozco: muralism and the use of the monumental human form. On May 21, 1961, in response to a request from Belkin's cousin in Los Angeles, Lebrun's wife Constance sent Belkin photographs of Lebrun's 1960 mural *Genesis* (Fig. 11). She also sent photos of *Buchenwald Cart* (Fig. 12) and *Buchenwald Pit*—themes of particular resonance for Belkin, who as early as 1959 had painted a large mural canvas for the Jewish Community Center of Vancouver, Canada, called *Warsaw Ghetto Uprising* (see Fig. 22). The photographs sent to Belkin by Constance Lebrun formed the basis of a glowing tribute to Lebrun by Julio González Tejada in *Mañana* magazine.[33]

Of the three senior United States artists admired by Nueva Presencia, Lebrun, Baskin, and the printmaker Mauricio Lasansky, there is no doubt that Lebrun was the closest to them artistically and personally. Evidences of the influence of his style, intermingled with that of Orozco, are apparent in the work of several members of the group—Belkin, Sepúlveda, González, and to a lesser degree Icaza and Góngora. Others, including Cuevas, Corzas, and Ortiz, remained untouched. Lebrun also had an unusually sweet disposition, and was willing to go to a great deal of trouble to support and help the younger artists. He early took considerable pains for Cuevas (introducing him to Los Angeles galleries and collectors) and later for the Nueva Presencia group when they were attempting to establish a Los Angeles base; his final gesture of help, when already mortally ill, was on behalf of Sepúlveda,

11. Rico Lebrun, *Genesis*, 1960, vinyl acetate. Pomona College, Claremont, California. Courtesy Pomona College News Bureau; photo by Robert C. Frampton.

12. Rico Lebrun, *Buchenwald Cart*, 1955, oil on canvas, 84 × 114 in. (213.5 × 290 cm.). Courtesy of the Pennsylvania Academy of the Fine Arts, Lambert Fund Purchase; photo by Phillips Studio.

whom he recommended for a Guggenheim Fellowship to study muralism.

The internationalist and bilingual aspirations of the fourth issue of *Nueva Presencia* reflect the constantly growing trend toward international cultural communication. In the thirties, the magazine *Contemporáneos* had been a short-lived effort to perform this integrating function, against the current; in the changed climate of the sixties the Spanish-English magazine *El Corno Emplumado*, which appeared from 1962 to 1969, printed a scintillating, world-wide selection of works from young writers and artists. Avant-garde in character, *El Corno Emplumado* emphasized humanism and inner liberation. Though *Nueva Presencia* itself never achieved bilingualism, it is not surprising that Interioristas like Cuevas, Belkin, and Góngora should have had drawings published by a magazine like *El Corno Emplumado* whose contributors placed emphasis on "the agrarian reform of the soul" and which had shifted its sights from Paris to New York, from surrealism to Zen and Beat.[34] Los Interioristas were, after all, moved by the same postwar romantic subjectivity as the New York abstract expressionists whose imitators they so bitterly opposed, although their aesthetic was figurative. Like the abstract expressionists, they were familiar with the writings of San Francisco's Beat poets (also printed in *El Corno Emplumado*) and French existentialists like Sartre and Camus.

As the underdogs in the struggle for artistic hegemony, the artists of Nueva Presencia would have replaced abstract expressionism if it had been possible, and in 1962 it certainly appeared to be possible. Instead, however, Pop art, a figurative art of a wholly different character, assumed leadership in the United States in the sixties, while the Mexicans and their United States counterparts remained in the minority. In the years 1962–1963, Los Angeles, then emerging as a major art center second only to New York, presented a microcosmic view of the neohumanist/

Pop encounter. On November 5, 1962, the first Nueva Presencia group show opened at the Zora Gallery. On November 25, FM radio station KPFK sponsored a one-day exhibit, "The Concept of Man as Seen through the Eyes of Southern California Artists," which included a cross-section of Los Angeles neohumanist artists: John Altoon, Flavio Cabral, John Coleman, Leonard Cutrow, Robert Frame, Ted Gilliam, Rico Lebrun, Arnold Mesches, Joe Mugnaini, Arnold Schifrin, June Wayne, Howard Warshaw, Charles White, and Joseph Young. However, Pop artists were to be equally represented on the Los Angeles scene: the month of February 1963 found Andy Warhol, Roy Lichtenstein, Jim Dine, Robert Dowd, Ed Ruscha, Joe Goode, Robert Indiana, Jasper Johns, Edward Kienholz, John Chamberlain, Claes Oldenburg, Robert Rauschenberg, Larry Rivers, and James Rosenquist showing at various museums and galleries—certainly a heavy contingent of the genre for a single city. Simultaneously, as a contrast to the Pop exhibitions, José Luis Cuevas opened with a lithograph show, "Recollections of Childhood," at the Silvan Simone Gallery.[35]

Pop art (which began about 1955 in the United States with early experiments by Rauschenberg) can be said to have superficial points of contact with neohumanism; it was a reaction to the subjective decorative surfaces of abstract expressionism; it restored "realism" and the human image to art and even (inadvertently) communicated the distress of the human condition. However, Pop art, with perhaps the exception of Jasper Johns' and Claes Oldenburg's ironies and the brutal social commentary of Edward Kienholz, Duane Hansen, and Paul Thek, was neither critical nor a form of protest like its prototype, Dada. It absorbed and synthesized the most trivial and banal products of a technological consumer society, neutralized them of feeling, detached them from reality, and united them with the aesthetic impulse, i.e., made them into paintable or sculptural objects, a sort of industrial still life. Human beings were similarly objectified: fragmented,

13. *Left to right*: Francisco Icaza, Rufino Tamayo, Arnold Belkin. Coyoacán. May 1962. Photo by Selden Rodman.

multiplied, trivialized, plasticized. Even the re-iterated themes of eroticism and violence were handled on a superficial level—experiences to be quickly consumed and forgotten. The central theme of neohumanism, expressed by the mon-strosities, deformations, and distortions of the human figure, was to reaffirm human potential by calling attention to the wounds inflicted by the present terms of existence. Negation was an act of criticism against society, what Herbert Marcuse called "the Great Refusal—the protest against that which is."[36] It was also an art of alienation, but one that called attention to the fact of alienation, not one that defused it. Neohu-manist artists of the United States were engaged in a genuine act of resistance to the dehumaniz-ing tendencies of contemporary art. Whether this was true for the Mexicans will be considered later.

Nueva Presencia No. 5

More than a year was to pass between the fourth and fifth issues of *Nueva Presencia*, a year dur-ing which the group consolidated its position and reputation in Mexico and, with Rodman's and Lebrun's help, established gallery contacts in New York and Los Angeles—specifically the fig-urative-oriented Cober and Zora galleries. As the

major spokesmen for the group, Icaza and Belkin became especially well known (without doubt a factor that exacerbated internal jealousies). There was even an attempted *rapprochement* with Ta-mayo (Fig. 13), with Selden Rodman acting as peacemaker. Tamayo was no more favorably in-clined toward neohumanism than he had been toward social realism. The artists who interested him most, he had said in an interview, were the abstractionists. Movements like that of Los Inte-rioristas did not bring anything new, he believed; they only tried to continue *orozquismo*. The word *interiorista* made allusion to psychological points of view, something that was completely foreign to painting in his opinion.[37] Despite peace-ful overtures, Tamayo was still hostile three years later during the 1965 Esso Salon, when he re-fused a prize to Benito Messeguer because of his neohumanist affiliations.

In August–September 1963, the final issue of *Nueva Presencia* appeared concurrently with two important exhibits: "Neohumanism in the Drawing of Italy, the United States, and Mexico," held in the San Carlos Academy galleries (Sep-tember 13–October 5), and "War and Peace," is-sued as ten portfolios by the Galería Misrachi, and expanded to an exhibit of almost two hun-dred works at the Salón de la Plástica Mexicana, "Drawings of Nueva Presencia: War and Peace" (August 20–September 7).

The "Neohumanism" exhibit, a product of the desire of Icaza and Belkin to organize an exhibi-tion of humanist artists that would place the Mexican artists within an international artistic panorama, opened September 13, 1963, a few weeks later than "War and Peace." Ten Mexican artists were included: Javier Arévalo, Belkin, Del-gadillo, Góngora, González, Icaza, Luna, Muñoz, Sepúlveda, and Xavier. From the United States came Manuel Ayaso, Mowry Baden, Leonard Baskin, Jacob Landau, Rico Lebrun, Arnold Mes-ches, Peter Paone, Ben Shahn, Don La Viere Tur-ner, and Howard Warshaw. The Italian repre-sentation came from a portfolio of lithographs, brought from Italy by Raquel Tibol, that had been the culmination of an early 1961 exhibit in Rome with the theme "Violence Still Exists." The Italian artists included Renato Guttuso, most prestigious of postwar Italian neorealists, as well as Ugo Attardi, Ennio Calabria, Fernando Farulli, Alberto Gianquinto, Piero Guccione, Giuseppe Guerreschi, and Lorenzo Vespignani.

There are notable stylistic and thematic similarities in the work of the three nationalities presented in this exhibit, a fact that sustains the claim that neohumanism was indeed an international movement with distinct characteristics. In 1962, when asked his opinion of the new humanism, Renato Guttuso had affirmed that it was the most widely discussed phenomenon of the time among both figurative and abstract painters. The discussion had been growing in the previous six or eight months, he said, but the real impetus for its universalization had been the 1959 "New Images of Man" show. At the same time, he cautioned that a valid approach to the contemporary human figure would not develop until it ceased to be a preoccupation of vanguardism, which put an emphasis only on certain problems (a possible reference to the premium being placed on transformation to the figure without losing the characteristics of abstract expressionism). A new humanism required that the problems of humanity be confronted as a whole, as a totality; not solely from the inside or the outside.[38] Because the Italian exhibit derived from a thematic portfolio, it was the most integrated (and also the most overtly political) of the presentations. It focused on war and torture, particularly in Korea and Algeria, carrying on the tradition of Goya in a modern idiom. Guttuso's *Massacre* (Fig. 14) is specifically contemporary: soldiers in the camouflage uniforms of modern war are engaged in hanging or butchering their victims. In *Algerian Still Life No. 2* Farulli has made a strong but grisly composition of torture instruments, with overtones of the Crucifixion. Calabria's *Africa* is a Rubensian whirlwind of dark bodies with a single white

figure at its hub, perhaps symbolizing the European presence in Africa and the revolt against colonialism that had already started in Algeria. One of the most haunting of the Italian works is Vespignani's *Television* (Fig. 15), in which a deserted child lies screaming on a disheveled bed in the glare of light from a television set that gives a wholly contemporary feeling to the sense of catastrophe that pervades the work. Guerreschi's *Little Girl of Milan-Korea* emphasizes the violence done to children in both Korea and his native Milan (by implication, everywhere) with the single, boldly drawn figure of a tattered, blood-stained child.

The United States contributions to the "Neohumanism" show were organized by Selden Rodman and the Cober and Zora galleries, representing the East and West Coasts. Lebrun, Turner, Warshaw, and Mesches were from Los Angeles. Landau, Ayaso, and Los Angeles-born and -trained Baden (a former pupil of Belkin's from Mexico City College, 1956–1957) had shown at Cober in New York, as had Paone, a friend of Rodman's. Baskin was also from the East Coast. Belkin owned the Ben Shahn lithograph *Head of Lincoln*, which was displayed. Rico Lebrun's large female nude from the *Island Bodies* series (1961) was contemporary with his illustrations for Dante's *Inferno* and done a year after the woodcuts he designed and Baskin cut for Herman Melville's *The Encantadas*; it is in the same metamorphic spirit. Spanish-born Ayaso, who came to the United States in 1947, had developed a poetic and delicate style in goldpoint (and other media) that so impressed Cuevas when he saw Ayaso's drawings at the Cober Gallery that they became close friends and traded works. *Owl Family with Poet* (Fig. 16) with its harpy-poet and anthropomorphic owls is both fragile and mysterious, like something out of a child's dream. Though it has affinities with the more surreal, fantastic productions of Cuevas and Emilio Ortiz, both stylistically and thematically it is quite distinct from the Mexican works. Jacob Landau's

14. Renato Guttuso, *Mas-sacre*, 1961, lithograph, 13 × 18⅝ in. (33 × 47 cm.). Collection of Raquel Tibol. Photo by Arnold Belkin.

15. Lorenzo Vespignani, *Television*, 1961, lithograph, 13 × 18⅝ in. (33 × 47 cm.). Collection of Raquel Tibol. Photo by Arnold Belkin.

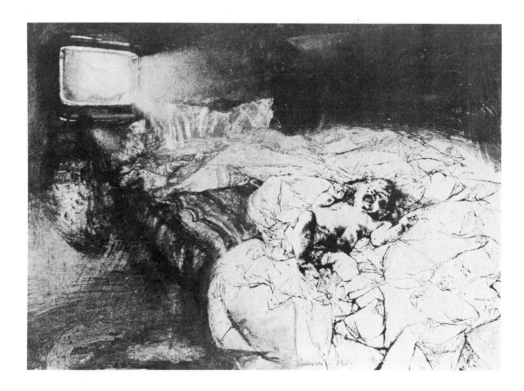

16. Manuel Ayaso, *Owl Family with Poet*, 1962, watercolor, pastel and ink, 17⅜ × 22¼ in. (44 × 56 cm.). Collection of Mrs. Lucia Ayaso. Courtesy of the artist.

17. Jacob Landau, *Tragic Hero*, ca. 1963, watercolor and pastel. Private collection. Courtesy of the artist.

18. Arnold Mesches, *The Rising of the Phoenix*, 1958,
pen and ink, 11 × 19 in. (28 × 48.5 cm.). Collection of
the artist.

Tragic Hero (Fig. 17), dominated by strong red
tonalities contrasted with green and white, is
more Orozcoesque and existential in nature.
From the tangled, centrifugal web of bodies and
heads that is Landau's hallmark emerges the solitary hero. He is tragic because, despite his power,
he is blindfolded and his fate is determined by
chance, symbolized by two playing cards he
holds aloft. One thinks immediately of Orozco's
similarly blindfolded figure in Guadalajara who
has lost control of his fate. In 1958, Arnold Mesches, then in his most pronouncedly Orozco
phase, had done a series of eighty-five drawings
(later translated into oil paintings) called *War
Images*, which were subdivided into *Rape*, *Survivors*, *The Rising of the Phoenix*, and *Metamorphosis* phases, all treating of his reactions to
World War II concentration-camp victims and

survivors. In *Metamorphosis* and *The Rising of
the Phoenix* (Fig. 18), Mesches dealt with a bird/
man symbiosis: in the former, scavengers feed on
the bodies of the victims, whose flesh is thus
transmuted into the bird form; in the latter the
victims achieve final triumph as their spirit
rises above them in the form of the legendary
phoenix.

Several weeks earlier, on August 20, 1963, the
exhibition "Drawings of Nueva Presencia: War
and Peace" had opened in Mexico to critical acclaim. Enrique F. Gual declared, "The group of
painters of Nueva Presencia, reinforced by a
number of artists with affinities to their ideals,
are presenting . . . an exhibition . . . which makes
available one of the strongest events we have had
in Mexico for many years."[39] The critic for *Tiempo* [Time] magazine in Mexico wrote: "Rarely

has such a large group of excellent drawings, almost completely unknown to the great public, been seen in Mexico."[40]

Nueva Presencia No. 5 was dedicated to the theme of war and peace. It should be noted that thematic portfolios around a political theme had long been utilized by the Taller de Gráfica Popular, drawing on the tradition of Posada. Just a year earlier, in August 1962, the Taller had produced a graphics exhibit on the theme "For World Disarmament and Peace," which may very well have suggested the similar endeavor by Nueva Presencia. A major difference between the two groups was the former's use of prints on inexpensive paper for maximum distribution at low prices, while the ten portfolios of Nueva Presencia were all original drawings to be sold to collectors. The Taller's choices were politically determined; they were addressing a mass audience and therefore chose media like the linoleum block for speed and quantity reproducibility. They avoided color (using colored paper instead) not, like Nueva Presencia, for aesthetic or philosophical reasons, but in the interests of saving time and money. The core of Nueva Presencia artists never considered themselves primarily as graphic artists (as did Leopoldo Méndez, leader of the Taller)—though their style was particularly felicitous for the medium and two of their masters, Baskin and Lasansky, were printmakers—but as painters who also made drawings and prints. In the collector's market, paintings brought larger prices (and profits) than prints and drawings, though the latter had their "uses" for young, less prosperous collectors.

The fifth issue of *Nueva Presencia* was keynoted by a poem that makes clear what the group hoped to accomplish with its portfolios. Signed by Lanzo del Vasto, the poem read:

¿Dónde castigar el enemigo?
En el centro.
¿Cómo? ¿En la cabeza? No.
¿En el pecho? No.

¿En el vientre? No.
¿Dónde, entonces?
En el centro: en la conciencia.[41]

Introducing the major theme was an essay on dehumanization by nineteen-year-old Argentinian poet Ezequiel Saad, who had been traveling throughout Latin America with a packful of Beat poetry translated into Spanish. Saad had opened the inauguration of the "War and Peace" exhibit with a poetic recital, and his brief discourse on that occasion was now put into print. Humanism in art, he said, is a position that the artist has taken in order to affirm human existence, not by merely accepting the no-atomic-war that has taken the place of peace, but by confronting the danger of dehumanization by the machine and the government.

Opening up the *revista-cartel*, one finds a quotation from Kant's *Perpetual Peace* and an apocalyptic "sermon" signed: "from the 18 of November [*sic*] to the 23 of the same month in the year 1962. In the *Sagrario* of Quito Cathedral, Ecuador. During the political crisis between the U.S. and the Soviet Union."[42] Then followed excerpts from Bertrand Russell's 1917 essay *Political Ideals*. Nueva Presencia had planned to dedicate the whole issue to Russell, the leader of the world peace movement, and had written to ask him for a personal message on behalf of a group of "painters, architects, writers, scientists, filmmakers, and intellectuals" who promised to organize for peace in Mexico and identify themselves with the international peace movement.[43] "We were actively anti-bomb and vociferously pacifistic (Russell style)," says Belkin.[44]

In the center spread of the *revista-cartel* was the entire text of Beat poet Lawrence Ferlinghetti's poem (probably provided by Saad) *Tentative Description of a Dinner Given to Promote the Impeachment of President Eisenhower*, illustrated by Belkin's monumental image of a flayed man (Fig. 19) inspired by the medical woodcuts of Vesalius (Fig. 20). Ferlinghetti's poem, couched in terms of biting sarcasm, took thrusts at the president, who

was doing everything
in his power to make the world safe for nationalism
his brilliant military mind never having realized
that nationalism itself was the idiotic superstition
which would blow up the world.

He painted word pictures of "spastic generations and blind boneless babies" resulting from the "strange rain" (atomic fallout) that would never stop—pictures analogous to the riddled and mutilated human figures of *interiorismo*.[45]

As originally conceived in January 1963, *Nueva Presencia* No. 5 had been a much more bellicose document. An undated draft contained a new manifesto that read, "We appeal to artists and intellectuals the world over to take an active stand against any possibility of war. We call upon the artists of all aesthetic tendencies, in all parts of the world, to protest through their work against militarism, war, and its consequence: 'Because art was, is, and always will be an instrument in the peaceful growth and spiritual evolution of the human race.'" In the style of Emile Zola's *J'Accuse*, the manifesto continued on to accuse

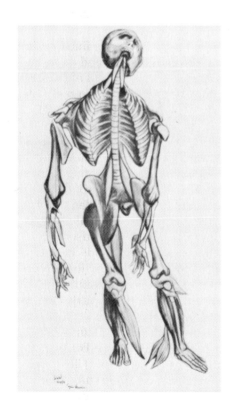

19. *Nueva Presencia* No. 5, center spread, August–September 1963.

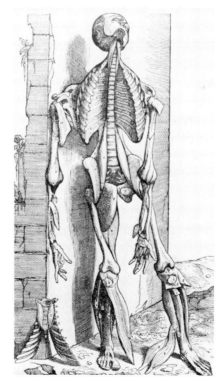

20. Andreas Vesalius, Eighth Plate of *De Humani Corporis Fabrica*, 2d ed., 1555, reprinted in *The Illustrations from the Works of Andreas Vesalius*, 1973. Courtesy Dover Publications, Inc.

countries that manufacture weapons; governments that maintain armies; scientists who will-
ingly become criminal accomplices in the destruction of the human race; those who are
connected with the big industries that produce
weapons, thus capitalizing on death; those who
traffic in tension, anxiety, and hatred, thus creating a war psychosis; and those who remain
in ignorance and voluntary indifference in the
face of atomic tests and wholesale stocking
of arms, bombs, and missiles. It ended by demanding total disarmament and the suppression
of militarism.

This version never appeared in print. "We felt
it was childish," said Belkin in 1975. Nevertheless, the idea had been planted, and it was reinforced when Belkin made a trip to Los Angeles
in March 1963, during the course of which he
attended a peace demonstration coordinated
by Women Strike for Peace. He jotted down the
slogans of the placards and retained one of the
handbills (Fig. 21) for future reference.

The changes and revisions in *Nueva Presencia*
No. 5 from its first conception to its final appearance are perhaps indicative of the contradictions
and indecisions characteristic of the group; the
same tendency to generalize, diffuse, and dissi-
pate their focus also appears in their art. It was,
perhaps, a reaction against the very real political
and artistic pressures exerted by social realism,
as exemplified by the Taller in this instance.
Nueva Presencia felt the need to occupy a me-
dian position, in neither the social realist nor the
formalist camp. No one has ever claimed that the
proverbial position of fence-sitter is either comfortable or secure!

Nueva Presencia No. 6 (Projected)

Despite the fact that the group had splintered
and separated by the beginning of 1964, Belkin
nevertheless planned another issue, with the
hope that it might reunify the members. It was to
include a letter from Belkin to the Instituto Nacional de Protección a la Infancia concerning the

destruction of his 1963 mural *It Rests with Our
Generation to Decide* (see Chapter 6, Figs. 34 and
35), an unspecified article by the critic Adrián
Villagómez, and an homage to Rico Lebrun, who
had died May 9, 1964. However, Belkin and Icaza
(the main persons involved with the publication
of the *revista-cartel*) had parted ways, and the
other artists were unresponsive. The impetus to
publish died, and *Nueva Presencia* No. 6 never
appeared.

Disintegration of Nueva Presencia

Peace, for the decade of the sixties, was a central
issue that connected the agony of World War II
with that of Korea and Vietnam. The pall of the
atom and hydrogen bombs hung like a blight
over all human activities and impinged on the
consciousness of an entire generation. For Latin
Americans the threats of war and imperialism
centered on Cuba, which, for a brief moment,
had become the locus of a clash between the two
superpowers. It was impossible to be isolated in
this world either as an individual or as an artist.
Every event, every attempt at self-determination
by a colonized nation, reverberated throughout
the strands of the world-wide web. The Nueva
Presencia artists, like artists everywhere who
lived with a consciousness of social responsibility, felt impelled to join forces to affirm a
common humanity and resist annihilation and
dehumanization. This is the most logical interpretation of the group's activities in 1963, activities that brought their artistic efforts to a culminating high point that strained every sinew of
a basically unstable organization.

It is hard to pinpoint an exact date or reason
for Nueva Presencia's demise. It was caused by a
combination of petty jealousies, misunderstand-
ings, and tensions about money, as one artist or
another accused the galleries of favoritism or of
not handling money matters equitably. There was
envy of the leading positions of Icaza and Belkin,

THIS IS WHY WE WALK ■FOR PEACE!

We have used our pens to write, we have used our voices to speak; we now offer our physical presence to witness for peace on earth and brotherhood among men. We believe that the times call for courage to stand up and be counted. We take our stand for sanity in a world bent on madness. We take our stand for man whose life on earth is imperiled by a wasteful, foolish arms race. We take our stand for the children we have brought into the world, and for unborn generations, that they may have abundant life, physically, mentally, socially and culturally. □ We walk to arouse the indifferent and apathetic members of our society. We covet their presence and cooperation in our efforts to promote human welfare and insure the survival of the race. We invite them to join us seeking to preserve human values built up in time. □ We walk to impress those who occupy places of leadership in our own and other nations. We would remind them of the solemn responsibility they bear for the destiny of millions of human beings whom they represent. We appeal to them to act with wisdom and patience in this decisive hour of human history. We pray that they may meet the test of greatness in a "time for greatness."

PERMANENT PEACE *IS* POSSIBLE
AND PEACE IS *OUR* RESPONSIBILITY

■ PEACE SATURDAY 1963 ■

Coordinated by: Women Strike for Peace, Box 69611, Los Angeles 69, Calif.

21. Women Strike for Peace, *This Is Why We Walk for Peace*, handbill, March 1963. Belkin Archives.

who were constantly in the press as spokesmen for the group; at the same time the members of the group tended to leave organizational activities in their hands.

By the end of 1963, Nueva Presencia was disintegrating. Selden Rodman, visiting Mexico in early 1964, noted that Nueva Presencia was now defunct.[46] Emilio Ortiz had broken with the group for its politics; both he and Muñoz thought humanism too firmly in the saddle to require Nueva Presencia or any other movement to promote it. Corzas also disaffiliated himself: "I do not wish in any way to ally myself, publicity-

wise philosophy-wise or exposition-wise with the 'New Presence' or 'Interiorist' group," he wrote to his gallery.[47] Icaza was apparently tiring of the "social savior" role. In the late fifties and early sixties he had done a number of works attacking corrupt politicians and capitalists and commiserating with the poor. By the end of 1963, however, he felt he was not the man to change the world: "That is where I differ most from Belkin, the friend I love best, who is the real ideological dynamo of Nueva Presencia," he said. He had begun to explore abstraction, to "let the imagery come naturally," which was, according to

Rodman's definition of "insiderism," the first signs of abandoning humanism. He told Rodman: ". . . I want to express less obvious social ideas, and emotions deeper within myself. I know now I can't do anything for the misery of humanity through my painting . . . I must paint myself out of this confusion! Not invent theories or follow other people's, like yours or Belkin's!"[48] Even Belkin began to change in his unflinching dedication. "Humanism," he said, "can be expressed in other ways than through the human figure,"[49] and indeed 1964 was a year in which Belkin experimented with organic abstraction, restored color to his palette, and substituted impasto texture for the thin, almost monochromatic acrylic washes and linear webbing of his earlier work. He never, however, totally abandoned the recognizable human figure, the *sine qua non* of his artistic being.

When Icaza definitely broke with Nueva Presencia, the group came to an end. The artists continued to be friends, but they went their separate ways. Causes of the demise can, perhaps, be briefly summarized: the tenuous character of the affinities that brought the group together; philosophical and political disagreements; the centrifugal tendencies of individualism; and internal jealousies and the pressures of the art market. In this connection it is important to note that the major organizers were competing artists and not literary figures, like Marinetti for the futurists or Breton for the surrealists, and that there was no strong ideological cement to hold the Nueva Presencia artists together, as there had been with the artistic organizers of the mural movement or the Taller. Nueva Presencia had served its function: it gave formal definition to a submerged artistic expression that had been developing since the mid-fifties, with Cuevas as its outstanding figure; it brought artistic recognition to its original seven members and some of its adherents; and it gave impetus to a revival of figurative expressionism, which is, in the final analysis, one of the cores of modern Mexican art.

Outsiders As Well As Insiders

5

The profession of political theorist or philosopher is an honorable one. But history leaves no doubt that the world's most urgent need is for dreamers and magicians.[1]

. . . Dostoevsky [had] a deeper feeling than a desire for social revolution.[2]

If Selden Rodman's The Insiders can be considered Los Interioristas' artistic testament, Colin Wilson's The Outsider was their literary/philosophical one. Wilson, dubbed one of England's Angry Young Men, published this first book in 1956; it became an immediate success on both sides of the Atlantic and within eighteen months appeared in fourteen languages. Belkin read it before The Insiders had even been published, probably between 1958 and 1959; it impressed him so strongly that he reread it, and Wilson's subsequent books, and sought out the books mentioned in its text. The Outsider, says Belkin, can be considered the literary counterpart of Nueva Presencia, and indeed many of the authors from whom Los Interioristas derived their ideas (some by reading; some by absorption from the intellectual currents of the day) were part of Wilson's philosophical/psychological system. The authors who mutually interested Los Interioristas and Wilson were Jean-Paul Sartre, Albert Camus, Hermann Hesse, Franz Kafka, Friedrich Nietzsche, William Blake, Fyodor Dostoevsky, George Gurdjieff, and Gurdjieff's major disciple, P. D. Ouspensky.

It is interesting to note that Selden Rodman was very much aware (unfavorably) of The Outsider. There is even a possibility that the title "Insider" was a conversion of Wilson's own, though in fairness it must be pointed out that Lebrun and Cuevas both used the term before Rodman's book appeared. Of the two writers, Colin Wilson appears the more original thinker. What is of importance here is that, for Belkin and Icaza, Wilson left the deeper philosophical impress, without the qualifiers and hesitancies that followed the initial acceptance of Rodman's

ideas. What obviously occurred is that The Insiders followed hard on the heels of The Outsider, in which Belkin was immersed at the time, and the two books were complementary—one literary and the other artistic.

The Outsider is not a religious book in the sense of dealing with historic or institutionalized religious dogma, but it is about spirituality, that spirituality that is the essence of every Outsider, according to Wilson. The major characteristics of an Outsider are that: (1) he stands for Truth at all costs; (2) he is self-divided (the human-animal nature of Hesse's Steppenwolf is typical, but there are examples of multiple aspects of a single human personality as well); (3) he sees deeper than other people (sometimes to the point of being a visionary like William Blake); (4) he is sensitive, at times to the point of neurosis or insanity (Van Gogh, Nijinsky, and Nietzsche); (5) he cannot live in the comfortable, insulated world of the bourgeoisie ("Man is a bourgeois compromise," said Hesse); (6) he sees the world as anarchic and chaotic, not rational and orderly; (7) he seeks a course of action that will maximize self-expression; this is necessary because he is not alive in himself, but acts as a conduit for life; (8) he has a sense of purpose in life; eventually, if the truth is told, there will be a restoration of order. Thus emerges the Outsider (Colin Wilson) or the Insider (Selden Rodman). What differentiates each from early existentialism is the sense of purpose that each considers part of the equipment of the rebel. Without a sense of purpose, all is despair. By the late fifties, existentialism (like Dada before it) had reached a dead end and sought modifications in psychology (Wilson, Rodman) or Marxism (Sartre).

For Los Interioristas, especially Belkin and Icaza, a sense of purpose was of major significance. It offered a way out of the existential nihilism in which they had been immersed for a decade. Colin Wilson's sense of purpose provided Los Interioristas with the philosophical foundation of their "third direction." At the nexus of the break with social realism was the desire to find a *positive* philosophy to embody the humanism they had absorbed, so to speak, from the very essence of Mexican art. The fact that Wilson's "new existentialism" was elitist did not seem to trouble them.

Not only did the elitism not bother them, they adopted it. In lieu of remaining an outcast, the Outsider could view himself as a Superman: "let him see himself in the role of predestined poet, predestined prophet or world-betterer, and a half of the Outsider's problems have been solved."[3] It was in this role, I believe, that Belkin and Icaza and Los Interioristas were pleased to see themselves. It allowed them to turn outward toward the obvious and glaring social problems of Mexico as predestined "world-betterers" without sacrificing their introspection. It was a nonideological position, since each Outsider was free to evolve his own ethical direction. Most importantly, it allowed them to attack the evils of capitalism without identifying themselves with Marxism. This was the philosophical essence of the "third direction." The Superman was the artist himself—not, as for Orozco, a Promethean personality in his art. Unlike the abstract expressionists (also existentialists), who remained wholly submerged in their inner necessities and whose external manifestation was the act of applying paint to exteriorize the turmoils of the psyche, the Outsider/Insider was one who felt "drawn to values outside himself strongly enough to examine them in his work."[4]

Many of Los Interioristas' values were drawn from books that comprised, if not an ideology, then at least a general outline of ideas. Several of the books that had currency not only with Los Interioristas but also with others of their generation were P. D. Ouspensky's *A New Model for the Universe* and a best-seller by Louis Pauwels and Jacques Bergier, *The Morning of the Magicians*. Along with the later books of Colin Wilson, they formed a continuum of thought that brought together psychology, esotericism, science, science

fiction, and art in the search for the highest levels of human experience and attainment. The key term is *mind-expansion*; the object, the possibility of a superior human species achieved through various types of superconsciousness. Just as Colin Wilson endorsed post-Freudian psychology (specifically that of Abraham Maslow), so did these ideas comprise a post-surrealist mystique. Many of the mind-changing experiences that linked the Beat movement to the counterculture of the late sixties, from Far Eastern religions and mental disciplines to hallucinogenic drugs (Wilson, for example, experimented with mescaline) can also be found in the writings of Ouspensky and Pauwels/Bergier.

Pauwels' type of mind-expansion was that of an ultraconsciousness that he named "fantastic realism"—a transcendental "awakened state" that he contrasted to that of the surrealists, who had explored the regions of sleep and the subconscious; in both cases the mind was permitted to surpass itself. In other words, he updated Ouspensky in the light of contemporary science and Freudian psychology. It comes as no surprise to discover that he was a close friend of André Breton. Colin Wilson used the term *peak experience* in lieu of Pauwels' *ultraconsciousness*, but the concepts have similarities.

The incorporation of these ideas into the Mexican setting of the early sixties (with its own history of magic, the fantastic, and a Mexicanized surrealism) affected what might be called Mexican neosurrealism. It retained many of the elements of pre-Columbian folk magic; was interested in the ideas of Jung; was delighted with technology (especially space travel) which replaced the mechanomorphic constructs of Dada and surrealism; evoked a frank eroticism; and retained the concept of metamorphosis, so characteristic of European surrealism.

One final book, on a wholly different level, must be mentioned before leaving the subject of general literary influences: Oscar Lewis' *Five Families*, published in 1959, an anthropological study of lower-class families living in a slum tenement in the heart of Mexico City. Not all Mexicans accepted the verity of *Five Families*, or of *The Children of Sánchez*, which followed it, but both have since become classics and have been widely reprinted. A journalist for the liberal magazine *Siempre!* attacked a group in Mexico for obtaining a judicial order prohibiting the sale of *The Children of Sánchez* because they felt it denigrated Mexico, its government, the army, justice, and religion.[5] Obviously both books, by focusing attention on the living conditions of the urban poor, embarrassed the government, which was trying to present a modern appearance to the world. At the same time they probed the intimate feelings and responses of the poor in a manner that emphasized the human qualities and sufferings of palpable people. They were harder to ignore than statistics. *Five Families* appeared during the incubation period of Los Interioristas, and it added fuel to their social concerns. It is not accidental that the marginal poor, those who worked in restaurants, markets, factories, as taxi drivers, lottery ticket vendors, peddlers, and the destitute, thieves, prostitutes, rag pickers, gamblers, and drunkards are major themes in the work of Los Interioristas. *Five Families* gave flesh and blood to the concept of the "victim" who appears repeatedly in the tragic images of *interiorismo*.

It is of central importance that Los Interioristas were simultaneously concerned with the "culture of poverty" depicted by Lewis and immersed in utopian literature that concerned itself with the other end of the spectrum: the enlight-ened, the gifted, and the superior. If, as I have suggested, they identified themselves with the Superman image, it is not surprising that their relationship to the poor was paternalistic. Instead of imparting the idea that innate reserves of strength, resourcefulness, courage, and dignity permitted the poor to survive their environment in spite of deformations, they extrapolated images of unrelieved misery. Their renderings of the poor were determined by their own identification with the middle class as well as the attitudes toward the poor of the collectors who purchased their work. It is not a new phenomenon in the history of art for the middle class to find catharsis and a pleasurable foil to its own way of life in humorous or didactic images of the lower classes.

In closing, it should be noted that the literary sources dealt with here are by no means exhaustive. The close connection between literature and art, in the tradition of nineteenth-century Europe, has never abated in Mexico, and offers a striking contrast to the antiliterary position (despite friendships between artists and writers) of Europe and the United States in mid-twentieth-century, when every effort was expended to erase all "literary" or "story-telling" suggestions from the painted surface, and artists treasured their own verbal inarticulateness. There is surely a correlation between the antiliterary attitude (which became frozen into an ideology) and the work produced under its aegis, and between the high degree of literacy among neohumanists throughout the world and their art forms.

22. Arnold Belkin, *Warsaw Ghetto Uprising*, detail,
1959, acrylic on canvas. Jewish Community Center,
Vancouver, British Columbia, Canada.

Belkin, Icaza, Cuevas:
The Artistic Genesis of *Interiorismo* _____

6

Arnold Belkin

I think I shall never finish illustrating the Bible, nor shall I ever stop drawing the victims of the Nazis, nor those of Hiroshima, nor the fugitives from the twisted justice of our time. I shall always draw the lovers, the Just and the Prophets.[1]

Arnold Belkin's artistic development has been two-faceted: he had the rare opportunity (for one of his generation) to be able to express himself in both murals and easel painting. In the former, he was able to develop a monumental style and a more complex statement; in the latter, a greater degree of intimacy and mystery. Many of his easel works (like those of other muralists) are directly related to muralism, in which context they attain greater richness; though they stand as independent works, they must be seen in this light. His propensity to have a figure "push" at the frame of a painting, as if requiring additional space, or to have a figure overflow several canvases to form a diptych or a triptych, or to work on a large scale, is a muralist legacy and distinguishes him, and the several other muralists who were part of the group, from those Interioristas who can be considered "intimists."

To the degree that he was a muralist, Belkin conceived of himself within the social realist aesthetic—though there were important differences, as discussed below. His career as a Mexican artist began in the phase of Mexico's history when the country was changing into a fully capitalist-industrial nation and before the 1955–1965 period of artistic confrontation had begun. His arrival in Mexico from Canada in 1947 at the age of seventeen was part of the continuing migration, spanning several generations, of idealistic and socially conscious artists from many parts of the world, drawn by the fame of the mural movement and the Taller de Gráfica Popular. Their hope was to learn and to contribute. Some stayed temporarily; others, like Belkin, Pablo O'Higgins, Elizabeth Catlett, Roberto Berdecio, and Mariana Yampolsky, remained permanently. This group of artists can be seen as distinct from the European refugees, many of whom came at the express invitation of the Mexican government to escape war conditions in Europe. (This was especially true for the Spanish refugees, who benefited from the Cárdenas policy of support to the Spanish Republican government.) Like that of Paris for the expatriates of the prewar periods, the artistic climate of Mexico offered foreign artists such brilliant possibilities in contrast to those of their native lands that they were willing to give up residences, family ties, and in many cases citizenship to relocate in Mexico.

Considering his age at arrival, it is hardly likely that Belkin's artistic and intellectual ideas were clearly formulated beyond the idealism of youth and the left-wing antecedents that had brought him to Mexico in the first place. Born in 1930, he studied at the Vancouver School of Art at fourteen and received a scholarship to the Banff School of Fine Arts at fifteen. By this time, he had apparently exhausted the Canadian possibilities. Thus the Mexican experience can be considered decisive in his formation.

In 1948 Belkin joined the Taller de Ensaye de Materiales de Pintura y Plásticos (Workshop for Testing Paint and Plastic Materials) of the Instituto Politécnico Nacional, working with José L. Gutiérrez, who had been with the 1936 Siqueiros Experimental Workshop in New York,[2] and in 1953 he was named assistant professor of mural techniques and art history at Mexico City College, succeeding Gutiérrez.

Between 1949 and 1950 he was a Siqueiros assistant for the mural *Patricians and Parricides* (ex-Aduana de Santo Domingo) and the Cuauhtemoc murals in the Palacio de Bellas Artes, and in 1957 he did a series of fresco panels on Don Quixote (a very popular theme in Mexico) at the Casa de Piedra Hotel in Cuernavaca, after completing several minor murals between 1952 and 1957.[3]

Belkin's social and Judaic interests and the first evidences of his personal style came together in his 1959 portable mural-size triptych, *Warsaw Ghetto Uprising* (see Fig. 22), painted and exhibited in Mexico before permanent installation at the Vancouver Jewish Community Center. The Orozco influence is evident in the flamelike brushwork and elongated figures (rather limp, since Belkin did not have the structural discipline that Orozco derived from his studies of Michelangelo and the dynamic symmetry theories of Jay Hambidge). In this mural Belkin evolved the archetypal human form that would serve (with refinements) his later expressive needs: a gaunt, distressed figure, generally unclothed, defined through flickering strokes of dark and light.

Thematically the mural must have evoked Belkin's most profound feelings, especially since its subject stood in a larger sense for universal injustice and brutality. His association with the Centro Deportivo Israelita (which used scenes from the mural for its 1962 commemoration of the Warsaw ghetto massacre) heightened his response to Jewish history and gave it a communal context. It was after he finished the Warsaw ghetto mural that he became actively interested in his Hebraic roots.

Warsaw Ghetto Uprising shows conviction and a sense of the tragic. It encompasses a number of issues: the evils of Nazism, which systematically liquidated the Polish Jews; the heroism of the Jews, who fought desperately for their survival, though practically all perished; the final hope of a "promised land" (Israel), which appears on the right as a fenced city surmounted by a menorah. Three themes prevail: evil (and its victims), heroism, and hope. At this point one encounters a paradox. In the creation of the Warsaw ghetto mural, Belkin confronted his Jewishness and his responsibility to the Jewish community to make a statement that would reflect its feelings. However, Colin Wilson in *The Outsider*, while conceding that Warsaw, Belsen, Buchenwald, and Hiroshima were appalling events, says that they do not hover over us with a sense of being ines-

capable. Real evil, in his view, attacks the mind, not the body, and Hitler was as defenseless against it as were the Jews of the ghetto. Evil and preservation from evil are abstractions of the mind and can be encountered only on the level of consciousness, which for the Outsider means strengthening his mind, resisting evil, and achieving freedom for himself. The paradox is one that arises out of the contradiction between, on the one hand, the history of the Warsaw ghetto, its act of communal resistance, and the communal nature of the commemoration of the ghetto uprising; and, on the other hand, the philosophy of existentialism that addresses itself to *personal* salvation. How is the artist to reconcile two self-imposed imperatives: that of social responsibility and that of individual salvation? As he was to do with Rodman's theories a year later, Belkin neither resolved nor rejected these ideas. He simply expressed or contravened them in his paintings as the occasion arose. It might be suggested that the imprecise character of the Nueva Presencia manifesto and its lack of intellectual rigor reflect these unresolved contradictions, which were never synthesized.

In Belkin's 1961 mural *We Are All Guilty* (Fig. 23), painted without charge for the penitentiary outside Mexico City, Jewish anguish became existential anguish. Ostensibly the mural's message was roughly akin to that of Oscar Lewis' *Five Families*: misery, slums, and poverty produce wasted human beings and criminality. The mural purported to be sociological, didactic, and therapeutic for the inmates of the prison.[4] It was typical of Belkin's inclinations that, in preparing to paint the mural, he turned to readings both in the area of criminology and in the works of a favorite author, Dostoevsky, whose *Crime and Punishment* dealt with the psychology of the criminal and also with the concept of redemption. (He also read Dostoevsky's *House of the Dead*.) These sources provided him with a socioexistential thematic framework for the mural. The ideas spelled themselves out laterally from

23. Arnold Belkin, *We Are All Guilty*, 1961, acrylic on cement, 9⅞ × 85¼ ft. (3 × 26 m.). Penitenciaría del Distrito Federal, Santa Marta Acatitla.

24. Arnold Belkin, *We Are All Guilty*, detail, 1961.

74

25. José Clemente Orozco, *False Leaders*, 1936–1937, fresco, 513½ sq. yd. (430 sq. m.). Universidad de Guadalajara. Courtesy of the Orozco family.

26. Arnold Belkin, *Torso* (or *Resurrection*), study for *We Are All Guilty*, 1960, acrylic on canvas, 45¼ × 35⅜ in. (115 × 90 cm.). Collection of Antonio González de León. Photo courtesy Instituto Nacional de Bellas Artes.

left to right in specific compositional areas.[5] The story of the mural (and Belkin was never opposed to telling a story; he believed narrative was fundamental to the plastic arts) concerns a lawbreaker who is caught, jailed, and finally freed. The skyscrapers (connected with the lateral wall by a series of geometrical lines) are overlaid with a jail-like grid that suggests a cage, from the bottom of which issues the slag heap of discarded humanity. Connecting *les misérables* and the family group at the right, shown in its anguish and tenderness, is the potential criminal. Only with the family does he have a tenuous contact. Then follow the crime, its adjudication, and his punishment (Fig. 24), during the course of which the criminal begins to acquire a consciousness of his destiny. The final step is his liberation—actual and spiritual. Arnold Belkin, as Raquel Tibol pointed out, undertook to represent the criminal as a rebel who takes refuge in antisocial acts because he cannot channel his rebellion. He also expressed the idea that the human spirit cannot be imprisoned.[6]

In keeping with the melancholy theme (and also Belkin's preference for subdued color) the mural was executed in burnt sienna, raw sienna, gray, burnt umber, black, and white—a color scheme frequently employed by Orozco. Since the stone wall on which he was working had a porous surface, he made an aesthetic virtue out of a technical difficulty by not refining the bold manner he was forced to adopt to cover the wall. Abstract expressionist influence (to which Los Interioristas were by no means immune) may also have affected the painterly quality of the brushwork; similar brushwork appears in Belkin's easel paintings, where the technical problem did not exist. Another expressive technique was borrowed from the movies, of which Belkin was an enthusiast. When Alain Resnais' film *Hiroshima mon amour* was released in Mexico, Belkin was so impressed that he went to see it five times. As it coincided with the planning stage of the mural, he adapted Resnais' technique of sharp contrast for alienated figures and mistiness for group figures (the Outsider versus the masses) for his mural.

Was the mural as therapeutic as the artist intended? There is some evidence that it was. Apparently a good deal of controversy developed among prison officials and prisoners about the propriety of painting a work that would "depress" the inmates. In an interchange overheard by the artist, one prisoner complained about the "gloomy death mural" and wanted to know why it was being painted in the prison, whereupon another prisoner responded, "What do you want? Mickey Mouse? To be entertained all your life? Don't you want to know who you are and why you're here?"[7]

There are such striking parallels between *We*

Are All Guilty and Orozco's Guadalajara murals of the thirties that it is worthwhile to explore Orozco's style and conception in reference to Belkin's. Among Orozco's most poignant expressions of human misery are the broken and despairing figures in the assembly hall of the University of Guadalajara, where he pictures beggars and a starving child. On the central wall (Fig. 25) of the university hall, gaunt, mutilated figures standing before a curtain of flame shake their fists toward those who have misled them—the "goons" and "labor leaders" in overalls who point to the texts that are the source of their leadership. A side panel shows two "labor aristocrats" backed up by an enormous soldier. Bernard S. Myers considered the misleaders on the side panel to be "labor millionaires" and their soldier allies.[8] Orozco had universalized the image, but there actually was a historical model for his figures in Mexico's postrevolutionary labor movement: Luis Morones, the Jimmy Hoffa of his day. During the Obregón administration, Morones had built a powerful, corrupt union organization, CROM (Confederación Regional Obrera Mexicana), headed by a labor bureaucracy, which had become an appendage of the government and sacrificed the workers' interests to carry out government policy. Morones became even more powerful during the Calles regime, administering "rough discipline" to his opponents, and buttressed by the courts, the army, and the police. It seems clear that Orozco's mural attributes the misery of the masses to very specific causes, though he chose to attack corrupt union leaders rather than the bourgeoisie. It was part of Orozco's reaction to the betrayals of the Mexican Revolution that had begun with the Calles presidency. At the same time, the mass of suffering humanity could symbolize suffering humanity everywhere. Belkin's prisoner, on the other hand, is a signifier for the rootless rebel in defiance of society at large, a universalized abstraction. His story is a parable of the Outsider, separated from the crowd by his size and spatial isolation, introspectively experiencing his antisocial rebellion, his guilt, and his final flight into freedom. If, as Belkin said, society itself is a prison without walls and none of us is free, then every individual, regardless of class, can be identified with the prisoner. As a result, the sociological aspect of the theme crumbles. If we are all equally victims, and all equally guilty, then the culture of poverty is *not* the cause of criminality. We leave Oscar Lewis and join Dostoevsky, who was concerned not with class-derived behavior (despite the upper-class derivation of Raskolnikov) but with the acting out of large questions of good and evil. Belkin's version of a "man in flames" (Fig. 26), a study for *We Are All Guilty*, shows the transformation of the accused, surrounded by and isolated within the nimbus of his awakened state of consciousness. There is no doubt that this figure owes direct inspiration to Orozco's *Man of Fire* (frontispiece) but Orozco's image is more classical in the sense that it suggests another manifestation of Prometheus. *Man of Fire* is a religious statement humanistically oriented. The human being in merging with the divine becomes a god in his own right. It is also Nietzschean in the sense that Nietzsche believed the one who can reproduce the world recreates the world and himself, i.e., he is the great artist, usurping the function of the original creator. Orozco's mystic tendencies were always tempered by the need to question any given formulation, to attack any ideology, to challenge any accepted creed, even that of religion itself, which thereby became humanized. Belkin's philosophy was the fruit of a similar kind of skepticism. He had been influenced both by Sartre and Camus, representing the atheistic wing of existentialism, and by Colin Wilson, who must be considered a neoreligious existentialist. In the context of his mural, Belkin's "man in flames" is a quasi-religious figure: he has passed through conversion and martyrdom to sainthood, as his nimbus attests. One is tempted to speculate that Belkin passed from social realism to existentialism un-

der the influence of Orozco's iconoclastic anarchism and via his reawakened interest in the mysteries of Judaism.

Belkin finished *We Are All Guilty* in April 1961. Conceptually the mural was a work of its own time, expressing a type of introspection, individualism, and psychological orientation that would have been foreign even to Orozco. It is without question a statement of *interiorismo*. Though society has been vaguely defined as coresponsible for criminality (the slums), and has provided an arena for contemplation and rehabilitation (the jail), evil and salvation are still shown in personal terms.

During the time he was working on the mural, Belkin had written the review of *The Insiders* and established a correspondence with Rodman. He had resigned his teaching post at Mexico City College to become a full-time artist and, in the company of Icaza, had gone to visit Siqueiros in jail—the visit that gave birth to the *revista-cartel Nueva Presencia*. He had also established a warm correspondence with Rico Lebrun. In August the manifesto issue of *Nueva Presencia* appeared and Los Interioristas, whose first exhibit had opened in July, began gaining momentum as an idea and a movement already provided with international connections. Thus Belkin's first transition into maturity and major recognition began with the penitentiary mural, continued with the conception and planning of the manifesto, and resolved itself with the formation of Los Interioristas.

On April 15, 1961, at six o'clock in the morning, B-26 planes bombed targets in Havana, San Antonio de los Baños, and Santiago de Cuba. This event, which became known as the Bay of Pigs attack, was carried out by Florida-based Cuban mercenaries armed, trained, financed, and launched by the United States. With the 1954 overthrow of the Guatemalan "social revolution" still rankling in their minds, Latin Americans were understandably incensed at this latest instance of United States intervention in their sovereign affairs. Belkin's specific artistic response was two paintings originally called *Reflections on Aggression in Our Time* and then renamed *Invasion of Cuba*. Both paintings are of single masculine figures whose bodies occupy most of the pictorial space. Incredible discomfort is induced in the viewer by the contortion of limbs in positions impossible to the human body. One (Fig. 27) forms a cramped box of legs, arms, and torso that seems to have been produced by one of those notorious torture chambers that are too low to permit prisoners to stand and too short to permit them to lie down. The other painting shows a figure on all fours like an animal, with the head turned completely awry. Both exist in airless, claustrophobic space.

There can be little doubt about the effect on these two paintings of Rico Lebrun's works *Buchenwald Cart* (see Fig. 12) and *Buchenwald Pit*, photographs of which, along with those of the *Genesis* mural, Belkin had just received. The heightened emotion of the Cuban invasion and the receipt of the Lebrun photographs, taken together, resulted in paintings that sought new levels of expressiveness by free manipulation of the human form. The problem of portraying horror is a difficult one. Anyone who has seen documentary films or photographs of the German death camps, with bodies stacked like cordwood, parts indistinguishably and promiscuously mingled, will understand the difficulty that Lebrun faced in attempting an artistic synthesis of the unspeakable. Aesthetic distance is absolutely essential or the work will either sink into heavy-handedness or be so revolting as to alienate contemplation altogether. On the other hand, it is not a subject for an exercise in formalism. It was in Lebrun's *Buchenwald Cart* that Belkin found the authority to arbitrarily displace and reassemble the parts of the human body in space. Like Lebrun's, the limbs are attenuated, the joints pronounced, the forms skeletal, the skin stretched tightly across the bone; however, Belkin's adaptation of the formal qualities is not as integral to

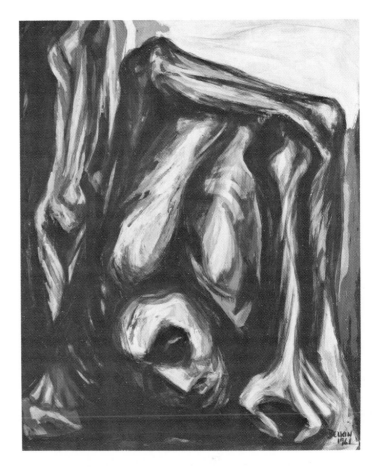

27. Arnold Belkin, *Invasion of Cuba No. 2*, 1961, acrylic on canvas, 52 × 42½ in. (132 × 108 cm.). Collection of the artist. Photo courtesy Instituto Nacional de Bellas Artes.

his subject as is Lebrun's. The latter started with a specific; the former with an abstraction. Belkin's figures are metaphoric rather than real images sublimated into art. In the case of Lebrun's works, the emaciated, interlaced bodies are transcribed from actuality. They are not expressionistic, but expressive.

Belkin was constantly engaged with four fundamental themes that he outlined as early as 1956: War and Peace, Man and His Works, Religion and Politics, and the Earth.[9] It is interesting to note that, in our secular world, he bracketed religion with politics, not philosophy. I understand that to mean (since Belkin was by no means orthodox in his Judaism but included it as part of a larger moral system) that he equated "religion" with the spiritual/transcendental, and "politics" with the working out of human encounter on the material level. He saw both, I suspect, as fixed rather than dynamic qualities. Thus when he undertook the theme of Job, it was in terms beyond those of the Biblical account, as is evidenced by such titles as *Hiroshima Job* or *Strontium Job* (which Lebrun had done before him) but under the sway of the idea of eternal injustice and eternal rebellion. To him, Job was a rebel, a symbol of suffering and anger. His name could be added to the list of existential rebels one encounters in Albert Camus' *The Rebel*—a book of great importance to both Icaza and Belkin in the pre-Interioristas period.

Belkin's Jobs are metaphysical, but also politically contemporary. Their contemporaneity derives from the parallelism between mythic and modern suffering. In the Bible the fire of God fell from heaven, the great wind came from the wilderness, and Job was smitten with sore boils, to test his devotion and faith. The fires, winds, and boils have their modern parallels in Dachau, Buchenwald, Treblinka, Hiroshima, and Nagasaki. Job is not passive: "Behold, I cry out of wrong, but I am not heard; I cry aloud, but there is no judgment" (Book of Job 19:7). As he is cast to the earth by misfortune, as the stream of fire descends, he lifts his head and directs his challenge heavenward (Fig. 28). He is the Biblical Job *and* the modern victim; he is each of us assuming responsibility for injustice by protesting it.

New refinement and linearity are apparent in Belkin's 1962 series of paintings, *Earth Beings*. These are more drawings than paintings and, like all of Belkin's work of the early sixties, are severely restricted in color, employing oil washes of black, sepia, or ochre on white canvas. The heavy, dramatic, darkly obscure figures of the 1959–1961 period, with their occasionally monotonous semicircular brushstrokes and flaccid form, have opened up to air and space, become brighter and more volumetric. Structure is held together with a web of lines. Though still in the

tragic vein, these paintings somehow appear freer and more joyous. Despite the dark quality of many of his works, Belkin is essentially an optimist. In addition, the affirmative note of *Earth Beings*, painted in the spring of 1962, might be linked with the upward trajectory of Nueva Presencia. Belkin and Icaza had been engaged in furious organizational activities for almost a year, sometimes to the neglect of their own paintings, and now this activity was being vindicated. After the appearance of *Nueva Presencia* No. 4 in April, they could work with renewed vigor and less distraction. Not the least result of the activities was the hope of alleviating the financial difficulties and hardships of, particularly, the younger and less well known artists of the group like Corzas, Góngora, Sepúlveda, and Muñoz. Recognition and gallery connections were obviously not just for the ego; they meant sales, commissions, potential teaching positions, and a degree of security for all of them.

Earth Beings also reflected the fact that 1961 and 1962 were momentous years for everyone interested in space travel—a subject that intrigued Icaza, Belkin, and their circle. It was intimately connected with their interest in science fiction and hermetic mysticism. Space travel had become a fact in 1957, when the Soviet Union succeeded in placing the first artificial satellites, Sputnik I and II, in orbits encircling the earth. These were followed by the United States Explorer I in 1958. Excitement and enthusiasm culminated in April 1961, when the Russian cosmonaut Yuri Gagarin became the first human being to orbit the earth successfully. In 1962, United States astronaut John Glenn repeated Gagarin's feat. For Icaza and Belkin, the series of space explorations had utopian significance. Discovery of other worlds in space, with the potential of planetary life, seemed to promise the possibility of greater harmony on earth, as if the human race would then have a cosmic perspective and be able to resolve its own differences. Like Marxism, this theory relocated the Golden Age from the

28. Arnold Belkin, *Job*, ca. 1961, acrylic on canvas,
63⅜ × 80¾ in. (161 × 205 cm.). Collection of Evelyn
B. Silver. Photo courtesy Instituto Nacional de Bellas
Artes.

29. Arnold Belkin, *Rock Man*, from the series *Earth Beings*, 1962, oil on canvas, 67 × 49 in. (170 × 124.5 cm.). Collection of Evelyn B. Silver.

past to the future; unlike Marxism, the transition from discord to harmony, the apparatus of change, was extremely vague. It was tenuously connected with ideas of pacifism, and was romantic to the last degree. Overwhelmingly writers of science fiction have projected conflict and war into their concepts of present planetary life or their visions of the space future. How it was possible for Icaza and Belkin to envision harmony and peace in that same sphere, except by an act of escapism, is difficult to imagine.[10] Nevertheless, the advent of

the Space Age seemed to provide a counterpoint to existential nihilism and, in the case of Belkin, to renew his sense of affirmation. Tamayo, he said, had reacted to the Space Age with fear, whereas Nueva Presencia had reacted with hope. Certainly the *Earth Beings* have this essence and are a departure from the "victims" stage. They not only reflect the optimism of space travel but also, in the face of that supremely technological achievement, celebrate human connection with the Earth, the planet that gave birth to *Homo sapiens*. In the group there are several rock/stone figures, including *Rock Man* (Fig. 29) (exhibited at the Guggenheim International Award Exhibition in New York, 1964), and *Man of the Rocks*, whose sources were the enormous craggy rocks overhanging the Pacific Ocean at Acapulco. These monumental iconic figures are related to *Seated Man* (Fig. 30), but are more sculptural, abstract, and remote. Man-mountains, they evoke the gigantic pharaonic sculptures of Abu Simbel or, closer to home, the huge Aztec stone carving of Coatlicue, goddess of birth and destruction. Belkin graphically suggests thinly layered granite forms opening at times into cavities or swelling into boulders.

Commenting on *Earth Beings*, Belkin said: ". . . in attempting to situate the human figure within the landscape of nature I have paused to observe the forms of nature, and have tried to identify and equate man's substance with the substance of the earth. At times the figure has been lost, or it has merged with the earth and rock forms, and if an almost abstract synthesis has been arrived at, I do not think the consciousness of man has been lost: human presence is implied."[11]

After seeing *Earth Beings* in 1963, Lebrun wrote to Belkin, commending his work, but also with a warning note: "I sensed in your work a tremendous urge, very healthy in many ways, for affirmation and even copiousness of statement. . . . Many of your large gestures in the show impressed me as good ideas ruined by haste . . .

30. Arnold Belkin, *Seated Man*, from the series *Earth Beings*, 1962, oil on canvas, 67 × 49 in. (170 × 124.5 cm.). Collection of the artist.

31. Arnold Belkin, *Flesh*, 1960, acrylic on canvas, 84¼ × 59 in. (214 × 150 cm.). Collection of the artist. Photo by Flor Garduño.

Take your time . . . control the frenzy of production and above all stop thinking of what you are *supposed* to say as a representative of the humanist movement." [12]

Even before he began the series *Earth Beings*, a new type of image began to appear in Belkin's work, an image that can be called the "flayed man." During the fifties Belkin had come across a half-tone reproduction of a flayed body by the Renaissance anatomist Andreas Vesalius in an architectural magazine. Later, during a visit to Los Angeles, he purchased a newly published fac-

simile of the sixteenth-century books containing the Vesalius woodcut illustrations (see Fig. 20). The pervasive tortured quality of the Vesalius figure studies has been experienced by many as a visual synonym for an existential or surreal view of life, and has attracted the interest of many contemporary artists. The "flayed man" began to appear in Belkin's work as early as 1960. It coincided with his fascination with butchered animal bodies, a theme treated earlier by two artists he very much admired: Rembrandt and Soutine. Rembrandt's *Beef Carcass* (1655) and Soutine's *Beef* (ca. 1925) are the obvious inspiration for Belkin's painting *Flesh* (Fig. 31). To the left hangs the opened beef carcass with its open cavity turned toward the right, overlapped by the standing figure of a man. The background is squared into small rectangles like the cubistic cityscape of the mural *We Are All Guilty*, suggesting that this painting was part of the evolution of his ideas for the mural. What did Belkin intend to express in this work? In the case of Soutine, it has been suggested either that he wanted to project the spectacle of putrid flesh out of morbid interest in decay, or that he viewed flesh in its character as primary element, the primordial material. [13] Belkin's title, his Biblical disposition, and his juxtaposition of the dead animal and the living human flesh suggest the latter interpretation. He had begun to accompany photographer Nacho López on visits to the slaughterhouse, where the rows of hanging carcasses were equated in his mind with human bodies in concentration camps, and to the autopsy room of a hospital to see human bodies cut up. He bought a chicken at the market (another Soutine device), photographed and then flayed it, and did careful drawings in pen and colored ink that were contemporary with López's photographs of dead chickens (See Fig. 124). As his conception evolved, he was no longer content to show the solid human flesh with only surface manifestations (limp bodies, tragic facial expressions) to betray inner spiritual turmoil; he wished literally to open up the body, to flay or dissect it so the "inner landscape" of the soul could be revealed. Thanks to the wood-cuts of Vesalius, he developed a dimension of *interiorismo*.

As a theme and a metaphor, the human ca-daver remained a constant in Belkin's work. It appeared in positive transformation in the *Earth Beings* and as a victim of destruction in *War and Peace*. In Western culture, flaying has generally been associated with terrible physical pain and the idea of punishment. Artists have shown the sufferings of flayed victims from the Christian martyrs to scenes of medieval torture chambers. Michelangelo, however, used a flayed skin in the *Last Judgment* as a synonym for spiritual rather than physical torment, and in his murals at Dart-mouth College Orozco showed a flayed Christ resurrected and chopping down his cross in de-spair at human brutality. Mexican mythology provides another, very different image; the Meso-american deity Xipe-Totec, whose priest is de-picted wearing the flayed skin of a sacrificial victim over his living body, symbolizing the res-urrectory potential of the live seed within the dead corn husk. These accreted meanings rever-berated in Belkin's flayed and opened bodies. The "flayed man" concept also suggests an anal-ogy to certain surrealist ideas. Surrealists were traditionally interested in exploring the "inte-rior"—the dream world, states of mental aberra-tion, psychosexuality, etc. Surrealism and exis-tentialism, which conceives of life as a lonely existence without formed essence in the "inte-rior" of a cosmos of Nothingness, represent the most subjective aspects of contemporary thought. "Inner landscapes" (like those of Belkin) that in-terpret *interiorismo* pictorially as an exposure of the viscera, the skeletal structures, and the mus-culature of the human body, give this interior do-main a mystical or metaphysical dimension com-parable, in its own way, to the metaphysics of surrealism. "Who am I?" they both ask, and find their answers in their own being: one in the li-bido, the other in rebellion.

Most eloquent of Belkin's "flayed man" images are those of the *War and Peace* series, which represent the culmination of a phase begun with the *Warsaw Ghetto Uprising*. The full synthesis of multiple inputs issued forth in this series as a developed style of clarity and purity. Immediate inspirations for these drawings in bistre, sepia, and Chinese ink were poems from the series *Mar de fondo*, *Poesía concreta* and *Desde abajo* by the Peruvian poet Alejandro Romualdo, who, at that time, had been imprisoned by the military junta of Peru as a leader of the Peruvian Libera-tion Front and editor of a theoretical magazine of the Latin American left wing, *Tareas del Pensa-miento Peruano*. It has been suggested[14] that the fondness for line and the ability to exploit it to the full derive from a bias toward illustrative art by Mexican artists, and that in Mexico the divi-sion between illustration and pure painting is hardly recognized. This may be another way of saying that Mexican artists have never fully yielded to the pressure to devaluate or abandon subject matter, and have never taken seriously the pejorative term *literary art*. Be that as it may, Mexico has a long history of narrative and graphic art, the former dating back to the pre-Columbian period, the latter to the colonial pe-riod, when Flemish prints were imported as a guide to church painters. Thus the literary, illus-trative, and graphic aspects of Nueva Presencia (in this case, Belkin's use of poetry) rested on a long and honorable tradition of which Posada and Orozco were the nineteenth- and twentieth-century representatives.

Romualdo's verses echo the sublimated inqui-etude that characterized Nueva Presencia; they are an exaltation of love and resistance, or per-haps resistance through love. Images of flesh, bone, blood, solitude, and anguish, as well as peace, light, sun, love, and hope prevail. War and peace, love and death come face to face in his poetry, making it the perfect vehicle for an artist like Belkin. To illustrate the verse

Para seguir amando, luchando y resistiendo,
Para seguir viviendo con tiempo y con espacio,
Aumenta a nuestra fuerza de amor y de entusiasmo[15]

Belkin showed two clasped lovers, flesh meta-
morphosizing into bone, unified in life and in
death. In another drawing (Fig. 32), a classically
delicate young woman bathed in light is confronted by a sphinxlike creature (perhaps an angel of darkness or the spirit of evil?) of whom she
seems unaware. In this drawing there are echoes
of Beauty and the Beast, the two natures of Steppenwolf, the carnal and the spiritual, and the
pre-Columbian equation of the equilibrium between darkness and light. In another (Fig. 33), an
accusing judge, a witness to the crime (the artist
himself? a portrait of the poet?), directs our attention, like Father Time drawing back a curtain
of revelation, to a fallen body. In a corner of the
drawing the poet is quoted:

¡Ay tierra mía, cielo por los suelos!
Lo que serás, seré junto contigo.
No puede ser posible. Esto se acaba.
No puede ser verdad. Pero hay testigos.[16]

Out of context the single verse loses some of its
social cogency. Romualdo was referring to *golpes*
(*coups d'état*) that had rent his land and set one
person against the other. It was hard to believe,
he said, that there was so much stubble on the
edge of love.

Belkin's mural for the Centro Pedagógico Infantil *It Rests with Our Generation to Decide* (Fig.
34), which was finished in December 1963, covered with a plastic sheet in January 1964, and
then painted over, grew directly out of the *War
and Peace* drawings. There is a similarity of style
and theme, even to the quotation from Bertrand
Russell's last book on pacifism, *Has Man a Future?* which provided the title of the mural. Plans
for the mural began auspiciously: Belkin worked
closely with architect Teodoro Maus during the
process of building the Centro, planned as a
school for handicapped children, to determine

the characteristics of the walls and surroundings
where the mural would be located. After approval of the sketches, Belkin finished the actual
painting in four months. The mural was composed in three sections (or "movements," as he
called them) corresponding to three states of the
spirit, or three strophes corresponding to the
three spaces. The right panel extended out toward the street and showed two monumental figures against a blue ground. One of the figures
reached back to a child in the central panel as if
to draw that child and the others toward the liberation of the outside world. The central panel,
in gray and sepia on a blue ground, was located
in a glass-enclosed vestibule that led into the ad-
ministrative section of the school. It was fronted
with a marble slab and showed a group of children whose faces reflected expressions of hope.
Over them inclined a large figure in a protective
attitude. In the section that faced the inner patio
(Fig. 35), on a ground of reds and oranges that
echoed the cobblestones of the yard, were children and adolescents clasping hands and playing
in a distant-horizoned open field. They were
guided by a winged figure. Through the familiar
device of the triptych, Belkin set up two directional tensions pulling outward from the central
group, one toward the world of the past (or the
present), the other toward the future. In both directions there is movement, while the core is
sedentary and perhaps symbolizes the nurturing
period in school, or the static quality of the present. A large reflecting pool, designed as an integral part of the composition, was intended to
give monumentality to the painting by extending
the reflections in space.

So well-integrated did the mural seem that it
came as a shock to the artist, who had left Mexico after its completion, to discover that it had
been covered and its future placed in doubt. He
quickly returned; a conference was held, and the
decision made to leave the mural covered until
the controversy that had arisen over its contents
had blown over. Several months later, without

32. Arnold Belkin, from the series *War and Peace*, 1963, colored ink on paper, 12¾ × 19¼ in. (32.5 × 49 cm.). Private collection. Photo courtesy Instituto Nacional de Bellas Artes.

33. Arnold Belkin, from the series *War and Peace*, 1963, colored ink on paper, 12¾ × 19¼ in. (32.5 × 49 cm.). Private collection. Photo courtesy Instituto Nacional de Bellas Artes.

34. Arnold Belkin, *It Rests with Our Generation to Decide*, 1963, acrylic on cement, 14¾ × 82 ft. (4.5 × 25 m.). Centro Pedagógico Infantil, Mexico City (destroyed).

35. Arnold Belkin, *It Rests with Our Generation to Decide*, left panel, 1963 (destroyed).

notification to the artist, it was destroyed.[17] Belkin and his supporters protested, and an open letter was sent to the government agency, all to no avail. It was pointed out in the press that not only had 65,000 pesos of public funds been misused (since the mural could have been stopped at any point from the presentation of the sketches) but, once it was completed, its destruction was a crime against the laws enacted to preserve works of art.[18]

The confrontation that led to the destruction of the mural was not based on controversial political content, but it demonstrated, nevertheless, the political power of the presidential office. It was through the direct intervention of Eva Sámano de López Mateos, wife of the president, who headed the agency of which the school was a part (a traditional role for first ladies), that the mural was destroyed. It is unlikely that the officials of the school would have gone so far without her authority; they had previously limited themselves to covering the mural and placating the angry artist. The whole event was a case study in degraded official taste and unhampered censorship. When the commission was first discussed, Captain José Luis Navarro S., general director of the Instituto Nacional de Protección a la Infancia (INPI), asked the artist to do a mural concerning the "mystery of the revolution as seen by Mexican children." Belkin replied that his generation did not paint inventories of the popular arts, or *huaraches* and *sarapes* (sandals and shawls), and that they did not believe in the trappings of nationalism. The doctor who had established the school wanted the artist to show a pile of discarded crutches and wheelchairs, with the image of Señora López Mateos reaching down to help the children. When presented with the mural sketches, Señora López Mateos considered them *muy triste* (very sad), but Navarro permitted the artist to proceed.

How valid were the objections to the mural? The strongest ones concerned the suitability of the pictorial treatment to the location. How suitable was this mural for handicapped children, and how closely did the artist adhere to the inspirational and optimistic text on which he based himself? Opinions varied. Julio González Tejada liked the mural; he felt that Mexico needed a generation (including the handicapped) that had grown up in an atmosphere of the kind of truth and honor that encouraged the growth of conscience and an awareness of the world and reality—not reduced to a folkloric version of civilization and culture.[19] Selden Rodman, examining the mural on a visit to Mexico, felt that Belkin had made great strides in simplification of the figures and clarity of the colors since the rather confused and "depressive" penitentiary mural. There was, he felt, an appropriate tenderness in the protective gestures of the adults, though all the people in the mural tended to look like spacemen or robots.[20] There is some question, however, as to whether immature children could see Belkin's images as those of hope. Could the didactic energy that produced images of existential anguish in the penitentiary mural, and flayed and mutilated bodies for *War and Peace*, sufficiently transform its *formal* characteristics (as distinguished from philosophical or thematic ones) to express a "world of glory and joy where minds expand, where hope will not be blasted"?[21] Belkin had been a tragic artist. His pictorial evolution had resulted in a purified, almost classical style that can be seen in the fine lines and proportions of the figures. He was still an expressionist, however, and the forms he used to express internal agony could not be left behind so easily. How would these bodies, elongated, emaciated, distorted, with crooked torsos, humps and hollows, exposed bone and muscle structures, and clumps of twisted fingers, appear to the eyes of a physically deformed child? How would the loops of calligraphic line, which tend downward, affect the spirits of a child who, without understanding the sophisticated context, would respond to the work on its most intrinsic—formal—level? From this point of view,

Señora López Mateos' remark about the sadness of the mural—though not couched in philosophical or aesthetic terms—can be considered a valid aesthetic criticism, quite apart from the deplorable consequences that followed.

In any case, judging from the photographs, the mural was one of Belkin's most beautiful works. There was an orchestration of architecture and painting such as rarely is possible for a muralist, and the movement of the figures in space and through reflections in the water was highly creative. Along with the *War and Peace* drawings, this mural represented a high point in Belkin's artistic evolution, which at other times had shown an unfortunate tendency to slip into repetitive facility and monotony.

Francisco Icaza

Icaza is an artist who cannot stand repeating himself. For him, images have a revelatory function. Consequently he cannot insist on discovery. For this reason, his work takes the form of series of varying lengths . . . [which] are the result not of projects but of progressions . . .[22]

By temperament, disposition, upbringing, and expectations, Francisco Icaza was the antithesis of Belkin. While Belkin's origins were provincial, Icaza's early life was cosmopolitan, with repeated changes of nations, homes, and schools which left a sense of rootlessness and disequilibrium that he sought unsuccessfully to adjust to in later years.

Born in the Mexican Embassy in San Salvador in 1930, Icaza was the oldest son of a diplomatic family. His grandfather had also been a diplomat in the years of Porfirio Díaz and, as was so often the case among high-level Latin American civil servants, was a poet and an intellectual, the first to translate Nietzsche into Spanish. Icaza and his two brothers were educated for the diplomatic service, and it must have come as a shock to the family when he was discovered to be something

of a "black sheep" and abandoned his studies in political science to become a painter. His rebellion at the age of nineteen was already symptomatic of the deep psychological dislocations from which he suffered as a result of rootlessness and his early and brutal contact with Germany, where his father was serving during the early stages of nazism. The nazi experience left a permanent and definitive scar on his personality, as he himself recognizes. Between 1940 and 1946 the family spent two years in Argentina, a year in Guatemala, and three in Mexico; then his father was sent to Beirut, while Icaza went to high school in Madrid, with tutors who had been recommended to his mother by the archbishop. The Icazas were *criollos* (Mexican-born Spaniards), related to the Spanish nobility. While being educated in Spain, Icaza stayed with his grandmother. The Spanish nobility was hostile to the Franco regime, not because they favored the Republican government that Franco overthrew, but because they were monarchists and wished for the restoration of the legitimate king whom Franco had displaced. Icaza himself was also anti-Franco—possibly, at first, because of the attitude of his aristocratic family, and then because he began to veer toward left-wing ideas. He went to the Prado every day, reinforcing earlier contacts with Renaissance and Baroque Dutch and Flemish masters as well as Goya, Velázquez, Ribera, Murillo, Zurbarán, and El Greco. Speaking several languages fluently, he had the opportunity to travel widely and saw many of the great artistic centers, absorbing their influences in a way that a tourist or a student of more mature years does not; they became part of his fiber.

Until 1948, when he matriculated as a political science major at the Catholic University of Louvain, Belgium, Icaza had done very little in the way of art. However, after a year of political science, rebellion erupted. He abandoned his career and went to study art for a year (his only formal training) at the Academy of Fine Art in Brussels, only to be thrown out as a rebel. Nevertheless he continued to paint every day. Of major importance during the Belgian stay was a trip about 1951 to Antwerp, where he discovered James Ensor's *The Entry of Christ into Brussels in 1889* during an Ensor retrospective. "I collapsed when I saw it," he said. Ensor's influence was to be an enduring one, perhaps partly because Icaza had a similarly lonely and misanthropic temperament. In addition, the many paintings employing skeletons and masks that emanated a kind of mad, fantastic humor, suggesting a world of hypocrisy and death, may have echoed what little Icaza knew of his own country; its native fantasy, its black humor, its *calaveras*, and its masking traditions.

Icaza did not leave Europe until about 1951. He was there throughout World War II; he saw the mobilizations, the destruction, the anguish in the faces of the people. He breathed an atmosphere full of violence and anxiety. He surely must have connected this with his earlier experiences in Germany, and conceived a hatred for the Nazis that may have expressed itself in his "monster" period of painting after he returned to Mexico. While in Belgium, Icaza met Tamayo, who visited the Mexican Embassy frequently and invited him to go to New York, where Tamayo had been spending part of each year since the late thirties. Icaza arrived in New York at age twenty for a two-year stay, worked for the Mexican Embassy, studied advertising and television, and painted very little.

During the latter part of his New York stay, he experienced the first profound emotional crisis of his life: all of the latent loneliness, alienation, rebelliousness, anxiety, and self-doubt, presumably exacerbated by a rupture with his father and his isolation in New York, exploded. For four months he stayed in bed, too depressed to get up. It was a truly existential experience, during the course of which he reread Schopenhauer and Nietzsche, listened to music, and asked himself, "Why am I here? What am I going to do?" The two gloomy German philosophers seem to have

had a salutary effect upon him. When he recovered from his crisis, he decided to reside permanently in his native land.

When Icaza returned to Mexico in 1953, his penchant for mysticism and idealism attracted him to Camus and Sartre, to Wilson's *The Outsider*, to science fiction (particularly that of Ray Bradbury), and to Pauwels and Bergier's *The Morning of the Magicians*. It was at this time that he made his final decision to be a painter—a decision that gave him a firmer grip on life. Art, for Icaza, was not only a means of expression but also a therapeutic activity by which he sought to probe the depths of feeling and consciousness. During the crisis period in New York, he had discovered that he was happy only when alone in front of a canvas; in fact, he painted in order to be alone. This feeling persisted into later years: "Painting for me is a religious exercise, a way of being alone with myself, to find myself."[23] We might suggest that this feeling was one of the reasons why Icaza's dedication to painting of social meaning was short-lived, and why he never seriously sought to be a muralist. Personal agony neither requires nor desires monumental scale. To be an artist of social conscience, certain sublimations above the self are required. The ego has to be submerged to address a larger issue. Icaza was capable of this at times, but because of his periodic private torments and survival needs, he could not consistently sustain concern for the Sartrian Other, for anyone outside his own individuality.

During Icaza's first years in Mexico, he worked in television, as a poster designer, and for *Mañana* magazine, for which he wrote articles on painting; it was during an interview for the magazine that he met Cuevas. Feeling like a stranger in his own land, he was also able to see Mexico with new eyes. He wished to identify with his native land and know his own culture, and he absorbed as much as he could. He immediately felt the mysticism and the magic. He traveled a great deal and drew in the streets, on the roads, in factories, and in the country, especially images of the working class.

In his early period in Mexico (up to 1963) Icaza dealt sporadically with social themes of hunger, poverty, anguish, and misery—themes he derived from what he actually saw in the streets and countryside that would have impressed any sensitive person not inured to such sights. Two factors distinguish the use of such themes in his work—and in that of any of the Nueva Presencia artists—from social realism: they were mingled with overtones of personal, existential anguish; and there was only the most superficial type of class-consciousness involved. In Icaza's case, his initial contact with the working class took place in Europe and was of brief duration. In Louvain, his friends were left-wing writers who were the children of miners and workers, able to attend the university because Belgium had a high standard of living and strong unions. Thus he experienced the working class indirectly, or at one remove.[24] The attraction of the working class, of socialist ideas, was equated with self-identification and rebellion in Icaza's mind. "As the son of a diplomat," he has said, "I was very lonely and had few friends. I was anxious to belong to something that was of the masses." He wanted to disengage himself from the bourgeoisie of which he was a part and make his own identity. This he did through art, and through artistic statements of protest. To attack the bourgeoisie had long been the honorable stance of avant-garde artists who were part of the middle class themselves. Icaza was no exception. However, the commitment—doubtless sincere enough at the time— was superficial. He tired of the role by the end of 1963 and, by so doing, gave the final *coup de grâce* to Nueva Presencia.

Like Orozco, Icaza was caught in the ambivalence between genuine sympathy for the misery of the poor and dispossessed and repugnance at the realities of their lives. However, Icaza was living in a different historical and social situation, in which leverage was not in the direction of social themes. It took a decade for him to realize the shift that had taken place. Within the exclusivistic role assigned to the artist after mid-century by the triumphant bourgeoisie of the revolution, abetted by cultural penetration, the product of the artist had become an elitist commodity addressed to those who could—or pretended to—understand it. Increasingly the themes and pictorial treatment of easel painting grew more personal and hermetic (whether figural or abstract), further circumscribing the audience. By late 1963, Icaza had accepted and endorsed this role for his own work. His work, even during the heyday of Nueva Presencia, was never directed to or intended for "the masses" (who never set foot in an art gallery) but for his coequals in the middle and upper classes, to invite the proper sense of anguish and guilt at the sufferings of the poor. At the same time, the choice of subject matter could be considered an act of defiance flung at the ruling bourgeoisie, which might not want to be reminded of the widespread poverty that underpinned its wealth. For a time, Icaza became a critic of society in the tradition of the muralists, but unlike them, as Selden Rodman astutely pointed out, he romanticized the poor.[25] The difference is crucial.

In 1957 Icaza received his first artistic recognition in Mexico when his painting *Figure* (Fig. 36) won first purchase prize at the Salón de Nuevos Valores. Margarita Nelken commented that from the time he first started to show his work, Icaza wanted to make his painting an antidote to customary realism. This figure, she said, was a point of departure for a body of Icaza's work inspired by themes of noble rebellion and protest.[26] *Figure, Hunger and Anguish,* and *Sisters with Fish* of the same year are paintings that contain stylistic elements of modern Belgian painting and Picasso combined with the harshness and angularity of German expressionism. Ensor's influence is most obvious in *Figure*, with its puppetlike, black-coated man hunched up claustrophobically in narrow space. His tall hat is repeated in

36. Francisco Icaza, *Figure*, 1957, oil on canvas, 59 × 22 in. (150 × 56 cm.). Collection of the Museo de Arte Moderno, Mexico City. Courtesy Instituto Nacional de Bellas Artes.

37. Francisco Icaza, *Self-Portrait*, 1957, 14⅛ × 10⅞ in. (36 × 27.5 cm.). Private collection. Photo courtesy Instituto Nacional de Bellas Artes.

the lonely silhouettes of the buildings. A tiny skull held in one hand, reminiscent of the sugar candy skulls sold in Mexico on the Day of the Dead, echoes his masklike face. The effect of the skull takes the painting out of the tragic into the mysterious, as does the nineteenth-century clothing; such elements mark Icaza as a romantic in the tradition of the Central European symbolists. Something of the dramatic quality of this romantic temperament can be seen in *Self-Portrait* (Fig. 37), an ink drawing in which Icaza looks fearful and pursued. He hunches into his shoulders in a protective gesture. Over the years Icaza was to do a number of very expressive and revelatory self-portraits.

Several years after arriving in Mexico, and almost at the time of Cuevas' asylum drawings (see Fig. 55), Icaza did a group of paintings of prostitutes. Like Cuevas, he had become intrigued with the red light district (an area he equated with Dante's *Inferno*), which he visited at night, doing paintings and drawings there for about a year and a half. As in the time of Orozco, there were hundreds of prostitutes standing in the streets in front of little rooms with couches in them. For Icaza, they were the last evidences of a dying culture, and they engendered a feeling in him that was very poetic, not in the least connected with anthropological or sociological considerations, or related to the real lives of these women. Icaza says that he was seeking the pre-Hispanic world, and could find it only among the *Lumpen*. This statement is not as enigmatic as it seems at first. The connection between the life of a social pariah, such as a prostitute, and the "uninhibited" life style of preindustrial peoples, i.e., peoples not bound by the rationalistic attitudes of the capitalist mentality, is an equation that was very attractive in the late nineteenth and early twentieth centuries—one which Robert Goldwater has called "emotional primitivism,"[27] which interiorized the "primitivism" imported from an exotic geographic locale. In this view, primitivism need not be limited to geography or level of technological development; it can be embodied in an emotional state, in children, in mad people, or in the *Lumpenproletariat*—prostitutes, tramps, beggars, thieves, etc. Icaza's view of prostitutes was of this primitivizing nature. Romanticism was implicit in the subject, but Icaza's depiction of the prostitute has nothing sentimental about it. She is garish and tawdry, hard-faced and dissipated. The viewer is forced to confront her and come to grips with her existence. She represents energy in an enervated world.

The prostitute and the clown, depicted—often sentimentally—as essentially unsullied vessels of goodness and tragedy, as symbols of emotions at a level of intensity not found in the events of

38. Francisco Icaza, *Ventriloquist*, 1959, oil on canvas, 51⅛ × 35⅝ in. (130 × 90.5 cm.). Collection of the Museo de Arte Moderno, Mexico City. Courtesy Instituto Nacional de Bellas Artes.

ordinary life, have a long history in modern art. Both these personages are found in Icaza's art, serving in this role (though never sentimentally portrayed). The 1959 satirical painting *Ventriloquist* (Fig. 38) introduces us to the clown, a theme Icaza expanded in his mural at the Hotel Casino de la Selva the same year. A grossly swollen figure with a mocking face holds a tiny skull in his hand and stands in the foreground of a desolate landscape that emphasizes (as in the painting *Figure*) the character's loneliness and separateness, his position on the fringes of so-

39. Francisco Icaza (assisted by Artemio Sepúlveda), *Carnival* (or *Revenge of the Actors*), 1959, acrylic on jute. Auditorium, Hotel Casino de la Selva, Cuernavaca. Courtesy of the artist.

ciety, and ever-present death. There is little doubt that the figure represented Icaza's own state of mind, thrown into disequilibrium by financial problems. Though these may not have been as severe as Icaza pictured them, they were real enough, and put him into a state of turmoil and crisis, during the course of which he went to Cuernavaca and got violently drunk. Friends there brought him to Manuel Suárez, owner of the Hotel Casino de la Selva, and an arrangement was worked out for him to paint a mural in exchange for food.[28]

The mural *Carnival*, on a lunette of the hotel theatre stage, was painted with the assistance of Artemio Sepúlveda (Fig. 39). Though the mural is painted to represent a stage peopled with circus characters facing the audience—a horn player, a trained animal, several clowns, and a melancholy harlequin in white-face—it is not a traditional circus. Icaza says the central figure, a seated dancer in a cabaret costume who suggests Marlene Dietrich in the movie *Blue Angel*, is a disguised portrait of Señora Adolfo Ruiz Cortines, wife of the president who completed his

40. Francisco Icaza, *Masks*, 1960, oil on canvas,
51⅛ × 74¾ in. (130 × 190 cm.). Collection of Con-
cepción Solana. Courtesy of the artist.

41. José Clemente Orozco,
La cucaracha [popular song,
"The Cockroach"], 1915–1917,
pen and black ink with washes,
12¼ × 18⅞ in. (31 × 48 cm.).
Collection of Museo Alvar y
Carmen T. Carrillo Gil, Mexico
City. Courtesy Instituto
Nacional de Bellas Artes.

term in 1957. Her attitude in the mural, says the artist, is one of indifference to the problems surrounding her, because she is "on stage." It was during Ruiz Cortines' term that television started to develop as an industry, and Icaza (who had worked in both U.S. and Mexican television) introduced a television projector into his mural as a symbol of the death of Mexican cinema, which had been a major spectator entertainment since the mid-thirties and a prime medium for the inculcation of nationalistic values. As cinema had displaced legitimate theatre, so television was slated to replace cinema despite the latter's governmental support. The two skulls represent the "fossils" of film production: outdated and aged film actors and actresses and producers who continued to present weary ideas.

Other characters besides the dancer have double meanings: the white-faced clown is also a gigolo; the fat clown on the right has two bags of gold and is meant to suggest a capitalist entrepreneur; the striped animal is a burro dressed like a zebra—symbol for a fool. According to Icaza, the images had to remain ambiguous—especially that of the former president's wife, who is presented in an unflattering light—if the mural was to survive. He went so far as to paint it on jute lightly tacked to the wall, instead of cement, so it could be easily removed in case of threatened destruction.

Ensor, says Icaza, gave him the feeling of the carnival that he used in the mural. There was no difference, in his opinion, between a carnival and a revolution; both were masquerades with a feeling of death. This latter idea is well expressed (perhaps better than in the mural) in *Masks* (Fig. 40), which is filled with sinister overtones and masked clowns, prostitutes, and assassins. The idea of the human carnival was expressed repeatedly by Orozco, whose series *The Truth* (one drawing of which appeared on the cover of the catalog of the first Interioristas show) dealt with clowns, fools, and prostitutes. Orozco had traditionally equated the corrupt elements of the rev-

olution (generals and their whores) with a carnival of lechery and drunkenness (Fig. 41). One might say that the misanthropic aspects of Ensor and Orozco, the death images of Flemish and Hispanic painting, and the equation of carnivals with human folly had been themes in Icaza's work from 1953 to 1961, and his mural was heir to these themes. Questions can be raised about the suitability of the composition, with its subjective emphasis, to its location, and about whether it really is a mural or simply an enlarged easel painting. The drawing is unsure; the use of space and disposition of figures unimaginative. It is not a wholly successful work and does not rank among Icaza's better paintings.

Unlike Belkin, whose evolution in the treatment of the human figure can be traced from one point to the next of his development, Icaza constantly experimented with style, technique, and content. The variety, even from 1953 to 1960, is amazing, and was noted by his contemporaries; he is weighted down, said critic Julio González Tejada in 1960, by a constant restlessness and invincible dissatisfaction; each moment he escapes us and appears even to escape himself. He has a decided conviction that every new canvas will mark a distinct route in his work. This search for "truth" is accompanied by the most painful self-examination, the marks of which are part of the works' aesthetic attraction.[29]

The events of 1960—the imprisonment of Siqueiros, the boycott of the Biennial, and Icaza's newly formed friendship with Belkin (whom he had known slightly since 1958)—marked a new phase for Icaza as well as for Belkin. For Icaza, the relationship with Belkin was providential, though he recognized the sometimes naïve aspects of Belkin's personality. It was more than an artistic association; it was a warm friendship and a partnership, the closeness of which Icaza acknowledged when he referred to Belkin in 1963 as "the friend that I love best."[30] These opposite but complementary personalities were brought together in the ferment and rebellion of the early

42. Francisco Icaza, *Dead Spain*, 1961, oil on canvas, 35⅝ × 51⅛ in. (90.5 × 130 cm.). Collection of Lic. Eugenio Rodríguez. Photo courtesy Instituto Nacional de Bellas Artes.

43. Francisco Icaza, *Los Juanes* [The John Does; average people, common men], 1961, oil on canvas, 34 × 55 in. (86.5 × 139.5 cm.). Collection of the San Diego Museum of Art; donated by Muriel and Sid Wenger.

44. Francisco Icaza, *Self-Portrait*, 1958, oil on paper on canvas, 39¾ × 26 in. (101 × 66 cm.). Collection of the Instituto Nacional de Bellas Artes, Mexico City. Courtesy Instituto Nacional de Bellas Artes.

sixties by a shared intellectuality and idealism, as well as an ambition to make their work known. Of the two, however, Belkin more consistently had his eye on history and his place in it. In the 1960–1961 period, Icaza reached a high point of anger against the misery and hunger in Mexico that seemed to parallel his increasing politicization. From the activities for Siqueiros' release, to the 1962 Cuban missile crisis, to the 1963 "War and Peace" issue of *Nueva Presencia*, Icaza was constantly active on political issues that might have helped to externalize some of his inner an-

guish and channel it into social concern. It is not that he suddenly became political at this time, or that he suddenly stopped being so in late 1963 when he turned to abstraction. It is just that he responded more directly to a whole series of events that occurred in Mexico and abroad and to his acclimatization as a Mexican.

Among Icaza's varied works in 1961 was the forceful, mocking statement of *Dead Spain* (Fig. 42), showing the alliance between the church, the aristocracy, the military, and other forces that had subdued Spain. This painting was influenced by Ensor and by Icaza's close friend, the exiled Spanish artist Antonio Rodríguez Luna. A series of paintings of the same year called *Los Juanes* is done in somber earth colors and thick impasto. While the figures in *Los Juanes No. 3* could be the anonymous men and women of any army, and even suggest a revolutionary or guerrilla group, another *Los Juanes* painting (Fig. 43) has a large foreground figure that strongly suggests Francisco Franco, and doubtless places the series in the same category as *Dead Spain*.

Another facet of Icaza's work was his portraits. The very nature of *interiorismo* indicated generalized statements about the human condition, while the portrait of necessity is individualized and specific. Since he was an expressionist, Icaza's portraits were frequently activated by his emotional feelings at the time; this is particularly true of the self-portraits, which are spread out over a period of years. One such, with a heavy Ensor influence (Fig. 44), shows the artist in the same setting and costume as *Figure* of 1957 (Fig. 36): cloaked, top-hatted, in a low-horizon desolate setting. In a predominantly cool color scheme, he pictures himself in a black-collared blue cloak with a white cape near a dark red column, silhouetted against a background of cold blues, whites, and siennas. The blue and black of his face and top hat are relieved by a band of bright red flowers. Through the heavy glasses, the eyes have an almost hypnotic stare. The elongation of the body, the flamboyant quality of the dress, and

45. Francisco Icaza, *Soaring*, 1961, oil on paper.
Private collection.

the sense of mystery and symbolism engendered by the blood-red flowers associate this painting with Icaza's earlier romantic phase.

The most important group of works of Icaza's development in the early sixties was the extended series based on the theme of metamorphosis that he worked on from 1961 until mid-1962, at one point doing seventy-five canvases in a three-month period without leaving his studio, and painting many over. While working on this series he went through a crisis so severe that he entered psychoanalysis, managing, however, to participate actively in the affairs of Nueva Presencia and carry on a spirited polemic with the detractors and attackers of the group. Public re-

ception of the *Metamorphosis* series was not up to his expectations; as a matter of fact, in a letter to Rico Lebrun dated August 31, 1962, he reveals his disappointment at the response and the fact that he was not as optimistic as Belkin about the success of the Nueva Presencia artists:

Two months ago I exhibited 52 works (oils) 8 of them of monumental dimensions. So much stupid literature was written about them that I have to smile bitterly. Nothing was understood, and the reaction was one of disgust, for it was something newer than that to which they were accustomed. . . . Those of our group that have exhibited are Góngora, Corzas, Zepúlveda [*sic*], Ortiz, and now Belkin. The same thing has happened to all of them, and the same will happen to Belkin, in spite of his illusions.

In the same letter he addressed himself to the problems of Mexican artists as compared to those of the United States:

. . . in a country like ours, the struggle is much more complex than in yours. The artist, like it or not, must participate in thousands of activities in which you never participate. Our market: that which gives us food and the ability to buy materials, is so rickety that we have to create our own sources of work.

And finally, he indicated the basis of Nueva Presencia's continued existence, despite problems:

The people who believe in us ask us "Why do you exhibit in Mexico where there are so many barriers?" We would be better understood elsewhere. *We exhibit in Mexico* because we are here, our roots are here, and we feel obliged to fight in our own country, because before thinking of the universal, we must start from our point of origin.[31]

The first indicators of Icaza's interest in the theme of metamorphosis were a series of oil drawings of birds: some delicate, some rapacious; some in black and white, some in color (Fig. 45). Thinly brushed, apparently taken from nature, they were, as Margarita Nelken called them, very eloquent sketches for a projected *Metamorphosis of a Bird*.[32] That Icaza was working from nature is suggested by the presence in his archive of a photograph of a hornbill bird that he had asked a friend to send him. Later the birds were to develop human characteristics (Fig. 46). In some cases the birds (or just their wings) emerge from strange, rocklike shapes. Some are sinister creatures, others benign and more completely evolved into dark human form (Fig. 47) or illuminated as if reflecting differing states of mind. (Belkin wrote in March 1962, "Paco [Icaza] is working on ten huge paintings and, as always happens, he is tremendously depressed and euphoric by turns.")[33] The color is dark and reduced, almost monochromatic, and the figures

flat—silhouetted against a dark or a light ground. Icaza seems to be foregoing all sensuousness to purify and abstract his imagery so as to draw closer to the essential form. Landscape and background disappear; the solitary figures stand alone in undefined space. These paintings, according to Icaza, were done with violence and emotion, never with reason, and his ideas about them came after the fact. Though many symbolic meanings can be read in, they give the distinct sensation of being autobiographical, located on the fine line between despair and hope. For example: though these are birds and their wings are outspread as if yearning to fly, they remain remorselessly earthbound, chained to the earth, reality, and the material in spite of spiritual aspirations. They might be seen as an incarnation of Steppenwolf, the character from one of Icaza's favorite authors, Hesse, who most graphically embodies the conflict between the animal and transcendental aspects of human nature. This ancient dichotomy has been expressed mythologically in the legends of the minotaur, the centaur, Icarus, and St. George and the dragon; philosophically as the Apollonian and Dionysian oppositions; and psychologically in terms of the id and the ego. Insofar as it is an animal, Icaza's bird is earthbound and expresses his melancholy, his torment, and his despair. The wings are his hope: symbols of the creativity that permits him momentarily to soar beyond the dead weight of the body. Immersed in the Icarus legend, one assumes that the metamorphosis is from man to bird, freeing the spirit to mount toward the sun. But at least one critic has pointed out that the figures are so enigmatic that it is not certain the transposition is not in the opposite direction.[34]

Given the prominence Prometheus has had as a Mexican theme, it was inevitable the imagery of this series should be compared to that of Icarus and Prometheus, who were seen as the two heavenly abductors.[35] The fact is that for Icaza—despite any private levels of meaning—the bird series represented what Prometheus had for

Orozco and his generation: the symbol of spiritual attainment and transfiguration. Icaza may have felt misunderstood, and doubtless he was. Nevertheless, an artist has to come to grips with the accreted meanings that adhere to an image borrowed, so to speak, from the "public domain" of iconography. In the case of the Icarus/Prometheus juxtaposition, it is notable that Icarus mounted toward the attainment of fire (the sun) as a supreme effort for his own sake, while Prometheus risked his life for the sake of the human race. It is perhaps a measure of the changed times and aspirations that one generation chose a demigod who was punished for bringing an incomparable gift to humankind, while the other pictorialized the failed dream of a wholly human protagonist. Perhaps this is why Icaza's birds can never fly: Icarus was hurled back to earth when he ventured too near his shining goal. Icaza wished to fly; he and Belkin conceived of space travel as utopia. The cosmonaut can be seen as a "space bird"—a modern Icarus who achieved the moon. Despite their darker and more sinister aspects, the bird paintings, created under tremendous duress, represented positive, hopeful symbols in Icaza's *oeuvre* in contrast with his former preoccupation with human misery and folly.

Metamorphosis of a Bird led to another series that might be considered the antithesis of the birds but is still metamorphic in character: rock men and women. *Rock Man*—chosen for the Fourth Guggenheim International Award exhibit—is the abstracted figure of a ponderous, petrified human being, the epitome of the earthbound. Icaza's *Rock Man* and *Rock Woman* series corresponded to Belkin's *Earth Beings* of the same year, a coincidence that surely was not accidental.

The simultaneous appearance of metamorphic imagery in Belkin's and Icaza's work was not unrelated to the emergence of neosurrealism in Mexico in the early sixties. Since it touched many of the Nueva Presencia artists, to greater or

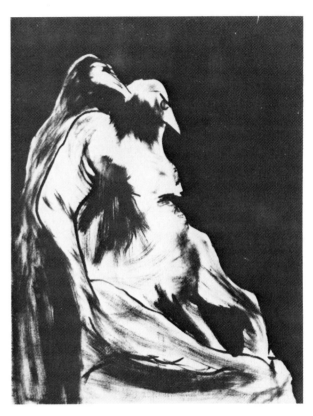

46. Francisco Icaza, *More than an Animal*, from the series *Metamorphosis of a Bird*, 1961, oil on canvas, 114⅛ × 90½ in. (290 × 230 cm.). Private collection. Courtesy of the artist.

lesser degrees, a brief digression to examine this phenomenon will be helpful.

After the brief flurry of the 1940 International Surrealist Exhibition of Mexico City, surrealism subsided. The true flowering of Mexican surrealism did not occur until the 1960s and was due primarily to the influence of Octavio Paz, who, fifteen years after the exhibition, conceived of surrealism as a new kind of revolutionary undertaking—a revolution no longer of social forces but of inner liberation. This was a seductive argument in the mid-fifties, when many young artists were casting about for a direction; it had the result of turning the attention of young writers and artists toward Parisian surrealism once more. Suddenly the influence of the surrealist refugees

47. Francisco Icaza, from the series *Metamorphosis of a Bird*, 1961, oil on paper. Private collection. Courtesy of the artist.

(who had come to Mexico during the war years and been relatively neglected) became widespread. Until that time, artists like Wolfgang Paalen (who had organized the 1940 exhibition), Alice Rahon, Remedios Varo, Kati and José Horna, Leonora Carrington (formerly associated with Max Ernst), and filmmaker Luis Buñuel had not been absorbed into the Mexican art world, which was under the hegemony of the mural movement. With the burst of eclectic freedom that characterized postwar painting, surrealism experienced a revival at approximately the same time that informalism and abstract expressionism (also partly influenced by surrealism) made their appearance in Mexico. Surrealism now no longer frightened the bourgeoisie; on the contrary, they

accepted it, approved of it, and enjoyed it.[36] In 1962, the writer Salvador Elizondo and a group of friends published seven issues of the magazine *S.NOB*, which attempted, artificially, to revive a surrealist ambience similar to that of Paris in the twenties and thirties. Among the collaborators were José Luis Cuevas, Alberto Gironella, and the Chilean theatre director, dancer, and writer Alexander Jodorowsky (who later introduced to Mexico such novel phenomena as science fiction, "happenings," "new wave" theatre, and comic strips as art forms).

Though the attempt to revive Parisian surrealism proved unsuccessful, its reverberations are still to be found among the young figurative artists of Mexico, for whom it represented both an allegiance to internationalism and an affirmation of artistic freedom. The artists of Nueva Presencia were not immune to its influences, and the constant transmutations that occur in surrealist thought and imagery can be cited as a possible source for the metamorphic earth/rock beings, as well as the bird series, which occupied Icaza and Belkin in 1962.

The influence on Icaza of Rico Lebrun, and particularly of his drawings for Dante's *Inferno* in which humans change into serpents, trees, and other forms, is not to be overlooked. Not only had Icaza seen these drawings in 1961, but Lebrun himself came to Mexico in February 1962, as Icaza was wrestling with the *Metamorphosis of a Bird* series, and they established the basis for a warm friendship. Icaza's *Rock Man* and, even more pronouncedly, the *Christ* series of 1963 show a distinct trend toward flatter, more monstrous creatures that can be attributed to Lebrun's work.

The *Christ* series surely presents some of the most unorthodox images of the Crucifixion in Mexican art. The solitary figure of the sufferer, unaccompanied by any of the traditional symbols, such as the crown of thorns or the nails, hangs upside down, a position unbelievably ignominious and humiliating in that it strips the

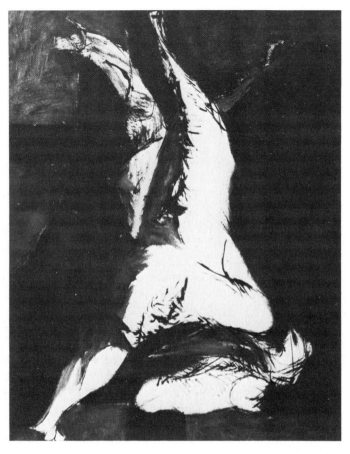

48. Francisco Icaza, from the series *Christ*, 1963, oil on paper. Private collection. Courtesy of the artist.

pain and indignity that had not been used before, if they wished to restate even some of the horror of a Grünewald in modern terms. Icaza struggled with every image and, in the process of doing so, began to achieve this kind of anguish. In one of the most moving of the *Christ* series, he opened up the hung figure to show entrails and bone. The cool gray-blue and ochre suggest decaying flesh, and the brilliant red, blood.

The *Metamorphosis* and *Christ* series mark Icaza's emergence from the period influenced by European expressionism into a plastic language of his own; they also signal his abandonment of social protest for existential themes—Christ symbolizing the ultimate "victim" in Icaza's work as Job did in Belkin's.

For the 1963 *War and Peace* portfolios, Icaza did a series of drawings of monstrous rats illustrating Camus' *The Plague*, in which the rats die after infecting the population with bubonic plague. In Camus' terms, plague is a metaphor for the social and spiritual ills that beset the human race, and each individual has the choice of fighting it or being part of it. As one character maintains, "On this earth there are pestilences and there are victims, and it's up to us, so far as possible, not to join forces with the pestilences." [37] The alternatives to enduring the plague are to seek release in death or to become a healer—and with this last alternative, Camus strikes the most positive note of the novel. Three of Icaza's rats (his symbols of plague) illustrate the phases through which the novel passes. The first is a brutal image, realistically realized, alive, menacing, vicious, and aggressive, like the plague itself; it confronts the viewer frontally as if ready to attack. This animal pertains to the early phase of the plague when the people face death directly and muster all their resources to counter it, but in so doing begin to question the "benign" aspect of the heavens. During the second phase of the plague, the will to fight is diminished. People are no longer capable of exalted emotion, and the memory of loved ones is becoming faint. The

human figure of any pretension to dignity (Fig. 48). If Belkin used a slung side of beef beside a human figure as a simile for the human condition, Icaza turned it into a metaphor. Because of the canonization of the Crucifixion, the supreme cruelty of this form of execution has been sublimated; through millions of denatured reproductions of the event since the Middle Ages, its character of blood-and-guts torment has been negated. As long as the figure is hung right side up, it is purified by familiarity of a wholly empathetic response, even when the victim is not traditional. To express the crucifixions of the twentieth century—of the body in Nazi concentration camps and at Hiroshima and of the mind through alienation—artists have had to seek new forms of plastic expression, visual equivalents of human people adapt themselves to the situation and to the habit of despair, only wishing dispiritedly for the end of the plague. "'It's high time it stopped,' people would say,"[38] reads the quotation on the drawing that illustrates this phase (Fig. 49). The rat is dead; its body lies in a vertical position confronting a melancholy white-clad figure (the human spirit?) that moves from a zone of black on the right toward one of gold in the center. The dead rat no longer terrifies; the human figure moves vacantly like a sleepwalker, oblivious of what surrounds it. The third rat (Fig. 50), stiff and dramatic in its horizontal position, is no longer a challenge. The plague has been conquered and the people rejoice, but the hero, Dr. Rieux, remembers that the plague bacillus never dies or disappears for good. The quotation reminds us that "Perhaps the day would come when, for the bane and enlightening of men, it would rouse up its rats again and send them forth to die in a happy city."[39]

Obviously *The Plague* can be read as a parable of war; the only way to achieve peace is to assume the responsibility of opposing war. "To my mind the social order around me was based on the death sentence," says one of the characters in the novel, "and by fighting the established order I'd be fighting against murder."[40] Icaza and Belkin assumed this responsibility in their art and in the publication of *Nueva Presencia* No. 5 with its pacifist message. According to their letter to Bertrand Russell, they were prepared to take their commitment into the political arena by organizing a pacifist movement in Mexico.

In 1964, the short-haired, white-draped figure of the *War and Peace/Plague* series reappeared in Icaza's paintings as a *Broken Angel*, thereby casting some light on the figure as originally

49. Francisco Icaza, from the series *The Plague*, 1963, watercolor and ink on paper, 32 × 23 in. (81.5 × 58.5 cm.). Collection of Selden Rodman.

50. Francisco Icaza, from the series *The Plague*, 1963. Private collection. Photo courtesy Joseph Young.

104

used. Icaza had entered another severe emotional
crisis; he was living with the prospect of divorce
from his wife (the divorce actually occurred in
the late sixties) and had entered psychoanalysis.
His feeling of mutilation was expressed in three
alternating themes: delicate, amputated "angels"
(another type of metamorphosed bird), sometimes silhouetted against a dark moon; barren,
solitary trees in deserted landscapes (Fig. 51) in
which nature is used to express an emotional
state; and self-portraits. "I painted one portrait,
one angel, and one tree every week," he has said.
There were also paintings of Auschwitz, and
these too Icaza considered autobiographical.

To a certain extent, all of Icaza's works are autobiographical in the same sense that Edvard
Munch's works, no matter how varied, return to
their starting point in his neurotic personality.
Raquel Tibol, who has had ample occasion to
know and observe Icaza well over the years,
draws the following summary conclusions: Icaza
is a highly talented young man who has self-
destructive tendencies, because when he takes a
particular artistic path, he himself destroys it.
After coming together with some of his colleagues to advance a movement, he was the first
one to destroy it. With all the ability to be the
guiding spirit of the movement, he at the same
time had a highly contradictory and tortured
temperament. His paintings of jails, scenes of
death, cadavers, and large rats are highly aggressive and desperate images; but at the same time,
if he could connect himself more to life in his
personal affairs, he could be one of the great artists of Mexico.[41]

José Luis Cuevas

. . . the world is to me a constant source of fascination
. . . what I see is a sweat-stained mass of businessmen,
priests, clerks, prostitutes, bank cashiers, and pregnant
women, who go their way without realizing what they
are, seeking oblivion. I make symbols of them, stripping them of all that is transient . . . I seek to render

51. Francisco Icaza, from the series *Tree*, ca. 1964, oil
on canvas. Private collection; photo by Crispin Vázquez. Courtesy of the artist.

them universal in their repulsiveness. It is for this reason that I draw zoomorphic monsters, gluttonously
obese, obscene with lust . . . It is not my intention
either to condemn or justify [the world]. I seek merely
to describe it in terms of my own sensibility.[42]

Two important clues to the personality of José
Luis Cuevas appear in the above quotation: his
universalization of "repulsiveness," the para-
mount characteristic of humanity in his view,
and the fact that his world view is totally or-
dered by his own subjectivity. "I do not perceive
him," said Luis Cardoza y Aragón, as an "il-

lustrator of his own time" in the same sense as Daumier, Lautrec, Grosz, Orozco, or Picasso, for example. He has no developed sociopolitical conscience. He does not see from the outside, but within himself.[43] Ida Rodríguez Prampolini noted the same characteristic: Cuevas is incapable, by nature, of following a program, a line of thought or feeling, or an attitude that is not his own.[44]

Though he cannot strictly be considered a "member" of Los Interioristas or Nueva Presencia, no history of the group would be complete without Cuevas, or without taking into consideration his extensive influence on his own generation. He established an image of success, through art and polemics, that reverberated throughout the art world and set an example for young artists. Since this book is concerned not with the biographies of artists per se, but with the biography of a movement, I shall not attempt to present a minutely detailed picture of Cuevas' activities, but rather to show how he affected the concept of neohumanism and the role he played in the organization of Los Interioristas. To do this, it will be necessary to look at his own evolution as well as his activities with the group.

As discussed in Chapter 2, Cuevas' precocious talent appeared on the Mexican scene at a crucial time in the development of Mexican art. Born in 1933 in Mexico City to a middle-class Yucatecan family, he gave his first exhibit in 1953 at the Galería Prisse in Mexico City (with the support of its artist founders) when he was only twenty years old. Practically all the critics agreed at the time that he possessed talent but was overly influenced by Orozco.[45] Indeed, despite his later attacks on the mural movement, Cuevas began his artistic career with a feeling of the deepest respect for the muralists, particularly the *tres grandes*, and did sketches in which he took Rivera and Siqueiros for his models. He soon rejected their influence, recognizing a natural affinity for Orozco.

What were the sources for Cuevas' monsters and grotesques, those creatures that he originated and that were so widely imitated? Once invented, they appeared so natural an expression of the Mexican spirit and of Cuevas' psychological makeup (and so successful with patrons) that he set himself deliberately to seek them out in later years. In the beginning they derived from his immediate environment. According to his autobiography,[46] his penchant for the monstrous and horrible goes back to his earliest years as a child, when his family lived, despite its means, in an area of Mexico City that abounded in scenes of human misery. The street outside his home was a promenade for the poor, homeless, diseased, and disfigured who became his models. He was fascinated by an all-night shelter for the poor where the ragged and filthy denizens of the city came at dusk, and by the painted and toothless prostitutes peering out of tiny windows waiting for men. This "human sewer," as he called it, absorbed his attention as a child and entered his later drawings. The line of hungry and indigent that formed before the all-night shelter is doubtless related to *Hungry Men* (Fig. 52), done when he was twelve; and the streetwalkers might have been the models for *Dance Hall* and *Sketch from a Brothel*. These images are not yet monstrous. They reflect the exaggerations and distortions of expressionism and are related to similar treatments by Orozco.

Another occurrence in Cuevas' early life that was momentous for his pictorial imagery and his later hypochondria and self-adulation was a serious illness at age ten that affected his heart and caused a long period of invalidism and introversion. He says of this period: "The tears and prayers of my family made me conscious of the importance conferred by misfortune, an importance which only the firstborn among children know [Cuevas was not the oldest child in his family]. I knew then that my days were to be fewer than those of other men."[47] The note of melodrama and fatalism that was to remain a permanent part of his personality is evidenced by the drawing done a year after his illness, *Sick*

52. José Luis Cuevas, *Hungry Men*, 1946, ink on paper, 11⅜ × 9½ in. (29 × 24 cm.). Collection of Horacio Flores Sánchez. Photo courtesy Instituto Nacional de Bellas Artes.

Self-Portrait (Fig. 53). The sad, wide-eyed youngster, confined to his chair, is surrounded by compassionate, protective women. Outside a sun and moon appear in the sky (to indicate the passage of time?). Pinned to the child's chest is a portrait of himself crying, which takes the place of his sick heart enclosed in a glass jar on the table beside his medicines. The surreal atmosphere produced by including a portrait within a portrait and a heart outside the body remind one of Frida Kahlo (*The Two Fridas*). The young, hooded woman at the right side of the drawing seems to spread her benign presence in the room like the images of the Virgin that appear, encased in a nimbus, in ex-votos dedicated to her.

In 1948 while studying engraving with Lola Cueto at Mexico City College (where he met Bel-

kin), Cuevas encountered Mireya, who became his model and lover for three years. He drew her repeatedly (Fig. 54), in "sketches full of affection and respect for a woman who asked for nothing."[48] Though he described her as thin and common, the great tenderness displayed in the drawings of Mireya is in distinct contrast to the brutal, unsentimentalized images of streetwalkers of 1953, although both have their source in a fascination with the *Lumpenproletariat* that also engaged Icaza several years later. In the Mireya portraits, we recognize the romanticized image of the pure-hearted, though vulgar prostitute (or working-class woman) whose attainments are hidden by her lowly station in life and discovered only by her sensitive middle-class lover—a theme that goes back to the nineteenth century and contains within it the seeds of guilt and patronization. Cuevas had begun to read Dostoevsky, particularly *The Brothers Karamazov* and *Crime and Punishment*. From the latter came the "Sonia" (the simple, docile, good-hearted prostitute who represents Raskolnikov's only possibility of redemption from his crimes) for whom Cuevas was searching when he first went to look for a woman, and whom he found in the person of Mireya. We are reminded that van Gogh, the great model for romantic expressionism, tried to redeem a prostitute as an expression of his own Christian virtue. It appears that many artists believe some kind of "basic truth" is revealed by observing and painting the outcasts and rejects of the working class as incarnations of suffering or evil. One can identify one's own psychic pain with the physical suffering and moral degradation of the *Lumpen*; at the same time the observer has an escape hatch and can return to the safety of the middle class at will.

Cuevas continued to draw the marginal people he had chosen as his thematic material throughout 1953 and 1954: mad people (Fig. 55), butchers, cripples, cadavers, women of all ages and shapes—thin, emaciated, or bloated—a veritable "human comedy," as he called one of his series.

53. José Luis Cuevas, *Sick Self-Portrait*, 1944, pen and ink on paper, 12½ × 9 in. (32 × 23 cm.). Collection of José Gómez-Sicre. Courtesy Museum of Modern Art of Latin America, Organization of American States, Washington, D.C.

54. José Luis Cuevas, *Portrait of Mireya*, 1949, ink and watercolor, 28¼ × 25½ in. (72 × 65 cm.). Collection of Mariana, Ximena, and María-José Cuevas. Courtesy of the artist.

55. José Luis Cuevas, *Madman*, 1954, ink, 38¼ × 25½ in. (97 × 65 cm.). Private collection. Photo courtesy Museum of Modern Art of Latin America, Organization of American States, Washington, D.C.

He sought out these models. His older brother, studying to be a psychiatrist, got permission for him to sketch in an insane asylum, and he went to the General Hospital to draw cadavers and the dying. His butchers are symbols of destructiveness; they are close to human bestiality and act out the sadistic and brutal in all of us. Cuevas' butchers can be seen at one end of a spectrum of which Belkin's carcasses and flayed humans provide the other end: the persecutors and the victims; the killers and the killed.

Cuevas' imagery was also fed by the repulsive and monstrous personalities to be found in Dostoevsky's writings. *Notes from the Underground*, for example, delineates not only the modest, hopeful prostitute Liza, who is deluded into placing her faith in the "hero" who she thinks can save her from the degraded life she leads, but also the half-mad, splenetic protagonist, who seems like the literary counterpart of Cuevas'

most bizarre creatures. Here, as in the works of Kafka, with whom Cuevas later identified himself, the antihero makes his appearance. The intense, gloomy personalities of Dostoevsky's novels, each carrying a metaphysical charge, were the literary fountains from which Cuevas began to create his "monsters."

At the same time that Cuevas was reading Dostoevsky, he also read "voraciously and indiscriminately"[49] in other materials, presumably including "pulp" books. His interest in popular culture and mass media began very early and forms what at first seems a contradictory bond between his art and that of the Pop phenomenon. Cuevas was not originally influenced by Pop (an art form that presupposes a type of consumer society that did not exist in Mexico in the early fifties), but he drew inspiration from some of the same sources, a process made easier by his constant travel and frequent residence in the United

States after 1954. Neohumanism and Pop art were more or less contemporary, and it should be stressed that no strict division separated them. (For example, Antonio Berni of Argentina, who had been a social realist and was associated with the European socially oriented Imago group and the 1962 Argentinian neofigurative movement that paralleled Nueva Presencia, combined politicized figuration with elements of Pop.) Cuevas admires the Pop movement, but his images never touch the aggressiveness, banality, or dehumanization of Pop; he is too wholly a product of Mexican humanism.

A form of popular culture which particularly impressed Cuevas was film, which he described as the most important influence on his work. He read everything he could find on film, from the theories of montage to gossip columns about the stars in magazines like *Novelas de la Pantalla*, *Cinema Reporter*, and *Mexico Cinema*.[50] Above all he enjoyed, and re-created in his art, the early Hollywood films with all their absurdities and incongruities. The gaunt, rubbery frame and deadpan expression of comic Buster Keaton and Fatty Arbuckle's pudgy, childlike features appear repeatedly. The more robust of his drawings owe as much to Arbuckle's voluminous figure as they do to pre-Columbian sculpture. Elements of bizarre terror were derived from old films like *Frankenstein* and *Dracula* (both 1931) and the even more horrifying film *Freaks* (1932), peopled with real Siamese twins, midgets, a half-torso man, and an armless, legless man. What Cuevas sought in film was the grotesque, the malformed, the frightening, the horrible. The result: an art which has nothing in it of "beauty" in the traditional sense, but which is closely tied to "black humor" and the absurd.

The artist who is constantly invoked in reference to Cuevas is Goya, and there is a great resemblance. Cuevas, who periodically studied artists of the past, was greatly interested in Goya's graphic art during the mid-fifties.[51] Even in the pessimistic world-view of Goya, however, one finds a more compassionate imagination than that of Cuevas. Viewing the totality of Goya's etchings, in which his most biting criticism appears, one quickly becomes aware that, though he could be corrosive about human stupidity, ignorance, superstition, greed, lust, brutality, and corruption, he also saw and recorded, like Orozco, the existence of innocence, courage, and dignity. In other words, Goya was selective about his criticism; he did not direct it against the entire human race. The art of Cuevas, on the other hand, is one of almost total negation, with rare exceptions, such as the portraits of Mireya. Cuevas lives almost completely in the distorted world he has created.

Rico Lebrun had a different opinion: ". . . when we speak of Goya the humanitarian we perpetuate a one-sided myth which takes no account of his complex, devious, and tormented nature . . . it is a fact that he courted violence . . . he would have been desolate in a world wise enough to have abolished both misery and the spell of monsters." Cuevas, Lebrun added, would also be "totally lost in a society without freaks and monsters."[52] Lebrun studied Goya deeply and knew Cuevas well; his opinion and estimation of these two artists merit the most serious consideration since they go beyond the hasty art-critical formulations that dump all neohumanists indiscriminately into a bag with Goya, Daumier, Toulouse-Lautrec, and the German expressionists (particularly in Mexico, where the invocation of the magic name of Goya emphasizes Hispanic nationalism). Goya's "complex, devious, and tormented nature" is evident throughout his work, especially in the *Disparates* (*Proverbios*), which were contemporary with his black paintings. The *Caprichos* of 1793–1798 and the *Disasters of War* of 1808–1812 were another matter: they reflect, in the first instance, his view of a Spain that was one of the most backward countries of Europe, a country of extreme social contrast, medieval survivals, stagnation, illiteracy, and ignorance, with an Inquisition that had lost very little of its power; and in the second instance, the Spanish nationalist insurrection against the French invasion. Both works, in addition, were set in a larger context: that of the French Revolution, which offered such a contrast to the abysmal situation in Spain. "Goya in his art," said the distinguished art historian Jakob Rosenberg, "records like a seismograph the deep revolution in philosophic, social and political concepts that shook the western European world in his time."[53] Both the *Caprichos* and the *Disasters* contain plates with veiled attacks on persons, church, and state, and it is believed that one of Goya's many friends who were disciples of the French Encyclopaedists may have assisted him with the texts accompanying the *Caprichos*.[54] In other words, many of Goya's statements that appear merely misanthropic are oblique, to avoid censorship or the Inquisition. They engage specific social evils upon which he could not comment freely. His "monsters" were distortions that sprang from the imperative of describing and commenting on pressing malformations of society. It is an oversimplification to suggest, as Lebrun did, that Goya produced "monsters" out of some internal attraction to misery. The question then arises: what imperative did Cuevas have for producing an art of uniformly miserable, degraded, and distorted personalities? What circumstances were there in the conditions of his personal life and that of his nation that called forth such pessimistic, if not outright nihilistic imagery?

This question can perhaps be answered by analogy. Bernard S. Myers has analyzed the social and emotional background behind the revolt of the German expressionists, for whom Cuevas and other Interioristas had such an affinity, in terms that might be applied to the Mexican situation. Not only was there a strong mystical/religious element in German thought, according to Myers, but German intellectuals were reacting against unsatisfactory emotional relationships with the patriarchal figures in their lives. The strictures of family life were reflective of general authoritarianism in society. Against the sense of frustration and helplessness engendered by such strictures (and we should note that both Kafka and Cuevas had domineering fathers), expressionist art "destroys the appearance of things to arrive at nonrational and spiritual values. Its often wild and demonic outpourings are as much reactions against blocked emotional fulfillment in everyday life as are those of an individual who expresses himself in a political or social manner."[55] Without attempting to translate German conditions to Mexico, or rejecting a psychological interpretation, we might carry the analogy further by suggesting that Mexico in the late forties and fifties was beginning to lose that sense of individual heroism that exemplified the activities of such revolutionary personalities as Pancho Villa, Zapata, and the *tres grandes* themselves (especially Rivera and Siqueiros, whose biographies are sprinkled with acts of derring-do that make them appear larger than life). In the course of the consolidation of the Mexican state under the firm control of the bourgeoisie, pressure was exerted on the working and middle classes to conform, to homogenize their individual and class strivings under the banner of Mexican unity. This pressure, both overt and covert, was very real. Its application in the art world, for example, ranged from the covert activities of the Biennials to the imprisonment of Siqueiros. These events reflected what was going on in the country at large. Cuevas opposed himself to this kind of "authoritarianism," using the government-supported Mexican movement as a scapegoat and (before his imprisonment) Siqueiros (transformed into an "art dictator") as a father figure. Cuevas' art did not deal with the social and political themes of the pre-1940 era, but with "demonic outpourings" that expressed his personal neuroses and narcissism primarily, and secondarily the reflections of the increasing oppressiveness of the Mexican state in which the middle class, as Octavio Paz pointed out, had no place in the new order of things, no political power, and no organization of its own. Its only role, therefore, was not to express itself as a class, but to act as a critic (as Cuevas did) in the hope that this would awaken other groups and classes to more positive action.[56] Paz saw the artist's role as neither moral nor political, but visionary. Cuevas' critical revolt was unfocused, coming as it did from a member of a powerless class, with no moral or political role. It aimed at whatever existed, without distinction. The implicit moral sense of a Goya or an Orozco is missing.

Mediating between the "naïve" imagery of Cuevas' youth (when he was still drawing from nature) and his maturing style (in which he turned primarily to literature, his imagination, and art of the past for imagery) were the circumstances of the Mexican art world. At this point, Cuevas' choice of "monsters" became programmatic. The original creation of these creatures was a natural development of the tensions between Cuevas as an individual and Cuevas as a social being within the Mexican ambience. The focus on monstrosity (to the point where he sought subject matter that allowed a play on the grotesque) occurred after Cuevas entered the international art market, assumed the role of *enfant terrible*, and became a spokesman for the younger generation in opposition to the Mexican School. To trace this shift, it is necessary to follow Cuevas' activities after his first professional show at the Galería Prisse in 1953. Beginning in January 1954, he was patronized by a private collector (Dr. Alvar Carrillo Gil) of considerable prestige. He had also been accepted into the warm confraternity of artists at the Galería Prisse and became a good friend of Vlady and Alberto Gironella. Within this coterie, new forms of art were discussed, foreign magazines and books were read, and official art circles were criticized. He met other artists and critics of the "opposition," one of whom, Felipe Orlando, wrote to José Gómez-Sicre about him in 1953. Cuevas and Gómez-Sicre met the same year, and in 1954

Gómez-Sicre offered shows at the Pan American Union to Cuevas, Gironella, and Enrique Echeverría, all part of the Galería Prisse group. Cuevas had instant success at his July 1954 show; the exhibition of forty-three ink and color drawings priced at fifteen to sixty dollars each sold out on opening night, and Gómez-Sicre himself bought a number of works for his private collection. Two were also purchased by New York's Museum of Modern Art. Cuevas was interviewed by *Time* magazine;[57] he claimed to be untutored and uninfluenced except for his admiration of Orozco and Tamayo. In the telescoped way that is typical of him, Cuevas had thus established himself as both artist and polemicist on an international scale and had obtained the personal support of the most powerful taste-maker of Latin American art.[58] Gómez-Sicre frequently met Cuevas in New York and took the young artist under his wing. Since he was a knowledgeable man with many connections, Cuevas accepted him in the role of mentor.[59] In 1955, Cuevas exhibited at the Edouard Loeb Gallery of Paris, from which Picasso purchased two of his drawings, and was the subject of a first monograph.[60] By 1957, he had achieved unusual international prominence for such a young artist. In that year his works were shown in France with those of Alexander Calder, Stuart Davis, and Morris Graves (United States artists very much his seniors) in an exhibit called "Four Masters of Line." Cuevas also had shows that year at the Metropolitan Museum of Art and the De Aenlle Gallery in New York and the Gres Gallery in Washington, D.C. He spent two months as artist-in-residence at the Philadelphia Museum of Art and did a series of drawings on New York for *Life* magazine.

Cuevas' rapid rise to fame would seem to be the success story par excellence. However, he owed his success not only to his talents as an artist, but also to a well-organized and prolific polemical campaign against the Mexican School that started as early as 1953. During his association with the Galería Prisse, he found a platform from which to launch his attacks in the pages of the newspaper *El Zócalo*; from that point on he missed no opportunity to criticize and even insult the artists he felt dominated the Mexican art world. In 1956, he launched his personal manifesto, "La cortina del nopal" ("The Cactus Curtain") in the cultural supplement "México en la Cultura" of the newspaper *Novedades*, edited by Fernando Benítez.[61] The wide bilingual dissemination of this article established polemics as a major weapon in the Cuevas arsenal, one that he later used with deadly effect against his former associates in Nueva Presencia. There is a possibility that, in choosing the three Galería Prisse artists for exposure at the Pan American Union in 1954, Gómez-Sicre was partial not only to Cuevas' artistic, but also to his verbal talents; the combination of these two qualities made him an obvious (and self-appointed) candidate to carry forward the war on social realism.[62]

Did Cuevas attack the Mexican School for political reasons? Obviously not, at first, though a later attack on Siqueiros as a Communist suggests an increasingly retrogressive politicalization on his part. Carlos Monsiváis has made some convincing suggestions: in 1956, he says, when Cuevas, then a young, "practically unknown" artist, brought his "Cactus Curtain" article to *Novedades*, he did so to confront the picturesque nationalism that dominated the cultural media, but equally, *to make himself known*. In order to guarantee himself public attention and affirm his personality, Cuevas had to manifest "arrogance" (through the extensive use of the first person in his diatribes) and to speak in a "high-pitched" voice. Anything less would not have been heard.[63] Cuevas' patron, Carrillo Gil, has stated the case with great lucidity and objectivity, giving due weight to polemical and artistic aspects of the Cuevas personality: "I admit that Cuevas' expansive and polemical temperament and his indiscriminate aggressiveness have contributed greatly to his being a well known and

controversial personality in our country and in the rest of America. Yet it is clear also that these aspects of his character would hardly enhance his prestige without a more important reason: Cuevas is a magnificent artist, intelligent, of great promise, and, as well, a man of noble sentiments. Otherwise nobody would have taken notice of him."[64]

Thus, it can be concluded that Cuevas violently attacked the Mexican School because it was the only serious target and because it brought him personal prominence. In the larger scheme of things, these attacks, in the name of freedom of expression and antinationalism, served an important function: Cuevas replaced Tamayo as the voice of protest (since he was more effective than the introverted Tamayo) and was accordingly given unprecedented publicity and exposure abroad.

In exploring the question of "monsters" in Cuevas' work, it is instructive to consider Marta Traba's book *Los cuatro monstruos cardinales*, which encounters this question head on and provides an ideological framework for Cuevas. (The four monsters of the title are Francis Bacon, Willem de Kooning, Jean Dubuffet, and Cuevas.) It is apparently central to Traba's concept that art associated in any way with politics, literature, or morality is considered devalued and limited, if not outright demagogic. In her view, the "alluvial expansion" of abstraction in the postwar period was necessary to cleanse the "criterion of salvation" that had infected German expressionism and the "confessional" aspect of social-tendency art of both left and right (Siqueiros and Bernard Buffet are given as examples). When neohumanism appeared, it was as exempt from the obligation to save humankind as abstraction had been. Its role was one of translating into figurative form the general human trauma of our epoch produced by the events of Hiroshima and the introduction of "nothingness" (*nada*) in the human domain. Abstract expressionism, according to Traba, was much more effective than neohuman-

ism in conveying this nihilism; however, it lost
its efficacy with informalism that passed from
parasitism to academicism. Neohumanism, which
was pictorial rather than moral or political like
traditional humanism, expressed the anxieties of
contemporary life through the use of surface in-
crustations, infections, corruptions, aberrations,
and mutilations representing internal malformations. It began with Soutine and continued with
Bacon, Dubuffet, de Kooning, and Cuevas.

Traba conceived of Cuevas' "monsters" as the
creations of another reality, not of a physical but
of a moral order. For him, she said, physical
order could result only from moral beauty, but
there was no moral beauty, and therefore perver-
sion of the physical was inevitable. Mutilation
gave the lie to physical integrity, which in itself
corresponded to the fiction of moral integrity.
This explanation, which sums up Traba's argument, seems to place Cuevas' figures in the long
line of tradition from the crustaceous monsters of
Bosch and Breughel (externalized visions of Biblical vice and sin) to those of Goya, Posada, and
Orozco (humanized corruptions, brutalities, and
weaknesses), which, because of their context
within socially derived systems of morality (even
if not the dominant moralities of their own times),
are outside the realm of simple misanthropy.
However, Traba herself removes this possibility
(accurately, in my opinion) by maintaining that,
though Cuevas was deeply sensitive to the strict-
est moral order, it was not one postulated from
outside, but one invented by him in an arbitrary
manner, i.e., a totally existential and individualistic morality. In this framework, human degradation, like human attainment, was totally unrelated to the social structure.

Although Cuevas (according to Traba) had ab-
dicated from the social and moral responsibilities of visual art in the early twentieth century,
he re-established these responsibilities through
literature—that of Dostoevsky and that of Kafka.[65]
Cuevas was first introduced to Kafka's writings
in 1954 but did not fully explore them until

56. José Luis Cuevas, *Study of Coney Island*, 1954, ink
on paper, 7⅞ × 12¼ in. (20 × 31 cm.). Collection of
Horacio Flores Sánchez. Photo courtesy Instituto Nacional de Bellas Artes.

three years later, when he was artist-in-residence for the Philadelphia Museum of Art and
did the drawings that became part of the book
The Worlds of Kafka and Cuevas.[66] The striking
similarity of Kafka's *Metamorphosis* and Cuevas'
work is perhaps best illustrated by a series of
drawings done in the amusement park of Coney
Island on Cuevas' first trip to New York in 1954.
The two figures of *Study of Coney Island* (Fig.
56) live on that borderline between human and
insect that is best expressed by Kafka's hero,
Gregory Samsa, who combines the features of an
insect with the mind and emotions of a man.
Cuevas' Coney Island creatures carry on a con-
versation, or at least the more humanoid of the
two is trying to communicate with the more insectlike creature, who seems indifferent. Coming
home from Coney Island by subway during a
rain, Cuevas got lost and soaked to the skin and
finally arrived at his hotel with a high fever. It
was in this almost hallucinatory state, he says,
that he read *Metamorphosis*. It produced so
strong an effect that during his sleep he dreamed
he too was transformed into an insect. Fevers,
not rare occurrences in Cuevas' life, often produced a hypersensitive state during which he experienced hallucinations. His drawings *I Am Not
Mad* and *In Memory of 8* (a series), in the Carri-

llo Gil collection, were produced during a high
fever in 1955. *Hallucination* (Fig. 57) from 1956,
a particularly fantastic drawing of a demon and
two dwarfs, seems drawn from both the demons
of folk art and the visions of another high fever.

It is suggestive that Cuevas' human images no-
ticeably changed in character in the period 1954
to 1956, when they began to resemble insects or
poultry, often armless, with compressed features
and distinct resemblances to the "plucked fowls"
of Goya's *Caprichos*. It was in the era following
Cuevas' Pan American Union show that he began
to withdraw from *apunte del natural* (drawings
from life) and turn increasingly to his imagination, literature, and art for artistic inspiration.
More and more his work featured monsters, grotesques, freaks, and aberrations—a trend that apparently began with his response to Kafka. These
characteristics appear in such works as *Grotesque Figures, Personages, The Possessed Ones,*
and *Figure for a Crucifixion.*

Two more unlike persons than Kafka and Cuevas could not be imagined. The former was a
sensitive, introverted individual, so repressed by
the strong, overbearing personality of his father
as to be rendered inarticulate except in his literature, and even there carrying forward an Oedipal
struggle in veiled form. He was an archetypical
German expressionist according to Bernard S.
Myers' definition and suffered from the prevalent
authoritarian patriarchal family and society. His
genius lay in projecting the repressed content of
the mind into mysterious events, and psychic situations into symbolic social ones. Cuevas, on the
other hand, is an articulate, extroverted personality whose proclaimed "solitude" is self-
imposed, or part of the larger role dictated by his
egomania. It is not my intention to enter upon a
psychological explanation for Cuevas' penchant
for misery and alienation beyond the obvious
statement that a precocious child with a retentive
memory, exposed to scenes of human misery,
could be expected to develop an almost morbid
fascination with such themes, while the positive

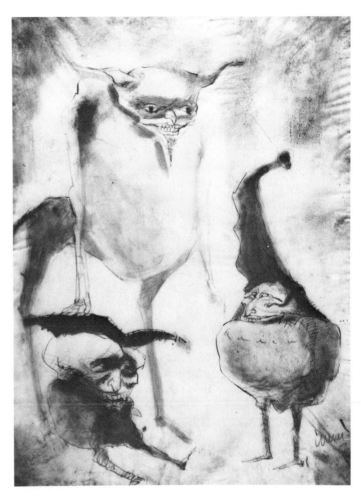

57. José Luis Cuevas, *Hallucination*, 1956, ink on pa-
per, 11¾ × 8⅝ in. (30 × 22 cm.). Collection of Horacio
Flores Sánchez. Photo courtesy Instituto Nacional de
Bellas Artes.

response of the art market tended to "fix" them.
The traumatic occurrence of his serious illness,
attended by a new and welcome solicitousness
on the part of his family (a situation exactly opposite to Kafka's experience), perhaps internalized in his mind the idea that disease and decay
and the proximity of death, while terrifying,
were also accompanied by rewards. His hypochondria and fear of death, acquired so early,
doubtless had much to do with the concentration
on self exhibited in verbal self-publication and
the proliferation of self-portraits, as himself and
as famous artists of the past. These were gestures

58. José Luis Cuevas, *Process of a Metamorphosis*, from the series *The Worlds of Kafka and Cuevas*, 1957, pen and wash, 8½ × 6 in. (21.6 × 15.2 cm.). Collection of the Philadelphia Museum of Art: given by Mr. Samuel Pesin.

of identity to stave off oblivion—fame and its attendant immortality having long been seen as the only antidotes to death. It has also been suggested that, while Cuevas found inspiration in the works of Kafka, Dostoevsky, and Quevedo, and in the paintings of Rembrandt, Dürer, and Goya, he actually used them for self-autopsy.[67]

No one who has read Kafka can fail to understand the rich possibilities of the ambiguities, mysteries, absurdities, and incongruities contained in his stories and books for the imagination of a fantastic artist like Cuevas, and it is not

surprising that he produced some of his most inventive, original images for *The World of Kafka and Cuevas*. For *Metamorphosis*, he not only did a series of insects but, in *Process of a Metamorphosis* (Fig. 58), showed the process by which the hero becomes one. In *Portraits of Kafka and His Father* (Fig. 59) he deploys the portraits across the page in such a way that father and son, though promiscuously mingled, never make contact, thus expressing Kafka's solitude even while living in the bosom of his family. Significantly, Cuevas "frames" several of the Kafka portraits (as he did his own weeping face in the 1944 *Sick Self-Portrait*), suggesting a play on the nature of reality by placing a picture within a picture. With this device, and by repeating the image of a single individual several times within one drawing, Cuevas destroys the unities of time and place. He establishes sequential time like that of the motion picture and the comic strip, which frame tiny segments of time that can be slowed into "stills" or speeded up into the illusion of motion. He also changes his viewing position: now up close, now from a distance, as in the close-up and panning techniques of film.

Just as there are many points of affinity between Cuevas and Goya but a profound disjunction in their world views, so one finds a similar discontinuity between Cuevas and Kafka. Kafka was acutely aware, even in his most mythic, fantastic, and painful symbolisms, of the causes of oppression. "In the network of meanings to be found in Kafka's work," says Michel Carrouges, "the social meaning holds an important place. It is the most obvious, for beyond the other hidden meanings his work is first of all a portrait of the worker alone, confronted with his job, unemployment, the city, mechanization, and bureaucracy, crushed between the necessities of earning his daily bread and the mysteries of an unfathomable and impersonal society."[68] Kafka despised bureaucracy, seeing in it an instrument of impersonal injustice, but also recognizing that the victim was not likely to be a member of the

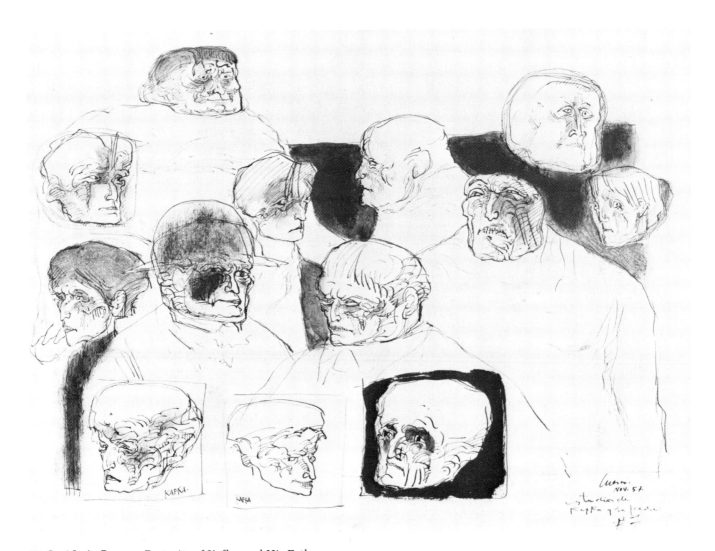

59. José Luis Cuevas, *Portraits of Kafka and His Father*, from the series *The Worlds of Kafka and Cuevas*, 1957, pen and wash on blue paper, 20 × 26 in. (50.8 × 66 cm.). Collection of the Philadelphia Museum of Art: given by Mr. Samuel Pesin; photograph by A. J. Wyatt, staff photographer. Courtesy of the artist.

propertied classes, who themselves held the reins of bureaucratic power. His protagonists are little people, caught in the chains of mysterious systems whose sources of power never appear on the scene: the traveling salesman of *Metamorphosis*, the bank clerk of *The Trial*, the unemployed surveyor of *The Castle*, etc. Despite their small pomposities, their ineffectualities, Kafka is basically sympathetic to them.

It seems obvious that Cuevas, operating from his view of an amorphous degraded "human condition," classless and ahistorical, did not respond to this level of meaning in Kafka's work. Following his own introspective visions, he skimmed the surface of Kafka's extravagant, absurd, and bizarre happenings. Occasionally he struck a particularly Goyaesque note, such as his images of the magistrates from *The Trial*, who are depicted in all their pomposity or equated with notoriously stupid animals (Fig. 60), as in Goya's *Back to Adam*, or seen as raucous birds. More often Cuevas' drawings are works of the purest and most appealing fantasy, lacking Kafka's mordancy: multiheaded personages; a circus bareback rider balancing on a wheeled, two-headed sheep, strongly resembling Nayarit sculpture and folk art toys; a circus scene with a dwarf, a fat lady, and a *calavera*—an image of the living dead like that of Kafka's story "A Hunger Artist," whose hero fasted to death as a sideshow attraction.

There is a body of Cuevas' work, done between 1958 and 1961, that appears to be political/historical, judging from the series titles: *Funerals of a Dictator* (1958), *The Spain of Franco* (1960), *The Conquest of Mexico* (1961), and *The Fall of Franco* (1961). The most obvious evidence that Picasso's influence, formally and perhaps thematically, entered into Cuevas' preoccupation with Spain at this time is the 1959 series *Tauromaquia*, which might be attributed to Goya if it were not for the use of the minotaur, a favorite Picasso theme. However, two other events, one political and one artistic, may have served to make the

transition from the more general *Funerals of a Dictator* to the specific anti-Franco series. From 1956 to 1958, the forces of Fidel Castro in Cuba were carrying on a desperate but finally successful struggle against the dictator Fulgencio Batista. The year 1958 was the crucial one of the fight, since the end of the Batista regime was announced on New Year's Day of 1959. Castro and pro-Castro sympathizers were heartened in February 1958 by the news that Marcos Pérez Jiménez, hated dictator of Venezuela, had been overthrown. Reflecting the overthrow of one dictator and the imminent fall of another, *Funerals of a Dictator* concentrates on images of dead dictators. Repeatedly a prostrate figure appears, extended horizontally or diagonally across the drawing. Sometimes the figure is alone, as in *Study for the Funerals of a Dictator* (Fig. 61); at other times there is an accompanying seated figure, suggesting a wake.

Possibly Cuevas' interest in Spain was stimulated by Antonio Rodríguez Luna's twenty-year retrospective that opened at the Museo Nacional de Arte Moderno in 1959, featuring over a hundred works, from his drawings in Spain during the Spanish Civil War in 1939 to his large body of anti-Franco works done in Mexico. In conjunction with Castro's victory the same year, this show served to focus attention on the Spanish dictatorship and the hope that its days too were numbered. Thus Cuevas' *Funerals of a Dictator* was organically connected to *The Spain of Franco* and *The Fall of Franco*. *The Spain of Franco*, like many of Luna's images, presents a circus society in which symbolic clowns and ballerinas confront each other, or a bulky figure lying in bed is observed by a monkey (traditional symbol of mendacity) seated on a high stool. The violence done to the Spanish people appears in a line drawing in which one figure hangs by the ankles, others are grotesquely flung about, and still others are tortured. The sense of violence and grotesquerie reaches its heights in *The Fall of Franco*, which seems to have been influenced

60. José Luis Cuevas, *Examining Magistrate*, from the series *The Worlds of Kafka and Cuevas*, 1957, pen and wash, 8½ × 6¼ in. (21.6 × 15.9 cm.). Collection of the Philadelphia Museum of Art: given by Mr. Samuel Pesin.

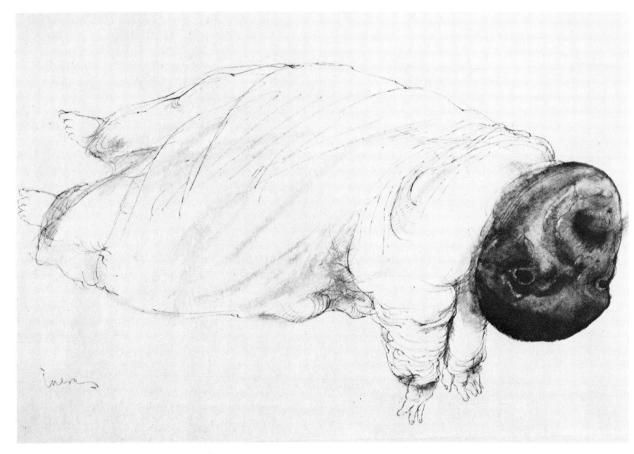

61. José Luis Cuevas, *Study for the Funerals of a Dictator*, 1958, ink, 14⅛ × 24 in. (36 × 61 cm.). Collection of the artist. Photo courtesy Instituto Nacional de Bellas Artes.

by Picasso's *Dream and Lie of Franco* as well as subsequent works leading up to *Guernica*. The dictatorship is symbolized by a group of very large drawings, one of which is a monstrous bellowing figure, part bull and part dragon, that fills the entire space and presses against the frame (Fig. 62). Another is more distinctly human; its large bloated body is stretched helplessly across the page; a long tubular nose, an open mouth with craggy teeth, and close-set crossed eyes complete the figure. It seems to be in its death throes. Still another figure of the series, called *Study for a Portrait of Francisco Franco*, shows the dictator, bare buttocks to the viewer, crawling away on all fours like an animal.

In connection with these series, Cuevas' biographer has pointed out that governmental tyrannies were insupportable to the artist, who set aside his "political neutrality" to take a position against the fascist Spanish dictatorship.[69] However, the timing of that opposition is significant in that it coincided with the fall of two very repressive Latin American dictators within a year's time. If Cuevas broke his silence on Franco (who, after all, had been ruling for seventeen years), it is reasonable to suppose that his choice of Fran-

62. José Luis Cuevas, *The Fall of Francisco Franco No. 1*, from the series *The Fall of Franco*, 1961, ink, 25 × 38 in. (63.5 × 96.5 cm.). Collection of Silvan Simone Gallery: photo by Jim Goss.

co was a convenient symbol for dictators closer at hand—the "funeral" and "fall" themes seem to bear this out. It is to be remembered (as mentioned earlier) that in 1960 Cuevas signed a public advertisement on behalf of the new Cuban Revolution, and boycotted the 1960 Biennial due to the dictatorial imprisonment of Siqueiros. These were sentiments and actions that temporarily brought him very close to the future Interioristas.

An evaluation of Cuevas' complex and convoluted personality would not be complete without some mention of his involvement with Mexican muralism. In spite of the fact that his international career was elevated on a platform of attack against the Mexican School—an attack that continued unabated for many years—Cuevas cherished ambitions to do murals himself. Surely in the back of his mind (despite his later disavowals of any influence from Orozco) was the thought that murals would finally affirm his position as "Orozco's heir" in Mexico. In 1967, he created a temporary "ephemeral mural" on a billboard. A "single massive figure" (Fig. 63) occupied the top half of the billboard to the right of a portrait of Cuevas signing his name in bold letters. The bot-

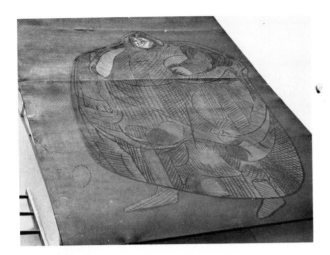

63. José Luis Cuevas, *Ephemeral Mural No. 1*, detail, 1967, vinylite on masonite (destroyed). Courtesy of the artist; photo by E. Olivar A.

tom half featured a horizontal line of vaporous abstract figures on a wash ground.[70]

It is, perhaps, unfair to judge Cuevas' muralist potentials from this mock "happening." In the "mural" there were big spaces with floating, trembling forms; there was a large, single figure; there was no message. With the best critical intentions, *Ephemeral Mural No. 1* functioned as an enlarged drawing, wholly inadequate to its space and the need for the formal simplifications and visibility at a distance that are requisite to the mural genre. The entire exercise casts an illuminating light on Cuevas' talents as an intimist draftsman and his dyspeptic career as a critic and "alternative" to the Mexican School. It does not diminish his stature in the former capacity as a leading figure of his generation—a figure without whose inventiveness contemporary Mexican painting might have taken a different route. But it does cast into sharp question any claim that he was of a stature even close to that of Orozco, whose mantle he has been given.

Artists of Nueva Presencia

7

Belkin, Icaza, and Cuevas (not necessarily in that order) were the generative forces of *interiorismo*. During the period from the first Interioristas show in July 1961 to the break-up of the Nueva Presencia group in 1964, there were also thirteen other artists who at one time or another were identified as "members" or supporters of the group: Corzas, Coronel, Muñoz, Ortiz, Sepúlveda, Góngora, González, Capdevila, Messeguer, Delgadillo, López, Xavier, and Luna. These artists are discussed here in terms of their contribution to the Nueva Presencia movement; consequently, attention is limited, in most cases, to the period ending in 1964. However, I have gone further back than 1961 in tracing the development of each artist in order to provide a sense of the evolution of ideas, plastic form, and social dynamics.

Francisco Corzas

Born in 1936, Corzas was one of the younger of the artists associated with Los Interioristas and Nueva Presencia. It is therefore difficult to evaluate his artistic achievements without going beyond the time limitations imposed by the existence of Nueva Presencia. Not until 1962 did his work begin to show some promise of maturing in the direction of the sensuous brushwork and luminous chiaroscuro, reminiscent of the baroque era, that characterize his later work. Some of his principal themes also began to make their appearance in 1962: the carnival figures, the painter and his model, and the nude. These, along with a series of portraits, provided the staple subject matter (under a variety of titles) of his mature work, long after the demise of Nueva Presencia, an episode that occurred during the period when his particular brand of realism was germinating.

Corzas' realism is charged with unseen presences. Trying to describe its nature in 1967, the writer Salvador Elizondo said that the work of Corzas contained unimpeachable evidence in favor of interior myths: mental cosmogonies that were eternally in the process of being realized.[1] Jacqueline Barnitz, writing in 1970, described "the drama in Corzas' unsettling world [that] comes from the painting itself and not the subject."[2] Whatever secret presence emanates from his paintings of these later years, its rudiments are to be found in the paintings of the Nueva Presencia years.

Corzas came of a working-class family in Mexico City and at fifteen entered "La Esmeralda" (Escuela Nacional de Pintura y Escultura), the art school that nourished a great many of the artists of his generation; he studied there for four years. A work from his student period of a group of working men drinking in a bar (*The Drunkards*, 1954) shows the stylistic influence of Pablo O'Higgins, who had taught at La Esmeralda for many years. A more important influence, and one that doubtless contributed to the mysterious melancholy "born of dreams and evocations,"[3] was that of his teacher Carlos Orozco Romero, whose lonely, semisurreal landscapes and lost personalities echo in Corzas' painting *Clown* (Fig. 64). Like many another young artist, Corzas expressed the early years of hunger and deprivation in gaunt, emaciated, and melancholy figures that corresponded to his state of mind and his actual living conditions—the poverty he suffered while studying in Italy (1956–1959). The style seems to owe a debt to German expressionism; however, the themes may have had a more immediate source in Corzas' poverty and the time he spent in jail and an asylum, and in the post-neorealist films made by Federico Fellini, Luchino Visconti, Vittoria de Sica, Roberto Rossellini, and Michelangelo Antonioni in the years between 1951 and 1957. Corzas' point of departure was both neobaroque and neoromantic, and it was these feelings that led him to Los Interioristas when he returned to Mexico.

In Rome, Corzas studied fresco and the nude at the Academy of San Giacomo and the Academy of Fine Arts respectively. In addition, he studied

64. Francisco Corzas, *Clown*, 1956, oil on masonite.
Collection of Lic. Adolfo Zamora. Photo courtesy Instituto Nacional de Bellas Artes.

first-hand the works of Italian art from Giotto to Modigliani and de Chirico. The works of Caravaggio left a deep impression that he expressed in his use of strong chiaroscuro and a basic dedication to realism.

By the time of his July 1962 exhibit at Galería Misrachi, Corzas was doing paintings strongly influenced by Cuevas' "monsters" and the family groupings of Coronel, but exhibiting personal characteristics as well. Among the twenty-seven works shown at Misrachi was *The Family*, in which tall-hatted creatures filled with some nameless terror peer out of a gothic darkness. Corzas continued to paint in this vein, as *My*

Mother's Visitors (Fig. 65) and *Exodus*, of the following year, attest. *Image of the Archway* (1962) is a painting of a batlike creature perched like a medieval gargoyle on a thick-walled Romanesque arch. Though Corzas' "monsters" are less graphic and original than those of Cuevas, and his figures less evolved as human presences than Coronel's, they evoke a nightmarish and foreboding feeling of dimly perceived creatures that appear fleetingly in a shaft of light and then vanish into darkness. The paintings seem to be set in the dark and magical world of the Middle Ages seen through the exalted sensibility of a romantic imagination, with just a pinch of Mexican magic thrown in. It is not surprising that Goya of the Black Paintings or the *Proverbios* comes to mind, or the shadowy medieval visions of certain of the symbolists. By 1962, all direct references to poverty, hunger, and misery seem to have disappeared from Corzas' work, but the sense of solitude and loneliness that pervaded his earlier work remained, taking a mystical and introspective direction.

Corzas was not of a literary turn of mind. He worked in an intuitive fashion, absorbing ideas and forms from the artists who were his friends and contemporaries, and inventing his own. Nothing as overt as existentialist or social philosophy, Dostoevskian morality, or Kafkian absurdity appears in his work. Instead there is a profound disquietude, the revelation of an intense spiritual unrest that placed him within the young generation for whom these characteristics constituted an aesthetic category.[4] Perhaps the most expressive symbol of this unrest is that of the *trashumantes*—the perpetual wanderers of the circus who live in constant transit between points, and who are related to the harlequins of Picasso's Rose Period. They appear as early as 1960 in the painting *Clowns*, and thereafter they turn up with sufficient regularity to be considered a leitmotiv. *The Three Antonios* (Fig. 66) is a typical treatment of the subject: three carnival performers, one mounted on a horse, emerge

65. Francisco Corzas, *My Mother's Visitors*, 1963, oil on canvas, 59 × 74¾ in. (150 × 190 cm.). Collection of Leslie Blanchard. Photo courtesy Joseph Young.

66. Francisco Corzas, *The Three Antonios* (or *Carnival Presences*), 1963, oil on canvas, 51⅛ × 66⅞ in. (130 × 170 cm.). Private collection. Photo courtesy Instituto Nacional de Bellas Artes.

67. Francisco Corzas, *Nude*, 1963, oil on canvas,
43¼ × 76¾ in. (110 × 195 cm.). Collection of Gelsen
Gas. Photo courtesy Instituto Nacional de Bellas Artes.

from an empty landscape. The horse (animal of transport, symbol of motion) almost always appears in connection with this theme, and the figures usually press together in the center of the canvas as if to escape the exterior desolation and alleviate their loneliness. From Toulouse-Lautrec to Ensor, Rouault, Picasso, and Orozco, clowns and harlequins have been popular, perhaps to express the rootlessness and alienation of modern society, but also as a romanticized symbol of individual freedom. One or both of these concepts infused Icaza's treatments of clowns and harlequins as well as Corzas'. These nomadic personalities offer an opposition to the settled respectability of the middle class, to its acquisitiveness and love of property, to its self-righteousness and smugness, to its plans for the future. Being performers, they are metaphors for the artist, ex-

pressing artistic aspirations, if not artistic actualities. They live perilously on the fringes of society and remain fixed at their own peril (symbolizing the need of the contemporary artist constantly to prove "growth" through change and originality?). Corzas' *trashumantes* are semitragic figures, caught in ghostly, luminous light and shadow, looking out at us for a brief moment before they move on.

Stylistically, *The Three Antonios* exhibits the neobaroque and neoromantic qualities that later became characteristic of Corzas' work. Despite the baroque stylistic borrowing, however, his works are wholly modern in content. The seventeenth-century baroque dealt in mysteries and dramas, it is true; but they were explainable within the context of religious, historical, or aristocratic sublimation. The personalities or miracles were known, or knowable; they were real or allegorical and were available to the senses as well as to reason. Nineteenth-century romanticism, on the other hand, used realistic means to suggest hidden, subjective qualities that had to be referred to the emotions (or the subconscious) rather than to the senses, or symbolic messages with a metaphysical dimension. Corzas' paintings do not state, as one would expect in a baroque work, "Here I am," but rather ask, "Why am I here? Where am I going?" One senses dis-ease and "lostness" in the way paint, light, and space are used—in what is left out as well as what is included. The "realism" is not real; it evaporates as we look, and leaves an uneasy void in the viewer.

In Corzas' art, the counterpart to the *trashumante* is the nude, which is life-enhancing rather than tragic or mystic. He has evoked the sensual nude that has been painted countless times from Giorgione to Modigliani and reflects his devotion to the great Italian artists of the past. Sometimes his image is fleshy and realistic, as in *Semi-nude* of 1962 and *Nude* of 1963 (Fig. 67), bringing to mind Titian's Venuses; at other times the flattened form is so strongly emphasized and stylized that the direct influence of Modigliani cannot be doubted. The model, in most cases, seems to be the same person: a slender, sinuous young woman, pink or golden-skinned, with a mop of wild, dark hair and eyes buried in shadow (a recurring mannerism that adds more than a little to the mystery of the works). Corzas seems to use shadow in a way that is the reverse of its use in baroque painting, in which chiaroscuro serves as a background from which figures emerge into light (whether real or symbolic) and are focused by it. His figures seem, instead, to retreat into the shadow, to become elusive and obscure. Frequently they are dark figures on a light ground, metaphorically voyaging from light into shadow.

Corzas' relevance to Los Interioristas and Nueva Presencia (he exhibited with the group throughout its existence) derives from the social themes of his early work and the more subtle disquietude and suggestivity of the 1962–1963 period. More a painter than a draftsman, he used a subdued and restricted palette and limited himself to the human figure. It was the tension produced by combining rather traditional formal means and decidedly nontraditional content that attracted him to Nueva Presencia. Though his work is suggestive of the symbolists, its "decadence" is of a wholly contemporary nature, embodying a degree of loneliness still unknown to the rebels of the late nineteenth century. Even his nudes, while sensuous, do not convey a healthy eroticism like those of Titian or, in a less idealized way, Rembrandt. Speaking retrospectively in 1972 about the work he had done in the previous twelve years, Corzas expressed those feelings that we sense beneath the surface of his paintings: "An artist paints his authentic corruptions, his genuine neuroses . . . The passion in which the painter is submerged is as monstrous as madness."[5]

In January 1964 Corzas emphatically disassociated himself from Nueva Presencia in a blistering letter to the Zora Gallery (see p. 65). For him, Nueva Presencia had served its function; he was ready to move out and follow his own predilections, which became increasingly ineffable and nostalgic.

Rafael Coronel

Rafael Coronel was a "member" of Los Interioristas for only a brief period. He exhibited at the first show at the Galerías CDI, and reproductions of his works appeared in the second and last issues of *Nueva Presencia*. He also made several efforts to exhibit with the group abroad, but these efforts were discouraged by Inés Amor, whose prestigious Galería de Arte Mexicano had begun to represent him as early as 1954. His direct participation in Nueva Presencia was very limited, although he remained on friendly terms with the artists in the group during the whole period of its existence.

Coronel was born in 1932 in Zacatecas City, grandson of a painter of saints and son of a musician. His brother, Pedro Coronel, six years older than he, had already achieved a considerable reputation as a painter and sculptor before Rafael left school, and helped him considerably in establishing himself in Mexico City. Despite the closeness of the brothers, who shared a studio at one time, their painting styles are very different; Rafael's work shows no influence from that of his brother.

In 1952, Rafael moved to Mexico City, where he studied architecture at the Universidad Nacional Autónoma de México, at the same time studying painting with Carlos Orozco Romero at La Esmeralda. He had his first individual exhibition in 1953 at the Ann Ross Gallery, White Plains, New York, and in 1954 exhibited for the first time at the Galería de Arte Mexicano. His early career was almost as meteoric as that of Cuevas, who was one year younger; both had solo exhibits in 1953. However, Gómez-Sicre and the Pan American Union (plus Cuevas' polemical talents— exactly the opposite of Coronel's) made a considerable difference in their subsequent careers. Though Selden Rodman felt in 1962 that Rafael was almost as successful as his brother Pedro,[6] he did not achieve Cuevas' worldwide reputation and prestige. His rapid ascent in the world of art was limited to Mexico, where in 1959 he was given an individual exhibition at the Museo Nacional de Arte Moderno. This was signal recognition for a young artist who, at the time, had had only three solo gallery showings and one exhibit the previous year at the official Salón de la Plástica Mexicana.

Coronel's paintings in the years 1956 to 1959 had developed into what Gilbert Chase has called "a phase of his work that was strongly expressionistic, verging on the macabre, obsessed by fear, confusion, dissolution."[7] Certainly such a work as the one exhibited at the Galería de Arte

68. Rafael Coronel, *No. 3*, from the series *The Witches of Salem*, 1959, ink and oil on cardboard, 25¼ × 19¼ in. (64 × 49 cm.). Collection of Horacio Flores Sánchez. Photo courtesy Instituto Nacional de Bellas Artes.

Mexicano, part of a series called *The Witches of Salem* (Fig. 68) and the 1959 "family" of portraits, *The One-Eyed Woman, The Catacombs,* and *My Bubble* have these qualities. There is something introverted, subterranean, and nightmarish about these figures, like images evoked from the subconscious—the interior of the mind. The violent contrasts of light and shadow, the almost grotesque faces, the menacing, haunted, or vacant eyes buried in shadow, the dislocations and exaggerations of the faces and bodies suggest a species of human that parallels the *Lumpen* worlds of Cuevas and Icaza. At the same time, Coronel's "families" differ from the semimythical ones of Corzas in that they unfailingly suggest real models: here are the tired sellers of news-

69. Rafael Coronel, *Posada's Sweetheart*, 1959, ink and oil on cardboard, 25⅝ × 19⅝ in. (65 × 50 cm.). Collection of Horacio Flores Sánchez. Photo courtesy Instituto Nacional de Bellas Artes.

70. Rafael Coronel, *Saturday Night*, 1959, ink and oil on cardboard, 25⅝ × 19⅝ in. (65 × 50 cm.). Collection of Horacio Flores Sánchez. Photo courtesy Instituto Nacional de Bellas Artes.

papers and lottery tickets huddled against the cold late at night, the trash collectors, the rag-pickers, the aged, the used-up, the crippled, the hungry, the exhausted, the drunks, the diseased, the sad and despairing faces of Mexico's streets to be seen at all times and in all weather. They are not so much individualized portraits as generic types[8] with which Coronel suggests a "truism" about humanity.

Posada's acknowledged influence is evident in a series of works from this period using the *calavera*: *Posada's Sweetheart* (Fig. 69), a clothed portrait of a skeleton; *Death*, a masklike skull, resembling those made of papier mâché or sugar for the Day of the Dead, with a large child's bow on its head; and *Death in the Spring*, a profiled

bust of a skeleton with a mop of dark hair and a large hat suggestive of Posada's well-known satire of nineteenth-century foreign fashion, *Calavera Catrina*. Orozco's influence was also not wanting in this period, as the painting of a prostitute in *Saturday Night* (Fig. 70) attests.

Coronel had made a considerable impact on the Mexican art world before the formation of Los Interioristas. He was financially secure and seemed to be a rising star. Like others of Los Interioristas, he was not opposed to the mural movement; he had painted a mural, *The Picturesque Zacatecan Woman* (now destroyed), for the auditorium of the Instituto de Ciencias of Zacatecas in 1959, and was to paint another (which was decorative in character) for the Museo Nacional

71. Rafael Coronel, *Charlot No. 1*, 1965, oil on canvas, 49¼ × 39⅜ in. (125 × 100 cm.). Collection of Lic. Francisco Martín Moreno. Photo courtesy Instituto Nacional de Bellas Artes.

72. Rafael Coronel, *Girl on the Staircase*, 1965, oil on canvas, 49¼ × 39⅜ in. (125 × 100 cm.). Collection of Francis G. Baldwin III. Photo courtesy Instituto Nacional de Bellas Artes.

de Antropología in 1964. However, he was of a generation that did not find its major expression in muralism and was primarily interested in the more private statement that could be made with easel painting.

Coronel shared two other interests with Los Interioristas. One was his fascination with silent movies (so much admired by Cuevas), although he was not drawn to freaks, comics, or monsters. Before his marriage to Ruth Rivera (daughter of Diego Rivera), his studio was covered with yellowed portraits of early twentieth-century "vamps": María Conesa, Celía Montalbán, Virginia Fábregas, Pina Menicella, with their garters, black stockings, feather boas, flapper dresses, and painted mouths.⁹ This modern version of the *femme fatale* possibly formed the basis of Oroz-

co's seductive schoolgirls (as opposed to his prostitutes), with their saucy eyes, big hairbows, and short skirts, who, despite their innocence, were seen as mantraps. Coronel's *Saturday Night* is in this tradition, though his squint-eyed woman with penciled eyebrows seems to be a professional rather than a schoolgirl.

His second interest is in the clown, which, in *Self-Portrait as a Clown* of 1959, he frankly identified with himself. In 1965, Coronel became intrigued with the image of Charlie Chaplin, whom he portrayed in *Charlot No. 1* (Fig. 71) as the wistful little tramp, part clown, part universal exemplar of the human condition.

From 1959 to 1963, Coronel's work continued in an expressionistic vein bordering on the macabre. By 1964 he had started to subdue the macabre quality, substituting external mutations for interior projections of deformities and anxieties. A new realism appeared, in which the single figures are meticulously modeled in simple compositions. They have been described as "the figures of old men and women, strangely dressed, [which] exist in their own right, in a dim light, between orange and gray, devoid of a message, of psychological conflicts, of all other values except intrinsic artistic force."[10] Nevertheless, works like *Girl on the Staircase* (Fig. 72) convey a brooding anxiety that seems to belie this analysis and mark Coronel as an artist who was squarely within the matrix of *interiorismo*.[11]

José Muñoz Medina, Emilio Ortiz, Artemio Sepúlveda

As Los Interioristas began to expand their horizons and become better known as a result of newspaper publicity and the publication of *Nueva Presencia*, three more artists joined the ranks as "members": José Muñoz Medina, Emilio Ortiz, and Artemio Sepúlveda. Their entry (as well as Leonel Góngora's) was not formalized until April 1962, when all four exhibited with the group for the first time under its new designation as Nueva Presencia.[12] When they did, it brought about a disagreement with Cuevas. He wrote a letter from out of town disaffiliating himself from the group because they had invited younger, less well-known artists to participate, an action for which he saw no need. From Belkin's and Icaza's point of view, new members were invited to join to "strengthen the group," which they saw in organizational as well as artistic terms, and they continued to invite participation on this basis.

José Muñoz Medina

José Muñoz Medina was born in 1928 in Mexico City. He studied five years at La Esmeralda, counting among his classmates and contemporaries Lilia Carrillo, Lucinda Urrusti, Vicente Rojo,

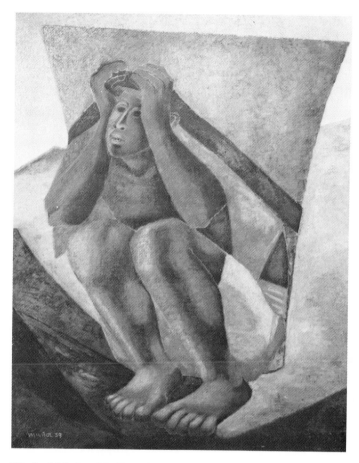

73. José Muñoz Medina, *Porter*, 1959, oil on canvas on fibracel, 47¼ × 36⅝ in. (120 × 93 cm.). Private collection. Photo courtesy Instituto Nacional de Bellas Artes.

Manuel Felguérez, Héctor Cruz, and Benito Messeguer; and among his teachers Diego Rivera, Frida Kahlo, Carlos Orozco Romero, Manuel Rodríguez Lozano, Jesús Guerrero Galván, Federico Cantú, Pablo O'Higgins, and the sculptor Francisco Zúñiga. To these instructors, he says, he owed a great part of his formation, not on the formal level necessarily, but on the spiritual level. They spoke to him of magical thought, which he considers the essence of the artistic spirit in all ages. Muñoz's early work, while containing the seeds of his later semiflat, static, and monumental style, shows an affinity to Tamayo mingled with the more geometrical aspects of Orozco Romero and Guerrero Galván. More precisely, 1959 works like *The Chat* and *Porter* (Fig. 73) utilize postcubist simplifications and planar structure that is both painterly and sculptural, while thematically reflecting social realist concerns: indigenous people at work or at rest. Thus Muñoz represents what was, for his generation, a very common fusion of social realism on the one hand and mid-century "modernism" on the other. At this stage of his development, the agitations and anxieties that characterized *interiorismo* had not entered his scope, or he had not yet found the means to express them. It is also evident in his work as a whole that he is basically a painter and a colorist in the tradition of Tamayo, using suffused, glowing, often monochromatic color in contrast to the starkness of *interiorismo*. Muñoz's figures are generalized and intangible. His subjects include the indissoluble bond yet separateness between men and women (the eternal Adam and Eve?) as in *Pair* (Fig. 74) and the serene bond between mother and child, as in his 1962 painting *Maternity* (Fig. 75). However, Muñoz also belonged among those artists of Nueva Presencia who were motivated by an active social conscience that was reflected directly in their art. The militant companionship of men united in a common endeavor (Fig. 76), emphasized by the similarity of blue coveralls, the stance, and the piling up of figures in shallow space (a technique akin to Rivera's), is immediately evident even if one knows nothing of the historical and political circumstances of the time. In June 1963 Muñoz had an individual exhibit at the Zora Gallery in Los Angeles, the major portion of which was devoted to a series called *Homage to the Mexican Peasant*. It also included the *Flagellants* series, *Death of a Revolutionary*, *Hiroshima*, *Homage to Patrice Lumumba* (Prime Minister of the Republic of the Congo, assassinated February 13, 1961), *Homage to Ruben Jaramillo* (peasant leader from Morelos assassinated with his family during the regime of

74. José Muñoz Medina, *Pair*, 1961, mixed media on canvas, 37⅜ × 27½ in. (95 × 70 cm.). Private collection.

López Mateos), *The Jaramillo Family*, and sixteen other works. The titles alone indicate the broad range of Muñoz's interests and his identification with assaulted peoples throughout the world; the paintings themselves were, as described by a Mexican critic at the time, "dense, humanistic, rich in formal and social explorations" that reflected what might be considered the artist's creed:

I want my painting to be a document of the world in which I live, of the human values and dignity that are daily pulverized. I would like, at some time, to be able to express the recovery of dignity, with the most intimate feeling of joy. I want my voice to be the voice of my people. This will happen whenever it can because

75. José Muñoz Medina, *Maternity*, 1962, oil on canvas, 51⅛ × 17¾ in. (130 × 45 cm.). Private collection. Photo courtesy Joseph Young.

76. José Muñoz Medina, *Workers*, ca. 1961, oil on canvas, 45¼ × 36⅝ in. (115 × 93 cm.). Collection of the artist. Photo courtesy Joseph Young.

I will not change myself into a puppet for the bored bourgeoisie, as has happened to many of my colleagues. And I hope to hurt this bourgeoisie, to prick them. The painter must feel about society the way the peasant and worker feel; he must be on the side of human beings and not among a pack of wolves. The mutilation of human life hurts me intensely . . .[13]

Muñoz's intense identification with the peasant movement probably began in 1955 when he taught in the Escuela Normal Rural de Tamatán in Tamaulipas and had a chance to observe the indigenous farming people—although the influence of Rivera and O'Higgins and the Mexican School should not be discounted. The early exposure to the life of the peasants and the brutal

repressions of rural strikes by the López Mateos government is reflected in his peasant themes from 1956 on.

From 1962 to 1963, Muñoz worked on a series of male figures that he painted in all conceivable positions of agony, called the *Flagellants*. The first painting of this series (Fig. 77) shows a distinctly Orozcoesque influence in the treatment of the male body: the emaciation, the protruding ribs, the gestures of sorrow and despair recall the figures at the University of Guadalajara, except that Muñoz's forms are more rigid and frontal. The "mutilation of life" to which he referred expressed itself on the very surfaces of these figures. For example, the immobile nudes of his

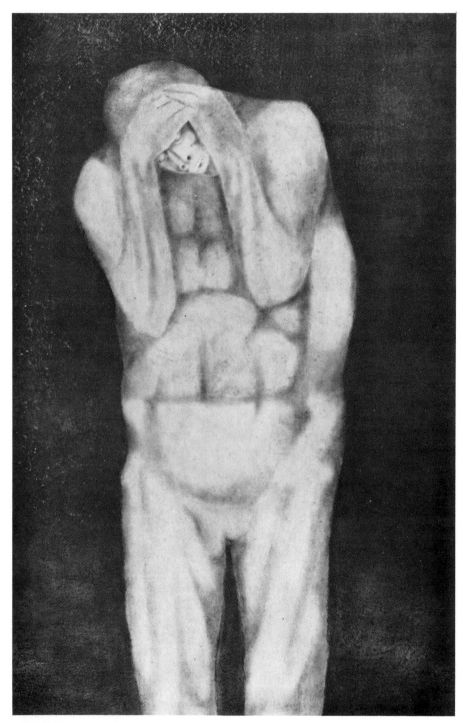

77. José Muñoz Medina, *Flagellants No. 1*, 1962, oil on
canvas, 57⅛ × 39⅜ in. (145 × 100 cm.). Collection of
the artist.

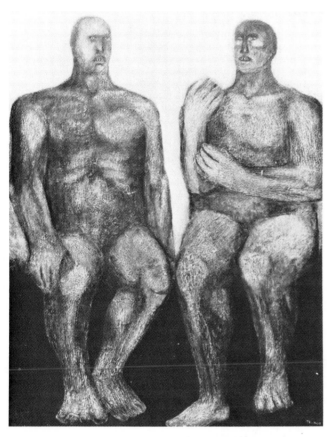

78. José Muñoz Medina, *Two Figures*, 1963, oil on canvas, 55⅛ × 43¼ in. (140 × 110 cm.). Private collection.

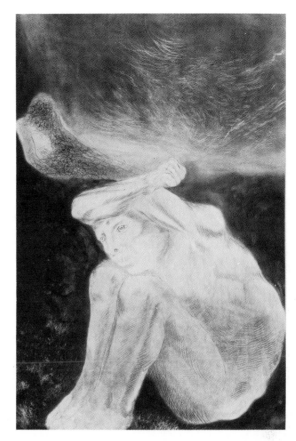

79. José Muñoz Medina, *Anguish*, from the series *War and Peace*, 1963, ink and charcoal on paper, 35 × 22½ in. (89 × 57 cm.). Collection of the artist. Photo courtesy Instituto Nacional de Bellas Artes.

painting *Two Figures* (Fig. 78) have surfaces encrusted and corroded as by the eruption of an interior disease or by searing fire. They bring to mind the similarly textured images of Leon Golub, whose *Burnt Men* of 1954 and 1960–1961 were originally intended as evocations of Buchenwald and Dachau, and later as referents to the increasing use of fire as a United States weapon on the battlefield and the bombsites in the Pacific, Korea, and Vietnam.[14] Muñoz's reaction to war and to Hiroshima in particular took a form similar to that of Golub, who ironically links the atomic and napalm fire weapons used against the Japanese and the Vietnamese as a

type of perverted Promethean retribution. Whether it was Golub from whom Muñoz drew inspiration for his *Flagellants* is not the major question; what *is* important is the fact that the "New Images of Man" perspective, of which Golub was a part, passed over and was incorporated into the artistic consciousness of Nueva Presencia in 1962, with obvious results in Muñoz's work.

The anguished imagery of the *Flagellants*, which already showed the influence of *interiorismo*, took on a new nervous energy in Muñoz's drawings for the *War and Peace* portfolios. In the drawing *Anguish* (Fig. 79), a seated man shields himself from an ominous, cloudy form that hovers over his head. Space is so compressed that it is hard to determine whether the figure is located in flat space in which an atmospheric presence (atomic fallout?) presses down on him, or whether he is in the foreground of an empty plain with storm clouds rapidly blowing toward him. Is there an outside threat, or is he shielding himself from his internal terrors? Faced, as in the works of other members of Nueva Presencia, with a "victim," with absolutely no clue as to the source of his anguish, we must conclude that it is existential in nature. The distance Muñoz had traveled from social realist tendencies is illustrated by comparing this figure to *Porter* (see Fig. 73). Though similar in pose, they offer the strongest possible contrast in meaning: from the indigenous worker struggling with the weight of his real load to the "universal man" carrying the "weight" of metaphysical anxiety.

Emilio Ortiz

At first viewing, one could hardly imagine an artist more unlike the other members of Nueva Presencia than Emilio Ortiz, though he shares stylistic characteristics with the rest of the group. A marvelous sense of fantasy bordering on the surreal; a playful irony and wit; the most fragile and delicate of etchings, ink and silverpoint drawings, and paintings of a created world of human creatures, insects, and animals seem to place him outside the existential concerns of Nueva Presencia. Upon closer inspection, however, one discovers more than one point of contact.

With Ortiz, the whole world of magic and witchcraft, of the *curandero* (healer) and the *brujo* (witch)—still a vital part of Mexican village life—come alive. A multiplicity of beliefs, centering on the darker, magical aspects of human thought and imagination, representing very old Indian, African, and Spanish concepts of cosmic organization (frequently in syncretic association with Catholicism), have provided one of the richest sources of Mexican folk art. Folk art and

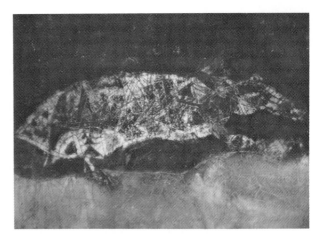

80. Francisco Toledo, *The Lizard*, 1973, oil on canvas, 47¼ × 62¼ in. (120 × 158 cm.). Collection of the Museo de Arte Moderno, Mexico City.

the magico-religious world it represents have been mined for forms by modern artists from Diego Rivera, Carlos Mérida, and Rufino Tamayo to Ortiz and Francisco Toledo, a Oaxacan artist (like Tamayo) and four years younger than Ortiz. Ortiz and Toledo were very good friends in the early sixties, when they worked closely together in printmaking classes at the Escuela de Diseño y Artesanías. Toledo's work falls within a magico-surrealist context that he has drawn, more directly than Ortiz, from his native background (Fig. 80).

The differences between Toledo and Ortiz are suggestive. Ortiz came to his interest in magic from an intellectual base, whereas Toledo's work is more intuitive, though he has drawn consciously on "primitive" sources and imbued them with a sexuality not present in the originals. To underscore this difference, it is helpful to know more of Ortiz's antecedents. He was born in 1936 in Mexico City to an upper-middle-class family. His lawyer father was opposed to his studying art, and he therefore attended the Escuela Politécnica for five years, until 1960. Three months before he would have received his master's degree, he made a gesture of independence, leaving both school and his home. Ortiz emerges as a typically alienated member of the middle class, rejecting its value system and life style.

He studied art at La Esmeralda for several months in 1959, and, after leaving the Politécnica, he enrolled in the Escuela de Diseño y Artesanías, where from 1960 to 1962 he studied lithography with Pedro Castelar, woodcut with Leopoldo Méndez, and etching with Guillermo Silva Santamaría. An interesting light is cast on the competitive isolation of the contemporary artist (in contrast to communal endeavors like muralism and the Taller de Gráfica Popular, of which Méndez was a major figure) by the fact that Ortiz found the collective experience of the print workshop preferable to painting in solitude. "Painters work in a very isolated way which I find difficult," he says. "The print workshop allows discussion and criticism. Painters get very egocentric." Possibly it was this feeling that interested him in Nueva Presencia, whose founders, Belkin and Icaza, he had met in the printmaking classes. There is little evidence that he shared their social concerns, except in the revolt against his family. Despite this, and though Ortiz claims no influence from his teachers, it is immediately evident that Colombian-born Silva Santamaría—trained in France and Mexico and a very influential teacher in Mexico—had a major formal impact on his work. A sense of the absurd, a dry humor about even the most serious subjects, and the folkloric quality of Silva Santamaría's personages—like animated wooden toys or cardboard figures—carry over into a delightful series of line drawings of anthropomorphic flies that Ortiz did about 1962. The fly becomes a witching presence, like an embodied spirit, hovering over the throne of a seated personage in a Tamayesque-colored painting of the same period. "Tamayo interested me for his color solutions," says Ortiz about this era. From this point, the fly undergoes transformations into insectlike animals and humans, such as the bird figure and person of *Waiting* (Fig. 81) and the bird of *Moonstruck Royal Peacock* (Fig. 82) of

81. Emilio Ortiz, *Waiting*, 1962, oil on canvas, 58 × 44¾ in. (147.3 × 113.7 cm.). Collection of Bernice Barth. Photo courtesy Joseph Young.

the same period. Critic Louise McCann characterized Ortiz as a young artist moving from a medium in which he reveals great control (drawing) to one in which he is still searching (painting) and is yet unsure of the development of form and mass. Such works as *Waiting* and *Moonstruck Royal Peacock* are actually drawings, using what the critic described as "maximum color vibration" that appears to "quiver on the wall,"[15] no small factor in their magical appeal.

Much of Ortiz's imagery looks as if it could have been derived from pre-Columbian sources; however, he says that modern folk sources have been more important:

136

82. Emilio Ortiz, *Moonstruck Royal Peacock*, ca. 1962,
oil on canvas with gesso, 36 × 50 in. (91.5 × 127 cm.).
Collection of Zora and Edward Pinney.

I was not interested in pre-Columbian, but in folk
magic, folk costumes—and later in toys. This was not
very conscious in the 1960s. My own family practiced
magic. My mother mixed magic herbs and was super-
stitious. Many well-educated and upper-class families
do so; they use love potions, black magic, spiritualism,
divination. They believe in the evil eye. They use
herbs to cure or cause sickness. As far as my own religious beliefs are concerned, I am an agnostic; I don't
deny God. I do believe that herbs can cause or cure
sickness. I don't practice magic, but I won't deny it
exists.

Ortiz entered the art world almost concurrently with the neosurrealist efflorescence.

Whether he, Toledo, or others among the young
artists who were attracted to the fantastic were
immediately influenced by specific aspects of
surrealism is only part of the question; they were
affected by new attitudes toward what was per-
missible in the arts, by the ideology that artistic
liberation equates with sociopolitical liberation,
and by the new direction offered representa-
tionalism by the surreal format. It was no longer
necessary to choose between social realism and
abstraction. Surrealism, in its highly appealing
Mexican variant, suffused with "genuine" primitivism, was finding patronage among collectors.
It appealed to the technology-weary (Toledo, for

example, has had great popularity in the United States, as has Tamayo) and offered an escape into the psychoprimitive.

Ida Rodríguez Prampolini has suggested that Mexican surrealism, in its original prewar manifestation, flowed naturally from living religions and magical sources. Unlike the European variety, which was a response to an excess of reason that had mutilated humanity and caused a conscious reversion to the instinctual, Mexican fantasy did not have to be induced or organized, in her opinion, and was based on collective rather than personal symbolic images.[16] So strong was this native effluvium, so pervasive its influence, that European surrealists who made their homes in Mexico often absorbed the peculiar qualities of their environment.

However, what of the younger generation, city-born and city-bred within an urban culture that had absorbed many of the rationalist, consumerist attitudes of the United States and Europe? (As a matter of fact, were their elders ever very far from European influence?) In the same way that we cannot draw firm lines between co-contemporaneous neohumanism and Pop art, we cannot draw lines between traditional surrealism and neosurrealism. It is hardly surprising that almost all members of Nueva Presencia were touched to some degree by surrealist ideas, if not in their artistic expression, then in their thinking. Ortiz expressed his fascination with folk culture and magic more directly than the others; it appears in his choices of images and the configurations in which he presents his personages, animal and human. Drawing these images out of his childhood memories, which were enlaced with the magic practices of the thirties, he weaves a spell for the present out of his subconscious: ". . . and I am here painting what I did not know I had in my head."[17]

A sense of mystery and the magical, of metamorphosis, of dreamlike empty landscapes where figures wander in loneliness, of darkness and sudden light, of "gothic" settings, of theosophist

doctrines and science fiction, of pre-Columbian magic pervades and forms the backdrop for Nueva Presencia thought. It is the product of a rebellious, disenchanted intelligentsia engaged in a struggle with the life-restricting ideologies and values of an industrial bourgeoisie. For this reason it is necessary to look with a critical eye at formulations that suggest that modern Mexican artists, for example, think from the solar plexus or some lower level of the nervous system and are, in some way, still related to the pantheistic world of ancient Mexico.[18] Nor can one agree with the critic who wrote that Ortiz's animals are "the direct expression of an artist who has been able to see his subject with a simplicity associated with the totemistic mind . . . an artist who has bridged [the] gap of millenniums."[19] These are assumptions that mistake the role of "primitivism" in modern romantic thought for residual pre-Columbian spirituality. When artists like Posada, Rivera, Kahlo, Tamayo, Cuevas, and Ortiz draw upon the rich vein of fantastic and macabre peasant art or pre-Columbian religious art, they detach these forms from their original spiritual meaning and transmute them into private symbols pertinent to their own time-space. The same thing was done earlier by Gauguin, Chagall, and Picasso with reference to the spiritual ecstasies or religious emotions adhering to the art of the Breton peasant, the Chassidic Jew, and the African tribesman. The contemporary artist is drawn to nativism by the stirrings of nostalgia for a lost simplicity, or a desire for the exotic, or the need to maintain roots in an alienated existence. The need of artists to capture the metaphysical and poetic qualities of their being through mystical references to the past is a symptom of growing dislocation from that past and the natural world, as well as an expression of the imagination. Indian peasants, after all, do not need to seek primary causes and effects; they *live* them mythologically within the parameters of a synchronic culture—and even for them, this culture is rapidly being destroyed by the encroachments of modern capitalism. Artists are city dwellers living with an international and technological culture. Their collections of masks, pottery, folk toys, pre-Columbian gods, and shamanistic mementos coexist with high fidelity stereo systems, imported automobiles, modern furniture, and refrigerators. It is an unbridgeable gap that art pretends to cross and does so only in terms of wish-fulfillment. The very act of extrapolating magico-religious symbols from their original context transmutes them into a paradigm of new meanings. There is no way back.

None of this gainsays the rich spirit of inventiveness with which the most talented young Mexican artists have treated their imagery. Ortiz, for example, created an entire zoological garden that was the interpretation of very profound human concerns, though done in an apparent spirit of play. We have already discussed his fanciful peacocks and flies; there were also a number of bulls, some animated, some static and cubic, many with an insectlike quality, and dogs, such as the one shown in Fig. 83, in this case oddly like Tamayo's humans reaching for the cosmos and faintly suggestive of the rib-exposed clay dogs of ancient Colima. The creatures of Ortiz's bestiary are benign, if strange; conceived in a totemic relationship to humans, like the werejaguar, born of the union between a jaguar and a woman; or the village shaman in the temporary guise of his guardian animal.

Playful and humorous tendencies are also present in *Mars as a Boy* and *War* from the *War and Peace* portfolios, works which make it possible to understand Cuevas' accusations of plagiarism. There are strong resemblances between these works and Cuevas' assaulted women; the chunky figure with thin, ropy arms had long been one of Cuevas' formal "types." Nevertheless, when one compares Ortiz's fragile, almost childlike personages with Cuevas' more forceful and vigorous images, one is aware that a different sensibility is at work, one more closely aligned with Klee than with Goya. The wit is gentle

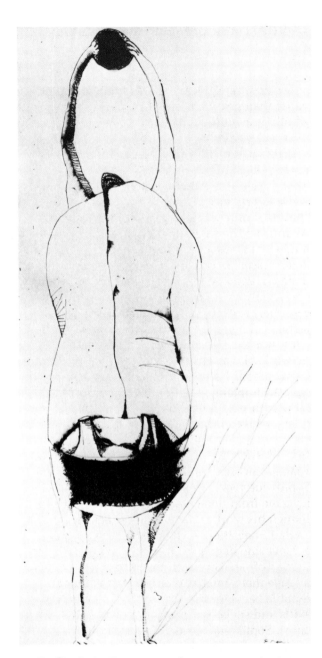

83. Emilio Ortiz, *Dog*, 1963, ink, 24⅜ × 12¾ in. (62.5 × 32.5 cm.). Collection of Horacio Flores Sánchez. Photo courtesy Instituto Nacional de Bellas Artes.

rather than sardonic, fanciful or melancholy rather than pessimistic. Ortiz's images of war are wholly unconvincing as such; they are toy rather than real soldiers.

Ortiz's association with Nueva Presencia endured almost to the demise of the group, but from the start he felt marginal to its principles and was primarily attracted by a vague sense of "protest," of rebellion against bourgeois norms. Apart from the desire for collectivity (a revealing holdover from social realist concepts in a period that stressed artistic individualism and competitiveness, and one that underlines the attitudinal complexity of the contemporary scene), Ortiz was apolitical. He shared the existential predilections of Nueva Presencia to a degree, but he felt it was absurd to do politically oriented artistic work. "I was always seeking to paint better, to create moods." Nueva Presencia, as Ortiz saw it, equated humanism with politics—a point of view with which he did not concur, and which finally caused him to abandon the group.

Artemio Sepúlveda

Among the artists of Nueva Presencia, Artemio Sepúlveda represents something of an anomaly: he came from poor, working-class parents and, though his work received critical acclaim in the United States (less so in Mexico), he did not achieve any degree of financial security. Shy, retiring, soft-spoken, with the apparent lack of confidence that sometimes characterizes those of humble backgrounds whose most elementary skills and social graces have been acquired with effort, Sepúlveda speaks eloquently in his art, which combines strength with a disturbing grotesqueness.

Born in 1935 in the tiny village of Los Rodríguez, Nuevo León, near the Texas border, Sepúlveda came from a miner's family. During the revolution his father had been an aid to a commissioner; later, both his father and his brothers were miners and union members, and Sepúlveda remembers a hunger strike in which they were

engaged and which they lost. In 1949 the family moved to Mexico City, part of the constant migration of jobless and underemployed to the capital in search of better opportunities. For Sepúlveda, who had drawn pictures since he was a child and had experimented with stone sculpture, Mexico City represented an opportunity to receive formal art training. He discovered, however, that at fourteen he was too young for the art schools, and he went to work, first as a carpenter, then for a year in Arizona as an illegal *bracero* (agricultural worker). By the time he was admitted to La Esmeralda at the age of fifteen on a meager three-year scholarship, Sepúlveda had experienced hard labor and real privation. His scholarship did not alleviate the grinding poverty, which continued for many years. When Selden Rodman visited his studio with Belkin in 1962, he described the living conditions as follows:

We entered a noisome, garbage-reeking hallway crowded with light meters, boilers and washtubs, and a steep winding stone-stepped staircase totally without illumination. "A true Insider's entrance!" Arnold and I exclaimed to each other in the same breath. The unshaven, intense young artist was working (simultaneously) on a big canvas of a spread-eagled grey-white "monster" that would have done credit to Baskin and Golub at their cruelest, and a remarkably bland frontal "portrait" of a society-type woman in social dress. It was easy to see from the dozens of bold sketches tacked to the walls where Sepúlveda's heart lay.[20]

Between 1952 and 1955, Sepúlveda studied with Carlos Orozco Romero (who seems to have left his imprint on this generation by virtue of his role as *maestro* and the appeal of his work), Manuel Rodríguez Lozano, and Enrique Assad. When Orozco Romero retired, he invited Sepúlveda to work with him in his studio. For a year Sepúlveda worked with Orozco Romero and helped him teach private classes. During this period, he did a portrait of the *maestro's* daughter. Two years after leaving Orozco Romero's studio

84. Artemio Sepúlveda, *The Timid One*, 1958, oil on wood, 24¾ × 18¼ in. (63 × 46.5 cm.). Collection of the Instituto Nacional de Bellas Artes, Mexico City. Courtesy Instituto Nacional de Bellas Artes.

to work independently, his painting *The Timid One* (Fig. 84) still shows the imprint of his teacher's postcubist structuralism and poetic quality. Commissioned as a portrait of his daughter by theatrical director Fernando Wagner, the painting treats the vulnerability of adolescence in a manner reminiscent of Munch's *Adolescent* (though without any neurotic overtones) and of Picasso's Blue Period.

The dichotomy between Sepúlveda's "genuine" work and the society portraits he was forced to do to keep alive is reflected in the technique and media of his work. The "society" works were generally in oil and finished in detail. His "own" work was more often done in ink, pencil, and, above all, charcoal rubbed and worked into the surface, with added white lines of gesso. When he used oil paint for his "own" work, it was often treated like a drawing material with thinly brushed washes of pale colors counterpointing the lines.

Sepúlveda intensely admired Orozco. He saw and studied all his murals in Mexico City, and the evidence of Orozco's influence never completely disappears in his work. It is particularly evident in *Aristocrats* (Fig. 85), part of the series *Landlords and Tenants*, which comprised his first individual show in 1961 at the Galería Chapultepec. Sepúlveda described this series as "imaginary portraits" of the humble people who were tenants. He treated the landlords satirically "because I didn't like to deal with landlords; I had trouble paying the rent." The large, gloved woman in the low-cut dress is a worthy descendent of Orozco's prostitutes and his caricatures of the rich. Her sharp, evil features are matched by those of her companions; together they form a "society" portrait far different from those with which the artist earned his living.

Sepúlveda's financial problems finally became so severe in the fifties that he spent a year under the total patronage and control of Manuel Suárez, living in servants' quarters at the latter's Hotel Casino de la Selva in Cuernavaca. In exchange for his room and board, he contributed his year's output—167 paintings and drawings—to Suárez.

Sepúlveda's life experience prepared him to identify with workers: their exploitation, their weaknesses, their vulnerability, their worn faces and hands, and their humanity. He responded to working-class types in a less romantic manner than many of his middle-class contemporaries. The expressionistic imperatives of his generation (and undoubtedly his own subjective torments) sometimes pushed him to produce ungainly monsters, but more often the distortions are integral to his conception of the subject. A penchant for exaggerated grotesquerie can be seen in some of his later work, such as the strange hydrocephalous baby suspended in mid-air (Fig. 86). These creatures have weight and volume, and it is most disturbing to observe their precarious

85. Artemio Sepúlveda, *Aristocrats*, from the series
Landlords and Tenants, 1961, oil on canvas,
33½ × 42⅛ in. (85 × 109 cm.). Collection of Sidney
Newman. Photo courtesy Instituto Nacional de Bellas
Artes.

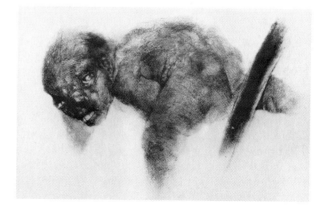

86. Artemio Sepúlveda, *Abortion*, ca. 1962–1963, ink
and charcoal on paper. Private collection. Photo courtesy Joseph Young.

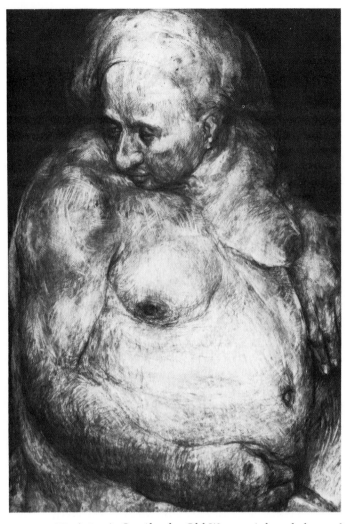

87. Artemio Sepúlveda, *Old Woman*, ink and charcoal on paper, 50 × 31 in. (127 × 78.5 cm.). Collection of Selden Rodman.

"levitation," which works against the solidity. When a Cuevas-like whimsicality is given weight and dimension, it becomes grotesque. Sepúlveda is at his best when he is firmly anchored in reality, the resources of which he transmutes into a nonrealistic psychological idiom.

Sepúlveda did not come to his working-class or *Lumpen* subjects from the outside and impose a transcendental meaning, but worked from the inside out to translate what he knew of their suffering bodies and souls into images that were pregnant with many of the social meanings of

interiorismo. Of all the Nueva Presencia artists, he produced some of the most powerful figures (though not necessarily lacking in tenderness), as demonstrated by his image of an old woman (Fig. 87). Within the circular volume of her body, encased by her arms, the head creates a subsidiary volume turned back on itself with the compactness of a sculpture. The worked-over surface has texture and luminosity; the scale is monumental. *Persecuted Man* (ca. 1963), a charcoal drawing of a man shielding himself with upthrown arms, is more traditional. The muscular structure of the body and the emotional expressiveness are reminiscent of Orozco's early studies for his Escuela Nacional Preparatoria murals.

For the *War and Peace* portfolios, Sepúlveda did a number of drawings of old women. One of the most monumental (Fig. 88) is a work done with tiny hatched strokes in ink, overlaid with lines of white gesso that impart a ghostly luminosity to the head. This woman appears to have some of the sturdy peasant quality and native shrewdness for survival that one associates with Bertolt Brecht's *Mother Courage,* while the arrangement of the large crossed hands has affinities with Käthe Kollwitz's bronze relief *In God's Hands.* There are also echoes of Cuevas, Lebrun, and Aztec sculpture; however, in the final analysis, the image is wholly Sepúlveda's own. Another drawing is restricted to the face (Fig. 89), wide-eyed, smiling, with large teeth and wrinkled features, which floats in nebulous space, leaving a trail of air behind it like a surreal, bodiless presence in the sky. Tension is produced by the contrast between the frightened eyes and the smiling mouth.

How did Sepúlveda view Nueva Presencia and his relationship to it? He was invited to exhibit with the group when Los Interioristas were re-forming themselves as Nueva Presencia. Icaza extended the invitation. "At that time," says Sepúlveda, "I was in agreement with the social ideas and principles of Los Interioristas, though I did not participate in the intellectual discus-

sions. Originally the group was supposed to
work as a collective, but later there were so many
exhibitions that things got confused. Belkin was
the key person, the one who had the most contacts, the organizer. The others were in their stu-
dios." Sepúlveda always considered his own
work and that of Nueva Presencia as within the
mainstream of Mexican painting, which he felt
was very much alive and vital in the work of the
younger artists. "There is no artistic decadence
in Mexico," he said in 1962. "What has existed
and still does is a constant renovation of painting, with different tendencies. The painter seeks
his own language, his own form of expressing
himself. He reflects the type of social thought
that is prevalent, and in which he participates
socially in the most complete way, given his sensitive temperament."[21]

88. Artemio Sepúlveda, from the series *War and
Peace*, 1963, ink, charcoal, and gesso on paper,
19⅝ × 11¾ in. (50 × 30 cm.). Private collection. Photo
courtesy Instituto Nacional de Bellas Artes.

89. Artemio Sepúlveda, from the series
War and Peace, 1963, pen and ink on paper, 13⅜ × 18⅝ in. (34 × 47 cm.). Collection of Leonel Góngora; photo by Bill
Burkhart.

From the very start, Sepúlveda was interested in muralism. The monumentality of his easel figures can be seen as an expression of this thwarted desire. Though he conceived of muralism as a natural idiom for himself, he had no illusions about the opportunities for young artists to paint murals in the sixties. He says: "Nueva Presencia was a resurgence, or a manifestation of the great painting movement of Mexico. We took ourselves, from the beginning, as part of the movement—which is to say we spoke of accepting the Big Three, but not the succeeding generations. The contradiction was that we wanted to return to the great movement, but we couldn't paint murals. There was no chance. There was no Vasconcelos; no commissions. They were all received by the Mexican School who had friends in the government." Sepúlveda never succeeded in obtaining a mural commission—for the same reasons, perhaps, that he, of all the Nueva Presencia artists (with the exception of Icaza, whose case is special and more due to personal idiosyncrasies than any other reason) did not become financially solvent. It was partially a result of his background, his nonaggressive personality, an inability to deal with the complex, highly competitive demands of a market and a publicity-oriented art world, his failure to acquire an aggressive dealer or someone close to him who would devote energy to advancing his affairs. Since he is not lacking in talent and can be compared favorably with other artists of his own generation, one must consider personal and class-derived characteristics as reasons why membership in Nueva Presencia did not serve in his case, as it did in others, as a stepping-stone to recognition and security.

Leonel Góngora

The two polarities (and obsessions) of Leonel Góngora's art are violence and sex—the former reflecting his experience with *la violencia* in his native Colombia during the forties and fifties,[22] the latter in reaction to the repressiveness of a strict Catholic upbringing. (The other face of Góngora's eroticism is anticlericalism, since he sees the Catholic Church as sex-repressive.) These two types of repression, both social in origin, have been internalized by the artist. His art can be seen on the one hand as a personal exorcism of the forces of sex and violence from his psyche, and on the other as an expression of twin phenomena that invest modern Latin American life. Dealing with his own obsessions in his art, he has become a moralist who erects dark presences and fears in order to reform or destroy them in his own name and that of society. He is passionately political and, at the same time, very personal. He sees no contradiction between the two, disagreeing with the mechanical Marxist attitude that is derogatory toward subjectivism. In this respect, he shares a view close to that of the New Left, with affinities to Herbert Marcuse, who stressed the fact that "psychological categories become political categories to the degree to which the private, individual psyche becomes the more or less willing receptacle of socially desirable and socially necessary aspirations, feelings, drives and satisfactions."[23] In other words, a liberated psyche (and sexuality) are political necessities in the struggle to achieve a nonrepressive existence. Says Góngora: "Sex is a manifestation of intelligence. Violence and sexual repression always go together. For Latin Americans, sexual deformation carries the weight of centuries. We have lived sexually and politically repressed."[24] Though this remark postdates the period with which we are concerned by some ten years, it is evident from Góngora's art of the early sixties that it is one he had held for a considerable time, even if in incipient form. Eroticism, which pervades his art, carries the charge of negating repression of all sorts; for Góngora it is a life-affirming force that effectively counterbalances the destructiveness of violence and Catholic dogma. Woman, therefore, is the fulcrum of his art, the main theme around which all else circulates.

In spite of this, there is an uneasy feeling that arises, like a miasma, from Góngora's artistic treatment of women. His is not the sexuality of free, liberated individuals joyously exploring the sensual possibilities of physical love—an approach implicit in Marcuse and the sexual philosophy of the later sixties. Góngora is obsessed by sex; it has remained a forbidden fruit, surrounded by sinful connotations that he cannot escape and therefore confronts blatantly. He apparently cannot avoid seeing women as tempters, sexual objects, desirable fantasies, or sinful traps. Since virgins (including the saintly) are, in his view, aberrations of nature rather than depositories of virtue, the traditional virgin-or-vamp dichotomy is somewhat rearranged: there are only vamps and sexually fulfilled women, the latter representing the intercession of the virile male— himself. (It is no accident, in my opinion, that many of Góngora's male figures physically resemble him—a variation on the old theme of artist and model given a new political/liberation orientation.) The male is central to most of Góngora's works; the woman is acted upon, either by one of the male characters or by the artist himself. When she acts, she is an aggressor or a threat. In this respect, Góngora perpetuates and applies to his own case a point of view he derived from German expressionism, one of the earliest influences on his art.

I have discussed this aspect in detail not only because it was (and is) a leitmotiv in Góngora's work, but because it was an unusual departure for Mexico, which does not have a history of erotic art. Except for a brief period of symbolism (with Julio Ruelas as a major exponent) there is little in the way of sexually oriented themes. Nudes are not absent; they appear in easel paintings and murals from the nineteenth century on, but they rarely carry the erotic charge of Góngora's women. More often they are historic, like Orozco's Malinche; or metaphoric, like Rivera's

dormant and fertile earth mothers in Chapingo; or symbolic, like Siqueiros' nude torso of liberation in the *New Democracy* mural. Among Góngora's contemporaries, images of women and of nudes (with the exception of those of Corzas) also lack specifically sexual connotations, though sensuality may be suggested negatively. Cuevas' and Icaza's prostitutes are images of decadence, like Orozco's, while Cuevas' *Mireya* and *Sonia* are Magdalenes, products of juvenile fantasizing. His other women are monsters. Belkin idealized his lovers to the point of asexuality; they were more the embodiment of ideas than flesh-and-blood men and women. Coronel, Muñoz, Sepúlveda, and González created working-class types and the poor, in which sex is a gender or a function, while Ortiz's toy-like images do not suggest an interest in eroticism.

The fundamental experiences that established Góngora's themes occurred before he was eighteen. He was born in 1932 in the colonial town of Cartago, Colombia (part of Colombia's banana and coffee economy) to an old family of landowners. He was sixteen when *la violencia* erupted, and Cartago was in the center of it from 1948 until Góngora left the country in 1952. The sights of horror, bloodshed, and torture left an indelible impression on his mind: "I saw people wounded, burned alive, have hands and feet cut off. At my parents' *finca* [farm] in the mountains, dynamite was put under the houses. We lived in constant fear. If I am paranoid, it is because I never knew if I would wake up alive. I was aware of the horrors of World War II and Hiroshima, but Colombian violence was more personal and immediate."

The other aspect of Góngora's Colombian experience also arose from the political situation: Colombia's Conservative president Laureano Gómez (from 1950 to his deposition in 1953) personified the clerical-authoritarian tradition of Franco's Spain. During his dictatorial regime, severe censorship was imposed on all freedoms, including those of press and religion. Góngora remembers Gómez bringing in fascist teachers from Spain and forbidding students to read literature proscribed by the Roman Catholic Index. It was during this time that his anticlerical attitudes took shape and, with them, his strong feelings about the repression of education, thought, and sexuality by the reactionary hierarchy of the Catholic Church. "My satirical works are against all repression," he says. "Art is liberation, psychological and social."

In 1950, Góngora's family moved to the greater safety of the capital, Bogotá, which he left in 1952 to attend the School of Fine Arts of Washington University in St. Louis. His teachers included painters Fred Conway, Walter Barker, and Philip Guston, and printmaker Fred Becker (associated with William Stanley Hayter's Atelier 17). But by far the most important influence came from the extensive Morton D. May collection of German expressionist art, located in St. Louis. It is clear from Góngora's early work that he studied closely the May collection's extensive holdings of paintings by Max Beckmann. Whatever evidences of Grosz or Kokoschka appear in his work over the years, *The Great Shower*, exhibited at the Galería Glantz during his first Mexican showing in October 1961, is characterized by typically Beckmannesque uptilted space divided by zigzag diagonals, interlocking human forms, and a kind of grim gaiety. The scene is set in a brothel where women rest, look in the mirror, or embrace each other while a maid ushers in the first clients—one convulsively clutching his mouth and sexual parts. For Góngora, Beckmann's appeal derived from a shared reaction to violence: in the latter's case, service as a medical orderly during World War I and the consequent humanistic psychosocial direction of his work. Beckmann's reactions to his world, says Bernard S. Myers, were "neither escapist nor occasional; they were a constant and powerful reaction against cruelty, stupidity, and tyranny, sometimes poetic in mood, sometimes brutal, but always filled with psychological meaning and form."[25] One

might say that these were also the aspirations of Leonel Góngora, working in a different time and context. If Beckmann expressed the sharpened disillusionment and despair of the interwar period in Germany, Góngora expressed his feelings about the fascist-type dictatorship and violence of Colombia. There was a certain crudity and verism in his early work that drew some hostile and uneasy criticism from Mexican reviewers of his first show in that country.

Before coming to New York and Mexico, Góngora had spent the years until 1959 in St. Louis, then traveled through Italy with his Sicilian-born artist wife, Vita Giorgi. To his experience of the Hispanic baroque (which pervades Latin America and forms a backdrop of anguished and ecstatic realism to contemporary expressionism) Góngora added the study of Italian early renaissance (Cimabue, Giotto, Mantegna, Crivelli) and baroque art, particularly that of Caravaggio, whom he found the most impressive. He admired Caravaggio because of his realism: when everyone else was doing idealized saints, he says, Caravaggio "put his feet on earth—and his feet were dirty." He considered Caravaggio's realism to be psychological and introverted and esteemed him as an outcast (the recurring Outsider) and for his anguish, which struck a responsive chord. "I have two styles," says Góngora; "in drawing I use the harsh lines of Bellini and Crivelli; in painting the brush stroke, fluidity of light, and color of Caravaggio." Góngora was attracted to the neorealist Italian film-makers (who had also affected Corzas during his Italian stay) and felt his art was tied to both the movies and literature. While in Italy he met the Sicilian-born realist artist Renato Guttuso, as well as Lorenzo Vespignani—both of whom were included in the international neohumanist exhibition in Mexico City in 1963.

After eight years away from Latin America, Góngora felt it was time to return. "I am a Latin. I had to go back to my source which is Latin America, and Mexico was the best," he says. Mexico,

in 1961, offered Góngora the excitement of the
mural movement, many cultural activities, and a
first-hand encounter with Mexico's pre-Columbian art (the influence of which appears in his
painting *Golden Nose Piece*). It was natural for
him to be invited to join Los Interioristas, to
whom he was drawn by both personal and artistic affinities. Highly literate, intelligent, and
articulate, he read Dostoevsky, Sartre, Camus,
Ouspensky, Colin Wilson, the Kama Sutras, the
writings of the Marquis de Sade, and Latin American and Beat poetry. He was the kind of artist
Belkin and Icaza were anxious to have in the
group in order to share the responsibilities and
leadership of Nueva Presencia. Góngora himself
was enthusiastic about the group. "I felt Nueva
Presencia was the most dynamic, perceptive, and
prophetic movement in Mexico during the period. It got together those people who were envi-
sioning larger things. Even the difficulties we
went through, the attacks that attempted to destroy us, built us," he says.

Góngora's works during 1962 were either violent or mocking, like *Man with a Top Hat* (Fig.
90), *Sexton, Man of the Cloth*, and *Fallen Man*,
done in Washington, D.C., during the Cuban
missile crisis and reflecting the tensions of that
period. The brutal application of paint, which reminds one of Karel Appel, and the ferocious expression of the top-hatted man convey an intense
aggressiveness, an almost homicidal quality that
finds its counterpart in the terror-stricken aspect
of *Fallen Man*, who drops back in dread before
some apparition of danger that seems to be descending upon him. Both figures are cadaverous,
but our sympathy is engaged by the "victim."
The two churchly figures, inspired, says
Góngora, by the fact that he was working in a
church converted to a studio, have a sarcastic
and anticlerical intent.

Back in Mexico but under the influence of the
same negative spirit, Góngora did a series of
works after the suicide of a friend that he calls
his "dark paintings" (after Goya's "Black Paint-

90. Leonel Góngora, *Man with a Top Hat*, 1962, oil on
gesso board, 15 × 11 in. (38 × 28 cm.). Collection of
the artist; photo by Bill Burkhart.

ings"?) and that includes the violent *Sacrifice of
a Chicken* (1962), in which a violet-faced woman
holds up a struggling chicken at arm's length.
The *Morgue Drawings*, elicited by the suicide,
are very different in feeling. They almost appear
to be not cadavers, but ghosts of the dead, rising
upward in space. In the drawing of three corpses
(Fig. 91), the two major figures that float together
in a V-shaped composition are sexually distinguished and it is with a start that one realizes
the male figure is clasping his sexual parts as if
death also had its erotic aspects.

Góngora's development as a draftsman, still exhibiting the influence of the German school but

arriving slowly at a personalized style and statement, is apparent in a drawing from 1962, *Aggression* (Fig. 92), which pictures a leaping woman with bared teeth and a sharp weapon ready to strike a crouching and terrified man, a theme that lends itself readily to sexual interpretation. In several works of this period the artist exhibits a certain hostility toward his female subjects, whether it appears in suggested or overt predatory activities, while his drawing of a man (Fig. 93) underscores, like that of *Aggression*, the fragility and vulnerability of the male, who must, in both cases, protect himself. While we may see these works as projections of the violence that permeated Góngora's work in 1962, we might also seek the iconography of *Aggression* on another plane. Appearing during and after the Renaissance with some regularity was the image of a voluptuous woman riding the philosopher Aristotle like a horse. The original intent was didactic: to warn against the temptations and wiles of the female sex, which could overthrow the power of reason and reduce the philosopher to the level of a beast. Once established, numerous variations were played on the original iconography, some political in nature.[26] The imagery was revived in various sadomasochistic Pop art works such as Mel Ramos' kitsch-Pop *Hippopotamus* of the sixties, showing a commercially stylized young nude woman riding a shining eggplant-colored hippo that suggests both the kneeling man of the original imagery and a huge male organ.

The woman-mounted man appears again in a drawing dated August 5, 1963, from the series *Colombia: Middle of the Century* (Fig. 94). The drawing carries the legend "Forty-two men were put to death today and then decapitated in an uninhabited spot near the limits of the departments [provinces] of Tolima and Caldas . . ." A lovely nude woman rides a crouching man; both stare at the bloody, mutilated, headless torso beside them. The reference is obviously to a continuation of *la violencia*, the laconic tone of the legend suggesting it was taken directly from a

91. Leonel Góngora, *Morgue Drawing*, 1962, pen and colored ink, 12 × 8½ in. (30.5 × 21.5 cm.). Collection of the artist; photo by Bill Burkhart.

newspaper story. Does Góngora intend to equate the equestrian woman with political violence? Is she a symbol for the downfall of reason that violence represents? Or is a variant of the sadomasochistic theme being introduced here?

Góngora was still haunted by the scenes of death and mutilation he had witnessed as a child, as is apparent in another drawing of the same series, in which a bloody dead body, with staring eyes and exposed teeth, is spread across the page.

A different aspect of the erotic experience appears in a drawing of the artist-and-model variety (Fig. 95). In Góngora's lexicon of types, male "victims" are usually shown as thin, pitiable, hairless individuals—as though (perhaps sub-

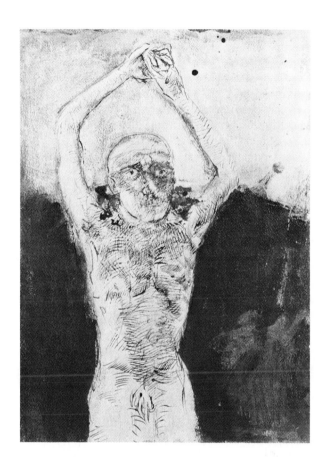

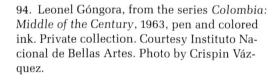

92. Leonel Góngora, *Aggression*, 1962, pen and colored ink, 11¾ × 8⅝ in. (30 × 22 cm.). Collection of the artist; photo by Bill Burkhart.

93. Leonel Góngora, Untitled, 1962, pen and colored ink, 12½ × 9 in. (32 × 23 cm.). Collection of the artist; photo by Bill Burkhart.

94. Leonel Góngora, from the series *Colombia: Middle of the Century*, 1963, pen and colored ink. Private collection. Courtesy Instituto Nacional de Bellas Artes. Photo by Crispin Vázquez.

95. Leonel Góngora, *Artist and Model*, 1963, pen and colored ink, 9⅞ × 7⅞ in. (25 × 20 cm.). Collection of Arnold Belkin; photo by Flor Garduño.

96. Leonel Góngora, from the series *Los brujos* [Male witches], 1963, mixed media, 27 × 22 in. (68.5 × 56 cm.). Private collection. Courtesy Joseph Young. Photo by Crispin Vázquez.

consciously) to put these types at a remove from the artist himself, who is fleshy and mustachioed (in later years, bearded), with a crop of dark curly hair. When the male appears as lover, Góngora shows him as a robust type (himself?) with mustache and beret, who, in this drawing, crouches admiringly at the foot of a bed on which is seated a dark-haired, infantile woman suggestively sucking her fingers like a Lolita. So intense is the man's gaze that he seems to absorb her with his eyes, while his folded hands indicate a restraint against any more direct action. This is perhaps intended to suggest metaphorically that artistic eroticism must be experienced vicariously through the eyes in order to be able to transmute the experience to art. It can also suggest that the

artist "possesses" his model on both visual and actual levels. The theme, of course, is an old one, from Vermeer's clothed model posing for the artist, to Picasso's numberless variations.

Enough has been said in modern feminist literature about the male-centered fantasy that the artist-and-model theme represents to make recapitulation here unnecessary.[27] It is sufficient to note that Góngora does not depart from the traditional relationships. In spite of his anticlericalism, he is too immersed in the Catholic attitudes toward women of baroque (and modern) Italy, Spain, and Latin America, and in the post-symbolist sexual neuroses of the German expressionists, to assign women other than their traditional roles. Whether they appear as sadomasochistic conquerors, as muses for his *brujos* (male witches), or as sex objects, they are simply updated versions of past types.

Góngora's *brujos* series appears to be a variation of the artist/model theme, though with a haunting and mysterious quality not previously present. The artist has described the way in which the *brujos* came into existence:

After a very depressed period in which I came to destroy all my paintings, I thought I wasn't going to paint any more or do anything connected with art. But slowly (it always happens) I started doing one drawing after the other and there was coming out a figure of obsession, an old man with a hat—a big one—that came out of another age. Un duende [a goblin]? un brujo? But this character was always surrounded by the halo of being capable of doing everything—By virtue of his hat or of his tricks? I don't know . . .[28]

Góngora did about fifty drawings in this series, using colored inks, acrylic glazes, and wax to produce an effect "almost like paintings with medieval-modern figures."[29] The *brujo* with his enormous hat-halo (mandala of power?) was drawn with Flemish-Renaissance precision and placed in juxtaposition to a female figure who may be sphinxlike (Fig. 96), loving, an idealized, unattainable illusion of which he dreams, perhaps a muse, or a victim of punishment who submits passively. Like the circus figures of some of Los Interioristas, Góngora's *brujo* seems to be the expression of a wish-fulfillment: the all-powerful magician-artist who dreams, loves, creates, and destroys his muse, and thus achieves control of the world and his own destiny. The desire to bypass material in favor of spiritual, magic, or utopian means of changing the world was not unique to Góngora. It was a major theme of *interiorismo*, whether expressed in *brujos*, earth mothers, magical animals, or birdmen. It is curious that the large "medieval" hat also appears in the work of Cuevas, Corzas, and Rafael Coronel, and, though one could argue, as Cuevas did, that he was being imitated, its roots seem to lie deeper, within a nostalgia for the past when

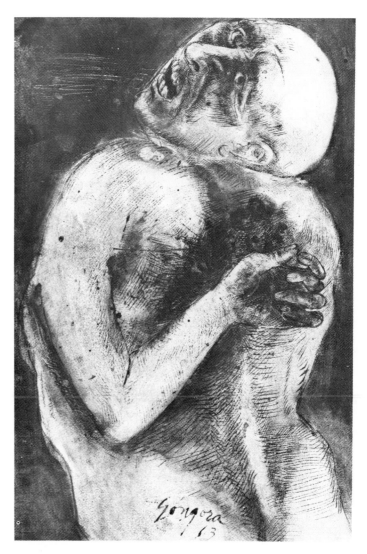

97. Leonel Góngora, from the series *War and Peace*, 1963, pen and ink, 18⅝ × 13⅜ in. (47 × 34 cm.). Private collection. Photo courtesy Instituto Nacional de Bellas Artes.

masculine religious and secular clothing was more extravagant and gave outward expression of an individual's function or position (or power?) in society. The conscious drawing upon the past, from the fifteenth to the nineteenth centuries, was not exclusive to thematic material, but also impregnated the stylistic attributes of *interiorismo*, placing the movement firmly within the romantic tradition, of which Góngora has personally proclaimed himself a part.

Did the terrifying quality of existence in the period of the Cold War and brinksmanship have any effect on the creation of Góngora's *brujos*? We have seen that he translated those terrible days in October 1962, while the events in Cuba were still in progress, directly into paintings. The *brujos* were created in the first few months of 1963. Perhaps it was not as easy to exorcise the fear of world annihilation with images of blood and mutilation as he did later in the year with *Colombia: Middle of the Century*. The possible consequences of the missile crisis boggled the mind. After its initial savage expression in the 1962 paintings, it is possible that the monstrousness of atomic destruction took a subterranean turn and issued forth in the dark and passionate presence of the *duende*. It is hard to say. All that is certain is that the *brujo* series was contemporary with Góngora's drawings for the *War and Peace* portfolios, which are existential statements par excellence. With excruciating body language, Góngora evokes once again the bald, emaciated "victim," who is subjected to tortures from an unseen source (Fig. 97) or crouches down in terror. Naked and vulnerable, these images express the artist's spiritual as well as political torment, and his sense of helplessness as contrasted to the magic power of the *brujos*. Even more than in *Colombia*, these are living bodies that are acted upon with no show of resistance, no clue as to the aggressor. It is the statement of an individual about *interior* torment. How else are we to interpret these naked, contorted bodies in neutral space? Lacking any specificity whatsoever, we must assume the expression of a general malaise, rather than the specifics of war.

The burden of Góngora's "message" must be found in the emotionality and frequently satirical intent of his images, and, though he claims they frequently come after the fact, his pungent titles obviously represent considerable thought and are not (as he claims) simply for identification. The *brujos* have such Goyaesque titles as:

The Final Result Is What Counts
We Are Left to Die
I Do a Bit of Business on Commission
Cases in Which Nothing Can Be Done
I Exorcise You
For the Good of All
*The State of the Situation Was Declared in
    Order to Help Things Return to Normal*
Am I My Brother's Keeper?
We Can Remedy the Evils of the World

In considering the titles, we become aware of a literate artist who gives his philosophy written, and his emotions pictorial, form. His drawings illustrate, in the best sense of the word, the sensibility of an artist who is moral, ironic, and fatalistic, and hovers at times on the fine edge of despair.

Gastón González César

Last of the artists to join Nueva Presencia, González was a newly graduated student from the San Carlos Academy when Nueva Presencia was formed. His first appearances with the group occurred in the "War and Peace" show of August–September 1963 and the September–October 1963 exhibition "Neohumanism in the Drawings of Italy, the United States, and Mexico." Though several Nueva Presencia artists have done sculpture (Belkin, Icaza, and Góngora, for example), González was the only member who worked primarily in this medium. His inclusion in the group, like that of the photographer Nacho López, was doubtless prompted by the desire to include multiple artistic disciplines as well as by the content and style of his work.

Youngest of the artists in Nueva Presencia, González was born in 1940 in San Felipe del Progreso, a small farming village near Toluca, in the state of Mexico at the foot of the mountains leading to Michoacán. Though his father was a doctor, he identified closely with the local farmers,

98. Gastón González César, *Visionaries*, 1959, clay, 15¾ in. (40 cm.) high, 5⅞ in. (15 cm.) wide, 5⅞ (15 cm.) deep. Private collection. Photo courtesy Wenger Collection.

99. Gastón González César, *Maternity*, 1963, Xaltocán stone, 23⅝ in. high, 31½ in. wide, 15¾ in. deep (60 × 80 × 40 cm.). Private collection. Photo courtesy Wenger Collection.

approximately 80 percent of whom were indigenous people. The family moved to the city of Toluca when González was eight years old, but he never forgot the early contact with the country. At fifteen he came to Mexico City and enrolled at San Carlos, studying sculpture with Ignacio Asúnsolo, Jorge Tovar, and Luis Ortiz Monasterio, for whom he worked as a teaching assistant after graduation.

In the early sixties, González worked in a style of simplified realism, treating his figures as organic masses that show the influence of multiple sources. His *Pre-Hispanic Dog* resembles the fa-

mous clay dogs of ancient West Mexican funerary art in its vibrant animation and in the emphasis on the bony structure of spine and ribs, but González has opened up the form to a greater interpenetration of space. The ancient Mexicans did not use metal armatures, and their sculptural composition tended to be more compact than González's free-swinging figure. *Visionaries* (Fig. 98) has a heroic monumentality that is related to outdoor civic sculpture like that of Asúnsolo and Monasterio, but it also quotes the stylizations, rounded forms, ponderous limbs, and clinging draperies of Francisco Zúñiga (Costa Rican-born artist and Mexico's best-known sculptor today) and his students José L. Ruiz and Alberto de la Vega. There is also a strong suggestion of Henry Moore (the most influential European sculptor for several generations of Mexicans) in the abstraction and interplay of concavities and convexities of body and drapery. These formal qualities are also present in *Woman* (ca. 1963, Wenger Collection), and *Maternity* (Fig. 99), though in the latter the emphasis seems more Brancusian. Its reduced volumes are related to the material,

100. Gastón González César, from the series *War and Peace*, 1963, 30 × 40 cm. Private collection. Photo courtesy Instituto Nacional de Bellas Artes.

stone (in contrast to the clay models that González hoped to turn into bronze if a commission were forthcoming), as well as to his admiration for Aztec sculpture, which he found impressive for its monolithic character.

Through the intercession of Monasterio, González had his first experience with monumental civic sculpture when he was only twenty-one, at which time he was commissioned to do a work for the Instituto Mexicano de Seguro Social (IMSS). In 1964 he received another commission for the same institution to do three stone sculptures of colonial doctors, one of which, the thirteen-foot figure of Gregorio López, researcher in

medicinal plants, was intended for the Centro Vocacional of IMSS in Oaxtepec, Morelos. By August 1964 he had also completed a large figure of the colonial priest Fray Bernardino de Sahagún for the Ciudad Industrial of Ciudad Sahagún, Hidalgo, and an eleven-and-one-half-foot *Guadalupe Victoria* for the city of Gómez Jalacio, Durango. These experiences made him an ardent advocate of architectural sculpture. He felt that sculpture, as one of the most ancient expressions of the art of Mexico, should more than ever be related to Mexican architecture. That Mexican sculpture had never achieved the same importance as mural painting was, he felt, the fault not of the sculptors themselves, but of the fact that they were not given the same opportunities as painters.[30] This judgment is only partially true. The real reasons must be sought in some combination of factors like the relative costs of sculpture and architectural painting, and their relative suitability and flexibility in conveying the social-historical-political messages of the revolution. That the "folkloric" charge leveled against Mexican muralism also afflicted sculpture is evident in González's 1965 analysis of the contemporary situation:

It is curious that many sculptors believe they are reviving the "Mexican spirit" when they make little Indians within a folkloric mold. But it is evident that what we have to revive is the cosmic, monumental, titanic spirit, the unifying feeling and the variety of forms that pre-Hispanic sculptures have. . . . In a sense, Zúñiga is our best contemporary sculptor. Aside from the plastic sense which we must call "Mexican" he has such good control of form that he tends to simplify it, to purify it. Unfortunately there still remain many anecdotal bad habits.[31]

González's criticism limited itself to being anti-academic and antifolkloric/nationalistic; he did not postulate a break with the past, but rather a purification of form and, above all, an elimination of "literary," i.e., anecdotal content. Implied, though not stated, was his disassociation from or disinterest in the tendency toward abstraction led by Mathias Goeritz and developed by some of González's contemporaries. Though he criticized young sculptors for not being willing to try new materials or ideas like the painters who, he said, were in a "historical hurry,"[32] he himself, in the early sixties, worked in the traditional materials of stone and bronze and produced figurative images.

Since he joined Nueva Presencia so late, González produced few works in the context of the group, and all of those are drawings. One of the most powerful is from the *War and Peace* series (Fig. 100), and shows the distinct influence of Rico Lebrun, with whom González identified

101. Gastón González César, *Zacharias*, from the series *The Prophets*, 1963, pastel, 29½ × 23⅝ in. (75 × 60 cm.). Private collection. Photo courtesy Instituto Nacional de Bellas Artes.

more than with any other artist from the United States. (As a sculptor, Baskin seems to have left no impression on him.) Though he recognized that his own quest had not reached the level of Lebrun's, he particularly admired the way in which Lebrun "broke up objects in order to reintegrate them in a new way." The sectioned, structural quality of this powerful fallen figure, headless and flayed open by some macabre massacre (which has also left behind a hanged figure whose knees appear to the left), refers us back to Lebrun's *Genesis*, which seems the immediate prototype for González's crablike image. "The figures are deployed," said Lebrun of the *Genesis* mural, "like opening a clam. The figures all have a barrel-like shape to repeat the tremendous curved shape of the arches." [33] The barrel-like shape of the figure, a compositional strategem for Lebrun, was used derivatively by González, as was the dramatic foreshortening, a device possibly borrowed from Siqueiros. A head of the prophet Zacharias (Fig. 101) has a curiously seamed and puckered physiognomy as if psychological wounds had produced exterior scars. González considered that one of the recourses of the artist, in trying to express human affectivity, was to produce an anatomy of internal problems (like that made by an X-ray) on the surface of the body, since the physical elements were the only ones available to the artist—a concept surely derived from *interiorismo*.

Francisco Moreno Capdevila, Benito Messeguer, José Hernández Delgadillo

Three artists, Capdevila, Messeguer, and Delgadillo, who exhibited under the banner of Nueva Presencia in October 1962 (and sporadically on other occasions), were slightly older than most of the other Nueva Presencia artists. All three were practicing or aspiring muralists, a fact that caused considerable disaffection in Nueva Presencia ranks. Two were Catalonian Spaniards. Capdevila, born in 1926 in Barcelona, came to Mexico in 1939, and Messeguer, born in Tarragona in 1927, came in 1943. Delgadillo was born in 1927 in Tepeapulco, Hidalgo, and moved to Mexico City in 1945. Delgadillo studied in the studio of Antonio Navarrete Tejero (1945–1954) and at La Esmeralda (1957). Messeguer also studied at La Esmeralda (in 1946) and was at one time its director. Capdevila studied (in 1946) at the San Carlos Academy, where he has been a professor of printmaking. He also took classes in printmaking at the Escuela de las Artes del Libro and studied privately with engraver Carlos Alvarado Lang.

Francisco Moreno Capdevila

Capdevila's initiation into the art world was as a printmaker, who illustrated many books, pamphlets, magazines, and posters over the years. From 1946 on, he illustrated extensively for the press of the Universidad Nacional Autónoma de México. He began exhibiting publicly in 1953, with a show at the Library of Congress, Washington, D.C., and continued with exhibits in 1954, 1955, and 1959 at the Salón Annual de Grabado in Mexico (sponsored by the Instituto Nacional de Bellas Artes), at two of which he won prizes. He had a second Library of Congress show in 1955. He showed in Yugoslavia (1956), Kamakura, Japan (1957), and Tokyo (1958), and participated in both the 1958 and 1960 Interamerican Biennials in Mexico City, winning a prize at the latter. In 1961, the year of the most intense controversy within the Instituto Nacional de Bellas Artes following the 1960 Biennial, Capdevila's prints were part of the official Mexican exhibit at the São Paulo Biennial (as opposed to the independent show mounted by Salas Anzures). In the same year, he also participated in a show sponsored by the Sociedad Mexicana de Grabadores (of which he had been a member since 1954), the participants in which were congratulated in an official government magazine for persevering in the path of the Mexican School without deviating from its principles or yielding to the demands of art speculators who followed the shortest, most spectacular road. [34] From this brief résumé, one can assume that Capdevila did not join Nueva Presencia in 1962 because he was unknown or needed the support of a collective; rather, this act can be seen as a gesture of identification with and support for artists who were his juniors by three to ten years and who shared, to a certain degree, his dedication to humanistic realism, social concerns, and a continuation of muralist (and Taller de Gráfica Popular) principles. In the range of ages covered by Nueva Presencia, Capdevila, Delgadillo, Messeguer, and

102. Francisco Moreno Capdevila, *Descending into the Valley*, 1954, metal relief in color, 11⅜ × 19⅝ in. (29 × 50 cm.). Collection of the artist. Photo courtesy Instituto Nacional de Bellas Artes.

photographer Nacho López (born in 1924) can be seen as the transitional figures between social realist humanism and neohumanism. Their links with the group, like those of Héctor Xavier and Antonio Rodríguez Luna (the oldest), were tenuous. None exhibited in the United States under the auspices of the group, though the Zora Gallery had been contacted in 1962 concerning Messeguer and Capdevila, and Icaza had written in 1963 announcing the membership of Delgadillo, González, and Xavier, all of whom, he said, would contact the gallery and arrange individual exhibitions.

To view Capdevila's work is immediately to become aware of his close ties in style and spirit to the Mexican School. The etching *Descending into the Valley* (Fig. 102) is a descriptive, pastoral scene. The dark horsemen are dramatically silhouetted against the distant vista of fields, mountains, and sky as dawn breaks. The strong contrasts of dark and light, the panoramic landscape, and the foreshortening are reminiscent of Leopoldo Méndez (though the feeling is more serene). Capdevila's use of etching and engraving in this period represented, in a large way, a deliberate political and artistic choice on his part— one of which he was very conscious. With some

exceptions, *grabado* (often used as the term for all graphic techniques) at the Taller de Gráfica Popular was limited to blockprints (most often linoleum) and lithography, media that would permit the largest number of prints to be pulled for the widest possible dissemination. Méndez, for example, worked exclusively with relief and lithography techniques. Etching, at the Taller, had been considered an unsuitable technique in a period when artists were not concerned with formal subtlety or the market requisites of limited editions. Intaglio was not wholly absent, but etching, aquatint, and drypoint did not come into their own until the fifties, or perhaps even later. When they did, the Mexican art market followed that of the United States, whose print market was an expanding one designed to draw the middle class and even the upper working class into art consumption, from which they had previously been excluded by cost. At mid-century in Mexico, the polarities between "people's art" and "middle-class art" were expressed by the Taller de Gráfica Popular, on the one hand, and the younger artists who were turning to etching, on the other. In 1974, speaking retrospectively, Capdevila summed up the situation as follows: "More people are making prints. A special inter-

103. Francisco Moreno Capdevila, *Self-Portrait*,
1960, oil on canvas, 15¾ × 11¾ in. (40 × 30 cm.).
Collection of the artist. Photo courtesy Instituto
Nacional de Bellas Artes.

est in print-making has arisen among practically
all the painters. The technical criterion has also
changed. Metal engraving, considered aristocratic until some years back, is profusely used
today. There is also beginning to be an interest in
lithography, though I don't know if the possibility of good reproduction exists here . . . Metal
engraving, particularly, is a technique of the
widest possibilities."[35] At the same time, Capdevila noted that art in Mexico had lost the possibility of saying anything. Artists, he said, had
entered into a type of "mutism" (*mutismo*) in
which it had become a matter of preference not
to express oneself clearly—a preference that he
did not share.

Capdevila's monumentality and sense of geometric structure is apparent in his *Self-Portrait*
(Fig. 103). The narrowed eyes in their large, geometrical, deeply shadowed eye sockets framed
by the structure of the cheek bones and forehead
seem almost hypnotic and lend a mysterious

quality to what otherwise would have been a
strongly painted but straightforward portrait.
This psychological (or mystical) dimension, superimposed on the framework of social realist
style and concern, make clear Capdevila's affinities with Nueva Presencia. On another plane,
his painting *Boots* (Fig. 104), while strongly indebted to Orozco and Siqueiros, places just sufficient emphasis on the large calligraphic brushstrokes to disintegrate the figurative objects into
an active abstraction. The skein of lines that form
an all-over pattern in shallow space look like a
particularly vigorous Mark Tobey painting and
have all the emotionalism and energy of abstract
expressionism. At the same time, they do not
lose their identity as boots, and the spurlike
strokes with which they are painted carry the
implications of machines, gears, perhaps even
barbed wire.

In 1961 and 1962, Capdevila did a group of
paintings based on faceless, robed figures that reflect a sense of desolation. *Tragedy* (Fig. 105) is
set in an ambiguous background, and the two
weeping figures seem carved of the same kind of
rock that makes up the landscape. The repetitive,
serried figures, the Biblical quality (that could
also apply to modern events), the stonelike rigid-
ity of this painting are very similar to that of *The
Exiles* (1961), whose row of masklike faces seems
to suggest a contact with African art. *The Exiles*
and *Exodus* (1961), in which a triangular wedge
of people is set in a barren landscape beneath a
stormy, threatening sky, both treat a subject that
has appeared repeatedly in the work of Spanish
painters in Mexico. More than thirty years after
his arrival in Mexico, for example, Rodríguez
Luna has continued to paint variations on the
"exodus" theme. Unlike Luna, Capdevila was
only thirteen when he left Spain for France and
then Mexico; nevertheless, the cataclysmic quality of the Spanish Civil War and the flood of refugees that left during the fighting and after the
defeat of the Republicans left their imprint on
his life. *The Exiles* and *Exodus* were responsive

104. Francisco Moreno Capdevila, *Boots*, 1961, acrylic
on canvas, 23⅝ × 49¼ in. (60 × 125 cm.). Collection
of the artist. Photo courtesy Instituto Nacional de
Bellas Artes.

105. Francisco Moreno Capdevila, *Tragedy* (or
Desolation), 1962, acrylic on canvas, 33⅞ × 22 in.
(86 × 56 cm.). Collection of the artist. Photo
courtesy Instituto Nacional de Bellas Artes.

to a historical event, but their tragic feeling carried over into much of Capdevila's work in the early sixties, whether he evoked lonely existential figures or recreated the fall of the Aztec capital in the mural *The Destruction of Tenochtitlan by the Spanish Invaders* (Fig. 109). One could read *Light* (Fig. 106) as another formulation of the refugee theme. Its most obvious reference is the Biblical one of Lazarus emerging from the tomb, but it is significant that the traditional iconography has been bypassed to exclude the figure of Christ and the emphasis on the miraculous. Capdevila focuses on the solitary figure emerging from the tomb, from darkness into light, freeing himself from his restraints (the wrappings of the shroud) as he goes. By changing the iconography he makes it possible to interpret the figure in new, nonhierarchical ways: as the refugee who escapes from the tyranny of the Spanish dictatorship; or more broadly and cogently, as an individual who, by his own efforts, frees himself from restraint and achieves per-

106. Francisco Moreno Capdevila, *Light*, 1961, acrylic on wood, 40⅛ × 23⅝ in. (102 × 60 cm.). Collection of Lic. Joaquin Lluhi. Photo courtesy Instituto Nacional de Bellas Artes.

107. Francisco Moreno Capdevila, *Genesis*, 1961, acrylic on canvas, 48 × 31½ in. (122 × 80 cm.). Collection of the artist. Photo courtesy Instituto Nacional de Bellas Artes.

sonal liberation; or as Lazarus, who attains his own resurrection without external aid. Resurrection accomplished, the liberated individual stands forth in *Genesis* (Fig. 107); birth and resurrection have become one. Capdevila's *Genesis* and Belkin's *Resurrection* both find their prototypes in Orozco's *Man of Fire*.

In spite of these similarities, which formed the bridge between Capdevila and *interiorismo*, his social orientation aligned him more closely to his social realist roots, and expressed itself in his art more completely than in that of any of the origi-

108. Francisco Moreno Capdevila, *Demonstration*,
1960, oil on canvas, 39⅜ × 49¼ in. (100 × 125 cm.).
Private collection. Photo courtesy Instituto Nacional
de Bellas Artes.

nal Interioristas. Paintings like *Demonstration*
(Fig. 108) are specific and political in nature. The
flags in the distance in *Demonstration* dispel
any notion that this is an elemental surge of unknown forces; the clothing (as against the nude
figures of existentialism) suggests working people; the thrust of the forms, the clenched fists,
and the open demanding hands make it obvious
that this is a mass demonstration of workers with
a sense of purpose to which the artist is sympathetic. This painting shows Capdevila's style at
its loosest, in which the lessons of paint application learned from abstract expressionism have
been integrated into the realist tradition.

*The Destruction of Tenochtitlan by the Span-
ish Invaders* (Fig. 109) was Capdevila's first mural, painted in 1964 in the Museo de la Ciudad de
México. The mural is a wedding of old and new.
The theme had been treated as early as 1923 at
the Escuela Nacional Preparatoria by Jean Charlot. The fact that it is specific and historical
places the mural within the framework of the
Mexican School. On the other hand, there are
elements and overtones of personal tragedy and

109. Francisco Moreno Capdevila, *The Destruction of Tenochtitlan by the Spanish Invaders*, 1964, acrylic on aluminum, 11½ × 32¾ ft. (3.5 × 10 m.). Museo de la Ciudad de México, Mexico City. Courtesy of the artist.

grandeur that associate it with Orozco's more metaphysical statements and with the contemporary existential bias that claimed to base itself on Orozco but actually represented a new deviation.

The theme of the mural concerns the final destruction by fire of Tenochtitlan, capital of the Aztec empire, in 1521—a year after Cortés had been humiliatingly driven out with great loss of life. Compositionally, the mural is framed by the image (at left) of Quetzalcoatl (whose predicted return to earth was confused by the Aztecs with the appearance of Cortés) surmounting two symbolic feathered serpents and that (at right) of the Spaniards, whose mounted horsemen cut down the Indians in a burst of flame. Quetzalcoatl gestures toward the destruction as if he had predicted it, and his prophecy connects metaphorically with the apocalyptic, Orozco-like Spanish horsemen. In the center of the curved mural are the defeated Aztecs, before whom advances the figure of Cuauhtemoc (last of the Aztec emperors); behind him is an image of Coatlicue, Aztec goddess of birth and destruction. In back of the entire scene, which appears to take place in the Tlatelolco marketplace, stretches a topographical view of the city with its temple-pyramids and canals—a view almost exactly like

that of Diego Rivera's mural *Great Tenochtitlan* in the Palacio Nacional.

Unlike Rivera, who maintained historical consistency in his murals, Capdevila plays out the drama/tragedy with the Spaniards dressed in armor but the Aztecs as nude figures; even Cuauhtemoc lacks the elaborate garb of the historical emperors. His figure has been taken from that of the painting *Genesis*, perhaps with the suggestion that the destruction of Tenochtitlan presaged the birth of a new people: the *mestizos*. Symbolically, the nudity of the Indians identifies them not just as victims of the Spaniards, but as eternal victims, giving the theme a contemporary application: the destruction of Tenochtitlan could be that of any city; the flames could be considered those of Guernica or Hiroshima, the victims those of World War II or a future atomic holocaust. It is the nudity that makes Capdevila's transpositions from Biblical, to Aztec, to modern times possible—even imperative. Clothed in historical dress, the characters would remain narratively fixed in historical time, although metaphorically symbolic of human potential. Capdevila tugs at these limitations in order to make a more universal statement, but is restricted by his historical theme and the specific references to

Tenochtitlan. Because he re-creates the city, the temples, the gods, and the Spaniards in armor, it is more difficult to disengage the Aztecs as universal victims, and a dichotomy is created. Thus there is an ambiguity and ambivalence in his statement: it attempts to be historical and ahistorical at the same time. It attempts to establish the victimization of the Aztecs and the heroism of Cuauhtemoc as human constants.

Capdevila attempted the type of wedding between the concrete and the metaphysical that characterized Orozco's murals. He was only partially successful, perhaps because Orozco expressed his philosophy with the help of such synchronic symbols as Prometheus and Christ and did not generally address the naked and unadorned "human condition" as eternal and unchanging. (To the degree that he did, perhaps even Orozco's symbols will cease to be "universal," or will become less so. For example, how long will the *femme fatale* as a symbol of corruption, or the Nietzschean Superman as a symbol of human potential, remain valid?)

In summary, it can be seen that Capdevila's work represents a mediation of artistic currents in the years 1955–1965 or, as it has been called, a "vital duality" between the Mexican School and the new currents of neohumanism and surrealism that have dominated figurative painting in the contemporary era.

Benito Messeguer

Benito Messeguer's changes and inflections of style over a period of about ten years were so varied as to be almost eclectic. His three-quarter portrait of a woman (Fig. 110) is almost classically baroque, in the tradition of Velázquez—even going so far as to include in the upper portion of the painting a small wall opening which leads into another area of space. This typical device from Velázquez is Mexicanized by the inclusion of toy animals and pottery—artifacts that the artist had long collected. Messeguer did not leave Spain until he was sixteen. He had the op-

110. Benito Messeguer, *Portrait of Licha*, ca. 1956, oil on canvas, 27½ × 21⅝ in. (70 × 55 cm.). Collection of the artist. Photo courtesy Instituto Nacional de Bellas Artes.

portunity to study painting in Barcelona with Enrique Assad, and also to see the rich, fluid architecture of Antonio Gaudi—an encounter that possibly contributed to his predilection for organic form and his feeling that an excess of rationality is detrimental to the human personality.

Messeguer's early paintings, like *Everyone's Bus* (Fig. 111) and *Musicians*, are anecdotal in the *riverista* tradition, though their plastic definition seems to owe a debt to Julio Castellanos. The painting *Ragpickers* (1957) shows a developed social conscience in the clear contrast between the modern illuminated downtown area of Mexico City, the implicit imperialism of a Coca-Cola sign (Coca-Cola being the ironic symbol par excellence of United States penetration in under-

111. Benito Messeguer, *Everyone's Bus*, 1956, oil on canvas, 26¾ × 34⅝ in. (68 × 88 cm.). Collection of the Instituto Nacional de Bellas Artes. Photo courtesy Instituto Nacional de Bellas Artes.

developed countries) and the shadowy existence of the ragpickers. *Fossils* (Fig. 112), exhibited at the Club de Periodistas Nueva Presencia show in 1962, pictures a terrifying beast with human characteristics sucking a group of humans into its maw. The geometric superstructure of the body and the plunging position are suggestive of pre-Columbian sculpture, but the head is out of a nightmare. Perhaps it was to this aspect of his work that the artist was referring when he said: "Sometimes I have part of an idea and later other things come forth as I am creating. I do not negate the subconscious; not everything is consciously thought out."

Very early on, Messeguer was interested in muralism, which he considers very vital and one of the most important art forms of the twentieth century. As a student at La Esmeralda he had received scholarships for mural study from the Instituto Nacional de Bellas Artes and the Taller

de Integración Plástica. In 1961, he painted his first mural, *Man as Creator*, in the Hotel Casino de la Selva in Cuernavaca. This was followed in 1963 by a mural in two sections called *Human Creation and the Economy* at the Escuela de Economía of the Universidad Nacional Autónoma de México. In 1964–1967, Messeguer did a spatially complex mural with unorthodox materials and with sound that he called *The Eyes and Ears of Man* in the Instituto Mexicano de Audición y el Lenguaje.

The location of the 1963 mural presented difficult problems of plastic unification between two sections that were opposite each other. The left side of the mural begins with a nebula that signifies original chaos. The Venus of Willendorf and images from the earliest cave paintings symbolize primitive food gathering and the creation of art. All this is developed within a dynamic feeling that points to the future, to the formation of the new man who initiates historical development. The right panel (Fig. 113) harmonizes with the other. From a tragic and sordid world in which appear signs of ignominy but also those of redemption, one passes to the multiform man as a being of infinite possibilities. He surges forth from two gigantic hands, luminous and potent, in order to create all the beneficial arts. The allegory culminates in a man who, with a decided attitude, marches toward the future in order to give new directions to history.[36] It is evident that the style (Orozcoesque) and the theme (a linear progression) make no great departure from ideas that have already been discussed at length in different contexts. Like Capdevila, Messeguer both continued and broke with traditional muralism by discarding a primarily narrative and historical approach, by utilizing metaphor without abandoning figurative expressionism, and by empha-

112. Benito Messeguer, *Fossils*, ca. 1961, oil on canvas, 55⅛ × 42½ in. (140 × 108 cm.). Private collection. Photo courtesy Instituto Nacional de Bellas Artes.

113. Benito Messeguer, *Human Creation and the Economy*, right panel, 1963, acrylic on asbestos cement, 9⅞ × 44¼ ft. (3 × 13.5 m.). Narciso Bassols Auditorium, Escuela de Economía, Universidad Nacional Autónoma de México, Mexico City. Courtesy of the artist; photo by Crispin Vázquez.

sizing plastic values that can be seen as abstract configurations of paint—a debt he owes to abstract expressionism. The luminous areas function as painterly compositions (sometimes at the expense of clarity); the "gesture" takes on an expressive meaning in its own right, independent of symbolism. This is why one viewer commented that the use of light had passed beyond a simple optical function and become a determining thematic factor; it represented the struggle of human culture against obscurantism and regression.[37]

José Hernández Delgadillo

While Capdevila's development toward monumentality was progressive (i.e., in stages from prints to easel paintings to murals) and dictated by his need to expand the terrain of statement, José Hernández Delgadillo seems to have been oriented toward the monumental from the beginning. Born the son of a poor farmer, he earned his living early at a variety of occupations, from farming and road construction to clerking in a grocery store. He had always shown artistic talent but received his first art training only when he came to Mexico City at age eighteen. He earned his living with commissioned portraits; however, at one point he was forced to return to his native village, where he worked as an artisan making wooden furniture until he could return to the capital and continue his artistic studies. The combination in Delgadillo's life of three factors— the experience of poverty and hard labor, the opportunity to receive an education as a child at the Escuela Normal in Tlaxcala, and some initial help in establishing his artistic career—enabled him to proceed with decision toward his goals without some of the terrible handicaps that Sepúlveda (who came from a similar background) had to overcome.

Delgadillo had his first one-person show in 1954 at the Galería López in Mexico City and received his first mural commission for the fresco *Indigenous Education* (done in the style of the

114. José Hernández Delgadillo, *Hiroshima*, 1961, acrylic on canvas, 60¼ × 48 in. (153 × 122 cm.). Private collection. Photo courtesy Instituto Nacional de Bellas Artes.

Mexican School) at the Escuela Belisario Domínguez in Mexico City in 1957. In 1959 he was commissioned to do a series of symbolic figures and a sculptural group in high relief (also in the Mexican School style) for the Ciudad Deportiva; and in 1960 he did a series of temporary concrete panel murals for the Pavilion of the City of Mexico at the VII Mexican Book Fair. The same year he received an honorable mention for his painting *My Time* at the Interamerican Biennial of Mexico; and in 1961, for his painting *Men*, a prize at the II Biennial for Young Artists in Paris, accompanied by a five-month scholarship to study in France.

As in the case of Capdevila and Messeguer, this history of "establishment" acceptance and/ or mural activity was anathema to certain mem-

bers of Nueva Presencia. Though Delgadillo did
not exhibit with the group until September 1963,
his expected participation doubtless added more
fuel to the fire that caused Ortiz and Corzas to
indicate that they intended to leave the group.

Two works on the theme of Hiroshima, though
still retaining the monumental and sculptural aspects of his earlier work, show a new symbolic,
poetic quality. *Hiroshima III* (1960) was perhaps
influenced by a Galería Misrachi show of African
and Mexican masks. *Hiroshima* (Fig. 114) of the
following year is a large, symbolic figure in shadow, forming an elliptical curve against brilliant
light, perhaps intended to suggest an atomic
explosion. The figure itself, solidly sculptural,
turns a frightened, furrowed face to the viewer.
Similarly, in Delgadillo's later series of paintings
*Memory of Auschwitz, Atomic Rain, Atomic
Era,* and *Vietnam,* one or two anguished or mutilated figures carry the burden of expression
whose historical or political connotation is explicit only in the title. In other words, the images
are primarily emotive and affective; they reflect
not the real happenings of the forties, but the
apprehensions of the fifties and sixties—the in-
calculable possibilities of the Cold War. Another
1961 painting, *Men* (Fig. 115) has two figures, one
with a rigid, masklike face, and both submerged
in atmospheric fog; the more solidly constructed
one on the right contrasts with the dark, skeletal
figure on the left like symbols of day and night or
life and death. This poetic and evocative quality
follows in the tradition of Ricardo Martínez, who
immerses his monumental figures in a penum-
bra that gives them a highly suggestive, ghostly
appearance.

At times Delgadillo varied his washes of paint
with a textural impasto as in *Three Figures* (Fig.
116), which is not lyrical or mysterious but conveys agony and strain. The emaciated bodies,
arms stretched upward as if hung in this position, introduce the "victim" common to *interiorismo.* The impasto suggests the external
corroded surface expressive of inner pain.

115. José Hernández Delgadillo, *Men,* 1961, acrylic on
canvas, 78¾ × 55⅛ in. (200 × 140 cm.). Collection of
the Museo de Arte Moderno, Mexico City. Photo courtesy Instituto Nacional de Bellas Artes.

In 1963 Delgadillo was invited to participate in
the *War and Peace* series, and his drawings included *War* (Fig. 117), in which war is shown as
a kneeling figure scattering skulls in all directions. The solid, muscular body of the figure and
the broad, square head with exposed teeth suggest a living person with the head of a *calavera*
that might have been drawn from Aztec sculpture. The victims of war are depicted in another
drawing of truncated limbs and fleshless heads

116. José Hernández Delgadillo, *Three Figures*, 1962, acetate on canvas, 47¼ × 61 in. (120 × 155 cm.). Collection of Dr. Mario González Ulloa. Photo courtesy Instituto Nacional de Bellas Artes.

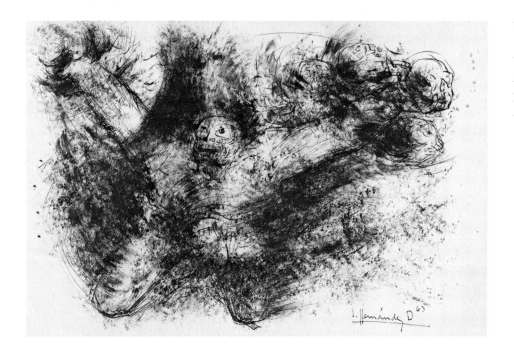

117. José Hernández Delgadillo, *War*, from the series *War and Peace*, 1963, ink and color, 12⅝ × 19¼ in. (32 × 49 cm.). Private collection. Photo courtesy Instituto Nacional de Bellas Artes.

from which one arm thrusts out in a gesture of pleading. In both drawings the artist has substituted feathery and speckled brushstrokes for the impasto texture of his paintings.

The changes that took place in Delgadillo's work from 1960 to 1961 (approximately) signaled a change in his outlook that seemed to be occurring generally among younger artists and was perceptively summarized by the critic Jorge J. Crespo de la Serna, who knew him well and followed his career for an extended period of time. The paintings of Hernández Delgadillo, he wrote in 1962, are the true outpouring of the problems of humanity. They signify a search for an expression that is constantly more subjective. It is surprising that an artist of so cheerful and apparently unapprehensive a personality reflects the kind of preoccupations and anxieties that appear in his latest works. Crespo de la Serna noted that Delgadillo's drawings were very robust but not lacking a hidden meaning. Within the framework of the famous Interioristas' vernacular, he felt Delgadillo was one of the strongest artists.[38] What can we deduce from this statement? Perhaps that some ineluctable pressure, subtle but imperative, was forcing Delgadillo in a direction not wholly compatible with his personality and predilections. His penchant was for monumental muralism and sculpture and, as Margarita Nelken pointed out, he had come to grips with the architectonic exigencies of large-scale painting and sculpture. Even in his smallest works, she said, these factors were determinants of his feeling for form.[39] With the opportunity for muralism and public sculpture diminishing, Delgadillo, who would probably have been a successful follower of the Mexican School under other circumstances, was frustrated in goals that were basically sympathetic to his nature. Easel painting, the private art market, and the gallery system had superseded public muralism; Delgadillo was forced into this world to continue as a creative artist, and he adopted the vocabulary and philosophy of *interiorismo* in his search for an expression more compatible with easel painting. Necessarily this expression, though still monumental, was increasingly subjective. It is clear, in comparing him with Capdevila, that he was not tragic by nature, and the tension produced by such contradictions was apparent in his paintings. Justino Fernández, commenting sympathetically on this fact, stated that Delgadillo's works exhibited a sense of monumentality and classicism, combined with personal expressionism. What appeared to be a contradiction in terms, he said, was not one, because Delgadillo had successfully synthesized the two currents—the classicism was manifest in the intellectualism of his forms and the clear presentation of his theme, and the expressionism in the emotionality and the sensuality of his color and texture.[40]

Ignacio (Nacho) López, Héctor Xavier, Antonio Rodríguez Luna

A photographer, a draftsman, and a painter made up the contingent of older artists who, at varied times and for supportive reasons, exhibited with Los Interioristas/Nueva Presencia. They do not complete the total roster of artists who were associated with Nueva Presencia, which also included Javier Arévalo, Michael Spafford, Alfredo Falfán, Jorge Alzaga, Felipe-Saúl Peña, José Manuel Schmill, Vlady, Roberto Donis, and Fanny Rabel; however, I have chosen those artists who were associated with the group over an extended period of time, or whose philosophies and/or styles were influential. In differing ways, this is true of López, Xavier, and Luna. All three exhibited with the group in 1961 when they were still known as Los Interioristas. Xavier became a "member." López had a close relationship with Belkin, while Luna served as a mentor to Icaza.

Ignacio (Nacho) López
Nacho López, born in 1924, is recognized today as one of Mexico's outstanding photographers.

He has also made several films, and considers the most important one to be the unfinished *In a Part of the World*, a history of the Cuban Revolution that he made in 1959–1960 at the invitation of the Cuban government and that was produced by Emilio Azcaraga Milmo. Money ran out, and the music and narration were never completed.

López's interest in photography started in adolescence, when he was living in Mérida, Yucatán, and received a camera as a gift. When his family moved to Mexico City in 1944, he applied (without success) for a position as a movie camera assistant at the Sindicato de Cinematográficos. Turning to magazines, he worked as a reporter and photographer for the movie magazine *Novelas de la Pantalla* and the magazine *Así*. From 1945 to 1947 he was an assistant to *Life* photographer Victor de Palma, who had settled in Mexico. López learned everything he could absorb from Palma, while simultaneously taking classes in the Instituto de Artes y Ciencias Cinematográficas de México, where he studied under Manuel Alvarez Bravo (the dean of Mexican photographers), Ricardo Razetti, Alejandro Galindo, Xavier Villaurrutia, and Francisco Monterde. Palma and Alvarez Bravo represent the two poles of his photographic aesthetic. Though Alvarez Bravo's influence is clearly evident in López's work—particularly in its more surreal aspects— it is primarily to Palma that he owes his technique and aesthetic training (as well as his contact with *Life* photographers Elliott Elisofon and Peter Stackpole). From Palma he learned composition, illumination, contrast, texture, and, just as important, how to look for good subjects. López himself says, "Palma taught me everything. I had great respect for him. I watched him: his technique, how he treated people. He gave me his photos to develop and showed me how that affected the result."

The years 1955–1960 were intensely active ones in which López established the body of still photography to which he now refers as his "classics." These works were created by the use of fine, sensitive lenses and natural light—never the frightening surprise of flashbulbs. They have been exhibited repeatedly, many appearing as parts of series at one-person exhibitions, first at the Salón de la Plástica Mexicana in November 1955 (with the sponsorship of Manuel Alvarez Bravo) and then at the Pan American Union the following year. On the latter occasion, José Gómez-Sicre wrote, "Although he employs a different medium, one which always retains the intrinsic values of photography as an art, quite independent of pictorial qualities, he nevertheless pursues substantially the same aim as his fellow countrymen José Guadalupe Posada, in engravings, José Clemente Orozco, in murals, and José Luis Cuevas, in drawings."[41] That aim was to express the life of Mexico's "lower depths" (as Gómez-Sicre phrased it) in a way that was not purely formal. According to Alvarez Bravo, "The imperious necessity of saying, of expressing something in photography, provides Nacho with the indispensable basis for what theoreticians call content, or in other words, it makes him conscious of the fact that the photograph, in the hands of a thinking person using more or less exact tools, is a language and he has felt the responsibility for what it says."[42] Since the distinction between a press and a "fine art" photographer (the distinction between artisan and artist) was of importance in the gallery world, Alvarez Bravo pointed out that López "treats his photographs not as mere items for mass reproduction but as objects which can be admired for their intrinsic qualities as finished works of photography, for the harmony of their tonal values, for their spatial composition, for the subject matter or lack thereof, and for the human reactions captured."[43] In spite of this, it must be pointed out that in the mid-fifties, photographs were not a viable gallery commodity; they lacked the uniqueness of a painting, a drawing, or even a print, and were uninteresting to private galleries because the selling price, and consequently the commission, was modest.[44] Thus the major ex-

118. Nacho López, *Responsum*, 1953, from the series *Death is a Siesta*, photograph, 13¾ × 10⅝ in. (35 × 27 cm.). Courtesy of the artist.

hibitors of photographers were generally institutional, and photographers like López earned their living in other ways. López himself recognizes the position of the photographer vis-à-vis the gallery world. "Much of my work," he says, "is prepared for the printed page, for reportage. Photographs don't sell; there is no diffusion [through galleries]." In this sense, the function and usage of the photograph can be compared to that of the public mural or, even more appropriately, to the political print produced in large editions for the widest dissemination. Paradoxically, a socially conscious artist like López found his avenues of dissemination primarily in the privately owned commercial magazines of Mexico and the United States, thus duplicating the phe-

Bravo and good friend of muralist José Chávez Morado, could say about his work, "My intention in photography—within my limitations—is to say something, to testify, to comment, using my technique and my eye honestly. I believe that such terms as 'humanist realism,' 'neo-humanism,' 'social realism,' 'sociological document' are highly pertinent to photography."[46] To stretch an analogy, we might say that a socially conscious journalistic photographer like Nacho López is a latter-day evocation of José Guadalupe Posada: an expressionistic-realist artist functioning in a sociopolitical context under the pressures of press deadlines and the need for relevancy. "I always thought photography could help resolve human problems and serve to denounce injustices," says López. With this as a philosophy, it is not strange that López was directly attracted by United States photography of the 1930s. "I think the great photography movement of the United States was that of the Photographic Unit of the Farm Security Administration. I feel related to it," he says. López also read the authors who were the influential voices of protest of the period: Sinclair Lewis, John Dos Passos, and Upton Sinclair. The Mexican artist who most affected him and whose subject matter and form were the principal influences on his work was Orozco— particularly his Escuela Nacional Preparatoria murals and his easel paintings and drawings. Despite the fact that he shared this aesthetic with Nueva Presencia, López also feels that the photographer is obliged to deal with the class struggle between the poor, middle, and aristocratic classes. He sees the human being as the entity in which these contradictions manifest themselves, and therefore the human being is his major subject. In the sixties, he found himself in disagreement with many artists who proclaimed the universality of art and forgot the class struggle; they were, he felt, not interested in what art is, or should be, but only in its production. Thus when he was invited to exhibit with Los Interioristas in 1961, he found sufficient commonality with their

aims and their manifesto to temporarily join their ranks.

López's themes and concerns were fully coalesced by the time of his show at the Pan American Union in 1956—two years after that of Cuevas. Titles of the ten series exhibited at that time, as translated from the Spanish by the Pan American Union, indicate the broad categories into which his artistic interests could be divided: (1) *Fiesta*, (2) *Proportion in Motion*, (3) *Once upon a Time . . .* , (4) *Hell Is for the Poor* (originally titled *Only the Poor Go to Hell*), (5) *Presence of the Unseen* (originally *The Sacred and the Magical*), (6) *Death Is a Siesta*, (7) *Windows on Life*, (8) *The Magic of the Commonplace* (originally *The Flavor of Simple Things*), (9) *The Shadow of Toil* (originally *Work without Dreams*), and (10) *Counterpoint*. Many of the photographs showed the life of the *Lumpen*, or the hard conditions in which people lived in the poor *barrios* (neighborhoods) of the city or in the country. The exhibit appeared a year after the attacks on Oscar Lewis, and a group of Mexican journalists created a scandal, saying López was exhibiting Mexico's "dirty linen." The Mexican representative to the Organization of American States was dismissed because he had inaugurated the exhibit. Like Lewis' books, López's exhibit exposed an aspect of Mexican life that President Adolfo Ruiz Cortines preferred to hide, since Mexico was in a period of great industrialization and modernization and he did not want this kind of image made public.

The unposed, narrative quality of López's work is apparent even in a solemn subject like *Responsum* (Fig. 118) from the series *Death Is a Siesta*. López works wholly in black and white (as part of his aesthetic), with strong value contrasts and dramatic composition. We are at no time invited to become either sentimental or metaphysical about death: the emphasis is on the reaction and emotion of the living and the ritual implements (candles, flowers) with which death is celebrated. Each of López's photographs is ac-

119. Nacho López, *Totoloque*, 1953, from the series *Work without Dreams*, photograph, 10⅝ × 13¾ in. (27 × 35 cm.). Courtesy of the artist.

tive; it is part of a process; a microcosm caught by the lens in a fraction of a second from the continuum of movement that comprises life. Unlike Alvarez Bravo, López does not, generally speaking, invite us to contemplation of the given. We have to supply what follows and what went before, and the significance of what is before us, as well as its context. In another, rather wry photograph of the same series, two prisoners in striped suits carry a decorated coffin through the barred gate of a jail. One of their comrades will finally attain his liberty through the release of death. The two men are not particularly sad and seem more concerned with the task of carry-

ing the coffin than the eventual purpose of their activities.

Totoloque (Fig. 119), from the series *Work without Dreams*, capitalizes on the circular rhythms of sombreros and tortillas seen from above as workers gather around an improvised grill for a "lunch break" in a rural area. The title refers to an ancient Indian game of quoits, and inferentially draws a parallel between the discus and the tortilla, both of which predate the Spanish conquest.

López's social realist vision is apparent in the contrast between rich and poor of *Supermarket* (Fig. 120). Though it is becoming increasingly

120. Nacho López, *Supermarket*, 1961, photograph, 8⅝ × 6¼ in. (22 × 16 cm.). Courtesy of the artist.

rare as the Mexican upper and middle classes adopt the more "democratic" ways of their United States counterparts, it is still possible today to see the *señora* of an upper-class family in the streets on the way to market followed by an aproned servant—usually Indian—who will carry back the purchases. It is not the *existence* of servants that offers the contrast (though they are still far more available to the middle class than is true in the United States and Europe; many upper-class families have three or more live-in servants), but their unliberated subservience, which conveys a feudal odor. The racial and attitudinal distinctions between the two women, as well as their dress, emphasize the separate qualities of their status. *Zapatistas* (Fig.

121), from the series *Windows on Life*, has a far different atmosphere. It was probably accidental that López photographed these former revolutionaries in a linear progression so reminiscent of Orozco's well-known 1931 painting *Zapatistas* (Museum of Modern Art, New York), but the coincidence could not have escaped his notice for long and is perhaps demonstrated by the fact that he chose the same title. There is a slight irony in comparing these middle-aged and old men lined up in a military manner, displaying their medals, with the relentless forward surge of sombreroed infantry, *soldaderas*, and mounted leaders of the Orozco painting. Yet there is no condescension; the same humble, anonymous peasants were capable of a revolution, and the memory of their participation in earth-shaking events is reflected in their proud faces half a century later. The spirit of the revolution might have ended for the bourgeoisie and middle classes in all but rhetoric, but it is still alive in the countryside, where agrarian reform was never fully implemented. In addition to drawing on Orozco for inspiration, López acknowledges the influence of the photographer Agustín V. Casasola, who persistently and thoroughly documented the Mexican Revolution, accumulating a pictorial record equal to that of Matthew Brady for the American Civil War. Casasola's photographs vary from panoramic overviews of troops in action to "candid" shots of the anonymous individuals who make up history to portraits of the heroes of the revolution like Villa and Zapata, whose activities and features his photographs made famous. López, as a press photographer, can be considered within this reportorial, documentary tradition that transcends its own transiency by producing memorable images.

In the strikingly dramatic photograph *Beggars* (Fig. 122) from the series *Only the Poor Go to Hell*, López gives us the faces of the poor that so preoccupied Los Interioristas, from Cuevas' and Coronel's street people to Icaza's *Lumpenproletariat* to Belkin's slum dwellers and criminals,

121. Nacho López, *Zapatistas*, 1950, from the series *Windows on Life*, photograph, 10⅝ × 13¾ in. (27 × 35 cm.). Courtesy of the artist.

122. Nacho López, *Beggars*, 1951, from the series *Only the Poor Go to Hell*, photograph, 10⅝ × 13¾ in. (27 × 35 cm.). Courtesy of the artist.

123. Nacho López, *Offertory*, 1954, from the series
Only the Poor Go to Hell, photograph, 13¾ × 10⅝ in.
(35 × 27 cm.). Courtesy of the artist.

124. Nacho López, *Poultry Man*, 1961, photograph, 5 × 9 in. (12.7 × 22.9 cm.). Courtesy of the artist.

Messeguer's ragpickers, and Sepúlveda's homeless women—the underbelly of Mexico's apparent prosperity. Their en masse actualization, with upturned faces ranging from the puzzled and vacant to the brutalized, in a realistic photograph—though mediated by the aesthetics of composition and value—permits us to apprehend the degree of poetic transfiguration that has occurred in the drawings and paintings. The simple act of moving from a single figure to a multiplication of individuals takes them out of the category of existential victim into that of class victim. We sense, in the photograph, that they represent not the universal, but a stratum of society, and their misery is defined in social terms. Such a mass of deprived humanity will not permit a solution like personal redemptive resurrection. And the future that includes such faces is ominous. The appearance of a "leader" (political or spiritual) would elicit a variety of responses from these men; nothing suggests the possibility of a united and onward movement of the masses such as is found in social realism. The feeling is more tentative, and underlines with great precision the differences between the triumphant postrevolutionary muralists who had seen just such people transcend (but also, in the case of Orozco, bru-

talize) themselves, and the feeling of hopelessness that animated the artists of the post–World War II period. The underlying implications of despair are clear.

Another memorable photograph from the same series is *Offertory*, (Fig. 123) which is so strange and surreal that it vibrates in the mind long after one has ceased to look at it. The two disembodied hands emerging from an iron gate are in the dreamlike tradition of Dali and Buñuel's film *Un Chien andalou* or Jean Cocteau's bodiless torch-bearing arms in *La Belle et la bête*. They resist explanation, like the stubborn image of a nightmare, even after one knows that they are the trembling and desperate hands of prisoners pleading for a cigarette through a hole in the door that closes their cell.[47] The photograph *Poultry Man* (Fig. 124) is of the same character: the sense of shock derives from the sudden awareness that the heap of dangling, plucked chickens is supported on the head of a man, forming a sort of large hatlike shape. His face and hands are obscured by the complex pattern of chicken bodies and necks. The juxtaposition of the dead and sightless chickens with the alive and alert face behind them and the vulnerability and obscenity of the naked corpses set up peculiar

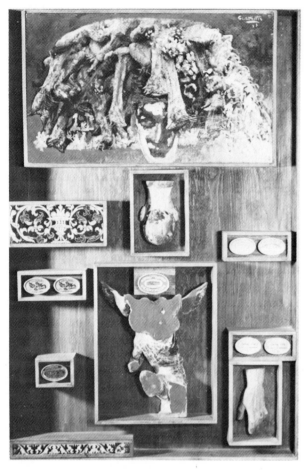

125. Alberto Gironella, *Queen Mariana*, 1964, collage, 72⅞ × 49¼ in. (185 × 125 cm.). Collection of Vicente Rojo. Photo courtesy Instituto Nacional de Bellas Artes.

resonances. The chickens become a metaphor for violated human bodies behind which is hidden a vital human soul, suggesting (as they did to Belkin, who was strongly influenced by this phase of López's work) the bodies of Buchenwald and Dachau. The chicken (or fowl) as a symbol of sacrifice is very old in human history, from the doves sacrificed to Greek deities to the cock of the Crucifixion to the sacrificial roosters of modern African tribes. It has had certain currency with modern Jewish artists, particularly Soutine, and it was under the double influence

of Soutine and López that Belkin made his drawings of flayed chickens. *Poultry Man* was integrated "whole" (and unacknowledged) into the art of yet another Mexican artist, Alberto Gironella, who pasted the photograph on the surface of a painting and substituted the hatlike configuration of López's chickens for the elaborate hairdo of the queen (Fig. 125) in one of his numerous variations of Velázquez's *Queen Mariana of Austria*. It has been said that there is a surrealism present in Nacho López's work independent of Nacho López himself,[48] i.e., that he produces surreal reverberations without intending to do so and without following any prescription. *Offertory* and *Poultry Man* do not resort to distortions or aberrations of reality; they are the result of the awareness of an acutely sensitive photographer who is constantly on the alert to the possibilities of what he sees.

One would assume that an identification with social realism and political criticism would have precluded López's identification with the artists under the banner of Salas Anzures. Such was not the case. Salas Anzures included López in the roster of artists associated with the Museo de Arte Contemporáneo de México—the common denominator being their mutual respect for the great iconoclast Orozco.[49] Like Salas Anzures, José Luis Cuevas also expressed his admiration for López: "I should also admit that the Mexico I have attacked is not the only one. There is another Mexico, one that I deeply respect and admire: the Mexico of Orozco, Alfonso Reyes, Silvestre Revueltas, Antonio Caso, Carlos Chávez, Tamayo, Octavio Paz, Carlos Pellicer, Carlos Fuentes, Nacho López."[50]

Héctor Xavier

Héctor Xavier (occasionally spelled Javier), born in 1921 in Tuxpan, Veracruz, and residing in Mexico City since 1930, is a self-taught artist, though he studied briefly at La Esmeralda in 1945. In Mexico he is considered one of the great contemporary draftsmen. His first major exhibition in Mexico City took place in 1945 at the Palacio de Bellas Artes, sponsored by the Dirección General de Educación Estética in line with its policy of opening doors to all artistic manifestations. The catalog issued at the time commented that although the first works of this young artist (then twenty-three) did not yet indicate a "consolidated personality" in the technical disciplines, they showed a sense of ambition, passion, and interest in searching out new roads that augured well for his future development. He did not, said the text, attempt to shine ostentatiously by seeking an originality based on the false recourses of foreign influences; instead, he was profoundly exploring the legitimate paths of Mexicanism.[51] In short, Xavier was continuing in the tradition of the Mexican School at this early date, exhibiting a *riverista* influence in some of his early works,[52] and an attraction for Orozco's expressive drawing.

Between November 1952 and 1954, Xavier traveled and studied in various European countries. In 1954 he was commissioned to decorate the interior and design a forged iron door for the chapel of Longueil-Annel at Oise, France. During this period, he initiated a new stage of his artistic development with the application of delicate color to his drawings.

From its inception Xavier had been associated with the movement of the most active artists of the rebellion against official art. His works were shown at the Galería Prisse in 1952–1953, and also at the Galería Proteo (where he exhibited regularly from 1955 to 1958) at the time the dissidents had consolidated their forces with Goeritz, Orozco Romero, and Tamayo. However, Xavier, like Cuevas, maintained a marginal relationship (for different reasons) with the Galería Proteo and other groups he joined, including Los Interioristas. Though close to the artists who comprised Salas Anzures' Museo de Arte Contemporáneo de México, he was not part of it. Nor does his name appear on the roster of artists at the 1960 Interamerican Biennial, though he *was* one

126. Héctor Xavier, *Gray Mangave*, from the series *Silverpoint/Bestiary*, 1958, silverpoint, 10⅜ × 13⅝ in. (26.5 × 34.5 cm.). Collection of Ing. Martín Kreimerman. Photo courtesy Instituto Nacional de Bellas Artes.

of the printmakers and draftsmen sent to the 1961 São Paulo Biennial as part of the official Mexican entry. Thus he, like López, appears to have moved easily between seemingly antagonistic worlds, demonstrating thereby how fluid the boundaries actually were. As for Los Interioristas, Xavier exhibited with them in October 1961 at the Escuela Nacional de Artes Plásticas (San Carlos); again at the Galería Ariza in July 1962; and at the two major shows of 1963; only in 1963 did he decide to become a formal member. In toto, therefore, his association must be seen as peripheral, like

127. Héctor Xavier, *Portrait of Miriam*, 1959, silverpoint, 20⅞ × 15 in. (53 × 38 cm.). Collection of the artist. Photo courtesy Instituto Nacional de Bellas Artes.

that of López and Rodríguez Luna. He maintained a wry, detached, and critical attitude toward Los Interioristas/Nueva Presencia, as he had done toward the Galería Proteo "opposition" group and the Museo de Arte Contemporáneo de México.

Xavier's age and artistic maturity precluded his coming within the *cuevista* sphere of influence, and despite such works as *Anguished Man*, *The Duality of Man*, *Our Interior Monster*, and *Anxiety*, the darker aspects of his work, when they

appear, seem to derive directly from Orozco or European expressionistic sources, rather than from *interiorismo*.

Some of the purest distillations of Xavier's style appeared in his *Silverpoint/Bestiary* series, done in silverpoint, a technique very popular in the Renaissance. Xavier used a wire of Mexican silver, filed to a point, and drew on paper coated with Chinese white. For eight months he worked inside the cages of the Chapultepec zoo, producing drawings of power and delicacy in which the lines vary from very light to very dark, and texture is achieved by multiple tiny strokes or crosshatching. *Gray Mangave* (Fig. 126) shows a wide variety of textural effects and value changes and manifests the artist's complete control of this difficult medium. The Dürer-like *Rhinoceros* is more vigorous—in keeping with the character of the animal—and shows attention to the creased and leathery quality of its skin. Other drawings eliminate almost all interior description, relying on a sensitive contour line to suggest volume. So successful were these drawings that the critic Crespo de la Serna urged Xavier to continue in this direction, comparing the clarity of form and linear stylization of the object to those of such great masters of drawing as Holbein, Ingres, Picasso, Rembrandt, Dürer, Pisanello, and the Japanese printmakers.[53] Though the praise tends to the superlative, there is no question about the fineness of this collection of drawings. In 1958 they were published as an album of twenty-four plates with a text by Juan José Arreola, in an edition of 500 copies.[54]

Two portraits from 1959, *Portrait of Miriam* (Fig. 127) and *Portrait of Emilio Carballido* show a similarity in expressive distortion of form, and the range of technical possibilities available to silverpoint—from pure contour to fully developed tonal dimension.

The following year Xavier developed an extraordinary new style of heavily outlined forms suggesting stained glass, with distinctly religious subject matter. It was a transition from drawing

128. Héctor Xavier, *Man*, from the series *Stained Glass*, 1960, ink and color on paper, 39⅜ × 26¾ in. (100 × 68 cm.). Collection of Lic. Jorge González Ramírez. Photo courtesy Instituto Nacional de Bellas Artes.

129. Héctor Xavier, *The Dead Poet*, from the series *The Old Ones*, 1963, ink, 39⅜ × 26⅝ in. (100 × 67.5 cm.). Collection of the artist. Photo courtesy Instituto Nacional de Bellas Artes.

to painting, though often limited to black and white. It is impossible not to think of Rouault in connection with these works, or to note that in drawing upon the French "Fauve" master, Xavier was paralleling the profound influence exercised on Los Interioristas by the German expressionists. *Man* (Fig. 128) from the *Stained Glass* series is obviously Christ, while a mother and child from the same series can only suggest a Madonna and Child; however, these sacred personages lack the serenity associated with them in traditional

imagery. Without varying the iconography, Xavier has suggested a feeling of nervousness and tension—particularly in the Christ—by the busy abstract splashes of ink animating the surface, a purpose also served by the stipplings of the mother and child. In fact, these are like the corroded as well as the fractured surfaces of *interiorismo* and infect all the works of this series.

In 1963, employing a modification of the "stained glass" technique, Xavier did a series of impressive works called *The Old Ones* in which

El fin y los medios.

130. Héctor Xavier, *The End and the Means,* from the series *War and Peace,* 1963, ink, 12⅝ × 19¼ in. (32 × 49 cm.). Private collection. Photo courtesy Instituto Nacional de Bellas Artes.

the influence of Orozco (his flickering brush-strokes in particular) seems to have given stronger linear definition to the forms and the grid. *The Dead Poet* (Fig. 129) is based on an old Mexican custom of painting portraits of the dead, either in their coffins or propped up in a seated position, as is the case here. The accurate description of fallen hair, sunken eyes, and sharp, bony features (as well as the pillow supported from the back by an attendant) reminds one of the long romantic tradition, from Géricault to Munch, of observing and recording the process of decay in detail. It also finds its prototypes in the *gisants* carved on

131. José Clemente Orozco, *After the Combat,* 1940, fresco. Biblioteca Gabino Ortiz, Jiquilipan. Courtesy of the Orozco family.

132. Héctor Xavier, *I Love, You Love: The Verb Is Man*, from the series *War and Peace*, 1963, ink, 19⅝ × 12¾ in. (50 × 32.5 cm.). Private collection. Photo courtesy Instituto Nacional de Bellas Artes.

tombs, the death mask, and other realistic renderings of the deceased. Such images, often used as the last memento for the family, are different in kind from the *calavera*, which shows the structural remains of the body rather than a final physical likeness before decomposition sets in, but they both represent a "taming" of death—stripping it of its repulsive and oppressive aspects so as to come to grips with it as a process.

Orozco's graphic style is very apparent in Xavier's drawing for the *War and Peace* portfolios, *The End and the Means* (Fig. 130). The dramatically drawn dead horse echoes the agonized horse of *Guernica* and Orozco's struggling and dying horses from the black and white frescoes at the Biblioteca Gabino Ortiz in Jiquilpan (Fig. 131)

(though Xavier's immediate source was a dead horse used for meat in the zoo). As in these two works, the horse is a metaphor for the human condition, for the victim, and as such it is a moving symbol of war. The gaunt forms splaying out in space, the jagged contour, and the sharp, pointed shapes of the negative space that seem to thrust into the horse's body speak eloquently of pain and death. In complete contrast are the monumental, rounded forms of a dark-skinned man and a light-skinned woman, clothed in robes that appear Biblical, of *I Love, You Love: The Verb Is Man* (Fig. 132). This is one of the few positive statements that appeared in the *War and Peace* portfolios, and, like Xavier's "stained glass" images, had an obliquely religious feeling.

Antonio Rodríguez Luna

If López and Xavier were transitional artists, mediating between old and new in their relationship to Nueva Presencia, Antonio Rodríguez Luna was wholly of the "old school"—not of Mexico, but of Spain, where he was born in Montoro, Córdoba, in 1910. Twenty years after his arrival, and despite his Mexican citizenship, Luis Cardoza y Aragón could still describe him as "an exile, with Spain in his heart."[55] Luna had been a well-known and respected artist before he came to Mexico in 1939 at the conclusion of the Spanish Civil War. The entire trajectory of his art is contained in that fact. His paintings and drawings then, and for years to come, were filled with bitter mockery of the Franco dictatorship and the alliance between the aristocracy, the military, and the church that supported that dictatorship. Every painting as well bears witness to special formal and expressive qualities that can be considered Spanish: his deep blacks, grays, umbers, ochres, tinted whites, blues, roses, and scarlets; his hard, dry textures or gleaming, varnished surfaces like those of the baroque era; the spatial organization and strong chiaroscuro. All this is combined with a unique type of cubistic structure and stylization that makes jointed puppets

133. Antonio Rodríguez Luna, *War*, 1935, from the series *War Drawings*, pen and ink, 18¾ × 23⅝ in.
(47.5 × 60 cm.). Collection of the artist. Photo courtesy Instituto Nacional de Bellas Artes.

of the figures he wishes to mock, but is softened
with compassion when he deals with the victims. Margarita Nelken considered Luna the heir
to the macabre mockery of the Spanish school,
and attributed his buffoons, clowns, skeletons,
and skulls to the influence of Juan de Valdés
Leal (whose most famous paintings are in Se-
ville, where Luna studied art for four years) and
that of Goya and Picasso.[56] These influences appear in an early series of twenty drawings, done
in 1935–1937, some predating and some in response to the Civil War. Just as strong, however,
is the influence of the Flemish primitives (so
richly displayed at the Prado) and the Neue
Sachlichkeit artists George Grosz and Otto Dix.

One of these drawings, *War* (Fig. 133), was exhibited with Nueva Presencia's "War and Peace"
exhibit at the Salón de la Plástica Mexicana. It
features a vast Bosch-like landscape pockmarked
with craters filled with dead and dying bodies,
skeletons, and ripped flesh. The sky is dominated by a kind of female/bird or insect[57] whose
exposed viscera are composed of symbols of corruption: fascist currency, a munitions factory, a
cannon, a bloated priest, a lecherous military
man, etc. The surfaces are covered with insects,
snakes, fragmented limbs, and ulcerated sores.
Below, between the death-filled craters on the
right and the city on the left, a tattered resistance
figure defends the mountain pass. The image

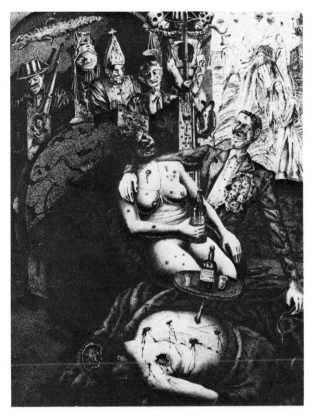

134. Antonio Rodríguez Luna, *Andalusian Land-owner*, 1937, from the series *War Drawings*, pen and ink, 8⅝ × 7⅞ in. (22 × 20 cm.). Collection of the artist. Photo courtesy Instituto Nacional de Bellas Artes.

is more than a statement of personal anguish (though Luna's emotional involvement is apparent); it is a complex, partisan prophecy of the Spanish Civil War, though it was triggered by Mussolini's invasion of Ethiopia on October 3, 1935. It predicts the struggle of the Spanish people against the coming monstrosity of the fascist-backed Franco rebellion, and it ties that rebellion to the capitalist-military-church alliance that stood behind it.

Luna's anger and disgust with Spain's ruling class is acidly expressed in *Andalusian Land-owner* (Fig. 134), with its strong overtones of Grosz, Goya, and Bosch. Seated on a bed with an ulcerated prostitute on his knee and holding a

whip in his hand, the landowner plants his table in a martyred body (Spain?), while the poor gather outside his window. Behind the headboard are the sources of his power: the army, monarchists, clergy, and judiciary. The general wraps his rifle in a banner of the Virgin and the Child, the cardinal holds a box of money, and the scales, held aloft on the skeleton of a snake and two skulls, form a halo over the judge. These satirical touches are worthy of Luis Buñuel, the Spanish film-maker now residing in Mexico, whose bitter anticlericalism has become a trademark of his films. In *Defense of Madrid* (Fig. 135), Luna pictures the defenders of the ravished city behind the barricades. This tableau, created a year before *Guernica*, has an uncanny number of features in common with the Picasso painting: the unique position of the fallen horse with its head thrust toward the sky (repeated in Luna's 1939 etching *Concentration Camp Argelés-sur-Mer*), the reclining soldier on the left, the woman's figure on the right, and even the architectural remnant whose "window" frames two figures. In both style and content, of course, the two works are totally different. Luna's fully modeled, sharply highlighted figures, done in an expressionist-realist mode, are highly charged with emotion and partisanship, as compared to the "cool" flatness and mythic-universality of *Guernica*. There are no figures with swords or references to the bullfight in Luna's work: his defenders are armed with rifles, grenades, and other contemporary weapons of war, and the devastation of the city beyond is caused by bombs. Though both share the image of the fallen horse as symbol of the Spanish people, Luna's people fight back. It must be remembered, however, that the historical circumstances of Guernica and Madrid were different; the former was a "trial run" for saturation bombing against a wholly unprepared civilian population, while the latter was a large city, the capital of the country, and the ground on which the battle for Spain was fought out. Nevertheless, the artistic and po-

135. Antonio Rodríguez Luna, *Defense of Madrid*, 1936, pen and ink with color, 17¾ × 23⅝ in. (45 × 60 cm.). Collection of the artist. Photo courtesy Instituto Nacional de Bellas Artes.

136. Antonio Rodríguez Luna, *Bombing of Barcelona*, 1938, pen and ink, 15¾ × 19⅝ in. (40 × 50 cm.). Collection of the artist. Photo courtesy Instituto Nacional de Bellas Artes.

litical choices made by these two artists are significant of their points of view.

In *Bombing of Barcelona* (Fig. 136), Luna sets the scene within a home through whose window can be seen the devastated city and the harbor beyond. Within, the destruction is complete. Seated by the lacerated heads of two adults buried under the rubble of their household furnishings is a bleeding child, seemingly alive, though its skull opens to reveal the brains. The crowding and telescoping of space, the unreal changes in scale, the profusion of detail, the extraordinary realism, the common objects that take on a new dimension, closely ally Luna with Parisian surrealism. He calls his style "social surrealism" because his drawings are expressions of the situation through which he was living in Spain. Thus he separates the *living* nightmare of Spanish agony that he witnessed and recorded from the induced and Freudian-oriented dreams of the Bretonians.

Luna's biographer Juan Rejano considers his *Exodus* (1936) and the *Masquerade for a Tyrant*

series, though separated by fifteen years and residence in a new country, the most characteristic of Luna's work and integrally related through a logical sequence, though they share no external characteristics.[58] A painterly style, reminiscent of Goya and Daumier, succeeded the earlier Greco- and Picasso-like elongations and applied to all subject matter until the mid-fifties, when works like *Iberian Bulls* clearly signaled the end of Luna's expressionist and painterly phases and the beginning of a new structuralism that corresponded with the beginning of the series *Masquerade for a Tyrant*.[59] The characters of his earlier work undergo a metamorphosis, like actors who change their makeup, costumes, and scenery to play new roles. It is as if Luna laid aside his expressionist, fluid style when he ceased to be an advocate in an ongoing struggle and became an exiled critic—the only valid role he could picture for himself as the Franco dictatorship became entrenched, accepted, and part of the United States–European defense network during the Cold War. Satirical criticism demanded

137. Antonio Rodríguez Luna, *Buffoon*, 1957, oil on canvas, 46⅛ × 53½ in. (117 × 136 cm.). Collection of Mrs. William Kennedy. Photo courtesy Instituto Nacional de Bellas Artes.

caricatures, and the caricature by nature is a form of abstraction and exaggeration; it strips away realism and the human dimension to reveal the nature of types, or the most condensed and salient features of individuals. Luna undertook to satirize the upper and ruling classes of Spain, and for this purpose he invented a world of rigid, posturing, puppetlike figures who represented what he calls the "dead weights" of Spanish society: the church, the aristocracy, and the army, usually accompanied by images of death, which in Franco's Spain was spiritual as well as physical. He plunged this world into darkness and picked out his characters in the contrasts of brilliant chiaroscuro. The dark colors were applied in rich layers of oil glazes and the surfaces highly varnished, thus blending—or even creating—a tension between the ultramodern cubist style and the baroque lighting and surface finish.

In addition to the satirical characters, and sometimes combined with them to heighten the irony, are circus people, animals, lunatics, prisoners, beggars, etc. In other words, the whole

array of types we find in the works of Goya, Orozco, Cuevas, and other humanists, though I wish to reiterate the differences in *content* in their treatment by the two former artists and by the neohumanists. Luna could more correctly be classified with Goya and Orozco than with Cuevas, though his style owes little to either. A work like *Buffoon* (Fig. 137) is only ostensibly about a circus personality. The monkey is a traditional symbol of mendacity, used by Picasso and others, and the presence of the laughing spectators who are fully aware that the performance is only for the gullible makes this a comment on the vulgar contortions of the Spanish rulers in their effort to appear creditable. *Tortured Prisoners* (Fig. 138) reveals the bleak realities of the regime, and it is notable that Luna softens his angular style somewhat to humanize these figures. Their nakedness seems to relate them to the naked "victims" of *interiorismo* except for the vital inclusion of the barred window. Eliminate that, and they become anguished existential images, stripped of social context, even that of clothing. The smug faces of

138. Antonio Rodríguez Luna, *Tortured Prisoners*, 1959, oil on canvas, 41⅜ × 29½ in. (105 × 75 cm.). Collection of Shirley Wallentin. Photo courtesy Instituto Nacional de Bellas Artes.

139. Antonio Rodríguez Luna, from the series *Masquerade for a Tyrant*, 1963, oil on canvas, 47¼ × 70⅞ in. (120 × 180 cm.). Collection of the Museo de Arte Moderno, Mexico City. Courtesy Instituto Nacional de Bellas Artes.

the *Satisfied Ones* (1961), bloated and withered
members of the Spanish ruling class, are part of a
cast of characters many of whom also appear in
the *Masquerade for a Tyrant* series (Fig. 139).
Dominated by a skeleton in a large feathered hat
(reminiscent of Posada), symbol of the dead hand
of the past, members of the military and the judiciary have come together. Their masked faces
have a conspiratorial expression treated with no
small degree of humor and sarcasm by the artist;
they are bulky presences who glance from left to
right as if they needed to keep secret and hidden.
Deep blacks, silver grays, and umbers contrast
with brilliant white, cerulean blue, and rose, applied layer upon transparent layer, adding depth
to the otherwise shallow space of the composition. The figures are all disposed frontally in
carefully arranged groups as if performing for an
audience, but since they are engaged in a conspiracy, it seems as if a curtain had suddenly
been raised on their doings.

Rejano has suggested that the phantasmagoric
beings of the *Masquerade for a Tyrant* series
are the reverse of Goya's *Family of Carlos IV*, in
which the Bourbons externally have the physical appearance of human beings, but where it is
easily understood that within they are despica-
ble, ridiculous marionettes, puppets of a tragic
carnival. Luna's, on the other hand, are abstractions, ghostly beings that appear like puppets on
the outside but are actually masks that cover a
sinister entity.[60]

Everything begins with the tyrant himself, says
Rejano. One painting of the series was *The Tyrant* (Fig. 140). Within context, there is no doubt
that this beribboned general with epaulettes and
sword is Franco, though he could symbolize all
the military engineers of coups d'état so plen-
tifully available in Latin America. His corrupt
and cynical expression and the sagging jowls of
his face are repeated in the grinning skull at his
feet to which the diagonal of the sword leads
one's eye. Here indeed Rejano's reference to
Goya's Carlos IV is well taken: the short bulky

140. Antonio Rodríguez Luna, *The Tyrant*, ca. 1958,
from the series *Masquerade for a Tyrant*, oil on canvas. Private collection. Photo courtesy Instituto Nacional de Bellas Artes.

person of Franco standing frontally in the fore-ground of the narrow "stage" is like that of a malignant Carlos whose faults have been exter-nalized. The difference lies in that Goya por-trayed Carlos as stupid, whereas Luna's Franco is sinister.

Luna's prestige and influence as a teacher was at its summit by the late fifties, when he became Icaza's mentor and friend.[61] Luna's use of car-nivals, masked figures, and circus folk must have struck a responsive chord in Icaza, much as the works of Ensor had previously done.

Luna is not much inclined to explain himself in words. A quiet and gentle man, he becomes animated only when showing his paintings. He particularly recalls a quotation of Ortega y Gasset to the effect that a painter should speak with his works, because when he uses words, they emerge as tonterías (stupidities). Nevertheless, he did produce one statement that seems to sum up the spirit of his work very well: "I try to paint with the deep and intimate spirit of life a dignified portrayal wherein the elements we use to evalu-ate a picture—materials, composition, color and delineation—are as subdued as possible. I at-tempt, in my humble way, with the scantiest technique possible and with a craft whose purity has to be reconquered day by day, to paint a work which can describe man's long hours of anguish and the mystery and poetry of life and the ob-jects that surround us."[62]

Luna's relationship to Nueva Presencia was an extension of his relationship to Icaza: that of friend, teacher, mentor, and possibly sympathetic father image. Retrospectively, Luna himself con-siders Nueva Presencia as a gathering of very young artists whose existence as a group left lit-tle or no impact on Mexican art. He has con-cluded that they had no ideology because each went his own way after the demise of the group, and the principles of Nueva Presencia no longer played any role in their art or their lives in later years. (This is somewhat of an overstatement, in my opinion. A more precise evaluation of Nueva Presencia's role and achievement appears in the concluding chapter that follows.)

Conclusion

Social Realism and Neohumanism

Among the questions, implicit and explicit, that have been posed in the pages above has been that of the difference between social realism and neohumanism. This difference can perhaps be best exemplified by a comparison of the Spanish Civil War drawings of social realist Antonio Rodríguez Luna and the drawings of the neohumanist Nueva Presencia artists in the "War and Peace" exhibit. In making such a comparison, one should keep in mind the text of *Nueva Presencia* No. 5, which constituted the literary counterpart of the exhibit and which had a distinctly militant tone. (Perhaps the desire for social protest should be localized to Belkin and Icaza, who as editors of the *revista-cartel* articulated the philosophical and aesthetic directions of the group, but one must assume that they spoke for the larger aspirations of all the artists.)

It has been shown that Luna's "social surrealism" consisted in combining the fantastic and nonrealistic aspects of surrealism with a clearly articulated statement of class forces in conflict. His drawing *War* leaves no doubt as to the causes of the war, attributed directly to the alliance between the Spanish upper classes and the representatives of fascism, and no doubt about the resistance of the Spanish people. By comparison, Leonel Góngora, the only other artist to have experienced mass violence and death first hand, expressed himself with a series of single figures in vacant space that conveyed their feeling through painful, but self-induced body distortions and dislocations. The focus (and this was generally true for Nueva Presencia) was placed on individual suffering rather than the clash of social forces. Icaza's rat, Sepúlveda's ghostly old woman, Muñoz's mother and child buried in darkness, Delgadillo's skull-scattering figure of death, González's flayed figure, Belkin's petrified lovers, all share certain characteristics that provide a line of demarcation between their concepts and those of Luna's allegory. Most of the Nueva Presencia images are of one or two figures with little suggestion of or reference to background. As a matter of fact, despite the titles, many have little inherent relationship to war and peace, and a certain amount of wrenching is necessary to make the connection. They do not pictorialize the horrors of war as did, for example, Jacques Callot, Goya, or Orozco; there is no specificity about the indigenous characteristics of a particular war such as we find in Daumier's 1870 lithographs of the Franco-Prussian War, Manet's drawings of the Paris Commune, or the works of Käthe Kollwitz, George Grosz, and Otto Dix in response to World War I. There are no weapons, no signs of external violence or violation, no wounds, death, or brutality in most of the drawings. Rather there are human forms (or animal/insect forms symbolizing humans) that suggest certain affective states: melancholy, loneliness, grief, terror, pain, aggressiveness, tenderness—emotions that have no specific stimulus, no visible cause. They are states of consciousness given human form. Despite Tamayo's pejorative characterization of *interiorismo* as an art form that makes allusion to psychological points of view, an allusion that he considered foreign to painting, there are affinities between this aspect of *interiorismo* and Tamayo's own work in the period from 1946 to 1956. There is also a greater resemblance than would superficially be supposed between abstract expressionism, which externalized the residue of psychic and emotional states in abstract form, and *interiorismo*, which did the same with figurative imagery. It is not simply a question of adopting abstract expressionist brushwork; the issue ran deep into the marrow of neohumanism and produced a similarity of *content*, albeit with a figurative style. This is the most crucial issue.

It is important to consider the relationship between the psychological and existential imagery of Nueva Presencia and the aspirations of the artists to make statements of social concern. For genuine protest art to be truly effective as a prod to the conscience, what is under attack must be grasped as solidly and firmly as possible, which in turn means it must have been observed precisely and in some real measure understood from the inside.[1] To have understood war means to have comprehended it as the working out of social problems on a plane of violence. It is the mass scale of that violence and the legalized abandonment of almost all civilized restraints and considerations that distinguishes war from ordinary murder. Every scene of individual suffering implies a multiplication of that suffering; every act of heroic resistance is symbolic of general resistance. The narrative, allegorical, or symbolic protests against war by Goya, Picasso, Orozco, Siqueiros, or Luna imply this mass application in a way that the drawings of Nueva Presencia do not. Faced with the frightening possibilities of atomic warfare and the total extermination of the human race, "conventional" war imagery may have seemed insufficient to the younger artists. Perhaps all that was left was an affirmation of individual existence. Much of Nueva Presencia imagery does not have an external referent; it leaves open to question whether the victims have been "acted upon" or are simply exhibiting their internal anguish and despair. It produces a sense of helplessness, since existential *Angst* is a permanent state of being and cannot be alleviated or remedied. This ambiguity, this fracture between pictorial imagery and social purpose as expressed in the literary productions, might be seen as a clue to the inner paradoxical nature of Nueva Presencia as a group and as a philosophical position in the context of modern Mexican art. It can be seen that between the call to collective social change and the recipes for its enactment that we find in the heyday of the mural movement, between the clearly stated socialist alternatives of that movement (in spite of government proscription) and the intensely individual, ahistorical, and apolitical position of *interiorismo*, there is only the most tenuous of links. *Interiorismo* was a successful

deflection from the type of political nationalism that was a defense against imperialism and from social art that called for internal social change and thereby endangered the position of the national bourgeoisie. On the other hand, the cooption of the mural movement by the government, which increasingly represented the interests of the bourgeoisie; the failure of the mural movement to renovate its imagery and ideology to meet the challenge of changing times; and the failure of many muralists to understand that the incomplete revolution of the twenties had become a betrayed revolution by the fifties, and that revolutionary glorification *in the old terms* had become a regressive social and artistic statement, left a vacuum in artistic ideology that was filled by a critical-idealist position taken from the middle class. *Interiorismo* itself, however, did not play an adversary role; as we have seen, no adversary was made manifest. The artists hurled their challenge into the cosmos, which, as is usually the case, made no response.

Style

Mexican neohumanism had a characteristic style, but one at the service of a particular kind of humanism, which distinguished it from figurative formalism. Throughout their existence as a group, the artists of Nueva Presencia remained dedicated to the aesthetic principles established in *The Insiders*, though (or perhaps because) for them these principles grew out of Orozco and the Mexican ambience. Rodman had stipulated that an Insider was more naturally a sculptor than a painter, that color was secondary to drawing, and that multidimensional painting was superior to two-dimensional painting. From the beginning, Los Interioristas restricted their ranks to artists who worked within these parameters. Strong value contrasts, minimal color, expert draftsmanship with emphasis on line, thin washes, intimate scale (except for the few who were muralists), expressive distortion and monstrosity, large single shapes, and empty backgrounds are some of the most notable characteristics.[2] Many of these characteristics can be traced back to Cuevas, though his view that Los Interioristas were all merely carbon copies of him is somewhat exaggerated. The real source of the style was Orozco, modified by various European sources from the Renaissance to Picasso.

Content

It was Cuevas, however, who struck the pessimistic and existential note: the anguished and subjective *ensimismamiento* that was no longer a tool of self-definition, as it had been in the thirties, but a true reflection of post–World War II malaise and the psychological dimension of such political realities as the Cold War and possible atomic destruction. In this sense, *interiorismo* evolved both a style and a content that absorbed and transcended the past. It expressed a new concept for Mexico: that of alienation.

Alienation is certainly not a new phenomenon in history: in Marxist thought it is coeval with the creation of class structures in society. However, there is a question of degree, and it is generally recognized that the highly industrialized Western capitalist nations have reached an acute stage. Signals of this stage include not only the loss of the figure in abstraction but also the totally subjective direction taken by abstract expressionism—without, for example, any of the optimistic, universalized, Platonic considerations of early abstractionists like Kandinsky, Mondrian, or Malevich. Existentialism can be considered the modern philosophy that most closely pertains to alienation, and in assuming a vesture of existentialism, Mexican neohumanists were expressing a degree of alienation unknown by their predecessors. I have argued that the importation of abstract expressionism into Mexico, plus the enormous prestige lent to Tamayo and

Cuevas by institutions in the United States, had the purpose of undermining social realism in Mexico, its strongest, most effective bastion. There was also a tendency to import certain negative concepts about the human condition that may not accurately have reflected the internal situation. While it is true that the processes accompanying the development of Mexican capitalism and the growth of a bourgeoisie and middle class accelerated the development of alienation, it was not necessarily at that extreme state encountered among the developed Western societies. The recasting of Mexican nationalism in an internationalist and universalist mold led to a process of homogenization that consisted of equating the rootlessness and powerlessness of the Mexican middle class with the extreme malaise of the Western capitalistic world, regardless of its organic connection to the lives and living culture of a third world country. Convinced of the futility of struggle in the face of the crisis of life itself, inexplicable and incomprehensible (as described by Barry Schwartz, see above, p. 00), the middle class feels it must yield to its destiny. It ceases to resist encroachments from foreign imperialism or its own bourgeoisie; it ceases to have any hope or aspirations for the "lower classes." Instead it withdraws into passivity, self-contemplation, and personal salvation.

I think it becomes clear that, as the outmoded and rhetorical aspects of the Mexican movement became the artistic symbol of the bourgeoisie, neohumanism was an expression of the middle class: the new restless (and later, rebellious) student, artistic, technical, and professional population that arose as a result of Mexican industrialization and modernization after World War II. These people became conscious of themselves as a class in the late fifties (and were among the most important patrons of Nueva Presencia). They aspired to, but lacked the power of the bourgeoisie; and they were disillusioned with and cut off from the working and rural classes. It was to this group that Octavio Paz assigned the role of criticism, but without an explicit message or a doctrine, and without the power to effect social change (see above, p. 000). Neohumanism's "victims," its human figures that are "acted upon" by mysterious, unexplained forces, are an embodiment of the new sensibility of the middle class—an audience that social realism spoke neither to nor for.

At the same time, neohumanism was not the artistic form that expressed the ultimate alienation. As has been pointed out, nineteenth-century romantic freedom was a mode of alienation from society, while existential freedom is a way of maintaining one's integrity in society.[3] The profundity of neohumanism lay in its insistence on maintaining the human image and dimension in the face of more alienated art forms that, in their escapism from reality or their bland assumption of the validities of formalism, celebrated the vacuum instead of revealing it. The Mexicans, precisely because of their "retarded" status as a capitalist state and their continuous need to react against their own colonization, have not yet been able to digest the final abnegation that accepts its own alienation, as expressed, for example, in the capitulatory philosophy of a major United States theoretician, Wylie Sypher, who interprets the message of modern painting and literature as follows:

Is it possible, while the individual is vanishing behind the functionary throughout the technological world, to have any sort of humanism that does not depend upon the older notions of the self, the independent self that is outdated . . . by the operations of power on its present scale? . . . we must no longer confuse humanism with romantic individuality or with an anthropomorphic view that put self at the center of things.[4]

He concludes that alienation is necessary, or at least irreversible:

What we evidently need is a new impersonal sense of the person, a retreat to a self that appears after the assassination of the self occurring in an age dominated by nuclear physics. . . . Any such impersonal human-

ism will be tentative and defensive—may even seem to be desperate; but it will be authentic as any outworn idea of humanism cannot.[5]

The Mexicans have not yet arrived at this terrible impasse; whether they will depends upon the degree to which they accept or resist the incursions of United States cultural imperialism (concomitant with similar incursions in the economic sphere) and the course of their own bourgeoisie.

Many critics—both favorable and hostile to the group—have claimed that Nueva Presencia had little impact on Mexican art. In my opinion, this is a difficult thing to judge. The Mexican art scene since the sixties has been marked by widespread eclecticism that makes it difficult to discern the existence of a "movement" (if the idea of a "third direction" is taken seriously). Various modes of surrealism have been the most pervasive, but, as we have seen, this is also one of the components of *interiorismo*. While there are some younger artists in the post–Nueva Presencia generation who distinctly show some of the stylistic characteristics of Nueva Presencia (for example, Alfredo Castañeda, Guillermo Ceniceros, Ricardo García Mora, Octavio Vázquez), the question should be seen more broadly. At the crucial juncture, when the devitalized Mexican movement proved inadequate to express the new sensibilities of a changed social situation and the encroachments of cultural imperialism had produced an empty, formalist abstraction, Nueva Presencia did, momentarily, offer a "third direction." Its greatest accomplishment, considerable for the fragmented and eclectic art world of the early sixties, was the ability to appeal to and unite a diversity of young, disaffected artists and strengthen the figurative and humanistic tradition of Mexico. This tradition has since been strong enough to resist all but the most superficial importations of Pop, Op, and conceptual art that have swept so many Latin American artists in their wake, further alienating them from their own cultures and integral development. However, Nueva Presencia's existential-critical position was not strong enough to sustain a "movement." It is best seen as transitional: mediating between social realism (the "old left") and the intellectual and rebellious currents of the New Left. Its special role and responsibility was to link Mexican *interiorismo* to an international neohumanist trend without losing a sense of its own national traditions. This it accomplished.

Appendix: Chronology of Major Events in the History of Nueva Presencia

1956
Selden Rodman in Mexico for six months collecting information for his book *Mexican Journal*. First encounter with work of José Luis Cuevas; writes to him February 10, 1957.

1958
First Interamerican Biennial of Mexico at the Palacio de Bellas Artes, Mexico City. Includes extensive exhibit of abstract expressionists sent by the United States.

1959
Cuban Revolution. Fidel Castro takes over from Fulgencio Batista.

"New Images of Man" presented by the Museum of Modern Art in New York. Rodman buys paintings from the show, starts preparing his book *The Insiders*. Cuevas wins the International Prize for Drawing at the São Paulo Biennial.

1960
Second Interamerican Biennial of Mexico opens in the fall. Siqueiros imprisoned for an eight-year term (he serves four) for "social dissolution." A number of Mexican artists (including future Interioristas) boycott the Biennial; the Siqueiros case becomes a *cause célèbre*.

Rodman's book *The Insiders* is published. Cuevas gives Belkin a copy for review. Insiders' shows open at the Albert Landry and Cober galleries in New York and the Silvan Simone Gallery of Los Angeles. The latter includes Cuevas and Rico Lebrun, then working on his mural *Genesis* at Pomona College, Claremont, California.

1961
In January, Belkin's review of *The Insiders* appears in the newspaper *Novedades*; it is later reprinted in the *revista-cartel Nueva Presencia* No. 2. In February Belkin proposes an Insider show to Malkah Rabell, director of the Galerías CDI of the Centro Deportivo Israelita.

Icaza and Belkin visit Siqueiros in jail and decide to print a regular newspaper for him; it develops into *Nueva Presencia*.

On May 21, Lebrun sends Belkin photographs of his *Genesis* mural and *Buchenwald Cart*. On July 29 Julio González Tejada writes an article about the mural for *Mañana* magazine.

On July 6, Belkin and Icaza apply to the Comisión Calificatora de Publicaciones y Revistas Ilustradas of the Secretaría de Educación Pública for a copyright for *Nueva Presencia: El Hombre en el Arte de Nuestro Tiempo*. Copyright granted August 26, 1961.

On July 20, the first show of Los Interioristas at the Galerías CDI opens, including Belkin, Coronel, Corzas, Icaza as "members"; Cuevas, Luna, López, and Orozco.

In August the manifesto, *Nueva Presencia* No. 1, appears. 3,500 copies distributed and pasted on walls.

In September, *Nueva Presencia* No. 2: works by Belkin, Corzas, Cuevas, Icaza, López, Luna, and Orozco; texts by Belkin, Cuevas, and Tibol.

On October 16 the exhibition "Collective of Expressionism" opens at San Carlos Academy (Escuela Nacional de Artes Plásticas) with Belkin, Cuevas, Corzas, Icaza, López, Luna, Xavier; catalog by Raquel Tibol. Shortly after, Muñoz, Ortiz, and Sepúlveda are invited to join Los Interioristas. Group discusses changing its name.

November: Interioristas participate in committee to visit Nehru on behalf of Siqueiros.

December 29: *Nueva Presencia* No. 3 appears, dedicated to Siqueiros on his sixty-fifth birthday. Signed by fifty-five artists, writers, and intellectuals covering a wide spectrum of political opinions.

1962
February: Lebrun comes to Mexico. (Belkin and Icaza have been promoting a Lebrun show in Mexico, but it does not take place until 1968.)

April: Rodman comes to Mexico; meets all the Interioristas. *Nueva Presencia* No. 4 appears, illustrated with works by Lebrun and Baskin; texts by the two artists reprinted under the heading "The Documents of Neohumanism." *Nueva Presencia* distributed internationally.

April 11: group show opens at the Galería Mer-Kup under the name Nueva Presencia; includes Jorge Alzaga, Belkin, Corzas, Cuevas, Góngora (now officially a "member"), Icaza, Muñoz, Ortiz, Felipe Saúl Peña, Sepúlveda, Michael Spafford.

May: Cuevas disassociates himself publicly from the group.

July: Marta Traba attacks Nueva Presencia. Show at the Galería Ariza, "11 Painters Show Their Works."

September 11: Nueva Presencia distributes an open letter to the convention of the International Association of Art Critics on behalf of Siqueiros.

October: Nueva Presencia exhibits at the Club de Periodistas de México, A.C. Messeguer and Capdevila exhibit for the first time.

November: Group opens at the Zora Gallery (Los Angeles) and the Cober Gallery (New York).

1963
January: Cuevas continues public attacks against Interioristas. Icaza advises Zora Gallery of three new Nueva Presencia "members," Delgadillo, González, and Xavier.

August–September: *Nueva Presencia* No. 5: "War and Peace." Galería Misrachi commissions ten "War and Peace" portfolios with drawings from ten artists. "War and Peace" show opens at the Salón de la Plástica Mexicana—"Drawings of Nueva Presencia: War and Peace" (August 20–September 7).

September: Nueva Presencia shows at Morse Gallery of Art, Rollins, Florida, and is included in Organismo de Promoción Internacional de Cultura show "Pintores Neo-Humanistas" in San Antonio, Texas, and San Francisco.

September 13–October 5: San Carlos Academy show "Neohumanism in the Drawing of Italy, the United States, and Mexico."

October: "Voices of Mexico" opens at the Riverside Art Association, California. "Art in Mexico Today" opens at the Zora Gallery.

November: Selden Rodman Collection of paintings and drawings shown at San Carlos.

1964
Plans are made for *Nueva Presencia* No. 6; it never appears. Group dissolved.

Notes

Introduction

1. William Barrett, *Irrational Man: A Study in Existential Philosophy*, pp. 64–65.
2. Leonard Baskin, "The Necessity for the Image," *Mexico Quarterly Review* 2, No. 2 (October 1963): 116.
3. Arnold Belkin and Francisco Icaza, in *Nueva Presencia: El Hombre en el Arte de Nuestro Tiempo*, No. 1 (August 1961). The five issues of this publication will hereafter be referred to as *Nueva Presencia* followed by the issue number. Translations are my own unless otherwise noted.
4. For a fuller development of the two phases, see Luis Villoro, "La cultura mexicana de 1910 a 1960," *Historia Mexicana* 10, No. 2 (October–December 1960): 196–219, to whom I am indebted for this analysis.
5. Tourism is an extremely important factor in this development. The area of Mexico City known as the *zona rosa* contains a great many private galleries, as well as fashionable restaurants and shops that cater to the tourist trade.
6. Luis Cardoza y Aragón, *México: Pintura activa*, p. 149.
7. Antonio Rodríguez, "El gran premio a la mediocridad," *Siempre!* No. 627 (June 30, 1965): 28f.
8. Octavio Paz, *The Labyrinth of Solitude: Life and Thought in Mexico*, trans. Lysander Kemp, is the source used here.
9. Alma M. Reed, "La 'generación apaleada' de los EE.UU.," *Excélsior*, January 25, 1959, Diorama de la Cultura, p. 3-C. The influence of *beatismo* had been going on for about two years among North Americans with student visas, said Reed, and many Mexicans also adopted their dress as a sign of protest.
10. Letter from Arnold Belkin to S.M.G., November 8, 1975.
11. Galería Novedades, Mexico City, *Cincuenta imágenes de jazz* (October 19–November 4, 1962), statements by Pedro Cervantes, and Nacho López.
12. Quoted in Stefan Baciu, "Beatitude South of the Border: Latin America's Beat Generation," *Hispania* 49, No. 4 (December 1966): 733.
13. Barry Schwartz, *The New Humanism: Art in a Time of Change*, p. 20.
14. Sheldon Williams, "The Return of Involved Art," *Studio International* 173, No. 889 (May 1967): 224–225.
15. Interview with Raquel Tibol, Mexico City, August 1972. Tibol is one of many who hold such views.

1. The Mexican Mural Movement, Cultural Nationalism, and Social Realism

1. Octavio Paz, *The Labyrinth of Solitude: Life and Thought in Mexico*, trans. Lysander Kemp, p. 22.
2. In this connection, it should be noted that Siqueiros, the leading Communist painter of Mexico, was not just a member of the Party but occupied one of its top political posts at the time of his 1960 imprisonment.
3. In practice, however, things worked out somewhat differently; individual jealousies and ambition marked some of the early phases of the mural movement. Several instances are recorded in Jean Charlot's book *The Mexican Mural Renaissance, 1920–1925*, including Charlot's own encounters with Diego Rivera in the Ministry of Education when Rivera made life very uncomfortable for his three assistants, finally destroying their individual murals. By the early 1930s, early unity was fractured in a series of bitter political encounters between Rivera and Siqueiros.
4. Translated by Anita Brenner, *Idols behind Altars; The Story of the Mexican Spirit*, pp. 254–255. The original Spanish text is available in Raquel Tibol's *Siqueiros: Introductor de realidades*, p. 230. Siqueiros wrote it in late 1922; it was signed by all the Syndicate members and was publicly released in June 1923.
5. Unpublished manuscript cited by Charlot, *The Mexican Mural Renaissance*, p. 227.
6. Howard Warshaw, for example, even disassociated himself from the concept of neohumanism: "As far as I know I am not a neohumanist. I do not think of myself as coming, once again, to certain ideas—they were never abandoned. Neither Lebrun nor I ever even toyed with the notion of painting as a purely syntactic language, such as music or mathematics. There is no basis for such an assumption. Painting, like literature—even poetry—has always been a semantic language whose syntax is inextricably involved with its referential meaning" (letter to S.M.G., September 2, 1976).
7. Quoted by Francis V. O'Connor, *Federal Support for the Visual Arts: The New Deal and Now*, pp. 17–18.
8. See, in addition to the O'Connor book cited in note 7, *The New Deal Art Projects: An Anthology of Memoirs* and *Art for the Millions: Essays from the 1930s by Artists and Administrators*, which O'Connor edited; Richard D. McKinzie, *The New Deal for Artists*; David Shapiro, ed., *Social Realism: Art as a Weapon*; and Matthew Baigell, *The American Scene: American Painting of the 1930s*.
9. See Los Angeles County Museum of Art, *Rico Lebrun (1900–1964)*, pp. 25–26, in which the impact of Lebrun's year in Mexico on his work and spirit is outlined.
10. Los Angeles County Museum of Art, *Rico Lebrun (1900–1964)*, catalog essay by Peter Selz, p. 57.
11. Holger Cahill and Alfred H. Barr, Jr., eds., *Art in America in Modern Times*, p. 44.
12. Sheldon Cheney, *A World History of Art*, pp. 903–904.
13. Shaffer and Kadish were the only North American artists who worked on *Portrait of Mexico Today*, which is still in

good condition in a private home in Santa Monica, California.

14. Frantz Fanon, *The Wretched of the Earth*, trans. Constance Farrington, pp. 208–209.
15. Unpublished manuscript by Orozco, quoted by Charlot, *The Mexican Mural Renaissance*, p. 227.
16. I am indebted to Fanon's *The Wretched of the Earth*, p. 222 and passim, for the formulation of the three phases.
17. Three theoreticians who have tried to establish wider, more flexible parameters for socialist realism (to which social realism is related) are the Austrian Ernst Fischer, *The Necessity of Art: A Marxist Approach* (trans. Anna Bostock); Spanish-born Mexican philosopher Adolfo Sánchez Vázquez, *Art and Society: Essays in Marxist Aesthetics* (trans. Maro Riofranco); and French professor Henri Avron, *Marxist Aesthetics* (trans. Helen R. Lane).
18. Donald Drew Egbert, *Socialism and American Art in the Light of European Utopianism, Marxism and Anarchism*, p. 75, n. 153.
19. See Maynard Solomon, ed., *Marxism and Art*, pp. 242–244, for the text of Gorky's 1934 address.
20. Quoted from the Statutes of the 1934 Soviet Writers Congress in Avron's *Marxist Aesthetics*, p. 86.
21. Suggested in his introduction to *Social Realism: Art as a Weapon*, p. 28 n. 1, by editor David Shapiro.
22. The most obvious cases of destruction were those of Siqueiros' Los Angeles and Rivera's Rockefeller Center murals. The most publicized clash about alleged Communist propaganda occurred over the Coit Tower murals in San Francisco. See McKinzie, *The New Deal for Artists*, pp. 24–26.
23. Quoted by Raquel Tibol, *David Alfaro Siqueiros*, p. 113.
24. The development of synthetic paint proved to be consequential not only for Jackson Pollock (whose "drip" technique depended on its use) but for Arnold Belkin as well. Except for two early works (1950, 1952), all of Belkin's murals, as well as many canvases, have been executed in synthetic paints. In recent years (since 1971) he has been using stencils and airbrush-applied acrylics in easel painting, a technique Siqueiros pioneered in 1932.
25. David Alfaro Siqueiros, *70 obras recientes*, p. 20.
26. David Alfaro Siqueiros, "La crítica del arte como pretexto literario," *México en el Arte*, No. 4 (October 1948): n.p.
27. José Luis Cuevas, *Cuevario*, p. 150.
28. Quoted by Bertram D. Wolfe, *The Fabulous Life of Diego Rivera*, p. 223.
29. Quoted by Justino Fernández, *Orozco: Forma e idea*, p. 5.
30. José Clemente Orozco, *El artista en Nueva York: Cartas a Jean Charlot, 1925–1929, y tres textos inéditos*, pp. 138–139.

2. A Contemporary Overview: The Seeds of Confrontation

1. All data have been derived from Orlando S. Suárez, *Inventario del muralismo mexicano (siglo VII a. de C.)*, p. 389. Suárez indicates that his information was still being researched at the time of publication.
2. Henry J. Seldis, "Politics off the Palette in Mexico City," *Los Angeles Times*, March 17, 1974, Calendar, p. 64. Ramón Xirau himself was not free of United States influence, which aligned him against social realism. In 1953, he became director of the Centro Mexicano de Escritores, founded in 1951 by Margaret Shedd under the auspices of the Rockefeller Foundation. The Centro annually gave fellowships to young Mexican writers so they could do their work "somewhat relieved from economic pressures." Between 1951 and 1964, the Centro gave out ninety-two fellowships. See Ramón Xirau, "Variety and Contrast: The New Literature," trans. Juan M. Alonzo, *Atlantic Monthly* 213, No. 3 (March 1964): 143.
3. Tamayo's reputation was established in his native land with major showings in 1944 and 1947 at the Galería de Arte Mexicano.
4. Paul Westheim, "El arte de Tamayo: Una investigación estética," *Artes de México* 4, No. 12 (May–June 1956): 16.
5. Quoted by Robert Goldwater, *Rufino Tamayo*, p. 21.
6. Quoted by Emily Genauer, *Rufino Tamayo*, pp. 57–58.
7. A comparison between Tamayo in this phase and color field painting certainly suggests itself. Tamayo has stubbornly resisted this step toward total abstraction (it could be considered dehumanization, i.e., the loss of the human image). As his figures become less human, the sensuality of his color and texture increases as if in compensation. His appreciation and support of Mexico's nonobjective abstractionists can thus be seen as more than a "political" maneuver.
8. Jean Franco, *The Modern Culture of Latin America: Society and the Artist*, pp. 212–213.
9. It should be noted, however, that, like other factors, the Mexican palette was also European-influenced. Impressionist and postimpressionist colorist influences can be found in the works of Saturnino Herrán, Dr. Atl, Alfredo Ramos Martínez, Diego Rivera, and others.
10. Luis Cardoza y Aragón, *México: Pintura activa*, p. 144.
11. Antonio Rodríguez, "El muralismo mexicana, un enorme absceso que contagió a todos nuestros países: Carta abierta de Marta Traba sobre el problema del muralismo mexicano," *El Día*, May 14, 1964, p. 9.
12. Marta Traba, *Dos decadas vulnerables en las artes plásticas latinoamericanas, 1950–1970*, p. 179.
13. Antonio Rodríguez, "El muralismo de México: Gran y aparatoso adefesio de la historia, dice José Luis Cuevas," *El Día*, April 16, 1964.

14. Antonio Rodríguez, "El muralismo de México: Unos de los momentos culminantes del arte en este siglo," *El Día*, April 17, 1964.
15. For a distinction between these two types, see Robert Pincus-Witten, "The Iconography of Symbolist Painting," *Artforum* 8, No. 5 (January 1970): 56–62.

3. A Time of Confrontation

1. Octavio Paz, *The Other Mexico: Critique of the Pyramid*, trans. Lysander Kemp, p. 52.
2. C. Wright Mills, "Letter to the New Left," in *The New Left: A Collection of Essays*, ed. Priscilla Long, pp. 22–23.
3. For further information on the gallery scene, see Justino Fernández, ed., "Catálogo de las exposiciones de arte de 1960," Supplement to *Anales del Instituto de Investigaciones Estéticas*, No. 30. These catalogs are also available for subsequent years. Also see Inés Amor, "Art in Mexico: A Dealer's View," trans. Emily Flint, *Atlantic Monthly* 213, No. 3 (March 1964): 129, and Luis Cardoza y Aragón, *Pintura contemporánea de México*, p. 29.
4. Quoted by Selden Rodman, *Mexican Journal: The Conquerors Conquered*, p. 194.
5. Cuevas' best-known attack was "The Cactus Curtain: An Open Letter on Conformity in Mexican Art," *Evergreen Review* 2 (Winter 1959): 111–120.
6. Cuevas' position, as he saw it, was to stand against dogma and tyranny as represented by Siqueiros' famous dictum "There is no other path but ours" ("No hay más ruta que la nuestra"). This, he claimed, was the reason for his attacks against the Mexican School. In the United States, however, where for a number of years the Mexican revolutionary painters had been "quarantined," Cuevas was hailed as the salvation of Mexican painting and given, for a Latin American artist, an unprecedented amount of publicity and exhibitions in important galleries and museums. When he undertook to attack Siqueiros, not as a painter but as a Communist, he was publicly labeled a McCarthyite—an appellation he greatly resented ("Habla José Luis Cuevas," *Política* 1, No. 2 [May 15, 1960]: 51).
7. Max Kozloff, "American Painting during the Cold War," *Artforum* 11, No. 9 (May 1973): 43–54; Eva Cockcroft, "Abstract Expressionism, Weapon of the Cold War," *Artforum* 12, No. 10 (June 1974): 39–41.
8. Kozloff, "American Painting during the Cold War," p. 44.
9. Sol Yurick, "Book Review," *Artforum* 13, No. 9 (May 1975): 69.
10. Cockcroft, "Abstract Expressionism," p. 39.
11. Stanton Loomis Catlin and Terence Grieder, *Art of Latin America since Independence*, pp. 124–125.
12. For an example, see Leslie Judd Ahlender, "For Young Artists: Series of National Salons Begin in Bogotá," *Américas* 17, No. 1 (January 1965): 36.
13. "Oil Company's Art Show Wins Friends in Colombia," *Business Week*, July 2, 1960, p. 102.
14. See *Image of Mexico*, Parts I and II, *Texas Quarterly* 12, Nos. 3 and 4 (Autumn and Winter 1969).
15. See José Gómez-Sicre, "Córdoba's Biennial Comes Washington" [*sic*], *Américas* 15, No. 2 (February 1963): 16–19.
16. Sam Hunter, "The Córdoba Bienal," *Art in America* 55, No. 2 (March–April 1967): 85.
17. Amor, "Art in Mexico: A Dealer's View," p. 130.
18. Harold Rosenberg, "Art in Orbit," *Art News* 60, No. 6 (October 1961): 23–24.
19. See Cornell University and the Solomon R. Guggenheim Museum, New York, *The Emergent Decade: Latin American Painters and Painting in the 1960's*, catalog by Thomas M. Messer, 1966; Catlin and Grieder, *Art of Latin America since Independence*.
20. Rosenberg, "Art in Orbit," p. 25.
21. Institute of Contemporary Art, Boston, *Latin America: New Departures*, texts by Thomas M. Messer and José Gómez-Sicre, 1961.
22. For fuller details see Raquel Tibol, *Pedro Cervantes*, pp. 171–176, and "Solventes pictóricos," *Política* 5, No. 116 (February 15, 1965): 8–12.
23. "Una pintura para la 'Standard Oil,'" *Política* 5, No. 116 (February 15, 1965): inside back cover. Translation mine.
24. Edouard Jaguer, "Estado de urgencia," *Arquitectura*, Año 22, Vol. 16, No. 69 and 5 of art section (March 1960): 55. (The article was written in 1958).
25. Described by Cuevas as a "beachhead on the local scene where contemporary foreign art could be seen" (*Cuevas por Cuevas: Notas autobiográficas*, p. 216).
26. Ida Rodríguez P[rampolini], "La Leçon des 'Hartos' (Les Ecoeurés)," *Aujourd'hui* 6, No. 35 (February 1962): 3.
27. Raquel Tibol, *Documentación sobre el arte mexicano*, p. 113.
28. Rafael Anzures, "Segunda Bienal Interamericana de México," *Artes de México*, Año 9, Vol. 6, No. 34 (1961): 32.
29. Ibid., p. 21; Margarita Nelken, "Balance obligado III," *Excélsior*, January 4, 1959, Diorama de la Cultura, p. 11-C; Margarita Nelken, "Segunda Bienal Interamericana de México," *Cuadernos Americanos* 113, No. 6 (November–December 1960): 230; Dore Ashton, "Art," *Arts and Architecture* 75, No. 10 (October 1958): 4.
30. Nelken, "Balance obligado III," p. 11-C.
31. See Margarita Nelken, *El expresionismo en la plástica mexicana de hoy*.
32. Among the Mexican artists who abstained from participation in the Biennial were Ignacio Aguirre, Olga Costa, Jesús Guerrero Galván, Xavier Guerrero, Elena Huerta, José Chávez Morado, Antonio Pujol, and Alfredo Zalce.

The foreign artists who solicited an interview with Siqueiros were Jack Levine of the United States, Raúl Soldi and Juan Carlos Castagnino of Argentina, Emilio de Cavalcanti and Quirino Campofiorito of Brazil, Oswaldo Guayasamín of Ecuador, and Marina Núñez del Prado of Bolivia (all but Castagnino and Campofiorito were Biennial guests of honor).

33. This was an organization with a membership that represented a wide spectrum of artists, critics, and arts administrators but was dominated by the social realists, with whom Salas Anzures was on a friendly basis at the time.

34. See Miguel Salas Anzures, *Textos y testimonios*, for his own account of the events leading up to his resignation.

35. According to painter Fanny Rabel, the realists were given teaching jobs and exhibits in prestigious government galleries. Realism was the *official* art; but the formalists were promoted and purchased by the Instituto Nacional de Bellas Artes, and supported—especially abroad.

36. The monolithic character of Mexican politics has to be considered in this connection. A continuum is provided official policy by the bureaucracy and the top administrators of the ruling Partido Revolucionario Institutional (PRI), which is linked to the business and industrial establishment that grew up after World War II, and often functions on a "personalist" basis. Presidents are chosen from the cabinet of the preceding president: thus Adolfo López Mateos was secretary of labor under Adolfo Ruiz Cortines (1952–1958), and Gustavo Díaz Ordaz—who was responsible for applying laws of "social dissolution" to Siqueiros and other radicals while in the cabinet—was secretary of the interior under López Mateos. Despite the change in presidents and their power while in office, basic policy, reflecting pressures from power groupings in the country, is determined within the PRI. Administrators may be fired or resign due to pragmatic considerations, but reappear in various posts at later dates.

4. Insiders and New Imagists

1. Arnold Belkin, "Breve historia de un movimiento (algunas aclaraciones)," *Excélsior*, May 13, 1962, Diorama de la Cultura, p. 4.
2. Ibid.
3. Arnold Belkin, "Nueva presencia del hombre en el arte moderno," *Novedades*, January 29, 1961, México en la Cultura, p. 6.
4. Selden Rodman, *Mexican Journal: The Conquerors Conquered*, p. 49.
5. Quoted by Selden Rodman, *The Insiders: Rejection and Rediscovery of Man in the Arts of Our Time*, p. 19.
6. Ibid., p. 4.
7. Ibid., p. 62.
8. Ibid., p. 63.
9. Ibid., p. 97.
10. Manny Farber, "'Insiders' and Others," *Arts* 35, No. 4 (January 1961): 42.
11. Harold Rosenberg, *The Tradition of the New*, p. 43.
12. Letter from Selden Rodman to Rico Lebrun, March 17, 1960, carbon copy in Rodman Archive.
13. Peter Selz, *New Images of Man*, p. 9.
14. Quoted by Anita Brenner, *Idols behind Altars: The Story of the Mexican Spirit*, p. 145.
15. Julio González Tejada, "El segundo número de *Nueva Presencia*," *Mañana* 95, No. 954 (December 9, 1961): 88.
16. Personal communication from Arnold Belkin. The painting, *Carrera sin rumbo*, and its dedication are reproduced by Raquel Tibol, *David Alfaro Siqueiros* (n.p. for illustrations). Also involved were painters Juan O'Gorman, Cordelia Urueta, Fernando Castro Pacheco, José Chávez Morado, Jorge González Camarena, Tibol, and Horacio Flores Sánchez, new director of the INBA's Departamento de Artes Plásticas. See Tibol, *David Alfaro Siqueiros*, p. 77.
17. The climate of fear was very real. The major newspapers of Mexico City (including *Excélsior*, *El Día*, and *Novedades*) considered Siqueiros a great painter but a traitor to his country for criticizing the president. So pervasive was the McCarthyite atmosphere that Antonio Rodríguez, art critic for *El Día*, felt impelled to remove issue No. 3 from the five copies of *Nueva Presencia* on display with the show he organized for the group at the Club de Periodistas in October 1962. The Nueva Presencia artists went on record to the effect that this censorship occurred without their knowledge and appeared as one more breach of liberty in Mexico.
18. See "Los críticos responden," *Política* 3, No. 61 (November 1, 1962): 67.
19. Letter from David Alfaro Siqueiros to Francisco Icaza and Arnold Belkin, December 24, 1962, Belkin Archive.
20. Letter from Arnold Belkin to S.M.G., August 25, 1975.
21. Quoted in Selden Rodman Journals (unpublished diary), December 12, 1963.
22. José Luis Cuevas, "Aclaración de José Luis Cuevas," *Excélsior*, May 27, 1962, Diorama de la Cultura, p. 2.
23. Marta Traba, "Nacimiento del interiorismo," *Excélsior*, July 8, 1962, Diorama de la Cultura, p. 4 (reprinted from *Nueva Prensa*, Bogotá, Colombia).
24. Rodman interview with Icaza, quoted in Selden Rodman Journals, December 10, 1963.
25. Francisco Icaza, "Carta a Marta Traba," *Excélsior*, July 15, 1962, Diorama de la Cultura, p. 2.
26. Quoted by Malkah Rabell, "Los Interioristas contestan a Rufino Tamayo," *Ovaciones*, February 11, 1962, p. 4.
27. Antonio Rodríguez, "El 'interiorismo,'" *Política* 2, No. 39 (December 1, 1961): 72.

28. Raquel Tibol, "¿Fué Orozco un interiorista?" *Excélsior*, February 21, 1962, Diorama de la Cultura, p. 1.
29. Rodman, *The Insiders*, pp. 71–72. Rodman, for example, either was ignorant of or chose to ignore Orozco's role as a caricaturist during the revolution, and in the pages of *El Machete*, organ of the Syndicate, in 1923–1924.
30. Selden Rodman Journals, April 19, 1962. The Belkin Archive contains a number of letters from Latin America and the United States.
31. Leonard Baskin, "La necesidad del prejuicio," *Nueva Presencia*, No. 4 (April 1962); originally published under the title "The Necessity for the Image," in *Atlantic Monthly* 207, No. 4 (April 1961): 73–76, and reprinted in *Mexico Quarterly Review* 2, No. 2 (October 1963): 110–116. Quotes are from the original English version.
32. Rico Lebrun, "Apuntes sobre arte," *Nueva Presencia*, No. 4 (April 1962).
33. Julio González Tejada, "Un saludo a Rico Lebrun," *Mañana* 93, No. 935 (July 29, 1961): 58–59.
34. Jean Franco, *Modern Culture of Latin America: Society and the Artist*, p. 208.
35. For information on both camps, see "The Concept of Man as Seen through the Eyes of Southern California Artists," *Beverly Hills Times*, November 23, 1962, p. 8; and Gerald Nordland, "Pop Goes the West," *Arts Magazine* 37, No. 5 (February 1963): 61.
36. Herbert Marcuse, *One-Dimensional Man: Studies in the Ideology of Advanced Industrial Society*, p. 63.
37. Malkah Rabell, "Rufino Tamayo y la pintura actual," *Ovaciones*, February 4, 1962, p. 4.
38. Raquel Tibol, "Guttuso y la nueva figuración," *Excélsior*, July 22, 1962, Diorama de la Cultura, p. 1+.
39. Enrique F. Gual, "Más guerra que paz," *Excélsior*, September 1, 1963, Diorama de la Cultura, p. 4.
40. "La paz es el tema," *Tiempo*, September 2, 1963, p. 51.
41. "Where shall we punish the enemy?/In the core of his being./How? In his head? No./In his chest? No./In his belly? No./Where, then?/In his core; in his conscience." (My translation.)
42. The reference was to the October 1962 Cuban missile crisis, which many believed would be the start of World War III.
43. Undated (1963?) draft of letter to Bertrand Russell, Belkin Archive.
44. Letter from Arnold Belkin to S.M.G., November 8, 1975.
45. Ferlinghetti's poem was published in San Francisco by the Golden Mountain Press, 1958.
46. Selden Rodman Journals, January 25, 1964.
47. Letter (in English) from Francisco Corzas to Zora Gallery, January 25, 1964, Joseph Young Archive.
48. Selden Rodman Journals, November 18 and 22, 1963.
49. Ibid., March 20, 1964.

5. Outsiders As Well As Insiders

1. Colin Wilson, *Hesse-Reich-Borges: Three Essays*, p. 17.
2. Colin Wilson, *The Outsider*, p. 179.
3. Ibid., p. 155.
4. Selden Rodman, *The Insiders: Rejection and Rediscovery of Man in the Arts of Our Time*, p. 4.
5. Roberto Blanco Moheno, "Estos kukluxklanes de bolsillo: ¿Dónde las mentiras?" *Siempre!* March 10, 1965, p. 26.

6. Belkin, Icaza, Cuevas: The Artistic Genesis of *Interiorismo*

1. Instituto Cultural Mexicano Israeli, Mexico City, *Dibujos de Arnold Belkin* (1965), statement by the artist.
2. See José Gutiérrez and Nicholas Roukes, *Painting with Acrylics*.
3. The Quixote murals are reproduced in José Rojas Garcidueñas' *Presencias de Don Quijote en las artes de México*, Plates 79–81.
4. David Weber, "Mural Offers Psychiatric Aid," *Houston Now*, October 29, 1961, p. 30.
5. Julio González Tejada, "Arnold Belkin," *Mañana* 92, No. 923 (May 6, 1961): 38–41.
6. Raquel Tibol, "El mural de Arnold Belkin 'Todos somos culpables,'" *Excélsior*, April 23, 1961, Diorama de la Cultura, p. 1.
7. Selden Rodman Journals, April 24, 1962. Since Belkin had proselytized among the prisoners, it might be hard to judge how much understanding derived from discussion and how much from the mural itself.
8. Bernard S. Myers, *Mexican Painting in Our Time*, p. 151.
9. Galerías CDI, Mexico City, *Paintings* (1956), statement by Arnold Belkin.
10. It apparently escaped them both that, just as the futurist glorification of technology was linked to the imperialist policies of fascist Italy, so the glorifications of the Space Age were linked to the Cold War, which the United States hoped to win through a display of superior technology.
11. Zora Gallery, Los Angeles, *Arnold Belkin: Paintings and Drawings* (1963), statement by the artist.
12. Letter from Constance and Rico Lebrun to Arnold Belkin, August 1, 1961, Belkin Archive.
13. Maurice Tuchman, *Chaim Soutine, 1893–1943*, p. 35.
14. Toby Joysmith, "The Uniqueness of Mexican Art," in *Image of Mexico II (L–Z)*, *Texas Quarterly* 12, No. 4 (Winter 1969): 19.
15. Alejandro Romualdo, "Oración total," from the series "Poesía concreta," in Romualdo's *Poesia*, p. 136: "To continue loving, fighting and resisting/To continue living with time and with space/Increase our strength of love and enthusiasm."

16. Romualdo, "Así estamos," from the series "Poesía concreta," in ibid., p. 131: "Oh my country, heaven over earth!/What you will be, I will be with you./It cannot be possible. That is finished./It cannot be true. But there are witnesses."

17. "Nadie sabe, nadie supo, del misterioso caso del mural borradito: El pintor Arnold Belkin protesta contra el INPI," *Siempre!* No. 577 (July 15, 1964): 80–81.

18. "Nueva diversión," *Política* 5, No. 120 (April 15, 1965): 44.

19. Julio González Tejada, "Renace el muralismo mexicano," *Mañana* 20, No. 1050 (October 12, 1963): 45.

20. Selden Rodman Journals, November 21, 1963.

21. Bertrand Russell, *Has Man a Future?* p. 126. These words are taken from a long quotation originally intended for inscription on a marble plaque at the site of the mural.

22. Raquel Tibol, "Francisco Icaza entre la fantasía y la inconformidad," *Kena*, No. 308 (May 1976): 65.

23. Quoted in Selden Rodman Journals, November 24, 1963.

24. Siqueiros and Orozco were also of the middle class, but they experienced the revolution first hand—an experience that gave Orozco a permanent distaste for the working class, while Siqueiros went on to be a labor organizer.

25. Selden Rodman Journals, November 23, 1963.

26. Margarita Nelken, *El expresionismo en la plástica mexicana de hoy,* p. 121.

27. Robert Goldwater, *Primitivism in Modern Art,* p. 108.

28. A former revolutionary soldier who became a multimillionaire, Suárez owns the Hotel Casino de la Selva in Cuernavaca and the Hotel de México in Mexico City, both of which are meccas of muralism because of his massive expenditures for art. At the former are murals by Siqueiros, José Renau, Jorge González Camarena, José Reyes Meza, Benito Messeguer, and Icaza. The latter, located in the Parque de la Lama, includes the Polyforum Cultural Siqueiros for which Suárez commissioned Siqueiros (whom he knew from the days of the revolution) to do the 4,600-square-meter *The March of Humanity on Earth and toward the Cosmos,* the outside sculpture-painting *Homage to Diego Rivera and José Clemente Orozco,* and the outside panels of the Polyforum, on which Siqueiros worked from 1965 to 1971. After his jail term there was not much possibility that Siqueiros would receive further government commissions, and Suárez came to the rescue. He was not strictly a philanthropist nor, judging from a brief encounter I had with him in 1972, much of an art lover. Added to the pleasure of acquisition was a very shrewd sense of the commercial possibilities of modern art as investment and as tourist attraction.

29. Galerías México, Mexico City, *14 Artistas* (1960), introduction by Julio González Tejada and Enrique Gual.

30. Quoted in Selden Rodman Journals, November 22, 1963.

31. Letter from Francisco Icaza to Rico Lebrun, August 31, 1962, copy in Belkin Archive.

32. Margarita Nelken, "Exposiciones: Grupo 'Nueva Presencia,'" *Excélsior,* April 19, 1962, Diorama de la Cultura.

33. Letter from Arnold Belkin to Shelly Wexler, March 19, 1962, Shelly Wexler Bickford Archive.

34. Clair Wolfe, "The Nueva Presencia," *Connoisseur's World,* April 1964, p. 52.

35. Margarita Nelken, "Prometeo o Icaro," *Excélsior,* July 22, 1962, p. 2.

36. Ida Rodríguez Prampolini, *El surrealismo y el arte fantástico de México,* p. 103.

37. Albert Camus, *The Plague,* trans. Stuart Gilbert, p. 236.

38. Ibid., p. 170.

39. Ibid., p. 287.

40. Ibid., pp. 232–233.

41. Interview with Raquel Tibol, Mexico City, August 1972.

42. David Herbert Gallery, New York, *José Luis Cuevas* (March 1–31, 1960), statement by artist.

43. Luis Cardoza y Aragón, *Pintura contemporánea de México,* p. 98. Cardoza y Aragón was referring to a show in which Cuevas was called the "illustrator of his time" (see Museo de Arte Moderno, Mexico City, *José Luis Cuevas: Ilustrador de su tiempo* [1972]).

44. Rodríguez Prampolini, *El surrealismo y el arte fantástico de México,* p. 111.

45. Carlos Valdés, *José Luis Cuevas,* p. 8.

46. José Luis Cuevas, *Cuevas por Cuevas,* passim.

47. Ibid., p. 188.

48. Ibid., p. 192.

49. Ibid., p. 189.

50. José Luis Cuevas, "Mis recuerdos y el cine" (July 1965), reprinted in *Cuevario,* p. 195.

51. Cuevas has been compared with Goya by many critics, including Margarita Nelken, Toby Joysmith, and Cuevas' biographer, Carlos Valdés, in Mexico; Rico Lebrun, Jules Langsner, and Jerome Tarshis in the United States. Cuevas includes among his many self-portraits several "after Goya" in the early sixties.

52. Silvan Simone Gallery, Los Angeles, *José Luis Cuevas,* (March 23–April 13, 1962); introduction by Rico Lebrun, reprinted as "La imaginería de José Luis Cuevas," *Excélsior,* May 13, 1962, Diorama de la Cultura, p. 1+.

53. Quoted in *The Disasters of War by Francisco Goya y Lucientes,* p. 1.

54. Francisco Goya y Lucientes, *Caprichos,* p. 14.

55. Bernard S. Myers, *The German Expressionists: A Generation in Revolt,* p. 11.

56. Octavio Paz, *The Other Mexico: Critique of the Pyramid,* trans. Lysander Kemp, pp. 52–53.

57. "A Vision of Life," *Time* 64, No. 7 (August 16, 1954): 68.

58. There is no doubt that the Pan American show was decisive in establishing Cuevas' reputation. "I went to Washington in 1954," he says after detailing the rebuffs received from public and private galleries in Mexico,

"and for the first time was given an intelligent and understanding reception by the Pan American Union. After this my situation improved and I began to sell in Mexico with considerable consistency, but almost always to foreigners" (*Cuevas por Cuevas*, p. 215). Throughout the fifties and early sixties, with some exceptions, Cuevas sold his work outside Mexico, largely in the United States.

59. Interview with Shelly Wexler, former owner of the Cober Gallery (New York), San José, California, October 1976.
60. Jean Cassou, Philippe Soupault, and H[oracio] Flores Sánchez, *José Luis Cuevas.*
61. Later reprinted as "The Cactus Curtain: An Open Letter on Conformity in Mexican Art," *Evergreen Review* 2 (Winter 1959): 111–120, and included as part of the text in *Cuevas por Cuevas.*
62. I am not suggesting a conspiracy, or even a deliberate intention, on the part of Cuevas and Gómez-Sicre to wage a political campaign of this sort. It has long been understood that it is not necessary for individuals to conspire; the nature of a triumphant ideology is such that its imperatives are carried out *voluntarily*, with free will, by those subject to its mystique. This was widely demonstrated by the Esso Salons of 1965. The complexity of this accommodation is emphasized by the fact that Gómez-Sicre exhibited the Mexican School and members of Nueva Presencia both before and after his advice to Cuevas to break with the group for its Communist sympathies.
63. Carlos Monsiváis, "Prologue" to *Cuevario*, by José Luis Cuevas, pp. 9, 18, 22.
64. University of Texas, Austin, *Cuevas 1960* (December 9, 1960–January 9, 1961), introduction by Dr. Alvar Carrillo Gil. It is not unreasonable to assume that the lesson of Cuevas' rhetoric was not lost on those of his own generation.
65. Cuevas also admired authors like Beckett and Ionesco who wrote in the vein of the Absurd. It should be remembered that Kafka, along with Bertolt Brecht, was one of the transitional authors who transmitted the heritage of German expressionism to the avant-garde of a later date, part of which became known as the Theatre of the Absurd.
66. Louis R. Glessman and Eugene Feldman, eds., *The Worlds of Kafka and Cuevas* (1959).
67. Cardoza y Aragón, *Pintura contemporánea de México*, p. 98.
68. Michel Carrouges, *Kafka versus Kafka*, trans. Emmett Parker, p. 65.
69. Carlos Valdés, *José Luis Cuevas*, p. 22.
70. The entire mural appears in an article by Rubén Salazar, "The Cuevas 'Mafia's' Mexican Mural Revolt," *Los Angeles Times*, June 25, 1967, Calendar, p. 48. A study for the bottom half is reproduced in Carlos Fuentes, *El mundo de José Luis Cuevas.*

7. Artists of Nueva Presencia

1. Palacio de Bellas Artes, Mexico City, *Oleos, acuarelas y litografías de Francisco Corzas* (1972), introduction by Salvador Elizondo.
2. Center for Inter-American Relations, New York, *Young Mexicans: Corzas, Gironella, López-Loza, Rojo, Toledo* (1970–1971), catalog by Jacqueline Barnitz, p. 8.
3. Juan García Ponce, *Nueve pintores mexicanos*, p. 79.
4. Berta Taracena, *Francisco Corzas*, p. 19.
5. Quoted by Raquel Tibol, "Francisco Corzas en la Sala Nacional y la Sala Verde," *Excélsior*, June 28, 1972, p. 6-D.
6. Selden Rodman Journals, April 23, 1962.
7. Gilbert Chase, *Contemporary Art in Latin America: Painting, Graphic Art, Sculpture, Architecture*, p. 32.
8. Margarita Nelken, *El expresionismo en la plástica mexicana de hoy*, p. 127.
9. Elena Poniatowska, "Rafael Coronel ha entendido mejor que nadie que el genio es una larga paciencia; estos Coroneles deberían ser generales," *El Día*, January 13, 1966, Cultura de Hoy, p. 9.
10. José Gómez-Sicre, "World Art at São Paulo," *Art of the Americas Bulletin* 1 (1966): 19. For this kind of "family gallery" the painter won the special prize instituted by Kaiser Industries of Argentina for Latin American artists (the Córdoba prize, awarded at the São Paulo Biennial in 1965).
11. For a shrewd and sensitive critic, Gómez-Sicre flies so squarely in the face of visual evidence that one can only conclude the formalist bias was intentional. Emphasizing "intrinsic artistic force" over all other criteria is a well-known technique for defusing art of its humanist content or (as in this case) denying that such content exists.
12. Jorge Alzaga, Felipe Saúl Peña, and Michael Spafford also exhibited with the group for the first time, but did not remain associated with them thereafter.
13. "Provocative New Movement," *Política* 4, No. 75 (June 1, 1963): 48.
14. Lawrence Alloway, "Leon Golub: Art and Politics," *Artforum* 13, No. 2 (October 1974): 66–71. For further discussion, see Donald B. Kuspit, "Golub's Assassins: An Anatomy of Violence," *Art in America* 63, No. 3 (May–June 1975): 62–65.
15. Louise McCann, "Emilio Ortiz, Zora Gallery," *Artforum* 1, No. 10 (April 1963): 50.
16. Ida Rodríguez Prampolini, *El surrealismo y el arte fantástico de México*, p. 93.
17. Arthur Tooth and Sons, London, *Emilio Ortiz* (1967), statement by the artist.
18. Toby Joysmith, "The Uniqueness of Mexican Art," in *Image of Mexico II (L–Z), Texas Quarterly* 12, No. 4 (Winter 1969): 15 and passim.

19. McCann, "Emilio Ortiz," p. 50.

20. Selden Rodman Journals, April 24, 1962.

21. Quoted by C. L., "'En México no hay decadencia artística': Artemio Sepúlveda," *El Día*, August 23, 1962.

22. In 1948, the popular Liberal presidential hopeful Jorge Eliécer Gaitán was assassinated in Bogotá, triggering a confrontation between the Liberal and Conservative parties that rapidly spread over the country and caused the deaths, before it was over, of more than 300,000 people, mainly poor peasants. It has become known as "the violence."

23. Herbert Marcuse, *Eros and Civilization: A Philosophical Inquiry into Freud*, p. viii.

24. Quoted by Raquel Tibol, "Góngora: Virtuoso y disciplinado," *Excélsior*, August 13, 1972, Diorama de la Cultura, p. 3.

25. Bernard S. Myers, *The German Expressionists: A Generation in Revolt*, p. 242.

26. For example, the 1642 engraving by a German portraitist, Peter Aubry, *A New Peasant Lament on the Unmerciful Peasant Riders of This Age*, depicts a landlord or bailiff riding on the back of a bridled peasant in a landscape dotted with similar scenes. The original misogynistic imagery has also persisted to our time: as examples, there are the 1902 drawing *Sokrates* by the Mexican symbolist Julio Ruelas, in which the nude Greek philosopher on all fours is mounted by a black-stockinged woman who galls him with a large compass, and the 1913 lithograph *Aristotle and Phyllis* from the *Chinese Wall* series by the Austrian expressionist Oskar Kokoschka.

27. For extended treatments of the subject, see Thomas B. Hess and Linda Nochlin, eds., *Woman as Sex Object: Studies in Erotic Art, 1730–1970*; Lise Vogel, critique, "Erotica, the Academy, and Art Publishing: A Review of *Woman as Sex Object: Studies in Erotic Art, 1730–1970*, New York, 1972," *Art Journal* 35, No. 4 (Summer 1976): 378–385; and Carol Duncan, "Virility and Domination in Early 20th-Century Vanguard Painting," *Artforum* 12, No. 4 (December 1973): 30–39.

28. Letter from Leonel Góngora to Zora Gallery, Los Angeles, April 1963, Joseph Young Archive.

29. Letter from Vita Giorgi de Góngora to Zora Gallery, April 30, 1963, Joseph Young Archive.

30. "Debe ligarse la escultura con la arquitectura mexicana," *Excélsior*, August 11, 1964.

31. Quoted by Gustavo Sáinz, "Escultura retardataría y las nuevas escuelas," *Novedades*, April 4, 1965, México en la Cultura.

32. Froylán M. López Narváez, "Gastón González, escultor," *Excélsior*, October 16, 1966, Diorama de la Cultura, p. 1.

33. Quoted by Elizabeth Poe, "Genesis: Lebrun," *San Diego and Point Magazine*, December 1961, p. 94, cited in Los Angeles County Museum of Art, *Rico Lebrun (1900–1964)*, catalog essays by Henry J. Seldis and Peter Selz, 1967, p. 59.

34. Other artists included in this exhibition were Fernando Castro Pacheco, Francisco Díaz de Leon, Erasto Cortés, Manuel Echauri, and Angelina Beloff (*Cuadernos de Bellas Artes* 2, No. 10 [October 1961]: 55).

35. Quoted by Raquel Tibol, "Moreno Capdevila: Contra un arte para tecnócratas," *Excélsior*, December 1, 1974, Diorama de la Cultura, p. 14.

36. Antonio Rodríguez, "Los murales de Benito Messeguer," *Norte*, 3ª época, No. 250 (December 1972): 35.

37. "'El hombre' de Messeguer," *Política* 4, No. 83 (October 1, 1963): 40.

38. Jorge J. Crespo de la Serna, "De aquí y de allá," *Novedades*, December 5, 1962.

39. Margarita Nelken, "De Hernández Delgadillo y del muralismo," *Excélsior*, December 12, 1962, Diorama de la Cultura.

40. Galería Mer-Kup, Mexico City, *Hernández Delgadillo: 30 pinturas recientes* (1962), introduction by Justino Fernández.

41. Pan American Union, Washington, D.C., *Nacho López, Photographer of Mexico* (1956), introduction by José Gómez-Sicre, p. 2.

42. Salón de la Plástica Mexicana, Mexico City, *Exposición de fotografía de Nacho López*, introduction by Manuel Alvarez Bravo, 1955.

43. Quoted in Pan American Union, *Nacho López, Photographer of Mexico* (1956), introduction by José Gómez-Sicre, p. 3.

44. Even in the United States, where the commercialization of art is far more advanced than in Mexico, photographs have not been considered a lucrative art commodity until recently. In the past, United States photographers received $25–30 per print. Within the last several years, the New York and Los Angeles art markets (utilizing all the merchandising apparatus available and capitalizing on the nostalgic wave of the sixties and seventies) have been able to raise the prices for rare and vintage photographs to thousands of dollars per print, though they are still unable to obtain such prices for contemporary photographs.

45. Walter Benjamin, "The Work of Art in the Age of Mechanical Reproduction," in *Illuminations*, ed. Hannah Arendt, trans. Harry Zohn, p. 224.

46. Galería Franco/Mexicana, Veracruz, *Fotografías de Nacho López: Nuevas, viejas y otras ligeramente usadas* (1975), statement by the artist.

47. Raúl Flores Guerrero, "Nacho López, fotógrafo de México," *Revista de la Universidad de México* 10, No. 8 (April 1956): 12–14.

48. Carla Stellweg, "Nacho López," *Artes Visuales*, No. 4 (Fall 1974): 24.

49. Miguel Salas Anzures, *Textos y testimonios*, p. 40.

50. José Luis Cuevas, *Cuevas por Cuevas: Notas autobiográficas*, p. 204.

51. Palacio de Bellas Artes, Mexico City, *Exposición: 21 pinturas y 4 dibujos de Héctor Javier* (1945), unsigned introduction.

52. Crespo de la Serna called his pencil drawing of a stunted mother and child from this period a "horrible dwarf" and considered it an all too obvious imitation of Diego Rivera's children in the attitude, the gigantic hands and feet, and the enlargement of the eyes ("Exposiciones de Héctor Javier y de Nicolás Moreno," *Novedades*, April 11, 1962, p. 3).

53. Ibid. Xavier has also been fascinated with Chinese art since he was a child.

54. Héctor Xavier, *Punta de plata/El bestiario*, with text by Juan José Arreola (Mexico City: Universidad Nacional Autónoma de Mexico, 1958).

55. Museo Nacional de Arte Moderno, Mexico City, *Antonio Rodríguez Luna, obra retrospectiva, 1939–1959*, introduction by Luis Cardoza y Aragón.

56. Margarita Nelken, *El expresionismo en la plástica mexicana de hoy*, p. 294.

57. A similar conception appears in Siqueiros' 1939 mural *Portrait of the Bourgeoisie*, in which a steel-plated eagle/dive-bomber surmounts the scenes of destruction below and might be indebted to Luna's death-dealing bird or insect. Luna worked on the eagle, but left the team before the completion of the mural because of his lack of vocation for mural painting (José Renau, "Mi experiencia con Siqueiros," *Revista de Bellas Artes*, nueva época, No. 25 [January–February 1976]: 17).

58. Juan Rejano, *Antonio Rodríguez Luna*, p. 19.

59. The structuralism can perhaps be traced to the year 1930, when the twenty-year-old Luna met the Uruguayan artist Joaquín Torres-García, then fifty-six and living in Paris, and became part of the Constructivist group he established. It was this style, emphasized by black outlines like those of Torres-García, that was later synthesized by Rodríguez Luna.

60. Rejano, *Antonio Rodríguez Luna*, p. 22.

61. Luna was appointed to a teaching post at San Carlos Academy in 1943, when he returned from two years in New York, where he worked under grants from the Guggenheim Foundation. In 1958 he served as a juror for the first Biennial, and in 1959 he showed more than one hundred paintings at the retrospective in the Museo Nacional de Arte Moderno that marked his twentieth year of residence in Mexico. The dates of Luna's Guggenheim grants offer an illustration of the changing attitudes of United States institutions toward social realism. In 1965, the Guggenheim Museum's Messer could express considerable hostility and contempt for Mexico's *tres grandes*, whereas in 1941–1942, a social realist like Luna had received grants from another branch of the Guggenheim complex. In 1938, when it was apparent that war was imminent, the Roosevelt government stepped up the Good Neighbor policy introduced in the early thirties, which for the first time purported to abandon the Monroe doctrine. By 1940, when Luna's application to the Guggenheim must have been made, the grants can be seen as part of the actions to engage the sympathy of Mexico (which had opened its doors to Spanish refugees) on behalf of an alliance against the Axis.

62. Statement sent to the Wenger Collection of La Jolla, California, from Mexico City, June 1, 1965, trans. Muriel Wenger; also appears in Rejano, *Antonio Rodríguez Luna*, p. 14.

Conclusion

1. John Fraser, *Violence in the Arts*, pp. 136–137.

2. The influence of abstract expressionism added others: blurred representations of the human figure in nebulous spaces and impasto brushwork that functioned independently as abstract form.

3. Wylie Sypher, *Loss of the Self in Modern Literature and Art*, p. 30.

4. Ibid., p. 14.

5. Ibid., p. 15.

Bibliography

Books

Alfaro Siqueiros, David. *See* Siqueiros, David Alfaro.

Avron, Henri. *Marxist Aesthetics.* Translated by Helen R. Lane. Ithaca, N.Y.: Cornell University Press, 1973.

Baigell, Matthew. *The American Scene: American Painting of the 1930s.* New York: Praeger Publishers, 1974.

Barrett, William. *Irrational Man: A Study in Existential Philosophy.* Garden City, N.Y.: Doubleday Anchor Books, 1962.

Belkin, Arnold. *Two.* Ten lithographs by Arnold Belkin. Poems by Jack Hirschman. Los Angeles: The Zora Gallery, 1964.

Brenner, Anita. *Idols behind Altars: The Story of the Mexican Spirit.* Boston: Beacon Press, 1970.

Cahill, Holger, and Alfred H. Barr, Jr., eds. *Art in America in Modern Times.* New York: Reynal and Hitchcock, 1934.

Camus, Albert. *The Plague.* Translated by Stuart Gilbert. New York: Vintage Books, 1972.

————. *The Rebel: An Essay on Man in Revolt.* Translated by Anthony Bower. Rev. ed. New York: Vintage Books, 1956.

Cardoza y Aragón, Luis. *México: Pintura activa.* Mexico City: Ediciones Era, 1961.

————. *Pintura contemporánea de México.* Mexico City: Ediciones Era, 1974.

Carrouges, Michel. *Kafka versus Kafka.* Translated by Emmett Parker. University: University of Alabama Press, 1968.

Casasola, Gustavo. *Historia gráfica de la revolución mexicana, 1900–1960.* Mexico City: Editorial Trillas, 1960.

Cassou, Jean, Philippe Soupault, and H[oracio] Flores Sánchez. *José Luis Cuevas.* Paris: Michel Brient Editeur, 1955.

Catlin, Stanton Loomis, and Terence Grieder. *Art of Latin America since Independence.* New Haven: Yale University Press, 1966.

Charlot, Jean. *The Mexican Mural Renaissance, 1920–1925.* New Haven: Yale University Press, 1967.

Chase, Gilbert. *Contemporary Art in Latin America: Painting, Graphic Art, Sculpture, Architecture.* New York: The Free Press, 1970.

Cheney, Sheldon. *A World History of Art.* New York: Viking Press, 1946.

Cuevas, José Luis. *Cuevario.* Prologue by Carlos Monsiváis. Mexico City: Editorial Grijalbo, 1973.

————. *Cuevas por Cuevas: Notas autobiográficas.* Prologue by Juan García Ponce. Translated by Ralph Dimmick, Lysander Kemp, and Asa Zatz. Mexico City: Ediciones Era, 1965.

Egbert, Donald Drew. *Socialism and American Art in the Light of European Utopianism, Marxism and Anarchism.* Princeton: Princeton University Press, 1967.

————. *Social Radicalism and the Arts: Western Europe, A Cultural History from the French Revolution to 1968.* New York: Alfred A. Knopf, 1970.

Fanon, Frantz. *The Wretched of the Earth.* Translated by Constance Farrington. New York: Grove Press, 1968.

Ferlinghetti, Lawrence. *Tentative Description of a Dinner Given to Promote the Impeachment of President Eisenhower.* San Francisco: Golden Mountain Press, 1958.

Fernández, Justino. *Orozco: Forma e idea.* 2d ed. Mexico City: Editorial Porrúa, 1956.

Fischer, Ernst. *The Necessity of Art: A Marxist Approach.* Translated by Anna Bostock. Baltimore: Penguin Books, 1963.

Franco, Jean. *The Modern Culture of Latin America: Society and the Artist.* Rev. ed. Harmondsworth, England: Penguin Books, 1970.

Fraser, John. *Violence in the Arts.* London: Cambridge University Press, 1974.

Fuentes, Carlos. *El mundo de José Luis Cuevas.* New York: Tudor Publishing Co., 1969.

García Ponce, Juan. *Nueve pintores mexicanos.* Mexico City: Ediciones Era, 1968.

Genauer, Emily. *Rufino Tamayo.* New York: Harry N. Abrams, 1974.

Glessman, Louis R., and Eugene Feldman, eds. *The Worlds of Kafka and Cuevas.* With texts by José Gómez-Sicre, Max Brod, Rollo May, and Franz Kafka. Philadelphia: Falcon Press, 1959.

Goldwater, Robert. *Primitivism in Modern Art.* Rev. ed. New York: Vintage Books, 1967.

————. *Rufino Tamayo.* New York: The Quadrangle Press, 1947.

Goya y Lucientes, Francisco. *Caprichos.* Introduction by Miroslav Mičko. Translated by Roberta Finlayson Samsour. London: Spring Books, n.d.

————. *The Disasters of War by Francisco Goya y Lucientes*. Introduction by Philip Hofer. New York: Dover Publications, 1967.

La guerra y la paz. Album. Text by Enrique Gual. Mexico City: Galería Central de Arte Misrachi, 1964.

Gutiérrez, José, and Nicholas Roukes. *Painting with Acrylics*. New York: Watson-Guptill Publications, 1965.

Helm, MacKinley. *Man of Fire: J. C. Orozco, an Interpretive Memoir*. New York: Harcourt, Brace, 1953.

Hess, Thomas B., and Linda Nochlin, eds. *Woman as Sex Object: Studies in Erotic Art, 1730–1970*. New York: Newsweek, 1972.

Larkin, Oliver W. *Art and Life in America*. Rev. ed. New York: Holt, Rinehart and Winston, 1964.

Lebrun, Rico. *Drawings*. Berkeley: University of California Press, 1961.

Lewis, Oscar. *The Children of Sánchez: Autobiography of a Mexican Family*. Harmondsworth, England: Penguin Books, 1961.

————. *Five Families: Mexican Case Studies in the Culture of Poverty*. New York: Basic Books, 1959.

Long, Priscilla, ed. *The New Left: A Collection of Essays*. Boston: Porter Sargent, 1969.

McKinzie, Richard D. *The New Deal for Artists*. Princeton: Princeton University Press, 1973.

Marcuse, Herbert. *Eros and Civilization: A Philosophical Inquiry into Freud*. New York: Vintage Books, 1962.

————. *One-Dimensional Man: Studies in the Ideology of Advanced Industrial Society*. Boston: Beacon Press, 1969.

Moliné, Héctor. *Mi soledad y los gordos*. Drawings by Leonel Góngora. Mexico City: Editorial Prometeo Libre, 1962.

Mondragón, Sergio. *Yo soy el otro/I Am the Other*. Translated by Margaret Randall. Drawings by Arnold Belkin. Mexico City: El Corno Emplumado, 1965.

Myers, Bernard S. *The German Expressionists: A Generation in Revolt*. New York: McGraw-Hill, 1963.

————. *Mexican Painting in Our Time*. New York: Oxford University Press, 1956.

Nelken, Margarita. *El expresionismo en la plástica mexicana de hoy*. Mexico City: Instituto Nacional de Bellas Artes, 1964.

O'Connor, Francis V. *Federal Support for the Visual Arts: The New Deal and Now*. Greenwich, Conn.: New York Graphic Society, 1969.

————, ed. *Art for the Millions: Essays from the 1930s by Artists and Administrators*. Greenwich, Conn.: New York Graphic Society, 1973.

————, ed. *The New Deal Art Projects: An Anthology of Memoirs*. Washington, D.C.: Smithsonian Institution Press, 1972.

O'Gorman, Edmundo, Justino Fernández, Luis Cardoza y Aragón, Ida Rodríguez Prampolini, and Carlos G. Mijares Bracho. *Cuarenta siglos de plástica mexicana: Arte moderno y contemporáneo*, vol. 3. Mexico City: Editorial Herrero, 1971.

Orozco, José Clemente. *El artista en Nueva York: Cartas a Jean Charlot, 1925–1929, y tres textos inéditos*. Prologue by Luis Cardoza y Aragón. Appendices by Jean Charlot. Mexico City: Siglo Veintiuno Editores, 1971. Translated by Ruth L. C. Simms as *The Artist in New York*. Austin: University of Texas Press, 1974.

Ouspensky, P. D. *A New Model for the Universe: Principles of the Psychological Method in Its Application to Problems of Science, Religion, and Art*. 1931; rpt. New York: Alfred A. Knopf, 1969.

Pauwels, Louis, and Bergier, Jacques. *The Morning of the Magicians*. Translated by Rollo Myers. New York: Stein and Day, 1964.

Paz, Octavio. *The Labyrinth of Solitude: Life and Thought in Mexico*. Translated by Lysander Kemp. New York: Grove Press, 1961.

————. *The Other Mexico: Critique of the Pyramid*. Translated by Lysander Kemp. New York: Grove Press, 1972.

Rejano, Juan. *Antonio Rodríguez Luna*. Mexico City: Universidad Nacional Autónoma de México, 1971.

Rhino Horn: Personal Interiors. Interviews with Peter Dean, Leonel Góngora, Jay Milder, Peter Passuntino, and Nicholas Sperakis by Dr. Jusep Torres Campanais [New York]: n.p., n.d. [after 1968].

Rodman, Selden. *The Eye of Man: Form and Content in Western Painting*. New York: Devin-Adair, 1955.

————. *The Insiders: Rejection and Rediscovery of Man in the Arts of Our Time*. Baton Rouge: Louisiana State University Press, 1960.

————. *Mexican Journal: The Conquerors Conquered*. New York: Devin-Adair, 1958.

Rodríguez, Antonio. *A History of Mexican Mural Painting*. Translated by Marina Corby. New York: G. P. Putnam's Sons, 1969.

Rodríguez Prampolini, Ida. *El surrealismo y el arte*

fantástico de México. Mexico City: Universidad Nacional Autónoma de México, 1969.

Rojas Garciadueñas, José. *Presencias de Don Quijote en las artes de México.* Mexico City: Universidad Nacional Autónoma de México, 1968.

Romualdo, Alejandro. *Poesía.* Lima: Juan Mejía Baca and P. L. Villanueva, 1954.

Rosenberg, Harold. *The Tradition of the New.* New York: Grove Press, 1961.

Russell, Bertrand. *Has Man a Future?* New York: Simon and Schuster, 1962.

Salas Anzures, Miguel. *Textos y testimonios.* Mexico City: Imprenta Madero, 1968.

Sánchez Vázquez, Adolfo. *Art and Society: Essays in Marxist Aesthetics.* Translated by Maro Riofrancos. New York: Monthly Review Press, 1973.

Saunders, J. B. deC. M., and Charles D. O'Malley. *The Illustrations from the Works of Andreas Vesalius of Brussels.* New York: Dover Publications, 1973.

Schwartz, Barry. *The New Humanism: Art in a Time of Change.* New York: Praeger Publishers, 1974.

Selz, Peter. *New Images of Man.* With statements by the artists. New York: The Museum of Modern Art, 1959.

Shapiro, David, ed. *Social Realism: Art as a Weapon.* New York: Frederick Ungar, 1973.

Siqueiros, David Alfaro. *70 obras recientes.* Mexico City: Instituto Nacional de Bellas Artes, 1947.

Solomon, Maynard, ed. *Marxism and Art: Essays Classical and Contemporary.* New York: Vintage Books, 1974.

Suárez, Orlando S. *Inventario del muralismo mexicano (siglo VII a. de C.).* Mexico City: Universidad Nacional Autónoma de México, 1972.

Sypher, Wylie. *Loss of the Self in Modern Literature and Art.* New York: Vintage Books, 1962.

Taracena, Berta. *Francisco Corzas.* Mexico City: Sep/Setentas, 1973.

Tibol, Raquel. *David Alfaro Siqueiros.* Mexico City: Empresas Editoriales, 1969.

——. *Documentación sobre el arte mexicano.* Mexico City: Fondo de Cultura Económica, 1974.

——. *Historia general del arte mexicano: Epoca moderna y contemporánea,* vol. 3. Mexico City: Editorial Hermes, 1964.

——. *Pedro Cervantes.* Mexico City: Sep/Setentas, 1974.

——. *Siqueiros: Introductor de realidades.* Mexico City: Universidad Nacional Autónoma de México, 1961.

Traba, Marta. *Los cuatro monstruos cardinales.* Mexico City: Ediciones Era, 1965.

——. *Dos décadas vulnerables en las artes plásticas latinoamericanas, 1950–1970.* Mexico City: Siglo Veintiuno Editores, 1973.

Tuchman, Maurice. *Chaim Soutine, 1893–1943.* Los Angeles: Los Angeles County Museum of Art, 1968.

Valdés, Carlos. *José Luis Cuevas.* Mexico City: Universidad Nacional Autónoma de México, 1966.

Wilson, Colin. *Hesse-Reich-Borges: Three Essays.* Philadelphia: Leaves of Grass Press, 1974.

——. *The Outsider.* London: Pan Books, 1974 (First published in 1956.)

Wolfe, Bertram D. *The Fabulous Life of Diego Rivera.* New York: Stein and Day, 1963.

Xavier, Héctor. *Punta de plata/El bestiario.* Text by Juan José Arreola. Mexico City: Universidad Nacional Autónoma de México, 1958.

Articles and Periodicals

Ahlender, Leslie Judd. "For Young Artists: Series of National Salons Begin in Bogotá." *Américas* 17, No. 1 (January 1965): 36–38.

Alfaro Siqueiros, David. *See* Siqueiros, David Alfaro.

Alloway, Lawrence. "Leon Golub: Art and Politics." *Artforum* 13, No. 2 (October 1974): 66–71.

Amor, Inés. "Art in Mexico: A Dealer's View." Translated by Emily Flint. *Atlantic Monthly* 213, No. 3 (March 1964): 129–131.

Anzures, Rafael. "Segunda Bienal Interamericana de México." *Artes de México,* Año 9, Vol. 6, No. 34 (1961).

Artes Visuales, No. 12 (Winter 1976–1977).

Ashton, Dore. "Art." *Arts and Architecture* 75, No. 10 (October 1958): 4.

Baciu, Stefan. "Beatitude South of the Border: Latin America's Beat Generation." *Hispania* 49, No. 4 (December 1966): 733–739.

Baskin, Leonard. "The Necessity for the Image." *Atlantic Monthly* 207, No. 4 (April 1961): 73–76; reprinted, *Mexico Quarterly Review* (Mexico City) 2, No. 2 (October 1963): 110–116.

Belkin, Arnold. "Breve historia de un movimiento

(algunas aclaraciones)." *Excélsior*, May 13, 1963, Diorama de la Cultura, pp. 2, 4.

———. "Nueva presencia del hombre en el arte moderno." *Novedades*, January 29, 1961, México en la Cultura, p. 6.

Benjamin, Walter. "The Work of Art in the Age of Mechanical Reproduction." In *Illuminations*, edited by Hannah Arendt, translated by Harry Zohn. New York: Schocken Books, 1973.

Blanco Moheno, Roberto. "Estos kukluxklanes de bolsillo: ¿dónde las mentiras?" *Siempre!* March 10, 1965, p. 26.

"La calle es también selva." *Tiempo*, October 30, 1961.

Canaday, John. "Growing Up with José Luis Cuevas." *New York Times*, May 23, 1965.

Chase, Gilbert. "Art in Mexico Today." *Mexican Life* 41 (September 1965): 25–28.

Cockcroft, Eva. "Abstract Expressionism, Weapon of the Cold War." *Artforum* 12, No. 10 (June 1974): 39–41.

Crespo de la Serna, Jorge J. "De aquí y de allá." *Novedades*, December 5, 1962.

———. "Exposiciones de Héctor Javier y de Nicolás Moreno." *Novedades*, April 11, 1962, p. 3.

———. "Leonel Góngora." *Novedades*, November 2, 1961.

———. "Perfil del pintor José Hernández Delgadillo." *Cuadernos de Bellas Artes* 2, No. 11 (November 1961): 53–60.

"Los críticos responden." *Política* 3, No. 61 (November 1, 1962): 67.

Cuevas, José Luis. "Aclaración de José Luis Cuevas." *Excélsior*, May 27, 1962, Diorama de la Cultura, p. 2.

———. "The Cactus Curtain: An Open Letter on Conformity in Mexican Art." *Evergreen Review* 2 (Winter 1959): 111–120.

———. "José Luis Cuevas and the 'Insiders.'" *Mexico Quarterly Review* (Mexico City) 2, No. 1 (April 1963): 32–34.

"Debe ligarse la escultura con la arquitectura mexicana." *Excélsior*, August 11, 1964.

Duncan, Carol. "Virility and Domination in Early 20th-Century Vanguard Painting." *Artforum* 12, No. 4 (December 1973): 30–39.

"En México no hay decadencia artística: Artemio Sepúlveda." *El Día*, August 23, 1962.

Farber, Manny. "'Insiders' and Others." *Arts* 35, No. 4 (January 1961): 42–45.

Fernández, Justino, ed. "Catálogo de las exposiciones de arte de 1960." Supplement to *Anales del Instituto de Investigaciones Estéticas*, No. 30. Mexico City: Universidad Nacional Autónoma de México, 1961.

Flores Guerrero, Raúl. "Nacho López, fotógrafo de México." *Revista de la Universidad de México* 10, No. 8 (April 1956): 12–14.

Goldman, Shifra M. "Siqueiros and Three Early Murals in Los Angeles." *Art Journal* 33, No. 4 (Summer 1974): 321–327.

Gómez-Sicre, José. "Córdoba's Biennial Comes Washington [*sic*]." *Américas* 15, No. 2 (February 1963): 16–19.

———. "World Art at São Paulo." *Art of the Americas Bulletin* 1 (1966): 19.

Góngora, Leonel. "Nueva Presencia en Nueva York." *Ovaciones*, January 28, 1963.

González Tejada, Julio. "Arnold Belkin." *Mañana* 92, No. 923 (May 6, 1961): 38–41.

———. "Nueva Presencia: El hombre en el arte de nuestro tiempo." *Mañana* 94, No. 937 (August 12, 1961).

———. "Renace el muralismo mexicano." *Mañana* 20, No. 1050 (October 12, 1963): 42–45.

———. "Un saludo a Rico Lebrun." *Mañana* 93, No. 935 (July 29, 1961): 58–59.

———. "El segundo número de *Nueva Presencia*." *Mañana* 95, No. 954 (December 9, 1961): 88.

Gual, Enrique F. "Más guerra que paz." *Excélsior*, September 1, 1963, Diorama de la Cultura, p. 4.

"Habla José Luis Cuevas." *Política* 1, No. 2 (May 15, 1960): 50–52.

"Hablando de fotografías: Visión mexicana de la muerte." *Life*, November 19, 1956, p. 11.

"'El hombre' de Messeguer." *Política* 4, No. 83 (October 1, 1963): 40.

Hunter, Sam. "The Córdoba Bienal." *Art in America* 55, No. 2 (March–April 1967): 84–89.

Icaza, Francisco. "Carta a Marta Traba." *Excélsior*, July 15, 1962, Diorama de la Cultura, p. 2.

———. "José Luis Cuevas, pinta actualmente en el manicomio." *Mañana*, March 5, 1955, pp. 48–50.

———. "Lavalle, pintor de la belleza." *Mañana*, December 25, 1954, pp. 47–49.

———. "Mario Orozco Rivera, 'no pintó para el pueblo sino por el pueblo.'" *Mañana*, January 29, 1955, pp. 40–42.

"In the Galleries: 'Nueva Presencia' Movement Growing." *Los Angeles Times*, April 27, 1964.

Jaguer, Edouard. "Estado de urgencia." *Arquitectura*, Año 22, Vol. 16, No. 69 and 5 of art section (March 1960): 55.

Joysmith, Toby. "The Uniqueness of Mexican Art." In *Image of Mexico II (L–Z)*. *Texas Quarterly* 12, no. 4 (Winter 1969): 5–20.

Kozloff, Max. "American Painting during the Cold War." *Artforum* 11, No. 9 (May 1973): 43–54.

Kuspit, Donald B. "Golub's Assassins: An Anatomy of Violence." *Art in America* 63, No. 3 (May–June 1975): 62–65.

Lebrun, Rico. "La imaginería de José Luis Cuevas." *Excélsior*, May 13, 1962, Diorama de la Cultura, p. 1+.

López Narváez, Froylán M. "Gastón González, escultor." *Excélsior*, October 16, 1966, Diorama de la Cultura, p. 1.

McCann, Louise. "Emilio Ortiz, Zora Gallery." *Artforum* 1, No. 10 (April 1963): 50.

Mills, C. Wright. "Letter to the New Left." In *The New Left: A Collection of Essays*, edited by Priscilla Long. Boston: Porter Sargent, 1969.

Monsiváis, Carlos. "Prologue" to *Cuevario*, by José Luis Cuevas. Mexico City: Editorial Grijalbo, 1973.

"Nadie sabe, nadie supo, del misterioso caso del mural borradito: El pintor Arnold Belkin protesta contra el INPI." *Siempre!* No. 577 (July 15, 1964): 80–81.

Nelken, Margarita. "Balance obligado III," *Excélsior*, January 4, 1959, Diorama de la Cultura, p. 11-C.

———. "De Hernández Delgadillo y del muralismo." *Excélsior*, December 12, 1962, Diorama de la Cultura.

———. "Del sentimiento trágico." *Excélsior*, August 27, 1961, Diorama de la Cultura, p. 2.

———. "Exposiciones: Grupo 'Nueva Presencia.'" *Excélsior*, April 19, 1962, Diorama de la Cultura.

———. "Exposiciones: La de Leonel Góngora." *Excélsior*, October 25, 1961.

———. "Exposiciones: La de Leonel Góngora." *Excélsior*, March 19, 1962, p. 4-B.

———. "Exposiciones: La de Sepúlveda." *Excélsior*, August 26, 1962, p. 12-C.

———. "El neohumanismo en la plástica actual." *Excélsior*, April 29, 1962, Diorama de la Cultura, p. 2.

———. "Prometeo o Icaro." *Excélsior*, July 22, 1962, p. 2.

———. "Segunda Bienal Interamericana de México." *Cuadernos Americanos* 113, No. 6 (November–December 1960): 225–239.

Neuvillate, Alfonso de. "El trágico mural de Moreno Capdevila." *El Día*, May 3, 1964, México en la Cultura.

Nordland, Gerald. "Pop Goes the West." *Arts Magazine* 37, No. 5 (February 1963): 61–62.

"Nueva diversión." *Política* 5, No. 120 (April 15, 1965): 44.

Nueva Presencia: El Hombre en el Arte de Nuestro Tiempo, No. 1 (August 1961); No. 2 (September 1961); No. 3 (December 29, 1961); No. 4 (April 1962); No. 5 (August–September 1963).

"Oil Company's Art Show Wins Friends in Colombia." *Business Week*, July 2, 1960, pp. 100–102.

Olea Figueroa, Oscar. "El erostratismo de Mr. Arnold Belkin." *Excélsior*, May 13, 1962, p. 4-B.

"La paz es el tema." *Tiempo*, September 2, 1963.

Pincus-Witten, Robert. "The Iconography of Symbolist Painting." *Artforum* 8, No. 5 (January 1970): 56–62.

Pinoncelly, Salvador. "Los manifiestos Belkin-Icaza." *Excélsior*, June 10, 1962, p. 4-B.

"Una pintura para la 'Standard Oil.'" *Política* 5, No. 116 (February 15, 1965): inside back cover.

"Poemas de Bertolt Brecht." Translations by Celso Amieva. Original drawings by Arnold Belkin. *El Día*, May 24, 1964, El Gallo Ilustrado.

Poniatowska, Elena. "Rafael Coronel ha entendido mejor que nadie que el genio es una larga paciencia; estos Coroneles deberían ser generales." *El Día*, January 13, 1966, Cultura de Hoy, p. 9.

"Provocative New Movement." *Política* 4, No. 75 (June 1, 1963): 48.

Rabell, Malkah. "Dos artistas colombianos en las Galerías CDI." *Revista C.D.I.* 11, No. 95 (May 1962).

———. "Los Interioristas contestan a Rufino Tamayo." *Ovaciones*, February 11, 1962, p. 4.

———. "Rufino Tamayo y la pintura actual." *Ovaciones*, February 4, 1962, p. 4.

Reed, Alma M. "La 'generación apaleada' de los EE.UU." *Excélsior*, January 25, 1959, Diorama de la Cultura, p. 3-C.

Renau, José. "Mi experiencia con Siqueiros." *Revista de Bellas Artes*, Nueva época, No. 25 (January–February 1976): 2–25.

Rivas, Benito. "Belkin como pintor rebelde." *Lunes de Excélsior*, April 25, 1966, p. 19-B.

Rodman, Selden. "Mexico's Enfant Terrible." *The American Way* 6, No. 12 (December 1973): 27.

――. "The New Presence of Mexico." *Mexico Quarterly Review* (Mexico) 2, No. 2 (October 1963): 95–102.

Rodríguez, Antonio. "El gran premio a la mediocridad." *Siempre!* No. 627 (June 30, 1965): 28f.

――. "Héctor Xavier: De la punta de plata a la pincelada violenta." *El Día*, May 25, 1964.

――. "El 'interiorismo.'" *Política* 2, No. 39 (December 1, 1961): 72–73.

――. "Manifiesto de dos pintores." *Política* 2, No. 34 (September 15, 1961): 44–45.

――. "Los murales de Benito Messeguer." *Norte*, 3ª época, No. 250 (December 1972): 35.

――. "El muralismo de México: Gran y aparatoso adefesio de la historia, dice José Luis Cuevas." *El Día*, April 16, 1964.

――. "El muralismo de México: Unos de los momentos culminantes del arte en este siglo." *El Día*, April 17, 1964.

――. "El muralismo mexicano, un enorme absceso que contagió a todos nuestros países: Carta abierta de Marta Traba sobre el problema del muralismo mexicano." *El Día*, May 14, 1964, p. 9.

――. "Sepúlveda: Un nuevo valor de la pintura." *El Nacional*, August 24, 1962.

Rodríguez P[rampolini], Ida. "La Leçon des 'Hartos' (Les Ecoeurés)." *Aujourd'hui* 6, No. 35 (February 1962): 3.

"Romualdo y Belkin." *Política* 3, No. 71 (April 1, 1963): 46.

Rosenberg, Harold. "Art in Orbit." *Art News* 60, No. 6 (October 1961): 22–25+.

Sáinz, Gustavo. "Escultura retardataria y las nuevas escuelas." *Novedades*, April 4, 1965, México en la Cultura.

Salazar, Rubén. "The Cuevas 'Mafia's' Mexican Mural Revolt." *Los Angeles Times*, June 25, 1967, Calendar, p. 48.

Seldis, Henry. "Politics off the Palette in Mexico City." *Los Angeles Times*, March 17, 1974, Calendar, p. 64.

Siqueiros, David Alfaro. "La crítica del arte como pretexto literario." *México en el Arte*, No. 4 (October 1948): n.p.

"Solventes pictóricos." *Política* 5, No. 116 (February 15, 1965): 8–12.

Stellweg, Carla. "Góngora: El pintor secreto." *Excélsior*, August 24, 1969, Diorama de la Cultura, p. 4.

――. "Nacho López." *Artes Visuales*, No. 4 (Fall 1974): 24–27.

Tarshis, Jerome. "Cuevas: Faithful to the Mexican Tradition." *Art News* 72, No. 5 (May 1973): 76–77.

Texas Quarterly 12, No. 3 (Autumn 1969), *Image of Mexico I (A–K)*; 12, No. 4 (Winter 1969), *Image of Mexico II (L–Z)*.

Tibol, Raquel. "Francisco Corzas en la Sala Nacional y la Sala Verde." *Excélsior*, June 28, 1972, p. 6-D.

――. "Francisco Icaza entre la fantasía y la inconformidad." *Kena*, No. 308 (May 1976): 65.

――. "¿Fué Orozco un interiorista?" *Excélsior*, February 21, 1962, Diorama de la Cultura, pp. 1–4.

――. "Góngora: Virtuoso y disciplinado." *Excélsior*, August 13, 1972, Diorama de la Cultura, p. 3.

――. "Guttuso y la nueva figuración." *Excélsior*, July 22, 1962, Diorama de la Cultura, p. 1+.

――. "Moreno Capdevila: Contra un arte para tecnócratas." *Excélsior*, December 1, 1974, Diorama de la Cultura, p. 14.

――. "El mural de Arnold Belkin 'Todos somos culpables.'" *Excélsior*, April 23, 1961, Diorama de la Cultura, pp. 1, 4.

――. "Rico Lebrun en México." *Calli International*, No. 31 (January–February 1968): 9–12.

Traba, Marta. "Nacimiento del interiorismo." *Excélsior*, July 8, 1962, Diorama de la Cultura, p. 4. Reprinted from *Nueva Prensa* (Bogotá, Colombia).

Valdés, Carlos. "Diálogo con Héctor Xavier." *Novedades*, August 27, 1961, México en la Cultura, p. 6.

Villoro, Luis. "La cultura mexicana de 1910 a 1960." *Historia Mexicana* 10, No. 2 (October–December 1960): 196–219.

"A Vision of Life." *Time* 64, No. 7 (August 16, 1954): 68.

Vogel, Lise. "Erotica, the Academy, and Art Publishing: A Review of *Woman as Sex Object: Studies in Erotic Art, 1730–1970*, New York, 1972." *Art Journal* 35, No. 4 (Summer 1976): 378–385.

Weber, David. "Mural Offers Psychiatric Aid." *Houston Now*, October 29, 1961, p. 30.

Westheim, Paul. "El arte de Tamayo: Una investigación estética." *Artes de México* 4, No. 12 (May–June 1956): 16.

Williams, Sheldon. "The Return of Involved Art." *Stu-*

dio International 173, No. 889 (May 1967): 224–225.

Wolfe, Clair. "The Nueva Presencia." *Connoisseur's World*, April 1964, p. 52.

Xirau, Ramón. "Variety and Contrast: The New Literature." Translated by Juan M. Alonso. *Atlantic Monthly* 213, No. 3 (March 1964): 142–145.

Yurick, Sol. "Book Review." *Artforum* 13, No. 9 (May 1975): 68–70.

Nueva Presencia Catalogs

Centro Deportivo Israelita, Mexico City. *Los Interioristas.* Introduction by Malkah Rabell. 1961.

Club de Periodistas de México, A.C., Mexico City. *Grupo Nueva Presencia: Los 'interioristas' y su nueva presencia en el arte de México.* Introduction by Antonio Rodríguez. 1962.

Cober Gallery, New York. *Nueva Presencia de México/Mexico's New Imagists.* 1962.

Escuela Nacional de Artes Plásticas, Mexico City. *Arnold Belkin, José Luis Cuevas, Francisco Corzas, Francisco Icaza, Nacho López, Antonio Rodríguez Luna, Héctor Xavier.* [1961.]

———. *El neohumanismo en el dibujo de Italia, EE.UU. y México.* Introduction by Enrique F. Gual. [1963.]

Galería Ariza, Mexico City. *11 pintores exponen sus obras: Belkin, Arévalo, Sepúlveda, Muñoz, Góngora, Ortiz, Xavier, Falfan, Corzas, Alzaga, Peña.* Introduction by Adrián Villagómez L. [ca. 1962.]

Galería Mer-Kup, Mexico City. *Inauguración.* Includes the "Primera Exposición del Grupo 'Nueva Presencia.'" [1962.]

Morse Gallery of Art, Rollins College, Winter Park, Florida. *Nueva Presencia: Contemporary Mexican Drawings.* 1963.

Secretaría de Relaciones Exteriores, Organismo de Promoción Internacional de Cultura, Mexico City. *Pintores neo-humanistas.* Introduction by Miguel Alvarez Acosta. [1963.]

Individual Artist Catalogs

BELKIN, ARNOLD

Escuela Nacional de Artes Plásticas, Mexico City. *Obras de Arnold Belkin.* 1960.

Galerías CDI, Mexico City. *Paintings.* Introduction by David Alfaro Siqueiros. Statement by the artist. 1956.

Instituto Cultural Mexicano Israeli, Mexico City. *Dibujos de Arnold Belkin.* Statement by the artist. 1965.

Zora Gallery, Los Angeles. *Arnold Belkin: Paintings and Drawings.* Statement by the artist. 1963.

CORONEL, RAFAEL

B. Lewin Galleries, Beverly Hills, Calif. *Rafael Coronel: Paintings, Drawings.* 1973.

Museo Nacional de Arte Moderno, Mexico City. *Retratos de Rafael Coronel.* Introduction by Sergio Pitol. 1959.

CORZAS, FRANCISCO

Palacio de Bellas Artes, Mexico City. *Oleos, acuarelas y litografías de Francisco Corzas.* Introduction by Salvador Elizondo. 1972.

CUEVAS, JOSÉ LUIS

Borgenicht Gallery, New York. *The Museum of Man.* Introduction by José Gómez-Sicre. 1965.

David Herbert Gallery, New York. *José Luis Cuevas.* Statement by the artist. 1960.

David Herbert Gallery, New York. *José Luis Cuevas.* Statement by the artist. 1962.

Museo de Arte Moderno, Mexico City. *José Luis Cuevas: Ilustrador de su tiempo.* 1972.

Phoenix Art Museum, Phoenix, Ariz. *José Luis Cuevas: An Exhibition of Recent Works.* Introduction by Ronald D. Hickman. Statement by the artist. 1974.

Silvan Simone Gallery, Los Angeles. *José Luis Cuevas.* Introduction by Rico Lebrun. 1962.

University of Texas, Austin. *Cuevas 1960.* Introduction by Dr. Alvar Carrillo Gil. 1961.

GÓNGORA, LEONEL

Café "Lautrec," Mexico City. *14 dibujos de Leonel Góngora.* Introduction by Alvaro Mutis and Luis Harro Leeb. 1962.

Galería Glantz, Mexico City. *Leonel Góngora, pinturas y dibujos.* Statement by the artist. 1961.

Pan American Union, Washington, D.C. *Leonel Góngora of Colombia: Drawings.* 1962.

HERNÁNDEZ DELGADILLO, JOSÉ

Galería Mer-Kup, Mexico City. *Hernández Delgadillo: 30 pinturas recientes.* Introduction by Justino Fernández. 1962.

LEBRUN, RICO

Los Angeles County Museum of Art, Los Angeles. *Rico*

Lebrun (1900–1964). Catalog essays by Henry J. Seldis and Peter Selz. 1967.

LÓPEZ, IGNACIO (NACHO)

Galería Franco/Mexicana, Veracruz. *Fotografías de Nacho López: Nuevas, viejas y otras ligeramente usadas.* Statement by the artist. 1975.

Galería Novedades, Mexico City. *Cincuenta imágenes de jazz.* Statements by Pedro Cervantes and Nacho López. 1962.

Pan American Union, Washington, D.C. *Nacho López, Photographer of Mexico.* Introduction by José Gómez-Sicre. 1956.

Salón de la Plástica Mexicana, Mexico City. *Exposición de fotografía de Nacho López.* Introduction by Manuel Alvarez Bravo. 1955.

MORENO CAPDEVILA, FRANCISCO

Galería Mer-Kup, Mexico City. *Capdevila: Pinturas y dibujos.* Introduction by Alfonso de Neuvillate. 1964.

ORTIZ, EMILIO

Arthur Tooth and Sons, London. *Emilio Ortiz.* Statement by the artist. 1967.

Galería de Arte Mendelsohn, Mexico City. *Galería Mendelsohn exhibe dibujos, pinturas: Los 22 perros de Emilio Ortiz.* Introduction by Horacio Flores Sánchez. 1964.

RODRÍGUEZ LUNA, ANTONIO

Museo Nacional de Arte Moderno, Mexico City. *Antonio Rodríguez Luna, obra retrospectiva, 1939–1959.* Introduction by Luis Cardoza y Aragón. 1959.

XAVIER, HÉCTOR

Palacio de Bellas Artes, Mexico City. *Exposición: 21 pinturas y 4 dibujos de Héctor Javier.* Unsigned introduction. 1945.

General Exhibition Catalogs

Center for Inter-American Relations, New York. *Young Mexicans: Corzas, Gironella, López-Loza, Rojo, Toledo.* Catalog by Jacqueline Barnitz. 1970–1971.

Cornell University and the Solomon R. Guggenheim Museum, New York. *The Emergent Decade: Latin American Painters and Painting in the 1960s.* Catalog by Thomas M. Messer. 1966.

Denver Art Museum, Denver. *German Expressionist Paintings from the Collection of Mr. and Mrs. Morton D. May: A Circulating Exhibition, 1960–1961.* Introduction by Otto Karl Bach. 1960–1961.

Galerías México, Mexico City. *14 artistas.* Introduction by Julio González Tejada and Enrique Gual, 1960.

Institute of Contemporary Art, Boston. *Latin America: New Departures.* Texts by Thomas M. Messer and José Gómez-Sicre. 1961.

Museo Nacional de Bellas Artes, Buenos Aires. *Pintura contemporánea de México.* 1962.

Unpublished Materials

Nueva Presencia. Undated draft for Issue No. 5; in English. Belkin Archive.

Rodman, Selden. Selden Rodman Journals. Diary. 1962–1964.

Letters

Alfaro Siqueiros, David. *See* Siqueiros, David Alfaro.

Belkin, Arnold. Letter to Shifra M. Goldman, August 25, 1975.

———. Letter to Shifra M. Goldman, October 30, 1975.

———. Letter to Shifra M. Goldman, November 8, 1975.

———. Draft of a letter to Bertrand Russell, undated (1963?). Belkin Archive.

———. Letter to Shelly Wexler, January 31, 1962. Shelly Wexler Bickford Archive.

———. Letter to Shelly Wexler, March 19, 1962. Shelly Wexler Bickford Archive.

———. Letter to Shelly Wexler, July 14, 1962. Shelly Wexler Bickford Archive.

———. Letter to Zora Gallery, July 4, 1962. Belkin Archive.

———. Letter to Zora Gallery, May 11, 1963. Belkin Archive.

Bickford, Shelly Wexler. *See* Wexler, Shelly.

Corzas, Francisco. Letter to Shelly Wexler, January 21, 1963. Shelly Wexler Bickford Archive.

———. Letter to Zora Gallery, January 25, 1964. Joseph Young Archive.

Cuevas, José Luis. Letter to Selden Rodman, May 19, 1959. Courtesy of the University of Wyoming, Archive of Contemporary History, Selden Rodman Collection.

Góngora, Leonel. Letter to Arnold Belkin, September 21, 1963. Belkin Archive.

———. Letter to Zora Gallery, April 1963. Joseph Young Archive.

Góngora, Vita Giorgi de. Letter to Zora Gallery, April 30, 1963. Joseph Young Archive.

Icaza, Francisco. Letter to Rico Lebrun, August 31, 1962. Belkin Archive.

————. Letter to Edward Pinney of Zora Gallery, May 16, 1963. Belkin Archive.

————. Letter to Shelly Wexler, January 15, 1962. Shelly Wexler Bickford Archive.

————. Letter to Zora Gallery, January 19, 1963. Belkin Archive.

Lebrun, Constance, and Rico Lebrun. Letter to Arnold Belkin, August 1, 1961. Belkin Archive.

Lebrun, Rico. Letter to Arnold Belkin, March 19, 1962. Belkin Archive.

————. Letter to Arnold Belkin, undated (1962?). Belkin Archive.

————. Letter to Arnold Belkin, April 24, 1963. Belkin Archive.

————. Letter to José Muñoz Medina, June 1963. Muñoz Archive.

Pinney, Edward (Zora Gallery). Letter to José Muñoz Medina, November 5, 1963. Belkin Archive.

Rodman, Selden. Letter to Arnold Belkin, July 21, 1961. Belkin Archive.

————. Letter to Shifra M. Goldman, April 22, 1975.

————. Letter to Rico Lebrun, March 17, 1960. Rodman Archive.

————. Letter to Rico Lebrun, November 15, 1963. Rodman Archive.

————. Letter to Rico Lebrun, December 7, 1963. Rodman Archive.

Sepúlveda, Artemio. Letter to Selden Rodman, end of December 1963. Rodman Archive.

Siqueiros, David Alfaro. Letter to Francisco Icaza and Arnold Belkin. December 24, 1962. Belkin Archive.

Warshaw, Howard. Letter to Shifra M. Goldman, September 2, 1976.

Wexler, Shelly. Letter to Arnold Belkin, June 29, 1962. Shelly Wexler Bickford Archive.

————. Letter to Arnold Belkin, August 22, 1962. Belkin Archive.

Zora Gallery. Letter to Arnold Belkin, November 12, 1962. Belkin Archive.

————. Letter to Arnold Belkin, July 16, 1963. Belkin Archive.

————. Letter to Arnold Belkin, September 27 (1963?). Belkin Archive.

————. Letter to Leonel Góngora, November 12, 1962. Joseph Young Archive.

————. Letter to Emilio Ortiz, April 14, 1963. Joseph Young Archive.

————. Letter to Artemio Sepúlveda, June 9, 1963. Joseph Young Archive.

Interviews

Bickford, Shelly Wexler. San José, Calif., October 1976.

Cuevas, José Luis. Mexico City, July 1972.

Góngora, Leonel. Amherst, Mass., June 1975.

González César, Gastón. Mexico City, August 1974.

Icaza, Francisco. Mexico City, July 1975.

López, Ignacio (Nacho). Mexico City, July 1975.

Messeguer, Benito. Mexico City, August 1972.

Muñoz Medina, José. Mexico City, July 1974.

Ortiz, Emilio. Mexico City, July 1975.

Rabel, Fanny. Mexico City, July 1975.

Rabell, Malkah. Mexico City, August 1972.

Rodríguez, Antonio. Mexico City, August 1972.

Rodríguez Luna, Antonio. Mexico City, July 1974.

Sepúlveda, Artemio. Cuernavaca, July 1975.

Stellweg, Carla. Editor of *Artes Visuales* of the Museo de Arte Moderno. Mexico City, July 1975.

Tibol, Raquel. Mexico City, August 1972.

Wenger, Sig and Muriel. La Jolla, Calif., September 1976.

Index _____